MODERN COLISEUM

MODERN COLISEUM

STADIUMS AND AMERICAN CULTURE

BENJAMIN D. LISLE

UNIVERSITY OF PENNSYLVANIA PRESS • PHILADELPHIA

ART HISTORY
PUBLICATION INITIATIVE

This book is made possible by a collaborative grant from the Andrew W. Mellon Foundation.

ARCHITECTURE | TECHNOLOGY | CULTURE
Series Editors: Klaus Benesch, Jeffrey L. Meikle, David E. Nye, and Miles Orvell

Published by
University of Pennsylvania Press
Philadelphia, Pennsylvania 19104-4112
www.upenn.edu/pennpress

Printed in the United States of America on acid-free paper
10 9 8 7 6 5 4 3 2 1

Library of Congress Cataloging-in-Publication Data
Name: Lisle, Benjamin D., author.
Title: Modern coliseum : stadiums and American culture / Benjamin D. Lisle.
Other titles: Architecture, technology, culture.
Description: 1st edition. | Philadelphia : University of Pennsylvania Press,
    [2017] | Series: Architecture, technology, culture
Identifiers: LCCN 2016049590 | ISBN 9780812249224
    (hardcover : alk. paper)
Subjects: LCSH: Stadiums—Social aspects—United States. |
    City planning—United States. | City planning—Social aspects—United States.
Classification: LCC GV415 .L57 2017 | DDC 796.406/8—dc23
LC record available at https://lccn.loc.gov/2016049590

CONTENTS

INTRODUCTION

STADIUMS FOR THE AFFLUENT SOCIETY

GRIFFITH STADIUM DREW FANS FROM ALL OVER the District of Columbia and its suburbs to attend baseball and football games in the 1950s—"like a street lamp draws mosquitoes," one area resident recalled.[1] The park was distinctive. Its stands framed an asymmetrical field; the outfield fence cut and jagged around the far reaches of the lot as if it were a
stumbling drunk, just dodging a massive tree and five row houses—property the builders
were unable to acquire in the ballpark's first days. The winking, mustachioed mascot for
National Bohemian beer peeked above the right-field wall as if he were trying to scramble
over it. Like so many other old ballparks, this one was squeezed by the neighborhood, producing an effect of either warm embrace or uncomfortable claustrophobia, depending on
one's mood and inclination. It was located on the east end of the U Street corridor—one of
the country's centers of African American life and culture. Howard University was blocks
away. Ralph Bunche, Josh Gibson, Langston Hughes, Zora Neale Hurston, and Thurgood
Marshall all lived nearby at one time or another. Duke Ellington had once worked at the
ballpark, selling peanuts, candy, and cigars.

Griffith Stadium—and U Street more generally—was one of the city's main sites of
interracial, interclass congress.[2] Loretta Parker Brown, who grew up in adjacent LeDroit
Park, remembered, "The only time that white people (other than policemen and firemen)
came onto our neighborhood was to attend events at Griffith Stadium."[3] The area had
changed since the end of World War II. Some of its more affluent black residents had left
with the loosening of residential segregation in the district and availability of newer, more
spacious homes—homes often vacated by whites who fled for the suburbs when *Brown v.*

FIGURE 1. Griffith Stadium in 1955. REPRINTED BY PERMISSION OF THE DC PUBLIC LIBRARY, STAR COLLECTION. © *WASHINGTON POST.*

Board of Education desegregated public schools in 1955.[4] The stadium was more difficult to get to than it had been in the past; the streetcar that once dropped people off at the mouth of the ballpark promenade on Seventh Street, in front of the stucco ticket booths, no longer ran. Those coming from elsewhere in the city or its suburbs could take some combination of commuter train, bus, or taxi to the stadium; more likely, they would drive themselves and endure streets clogged with game traffic. Once there, they would then have to find street parking (unless they were privileged enough to make it into the stadium's two-hundred-spot lot).[5] Stories of slashed tires and scratched hoods were often repeated, though exaggerated.[6] A trip to Griffith Stadium was no doubt a logistical trial, but it was also one charged with urban excitement—and perhaps the most sustained exposure to African American and working-class urban life for most white visitors. It was certainly one of the few times that white people had to walk African American turf.

The new District of Columbia Stadium opened in October 1961, and the experience of attending big-time sporting events in the city changed dramatically.[7] The stadium occupied a symbolic spot in the city landscape—directly east of the Capitol on the Anacostia River, in line with the Washington Monument and Lincoln Memorial. Though not far from the city center and the predominantly black neighborhoods of Kingman Park and Lincoln Park, the stadium stood apart from its surroundings; it lorded over its space, an abstract sculpture—750 feet in diameter and 135 feet tall at its highest point—in the midst of parking fields, curving roads, and grassy lawns. Sixty-six massive box girders lifted a signature undulating roof that was designed to provide uniform shade to inhabitants within. Most visitors arrived by car, though that was an ordeal not all that much better than driving to Griffith Stadium; the Anacostia Freeway, which would link the stadium to the suburbs of Virginia and Maryland, was still being assembled across the river. If the roads to games were just as clogged, the chance to secure a "supervised" spot in the parking lot adjacent to the stadium was far more likely; at the stadium's opening, there was space for 9,000 automobiles, with promises of 3,500 more spots by the spring of 1962.[8] Once parked, fans ambled into the stadium shoulder to shoulder with their fellow travelers in from the suburbs, on gradually pitched ramps and down wide aisles, sitting down together in a continuous circle of aqua and tan contoured theater seats that were three inches wider than those in most stadiums at that time. There were no bleachers—the traditional home of cheap seats and beer-guzzling rowdies. And neither were there view-obstructing support posts, thanks to the cantilevered upper deck. It was a stadium made as much for football as baseball—the first of its kind—in which the banks of seats on the lower level could pivot to accommodate both the rectangular gridiron and the fan shape of the diamond. After the opening game for the city's NFL team, a *Washington Post* reporter claimed that most of the fans, "perhaps recalling conditions at Griffith Stadium, must have felt they were the affluent society."[9]

All this modern progress came at a cost. A *Post* columnist noted, "Some of the old-line . . . fans complain the new D.C. Stadium doesn't have the 'intimacy' of old Griffith Stadium. . . . It's something like having a party in an austere drawing room after being accustomed to gathering in the kitchen."[10] The sense of urban intimacy and public contact, characteristic of old Griffith, had been lost in a new stadium remarkable for its spaciousness, comfort, and modernist novelty. It was in the city but seemed to share more with the suburbs. The outside world, save the sky above, was invisible to most inside. The circular stadium possessed its inhabitants as though they were in a protective womb. The experience of U Street, and the unpredictable city, had been eliminated.

Variations on this theme were played across the United States, beginning in the mid-1950s, as new modern stadiums were built for major league baseball and football teams—either to replace aging structures or to lure other cities' clubs to new pastures. At the end of

FIGURE 2. The new, sculptural District of Columbia Stadium under construction in the late 1950s. REPRINTED BY PERMISSION OF THE DC PUBLIC LIBRARY, STAR COLLECTION. © *WASHINGTON POST.*

World War II, most urban stadiums were privately owned affairs that had been built three decades before for professional baseball; they doubled as stages for professional and college football, political speeches, religious gatherings, concerts, and other big events. At the time of their construction, typically in the decade before World War I, these ballparks had marked a new era for spectator sport. Built of brick, concrete, and steel, their permanence contrasted starkly with the wooden firetraps they replaced. Their architectural flourishes marked them, in the eyes of their builders, as challenges to other forms of middle-class leisure like vaudeville theater and amusement parks. Many were even located in middle-class neighborhoods. But by the 1940s, after years of economic depression and war, most were nestled into materially deteriorating neighborhoods—neighborhoods that, like U Street, were either predominantly African American or becoming so. The ballpark scene had become mixed class, interracial, and often rather rambunctious. These were sites of genuine urban diversity, inside and outside the stadium walls.

The stadiums that replaced them in the decades after World War II erased much of that urban diversity. Postwar modern stadiums relocated sports space from old urban

FIGURE 3. President John F. Kennedy throws out the first pitch on opening day, 1963. The monumental scale and concrete regularity of the new District of Columbia Stadium contrasted starkly with old Griffith Stadium. The stadium would later be renamed in honor of Kennedy's assassinated brother, Robert F. Kennedy, in January 1969. CECIL STOUGHTON (HAROLD SELLERS). WHITE HOUSE PHOTOGRAPHS. JOHN F. KENNEDY PRESIDENTIAL LIBRARY AND MUSEUM, BOSTON.

FIGURE 4. A racially mixed crowd fills up the outfield bleachers at Griffith Stadium on the first day of the baseball season, April 1961, months before the opening of the new District of Columbia Stadium. REPRINTED BY PERMISSION OF THE DC PUBLIC LIBRARY, STAR COLLECTION. © WASHINGTON POST.

neighborhoods to open sites along freeways, convenient to booming white suburbs or as anchors to clean-sweep downtown redevelopment. Unlike aged ballparks stitched into neighborhoods, modern stadiums stood like monuments alone amid sprawling parking lots. Ballparks had been boxes, filling up every inch of their rectangular urban lots; modern stadiums were circles, allowing an easier (and more symmetrical) adaptation from baseball diamond to football grid. Old grandstands were stacked one atop the other on vertical support posts. New stadiums cantilevered their second decks, eliminating view-obstructing columns; this also allowed these stadiums to "breathe" by pushing fans further from the field and releasing some of the pent-up energies that could electrify an unruly crowd. Employing the stark and monumental geometries of engineered modernist architecture, these stadiums were material critiques of the old city and pronouncements of a new modern era—pronouncements that were always heavily subsidized, if not entirely funded, by public dollars.

Whereas the old urban ballparks were rough around the edges, the new stadiums were idealized as playgrounds for the affluent. Promoters pitched the sporting experience to the casual consumer with money to burn, applying the exuberant "populuxe" styling of postwar consumer culture.[11] They integrated new consumer spaces, like exclusive restaurants and private luxury boxes, into the stadium. Attracting women was a crucial strategy in marking these spaces as "classy" and appropriate to a modern mode of living. New technologies like video boards assured that there was never a dull moment for inexpert observers, who were the ideal customers in the eyes of promoters; these were people who wouldn't come to the stadium for sport alone but needed to be seduced from their suburban television sets with other in-stadium distractions. Postwar stadiums reconstituted sports spaces as modern, suburban, and technological, fundamentally altering stadium experience by shifting emphasis from games on the field to entertainments and consumption opportunities around it.

This book examines how such stadium changes unfolded after World War II, focusing particularly on the shift from old stadiums to new ones from the late 1940s through the early 1970s—from the "classic ballpark" to the modern stadium (dubbed the "superstadium" or "concrete doughnut" by its many critics over the years). I investigate why and how new, modern stadiums were built across the United States and the effects these structures had on how people experienced sport and public space.[12] This study attempts to square national trends in stadium design and culture with more particular accounts in specific urban settings. The postwar modernization of professional sports space—as modernization is wont to do—regularized the form of the modern stadium in city after city.[13] Critics of the modern stadium, who surely outweigh its advocates since the 1970s, often cite Pittsburgh Pirates third baseman Richie Hebner, who observed, "I stand at the plate in Philadelphia and I don't honestly know whether I'm in Pittsburgh, Cincinnati, St. Louis, or

FIGURE 5. Men play billiards in one of the Houston Astrodome's private luxury suites in 1968. The stadium interior is visible through the diamond-shaped window at their backs. PHOTO BY MARK KAUFFMAN/TIME & LIFE PICTURES/GETTY IMAGES.

Philly. They all look alike."[14] However, this modernization and standardization occurred in specific urban contexts. The peculiarity of the local always shifted the circumstances of stadium debate, planning, and construction, as well as the conversations about what these new structures meant and how they meant different things to different people.

Why do stadiums matter? Few other structures are so costly or so controversial as public investments.[15] Stadiums are massive components of urban landscapes and since the mid-1960s have played an important role in the reordering of central business districts. They are weapons in an arms race that pits city against city—part of the "cultural capital" that might attract corporate investment.[16] They are iconic structures, often symbolizing entire cities. No other buildings host such large and captive audiences so often—over four and a half million people attended events at the Houston Astrodome in 1965 alone.[17] Sports have long been among the most immediate ways Americans cultivate a relationship with place: the names of cities are written right there on the players' chests. Sports can also connect us to fellow rooters across time—others who have sat in the same stadium seats, across generations. The stadium is where relationships in place and across time are anchored and staged, where people experience a version of "the public" uniquely.[18] At a very personal level, they are places etched into the fiber of who we are, where many people register some of their most memorable moments. Altogether, the design of stadiums and the stadium experience—and debates over each—tell us a great deal about who we are, who we aspire to be, and who is seen to matter as a part of the stadium public.

Roy Hofheinz, the driving force behind the Astrodome's planning, execution, and management, understood quite clearly that stadiums are much more than concrete and plastic or mere containers for sports entertainment; as he put it, "You've got to have tangibles to sell intangibles."[19] What "intangibles" were being sold in the modern stadium? Stadiums like the Astrodome celebrated an era of consumption-oriented, technology-based comfort and convenience for a swelling middle class of white Americans. They packaged the present in the guise of the future—promising these Americans that a utopian future of democratic luxury was immediately available. They erected stages on which this vision of "progress" could be enacted in material form again and again, solidifying it as the way things were and should be. More than just reshaping the way sports were understood and experienced—significant in its own right—the modern stadium played a crucial role in shaping Americans' conceptions of the public, a narrowing that has had consequences for sport and society and whose legacy we witness today.

Stadiums are, like any built environment, social blueprints that order human experience and actions, marking what is appropriate and shaping people's senses of themselves. Society is defined and shaped through space; it simply cannot exist without places in which to exist and reproduce itself.[20] The built environment is a particularly effective mechanism for naturalizing dominant ideas and behaviors because it *seems* so stable. The solid brick and ancient girders of the old parks suggest permanence, as do the great concrete ramps encircling the modernist stadium saucer. The stadium is thus both medium and message. It is a place where people define themselves through their experiences; it is also a symbol upon which people project their anxieties and aspirations about themselves, their cities, and how each fits into the broader world.[21]

A place like a stadium is many things at once. It is material and spatial, empirical and mappable, constructed of concrete and plastic. The stadium is also something that exists in people's eyes and imaginations, which can be represented and interpreted in different ways. Architects and engineers draw plans and sketches, politicians and sports club owners make speeches and plant stories with chummy reporters, columnists celebrate or critique, and club marketers publish souvenir guides and distribute press releases. Together these groups—often in league with local newspapers and businessmen—produce dominant or official meanings for these structures. Fans, players, and journalists know, interpret, and represent stadiums in their own ways, sometimes embracing the dominant meanings, at other times partially accepting them, and at still others rejecting them outright.[22] They all *live* stadium spaces as embodied analysts, collecting memories and experiences of the place that become layered atop one another. Stadiums are thus material, representational, and lived.[23] They exist within broader structural and historical contexts—economic, political, social, and spatial—that influence how they develop, are represented, and experienced. This study connects these different threads and scales together, intersecting close readings of the language and visual representations of stadiums in the postwar era with previous work in sports studies, cultural and economic geography, and urban history.[24]

This story of the modern stadium starts in Brooklyn, at the iconic urban ballpark, Ebbets Field—the focus of the first chapter. Central Brooklyn underwent tremendous racial and economic change in the decade after World War II, and Ebbets Field was located amid much of that change. Though unique in many ways, Ebbets Field exemplifies the circumstances facing the prewar ballpark and central cities in a period of suburbanization and urban disinvestment. It is also where new possibilities for stadium design were most actively imagined—novel proposals that would dramatically reinvent the stadium, making it safe, convenient, and attractive to a new generation of affluent suburban consumers. Chapter 2 explores how postwar stadiums were being imagined and constructed as the national sports landscape shifted dramatically in the 1950s. Walter O'Malley, owner of the Dodgers, played a pivotal role in reshaping that landscape and redefining what a stadium could be. He garnered headlines nationwide by employing celebrity designers and futurists Norman Bel Geddes and Buckminster Fuller to reinvent the urban stadium as a mixed-use community center in Brooklyn. Ultimately O'Malley turned his back on Brooklyn, moving the Dodgers to Los Angeles, where he built one of the first—and certainly one of the most economically successful—modernist stadiums in 1962. O'Malley and the Dodgers weren't alone, as other major league clubs were also lured to new cities— or convinced to remain in old ones—by publicly built stadiums. Three subsequent chapters explore adaptations of the modernist stadium in places with different civic, economic, and sporting cultures: Shea Stadium in Queens (opened in 1964), the Houston Astrodome (1965), and Busch Stadium in St. Louis (1966). While these three stadiums were similar in many ways, they also reflect how the stadium meant various things to different communities. In each place, the modern stadium took on distinctive symbolic meanings in the hands of politicians, businessmen, and everyday citizens; through language and imagery, people projected their anxieties and aspirations about their places in the world onto these new monuments to sport. The final chapter considers the development of the modernist stadium in the 1970s and its influence on subsequent stadium design, culture, and urban life, from the 1990s to today. What was once an adventure quickly became routine, as functionalist multipurpose stadiums popped up like concrete mushrooms in city after city throughout the 1970s. These modernist monuments—outfitted in plastic seats and synthetic grass, swelling with televisual scoreboards and luxury suites, often topped by domed roofs—soon seemed a decade behind the times, out of place in a culture increasingly concerned with heritage, ecology, and authenticity. When cities had mustered the political and economic capital to build again, they made a seemingly dramatic departure from the modern form. Most commentators celebrated what seemed a rebuke of modernist stadium design, announced with the opening of Baltimore's Camden Yards in 1992—a baseball park outfitted in brick and steel, seemingly stitched into the cityscape not far from the popular Inner Harbor entertainment district. The modern concrete cylinder was splintered apart, revealing carefully framed vistas of skyscrapers downtown. Asymmetrical and idiosyncratic, it recalled the old classics like Boston's Fenway Park and Cincinnati's Crosley Field. The stadium, it seemed, had returned to its roots. Modernist universalism was replaced with local identity, history, and accents of authenticity. Inspired by Camden Yards, politicians and business elites across the country drove a new wave of stadium construction throughout the 1990s and 2000s, tearing down modernist stadiums that were deemed old and obsolete, replacing them with sporting monuments that seemed to celebrate a new spirit of democratic localism and diverse urbanism.

Washington had once been at the forefront of stadium redesign. When it opened in 1961, District of Columbia Stadium was the first of the multisport concrete cylinders. But by the end of the century, the stadium's only regular tenant was D.C. United of Major League Soccer, a league whose name was more aspirational than accurate. The original Senators, who had played all those seasons at Griffith Stadium, had flown west to the

FIGURE 6. Nationals Park and Near Southeast in 2008. The Capitol is visible directly north of the stadium. PHOTO BY G FIUME/GETTY IMAGES.

Minneapolis suburbs in 1960. Their replacement club, also known as the Senators, had lasted just eleven seasons in Washington before leaving for Texas. The city's NFL team had departed for the Maryland suburbs in 1997.[25]

But the old stadium got another shot at the big leagues. Major League Baseball relocated the Montreal Expos to the nation's capital in 2005, after the mayor promised that Washington would build the club and its owners a new baseball park. As the politics and planning for the new ballpark were worked out, the newly christened "Nationals" played three seasons at old D.C. Stadium (which had been renamed RFK, after the assassinated Robert F. Kennedy, in 1969). Baseball at RFK provoked some sentimentality among the city's older fans—those who could remember summer games played there over three decades before. But many treated RFK with scorn. Reporters called it a "heinous, mausoleum-like" stadium and a "dilapidated multi-use facility" that was "baseball's equivalent of a shack." When the initial designs for a new Nationals ballpark were publicized, columnist George Will hailed it as "the complete reverse of those dual-purpose monstrosities." Most other cities had slain their modernist monsters, but Washington's stadium, the original multipurpose monster, remained.[26]

The District of Columbia arrived to the new ballpark party unfashionably late when it opened Nationals Park in 2008. City officials hoped to distinguish their new park from those that had been built over the previous fifteen years—ballparks that had taken their cues from nearby Baltimore's much-celebrated, retro Camden Yards. Planners and politicians asked the architects to abandon what one journalist called the "trademark red-brick throwback style" and "create something fresh to symbolize the national pastime in the nation's capital." They hoped to design a building that would feel "indigenous" to the city—a reflection of the two faces of Washington, the federal and the local. Stone was meant to echo federal landmarks like the Capitol Dome. Glass façades were supposed to express the "transparency of democracy," as the lead designer put it.[27] The Capitol Dome and Washington Monument would be visible from upper-deck seats along the first-base line; the Anacostia River could be seen through the stadium's south-facing glass wall. The chief executive of the D.C. Sports and Entertainment Commission, which oversaw the project, said, "We want to create a piece of architecture that when people see it on TV, they immediately associate it with Washington, D.C." If the concrete cylinder of D.C. Stadium had obliterated a sense of place, Nationals Park was quite consciously designed to produce it.

One of the most popular markers of authentic localism was Ben's Chili Bowl, where fans stood in line for over half an hour on opening day to order Ben's famous chili dogs and "half smokes."[28] The original restaurant had opened in 1958 on U Street, mere blocks from Griffith Stadium. Ben's had witnessed the shuttering of the old stadium in 1961; it then helped open the new ballpark nearly a half century later. This seemed only fitting, as the new park and its setting so actively gestured to the old stadium and neighborhood.

Nationals Park was loaded with nostalgic references to Griffith Stadium: statues and plac-
ards of legendary players, memorabilia plastered on the walls of clubs and restaurants,
old-timey pennants hanging from rafters, and baseball history posters lining the concourses. The stadium's very structure—with stands hugging the field and views outside
the seating bowl—was a throwback to the form of the traditional ballpark. The new park
acknowledged its debt to the old grounds by replicating its outfield dimensions—their
shared asymmetries a direct rebuke to the standardized outfield of D.C. Stadium.[29] But
Nationals Park didn't just conjure echoes of Griffith Stadium; it also signaled a return to
its brand of urban life. The new stadium was intended to anchor vast redevelopment of
Washington's Near Southeast neighborhood, reproducing it in the image of a pre–World
War II urbanism—a dense streetscape of housing, retail, and entertainment.

But, of course, Nationals Park isn't Griffith Stadium. If we look past the themed celebrations of place and simulations of urban diversity, we see that today's stadiums differ
starkly from those they pretend to emulate. Glass façades might suggest a "transparency
of democracy," but only the people inside the stadium enjoy the view. Some of those in the
upper deck can see the Washington Monument, but only because those stands are perched
atop three levels of exclusive clubs, luxury suites, and premium seating.[30] The public paid
over $736 million for this; the Nationals and Major League Baseball pitched in just $31
million.[31] In spite of the public investment, the cost of non-premium tickets went up 30
percent with the new stadium's opening. And those seats were smaller than RFK's. Meanwhile, the Nationals' operating income went from $19.5 million to $43.7 million. Team
owners paid $450 million for the team in 2006; it is now valued at $1.28 billion. Private
profits from public costs.[32]

How did we get from Griffith Stadium to Nationals Park, from U Street to a gentrified
Near Southeast? That road passes through D.C. Stadium and many stadiums like it, built
across the country throughout the 1960s and 1970s. The modernist stadium has been dismissed as a strange functionalist failure in our sports and architectural history. It has thus
been largely neglected. But these modern coliseums tell us a great deal about who we were,
who we aspired to be, how we experienced space and the city, and how we conceived of
ourselves as a public. We see the legacies of these beliefs and behaviors in the disingenuous simulations of democracy that our stadiums have become.

CHAPTER 1

URBAN INTIMACY, URBAN ANXIETY

STADIUM CULTURE AND THE OLD CITY

OPENING DAY, APRIL 15, 1947, EBBETS FIELD, BROOKLYN. Dodgers supporters and sportswriters obsessed over who would replace iconic manager Leo Durocher, suspended for a year by baseball commissioner Happy Chandler for "conduct detrimental to baseball," which included assaulting a fan and hanging out with gamblers. As the Durocher saga dominated the headlines, the game went on. Everett McCooey, backed by the Fourteenth Regiment band, sang the national anthem. Borough president John Cashmore threw out the first ball. The famous Dodger band held up a sign entreating Chandler to free Durocher. Surprisingly, there were just 26,623 at the grounds; Arthur Daley of the *New York Times* noted, "It was a calmer and quieter Ebbets Field than we've known in a long while. It wasn't even a filled Ebbets Field because there were yawning spaces deep in the upper left-field stands. This was the same old story, of course. If a sell-out is mentioned, the crowds stay away in droves." Harold Burr of the *Brooklyn Daily Eagle* had promised in that morning's paper that "hordes" would "storm the gates early . . . a capacity crowd of 35,000 with the customers clinging to the rafters"; afterward he found the actual turnout "disappointing," speculating that the smallpox scare might have convinced some to stay home. On this stage, old-timer Pete Reiser laced a game-winning double against the right-field wall, just inside the foul pole; the laser knocked in Eddie Stanky, who had kicked off the inning with a walk, and the Dodgers' new first baseman, who had led off with a bunt.

While Durocher's name dominated the headlines in April 1947, that first baseman, Jackie Robinson, would become an icon.[1]

The day that Robinson broke baseball's color line was one that sportswriter Lester Rodney would remember as "oddly constrained." There were more African Americans there than at previous opening days, but hardly the black crowds that many expected and "some had feared," as Rodney put it.[2] Those black fans, many of whom may have been at their first major league baseball game, were reserved, heeding the advice of general manager Branch Rickey, who was worried that their exuberance might agitate fans and players who weren't fully on board with the project of desegregation. The players themselves had to adjust to a monumental change. One Dodger player said, "Having Jackie on the team is still a little strange, just like anything else that's new. We just don't know how to act with him. But he'll be accepted in time. You can be sure of that. Other sports have had Negroes. Why not baseball? I'm for him, if he can win games. That's the only test I ask."[3] Other players, managers, and fans would prove less philosophical in the games that would come, responding venomously to the presence of a black man in the midst of their lily-white boys club.[4]

Two years later, the scene was quite different. By then, Dodgers fans of all colors and ethnicities adored Robinson, and the club had added another black regular to the squad, Roy Campanella. Rodney remembered players like Carl Furillo, who had originally resisted the desegregation of the club, being embraced at the edge of the dugout by Robinson and Campanella—a scene witnessed by "those raucous, salty, kidding, good-natured, integrated Ebbets Field stands, unlike any before or since. You imagined the continuing crowd roar traveling far out into the Brooklyn night to merge with the cheers and animation of those listening to radio's Red Barber in Flatbush, Brownsville, Red Hook, Bay Ridge, Canarsie, Bensonhurst, Coney Island."[5] This was Ebbets Field—a ballpark that stretched from its single city block in central Brooklyn to every neighborhood in the borough.

Ebbets Field was the iconic urban ballpark, expressing the rambunctious diversity of the old city, a city of neighborhoods. Versions of this urban space existed in cities and towns across the country during baseball's boom years in the late 1940s. Of course, the makeup of the stands varied from place to place. None of them was Brooklyn, though Brooklyn seemed to travel with the Dodgers; Jackie and the Bums always boosted attendance at away games, adopted by baseball fans, black and white, in places like St. Louis and Chicago.[6] This was, after all, the team that had broken the shameful color barrier. But even when Brooklyn wasn't in town, the old ballparks were places where strangers congregated—old and young, rich and poor, baseball-loving women and men, people of color and ethnic whites. In Manhattan, this ballpark was Harlem's Polo Grounds, home of the Dodgers' archrivals, the Giants. In Milwaukee, it was Borchert Field, a park pinched into a narrow rectangular lot, surrounded on all sides by two-story, single-family homes and

FIGURE 7. The diversity of the Ebbets Field stands—a diversity of age, sex, and race—is on display in this photograph from around 1950. A brave Yankees fan turns a hand-cranked siren in the foreground. BROOKLYN PUBLIC LIBRARY—BROOKLYN COLLECTION.

duplexes. In Houston, it was Buff Stadium, snug against railroad tracks in an industrial area on the edge of the city's African American Third Ward. In San Francisco, it was Seals Stadium on 16th Street in the North Mission District, amid recently opened Latin American restaurants and *panaderías*, as well as working-class apartments and flophouses convenient to the jobs available south of Market Street and along the waterfront. From coast to coast, professional playing fields were *urban*—places that embodied and reckoned with urban diversity and change at a time when cities were changing profoundly. Ebbets Field and other ballparks like it were living examples of the prewar urban and served as foils against which a new, modern generation of stadiums would be defined. Walter O'Malley, owner of the Dodgers, led this reinvention of the stadium—first by recognizing, in the late 1940s, problems that faced urban ballparks in a suburban age; next by reconceptualizing the possibilities of stadium space, employing celebrity designers like Norman Bel

Geddes and Buckminster Fuller in the 1950s; and then by ripping Brooklyn's club out of the borough in 1957 and planting it in a gleaming new ballpark nestled in the Los Angeles hills. O'Malley mimicked the move millions of white Americans made in the postwar era—from cities to suburbs, from the Rust Belt to the Sun Belt—building a new split-level home for his baseball team with the help of public subsidy. Housing policy, real estate procedures, highway construction, urban renewal, and a new emphasis on consumption redefined the American landscape and with it how people experienced and understood the world they lived in. The stadium was both actor and stage for the restructuring of midcentury life.

The Neighborhood Ballpark

Ebbets Field, like most urban ballparks, had been long anchored in its neighborhood by the end of World War II. The baseball park had opened on April 5, 1913, on four and a half acres in Brooklyn in an area known as Pigtown. It was, as the name suggests, a popular spot for pigs that came to feed on the garbage pit locals had created there. The new Ebbets Field was little more than a block from the western edge of Prospect Park. It brushed up against Bedford Avenue, just north of Empire Boulevard, in a poor Italian area. The ballpark was on the fringes of the city in 1913, but it was accessible to most of Brooklyn via trolley lines and Manhattan by elevated train or subway; there was also a parking lot across the street from the field, for those few arriving by car. To acquire this promising block, club owner Charles Ebbets had formed a dummy company to buy up the lots, trying to maintain some level of secrecy for the overall plan lest owners raise their demands. Over four years, Ebbets quietly pieced together twelve hundred individual lots, owned by fifteen different people, at a cost of two hundred thousand dollars. The high cost of the land rendered Ebbets nearly broke, so he sold half the club's stock to finance the construction of the new baseball stadium. His new co-owners were politically connected contractors, Edward J. and Stephen W. McKeever, sons of Irish immigrants. With their backing, construction began at the site on March 4, 1912. In the end, the cost of the new baseball palace was seven hundred fifty thousand dollars.[7]

By Jackie Robinson's debut in the late 1940s, the stadium's Romanesque Revival façade marked it as a structure from another era—one in which baseball competed with vaudeville theaters and amusement parks.[8] Visitors passed under an awning at the main entrance at Sullivan Place and McKeever Place into a dramatic rotunda eighty feet in diameter, twenty-seven feet tall, with Italian marble walls and tile floors embellished with faux baseball stitching. From the center hung a themed chandelier consisting of twelve baseball light globes dangling from twelve bats. Doris Kearns Goodwin, recalling a visit to Ebbets Field as a child, claimed the rotunda was "like a train station in a dream, with doz-

FIGURE 8. Ebbets Field in Brooklyn. The ballpark is just east of Prospect Park, in the bottom right corner of the photo. Downtown Brooklyn is at the far end of Flatbush Avenue, which bisects the park. Manhattan is beyond that, at the top of the image. BROOKLYN PUBLIC LIBRARY—BROOKLYN COLLECTION.

ens of gilded ticket windows scattered around the floor."[9] Dodgers promotions director Irving Rudd remembered the rotunda as "a huge cavelike opening which on the hottest days was refreshingly cool."[10] From there, customers walked through tunneled ramps into the stadium, emerging from beneath the stands to find the reddish browns of the diamond, the rich green of the grass, the colorful advertising on the outfield walls, and the intense enclosure of the grandstands.[11]

Viewed from above, Ebbets Field was shaped like a soggy cardboard box with one side kicked out. Double-decked, roofed grandstands, propped up with support posts, surrounded most of the field, coursing alongside the first- and third-base lines and across left field to straightaway center. The bank of seats in straightaway center was slightly taller than the connecting stands along left field, as a few extra rows of seating at the top pushed the roof higher, giving the grandstand an awkward, incongruous accent mark. A low wall and

FIGURE 9. The main entrance to Ebbets Field, at McKeever and Sullivan places, marked baseball's arrival as a popular and lucrative middle-class entertainment. BROOKLYN PUBLIC LIBRARY—BROOKLYN COLLECTION.

fence separated fans from the field along the baselines; the outfield walls were lined with advertising—for men's deodorant, restaurants, beer, cigarettes, and gasoline—that spoke particularly to a male crowd. Banks of lights sat atop the roofs, their supporting frames angled forward to the roof edge, seeming to press the lights inward, squeezing the air above the field and accentuating the verticality of the stands, one deck poised above the other.

The intensity of enclosure was released in right field, where the proximity of Bedford Avenue barred the erection of a grandstand. Instead, there was just a wall dividing the field from the street. It was fifteen feet tall, sloping toward the infield at the base before straightening out perpendicular to the ground as it rose. The wall was covered with colorful advertising for products like Gem razors, Lucky Strike cigarettes, and Mobil gasoline. Atop this solid wall sat a wire fence, peaking at 40 feet tall, designed to keep batted balls inside the park (the right-field wall was a mere 297 feet from home plate at its closest point, before stretching to 397 feet from home in center field). Outfielder Floyd "Babe" Herman claimed that they built the fence because his home runs were "breaking all the windows on the other side of Bedford Avenue."[12] Balls hitting the wall usually caromed onto the field unpredictably and were best handled by Dodgers outfielders familiar with the screen's eccentricities. In the middle of the right-field wall was a broad, black scoreboard (itself nearly 30 feet tall), which protruded from the main wall, and was topped with a Schaefer beer sign that announced hits and errors (the "h" would light up for a hit, the "e" for an error). At the base of the scoreboard was the famous "HIT SIGN, WIN SUIT" advertisement for clothier (and future borough president) Abe Stark. On the other side of the fence was Brooklyn: apartment buildings, plastered with advertisements for Sani-White shoe polish and Marlboro cigarettes, squatted across Bedford Avenue. A DeSoto car dealership and gas station, its lots used for parking during games, sat beyond the first-base foul pole.[13] There were walls around the field, but the boundaries between city and ballpark seemed permeable.

Ebbets Field defied the limitations set by the bordering streets, swelling into the neighborhood and borough beyond. Overflow crowds not only stood in the aisles but also perched upon the roofs of the apartment buildings across the street, looking down upon the park below. The noise of the park, according to one historian, "spilled out Bedford Avenue and into the surrounding neighborhood. It was possible five blocks away to tell if the Dodgers were doing well or not in a particular game by the rise and fall of the sounds."[14] One fan, who grew up ten blocks from the ballpark, recalled, "Lying in bed at night listening to a Dodger game, I'd hear the roar of the crowd on the radio seconds before cheering wafted through the bedroom window."[15] The odors of the city and the ballpark intermingled. The smell of baking bread from the Taystee factory would follow fans from the Franklin Avenue shuttle into the ballpark.[16] Fans inside and out of the stadium could smell the steamed peanuts of vendors. Even the ballpark had a distinctive smell, like the colored ink used in the magazine insert of the *Daily News* according to one fan.[17] Ebbets Field could seem a piece of home itself; one regular referred to it as a "homey park," and as many as half the fans could walk home within twenty minutes to the residential neighborhoods surrounding the park.[18] Those who didn't walk rode subways that cut through Brooklyn's ethnically defined neighborhoods, picking up fellow travelers along the way, before they all emptied out together into the crowded streets headed to the ballpark.[19]

The Culture of Ebbets Field

In a figurative sense, Ebbets Field reached from Red Hook to East New York, Greenpoint to Coney Island. The Dodgers were famously central to Brooklyn identity—an identity that Brooklynites guarded closely. When asked if he was native New Yorker, Robert Gru-

FIGURE 10. The Ebbets Field right-field wall, backed by Bedford Avenue. Distinguishing features included the slanted lower portion of the wall to the right, the "h" and "e" of the Schaefer sign atop the scoreboard (lit up to indicate hits and errors), and the Abe Stark "HIT SIGN, WIN SUIT" advertisement at the bottom of the scoreboard. For a sense of perspective, note the outfielder poised for play. AP PHOTO/LINDSAY.

ber, a childhood fan of the Dodgers, would reply, "Not really, I was born and raised in Brooklyn."[20] The relationship between the borough of Brooklyn and the rest of New York helps explain the peculiar attachment between the Dodgers and their supporters. Indeed, the club had very good teams in the 1950s, Brooklyn had a large population to draw fans from, and the concentration of news media stoked the appetites of baseball aficionados. But the borough's second-class status to Manhattan—ever since the consolidation of the five boroughs at the turn of the century—is central to understanding the club's significance in the imaginations of Brooklynites. With consolidation Brooklyn became, in the mind of one historian, a "comic foil" to illustrious Manhattan, and the Dodgers represented a potential escape from "a humiliating burlesque role."[21] Forced to play second fiddle to Manhattanites—and continually dismissed as rubes—Brooklynites could mark their difference and claim their exceptionalism through their ball club.

Though various ballparks anchored neighborhoods and neighborhood identities in different cities, nowhere was the irregularity of built space so closely matched to the irregularity of behavior as it was in postwar Brooklyn. The Dodgers were essential to

the identities of Brooklynites, and Ebbets Field was at the core of the borough's identity. The vocal cast of characters in the stands was widely regarded as the most peculiar
in baseball—"our special type of fan," according to longtime *Daily News* sportswriter
Dick Young—and a fitting group of fans for distinctive Ebbets Field and Brooklyn.[22] *New
York Times* sportswriter Arthur Daley called the ballpark a "sanctuary for zaniness" with
"a warm and human touch rarely found in the coldly efficient confines of Yankee Stadium."[23] Red Barber, an everyday observer of Ebbets Field antics, called the park "the
rhubarb patch."[24] The unofficial mascot of the Dodgers and their fans was the "bum," a
figure popularized by cartoonist Willard Mullin of the *New York World-Telegram-Sun*.
The bum was a ragged, good-for-nothing, underdog figure expressing both the tragic
tradition of the Dodgers on the field and their fans' status as New York provincials, third
class to the more respected Giants and upscale Yankees.[25] Shabby, cigar-chewing, and
unshaven, Mullin's bum evoked an old, working-class masculine urbanity.[26] The Dodgers Sym-Phony Band (occasionally donning hobo costumes, in deference to the "bum")
provided a constant soundtrack at the park, harassing umpires and opposing players
with tunes like "Three Blind Mice" and "The Worms Crawl In, the Worms Crawl Out."[27]
The eccentric public address announcer, Tex Rickards, added a sense of carnival to the
grounds through his frequent misstatements and malapropisms; once when fans draped
their coats along an upper-deck railing, their colors interfering with the batter's vision,
he publicly requested that "the fans sitting along the rail in left field please remove their
clothes."[28] Gladys Goodding's organ was an institution through the 1940s and 1950s, as
she serenaded players with favorite songs and popularized "Chiapanecas" as standard
ballpark fare.[29] Hilda Chester, perhaps more than anyone else, epitomized the grounds.
A sizable woman with a taste for floral print dresses, Chester led the cheers with her im-
pressive voice and accompanying cowbell. Broadcaster Joe Garagiola claimed her voice
"sounded like the 10-second buzzer at Madison Square Garden. When she let out, you
heard every word."[30] Irving Rudd said of Chester: "Hilda was a sensitive, caring lady.
Once in a while some people didn't understand her and would talk to her as if she were
some demented asylum inmate. She would tell them to talk nicely. She was a dame who
just wanted to ring a cowbell."[31] Put together, these regulars and many others at Ebbets
Field conjured a memorable stadium culture. Baseball commissioner Kenesaw Mountain
Landis, considering the stadium's oddball elements, had once claimed, "This doggone
park is like a pinball machine."[32] Historian Harvey Frommer, tapping another Brooklyn
landmark for inspiration, referred to it as the "Coney Island of ballparks."[33]

Just as visitors to Coney Island thrived on the kinesthetic experience of the jostling
rides and ebullient crowds, the spatial and imaginative intimacy and energies of Ebbets
Field accentuated one another. Fans sat not only close to the field but also quite closely to
one another, and the rambunctious expressiveness of the stadium culture made those phys-

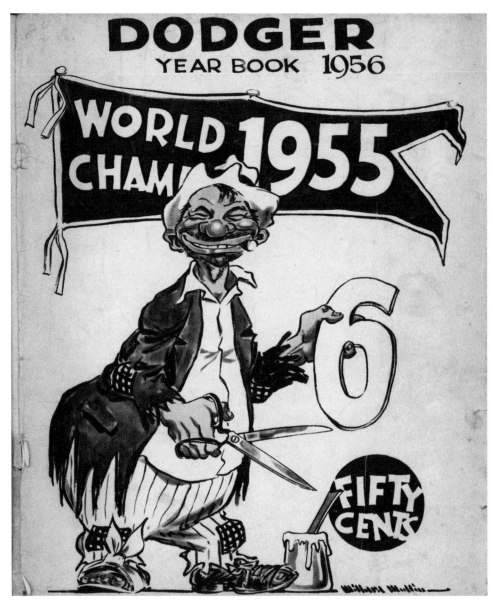

FIGURE 11. Willard Mullin's Dodger bum was embraced by Brooklynites—a defiant symbol of the borough's second-class status and the team's historic ineptitude. Being the reigning "World Champs" was unfamiliar ground for Brooklyn Bums in 1956. A. BARTLETT GIAMATTI RESEARCH CENTER, NATIONAL BASEBALL HALL OF FAME.

FIGURE 12. A man dressed as a Brooklyn Bum stirs up young fans at Ebbets Field in 1951.
BROOKLYN PUBLIC LIBRARY—BROOKLYN COLLECTION.

FIGURE 13. A cat named Rhubarb donates a dollar to the Dodger Sym-Phony Club in 1951, acquiring a club membership card for his troubles. BROOKLYN PUBLIC LIBRARY—BROOKLYN COLLECTION.

ical spaces seem even smaller. Brooklyn resident Howard Golden recalled that at Ebbets, "whether you sat in the box or reserved section, or you sat in the bleachers, you were part of the action." Broadcaster Red Barber took it a step further, suggesting that if you were in a box seat, "you were practically playing the infield." The density and expressiveness of fans made for a roiling, boisterous environment. This was a ballpark where you often knew your neighbors; one fan remembered, "You would go to the bleachers and sit in the same place every day and see and listen to the same people every day."[34] Jim Thomson, stadium supervisor and manager, claimed (with a sort of pride), "You either got along with the fellow sitting next to you, or you fought him. There was no in-between." Though they may have fought one another occasionally, fans more often antagonized those on the field—both the opposing team and their own squad. To reach the clubhouses, players and managers had to run a gauntlet of noise and fans, protected merely by an iron fence. Insults were sometimes accompanied by hurled tomatoes, raw eggs, half-filled cups of beer, and hot dogs.[35]

Players weren't even safe from Brooklyn's notoriously expressive fans once they left the stadium. The Philadelphia Phillies beat the Dodgers at Ebbets Field in the final game of the 1950 season. A Dodgers win would have meant a three-game playoff between the two teams for the league pennant; a Phillies win clinched the pennant for a team with an injured catcher and exhausted pitching staff. In the bottom of the ninth inning, Phillies outfielder Richie Ashburn, not known for his arm strength, threw out a Dodgers runner at home plate, preserving a tied game that the Phillies would win. Future Hall of Fame pitcher Robin Roberts, who was on the mound, called the throw "the biggest in Phillies history." Roberts also remembered that after the game, as he and Ashburn boarded a bus to the train station, "a woman kept calling Richie Ashburn by name. When finally he turned around to look at her, she spat right in his face. I had to grab Whitey [Ashburn] and push him into the bus to keep him from going after her. Some Brooklyn fans had taken that loss personally."[36]

The combative Brooklynite—she who would spit in the face of opposing players—lived in a tapestry of ethnic neighborhoods that didn't always coexist peacefully. Ebbets Field, at the center, was a rare site of cross-ethnic accommodation and synthesis, though one that was historically dominated by men.[37] There had long been a hint of violence about Ebbets Field—a place where opposing players were verbally abused, where objects were thrown, where players fought, and where pitchers threw at batters' heads. But the ballpark was changing into a new sort of place after the war—not just a place for working- and middle-class men, various shades of white, whose fathers and grandfathers had come to Brooklyn from different European nations. Now there were African Americans. Now there were more women as well—a third of the customers. No longer was the ballpark the domain of white, working-class men who had dominated the park before the war.[38]

The bleacher seats—traditional home of the hardiest supporters—had become diversified enough in 1948 to warrant attention in the *New York Times*. Ticket takers and police noted that the population of the bleachers had shifted since the war, hosting many more children, women, and African Americans. During afternoon games, "perhaps 40 percent of the bleacher clientele at Ebbets Field may be composed of noisy, assertive, self-reliant wiseguys no taller than a baseball bat," according to the reporter. Groups of young women, "unescorted by males," the reporter observed, "flock to the bleachers in pairs, trios and quartets. They are equally quick, and twice as shrill, as the boys surrounding them in appreciation of a fine point of the game." The club had been deliberately trying to attract women to the ballpark through discount-price Ladies' Days since the late 1930s. More adult women, accustomed to following the Dodgers' afternoon games from home through the radio (and, increasingly, television), began coming to Ebbets Field in greater numbers as well. More African Americans had been attending games since the arrival of Jackie Robinson the pre-

FIGURE 14. Barbara Anne Greene from Crown Heights and Anita Tinkoff of Brownsville, both eighteen years old, express lethal contempt for the Dodgers' rivals from Manhattan in 1952. BROOKLYN PUBLIC LIBRARY—BROOKLYN COLLECTION.

vious year and new catcher Roy Campanella in 1948. The reporter concluded, "The effect of more youth and femininity has been to give the bleachers a new look. The spirit is less alcoholic, the air less profane, the whole atmosphere softer, though not quieter. The conception of the typical bleacher fan as a middle-aged, vulgar, boozing loafer, dividing his idleness between the ball park and the poolroom, is no longer valid, if it ever was."[39]

The *Brooklyn Eagle*'s front-page coverage of the opening game of the 1952 World Series suggested just how diverse a crowd Ebbets Field hosted. A photograph taken outside the bleacher gate displayed a group of men, both black and white, some holding homemade signs. Below the photo, an article titled "Faithful Jam Ebbets Field" introduced readers to that day's crowd—one that was "jammed to the rafters" with "office boys mourning 'dead grandmothers,' . . . salesmen 'too sick' to report to work, celebrities from many walks of life, and characters of many types." Nearly all of the fans the reporters interviewed were women—though the writers didn't explicitly comment on this, suggesting just how commonplace the female fan was at Ebbets. Carrie Koschnick, who boasted that she had missed just fifteen games the Dodgers had played over the previous forty-two seasons, made the trip from Bedford-Stuyvesant and sat out in the rowdy bleachers. She was accompanied by a friend who claimed she could see the game better from her bedroom window—she lived just around the corner from Ebbets—but went along so she could give her husband a full report that evening. Fourteen-year-old Virginia Reime made a four-mile trip from Borough Park. She had been to one hundred games since she was four, though this was her first World Series game. She brought along a radio to balance what she saw on the field with Red Barber's perspective from the broadcast booth. Another article in that day's paper noted the impending birthday of ninety-eight-year-old Calista Bryson of Fort Greene; the title announced, "She Still Remembers Lincoln—And Roots for the Dodgers."[40] Alongside the Dodgers' more famous female fans—poet Marianne Moore, for example, and Hilda Chester—were many anonymous but committed and knowledgeable women at the ballpark.

New female fans joined these seasoned ones at the ballpark in the postwar years. Department store Abraham & Straus, Brooklyn's largest, took advantage of this by scheduling an A&S Ladies' Day Baseball Clinic where women could learn "the lingo of baseball" from the likes of Jackie Robinson, shortstop Pee Wee Reese, broadcaster Vin Scully, manager Charley Dressen, and owner Walter O'Malley. Rachel Robinson and Dorothy Reese would also attend. An advertisement for the event in the *Brooklyn Eagle*, titled "For Ladies Only!" instructed readers to "Drop the mop . . . leave hubby at home . . . it's time for the women of Brooklyn to become grandstand managers . . . firm Dodger rooters right along with the men. If you've been under the misapprehension that a *Pop Fly* was an insect's daddy . . . that [Dodger player] *Preacher Roe* was akin to Shad Roe . . . that *batter up* meant the wheatcakes were rising . . . Surprise the husband or boy friend with your new baseball lingo." After they had acquired the inside dope that would wow the men in their lives, women could also purchase items from the store's new line of Dodgers accessories. The advertisement's illustrations expressed many of the clichés about female fans—women puzzled over simple baseball terminology, fretted over a scorecard (under pressure from a condescending husband), delighted in ballpark food and drink, and flirted with the players.[41]

Though women participated in Dodgers baseball culture, both in and out of the stadium, they were hardly considered equals—as the Abraham & Straus advertisement reveals. Many men were quick to dismiss female fans as second-rate—an attitude expressed not just in the stands but through a sporting press well practiced in treating women like children and sex objects (particularly as depicted through photos). *Brooklyn Eagle* sportswriter Sid Frigand, for example, would write that his wife "doesn't know beans about baseball" and would continually ask him naive questions about the Dodgers at the end of each day. Cartoons in the *Eagle* consistently centered on supposedly typical female misconceptions of the game on the field or women's preoccupations with how attractive the players were. Photographs of female fans and players' wives often staged them as eye candy for a presumably male viewer.[42]

The rhetorical marginalization of women went hand in hand with an athletic masculinity that a sport like baseball rigorously maintained—particularly during the postwar era, as gender roles were being increasingly distinguished and enforced. In terms of athletic ability, most of the men in the stands would have been more athletically comparable to the female spectators alongside them than the remarkable players on the field; however, male spectators no doubt self-identified, by virtue of their shared sex, more with the men on the field, imaginatively stealing some of their rugged and vigorous masculinity for themselves.[43] The presence of more women in the stands complicated what had once been a more masculine space, but it didn't fully undo its masculine edge.

More women were coming to the ballpark; so too were kids. The Dodgers masterfully recruited new generations of fans—particularly boys who played in the Brooklyn Amateur Baseball Foundation, which benefited handsomely from donations raised by the club. By 1951, there were over a thousand teams playing in the various leagues at the Parade Grounds in the south end of Prospect Park. Dodgers scouts patrolled the grounds, and the club signed about ten local boys a year to their minor league system. They were given contracts at a pittance, but the signings encouraged young boys to imagine themselves someday playing on the revered Ebbets Field diamond. Italians, Irish, Jews, Greeks, and Scandinavians—ethnic groups that would often view each other antagonistically on the streets of Brooklyn—played with and against one another, most of them sharing, at the very least, a love of baseball and the hometown Dodgers. The Knothole Club provided another avenue for the Dodgers to incubate new fans. That organization supplied more than one hundred thousand free admissions to kids each year, including a whopping two hundred thousand in 1954 (20 percent of the total paid attendance that season). Young Brooklynites would get out of school early, be herded onto buses, and then be deposited in entire sections of the ballpark for afternoon games. These kids knew how to play the part of the proper Ebbets Field rooter; at one game in 1954, they targeted outfielders with what remained of their lunches. Umpires also complained of being on the receiving end of such behavior, noting that it was more often practiced at Ebbets Field than other parks.[44]

African Americans also came to the ballpark in greater numbers, as black players were finally allowed back into organized baseball.[45] Robinson's presence—in regular season games and preseason tours—always drew black fans through the turnstiles, wherever the game was played. The Montreal Royals, the minor league team where Robinson began his career in desegregated baseball in 1946, set a record for home attendance that year and played in front of three times as many fans on the road as they had in 1945. In places like Buffalo and Baltimore, up to 50 percent of the stands were filled with African Americans when Robinson played. Black newspapers often encouraged their readers to tamp down their exuberance, fearing a backlash from antagonistic white fans. It was, however, difficult for these fans to hold back; in fact, the black press often failed to take its own advice. Once Robinson made the big-league squad, many southern cities, including Dallas, Oklahoma City, Mobile, and Atlanta, lobbied the Dodgers to play in their cities in order to exploit both black and white interest. Responses in different markets would be mixed; in Atlanta, for example, black cheers were met with white boos, which in turn were overwhelmed by white applause.[46]

Many owners craved the attendance income that black players could stimulate, but others were, in fact, quite fearful of black attendance. A major league steering committee, chaired by Larry MacPhail of the Yankees and including both league presidents and the owners of the Boston Red Sox, St. Louis Cardinals, and Chicago Cubs, investigated (among other things) the "Race Question" in 1946—over two months after Robinson had played his first game with the Montreal Royals. MacPhail's concerns weren't with how to further desegregate the game but rather how to defend baseball's reputation against those who were demanding accelerated desegregation. Noting Robinson's impact on black attendance, he worried that signing more players would further spur an African American clientele in the stands. He fretted that the value of franchises would decline if African Americans made up a sizable portion of the audience. Furthermore, signing players away from the Negro Leagues could ultimately end in its demise—and the loss of jobs for black players. MacPhail was likely more concerned with how this would hurt the bottom line of white major league owners, as they regularly leased out their stadiums to the black ball clubs. MacPhail's report was rejected by the committee, but it would be thirteen years before every club had signed at least one black player.[47]

FIGURE 15. The Dodgers' signing of black players in the late 1940s attracted more black spectators to Ebbets Field. Here a multiracial crowd of supporters shares coffee as they wait to enter the ballpark in 1949. BROOKLYN PUBLIC LIBRARY—BROOKLYN COLLECTION.

Sportswriter Roger Kahn remembered one of the Yankees' top executives say, "after three martinis," that they wouldn't ever sign a black player: "We don't want that sort of crowd. It would offend boxholders from Westchester to have to sit with niggers."[48] The Dodgers, of course, weren't the Yankees, and many white Brooklyn fans idolized Jackie Robinson and celebrated the club's desegregation as an expression of American democracy. Ivan Hametz remembered his Greek Jewish immigrant father telling him, as a ten-year-old, that the Dodgers were adding a black first baseman. The son's nonchalant response—"Can he hit?"—evoked a spirited retort from his father, who, "in a thick Levantine accent, raised his voice in the stentorian manner of Pericles in Athens" before saying, "Think. Please stop and think. This is a giant step toward ending inequality in the United States. It is what we were fighting for in World War II. Justice!"[49] Bill Veeck, the renegade owner of the Cleveland Indians (who would sign the second African American player in the major leagues, Larry Doby, in 1947), claimed, "If Jackie Robinson was the ideal man to break the color line, Brooklyn was also the ideal place."[50] Robert Gruber, who grew up in Brooklyn in the 1940s, explained such logic:

So why was Brooklyn the ideal place to break baseball's color line? Significantly, its citizens were not content with the status quo. They were strivers: hard-working, first- and second-generation immigrants. They were ridiculed outsiders. They were underdogs who could sympathize with an underdog. More than a third of the Brooklynites were Jewish, with their tradition of social justice. Finally, frustrated Dodger fans wanted a winner and Robinson helped to bring them six pennants— and one world championship—in ten years. Winning can be a powerful force for tolerance.[51]

Gruber writes with the aid of hindsight, after a decade of success. Certainly Robinson didn't demand such reverence in his first year. Most Brooklynites weren't Jewish liberals, and yet even for many conservatives, Robinson became a symbol of the American prom- ise of equality.

The breaking of the color line occurred in a society that was largely segregated by ethnicity and race—even, or perhaps especially, in Brooklyn. However, Ebbets Field was a place where there was some sense of common purpose that could, at least momentarily, overcome such boundaries. Though the Dodgers, as a baseball team, sometimes struggled with the inclusion of the proud and occasionally abrasive Robinson and competition from young black players, external racism typically drew the team together in the clubhouse and on the field.[52] Just as the Dodgers team coalesced around Robinson, Campanella, and Don Newcombe, so too did most Dodgers fans, regardless of the biases they bore with them outside of the park. It was the Brooklyn Dodgers against the world, and the team's racial identity was just another factor that distinguished borough residents from those who had "always associated the Brooks with déclassé phenomena like El lines, cobble- stones and walk-up rooming houses," in the words of sportswriter John Lardner.[53]

While fans of all colors, classes, ages, and sexes would get behind the boys in Dodg- er Blue, racial biases and anxieties were more charged in the stands, on the streets, and in the imaginations of the borough's white residents in the decade after the war. After a surge of attendance in the late 1940s—peaking in 1947, when 1.8 million came to the ballpark—fewer people were making the trip to Ebbets Field. Attendance averaged just over 1.1 million from 1950 through 1957, in spite of the club winning four pennants and finishing second three times in a seven-year span. Suburbanization, increased use of and dependence on the automobile, and an expanding range of leisure opportunities all im- pacted attendance at urban ballparks. Throughout the 1950s, upwardly mobile white, eth- nic, working- and middle-class Brooklynites left the city for the growing suburbs. Many would continue to follow the club, albeit through their televisions and radio sets, in the comfort of their living rooms. Their departure from central Brooklyn would profoundly change the cityscape and people's perceptions of the urban public assembled in that old "rhubarb patch" of Ebbets Field.

Building the Suburbs and Constructing the Ghetto

The nickname "Dodgers" was short for "trolley dodgers." Indeed, Ebbets Field was a ballpark for the streetcar age, not the postwar automobile city with its new freeways and orbital suburbs. Use of the automobile exploded after World War II, both allowing the movement of people to suburban communities and driving the demand for those communities. The material and manufacturing demands of the war had squelched automobile purchases in the early 1940s; that would change dramatically in the coming years. While just 70,000 cars were built in 1945, 6.7 million were manufactured in 1950.[54] Americans bought 21.4 million vehicles in the half decade after the war, practically doubling the number of cars on the road.[55] Robert Moses, who lorded over city construction as the head of numerous offices—including the Triborough Bridge and Tunnel Authority—committed New York City to accommodating the private automobile; he constructed expressways, bridges, and tunnels that surged through the city and connected it to the developing suburbs beyond. The increased reliance on the automobile posed a major problem for the Dodgers, as Ebbets Field, which could seat nearly 32,000, possessed parking for just 700 cars and was locked in the midst of a dense urban neighborhood, miles from the nearest expressway. In a society embracing the automobile, Ebbets Field's location amid congested city streets made going to games a hassle for car-driving suburbanites increasingly unwilling to take commuter trains, subways, or buses. This posed a particular problem for O'Malley and the Dodgers because more and more of the team's supporters were becoming car-driving suburbanites moving from Brooklyn to the new developments of Long Island and New Jersey.

After World War II, a massive housing shortage forced many to live with extended families in small city apartments. This shortage was met by a boom in new housing construction, subsidized by the Federal Housing Administration (FHA) and the Veterans Administration (VA), which guaranteed long-term, low-interest mortgages.[56] In 1944, 142,000 housing units were started in the United States. In 1946, 1,023,000 housing units were started. In 1950, an incredible 1,952,000 housing units were begun. There would be over 1,200,000 housing starts per year through 1964. Most of these were single-family, owner-occupied suburban homes with private yards—FHA loan guarantees favored new properties in low-density areas that were geographically separated from business and industry.[57] The suburbs promised families something new and spacious, while the mortgage, when backed by the government, cost the same as (or even less than) rent.[58] In the postwar era, as historian Kenneth T. Jackson writes, "The middle-class suburban family with the new house and the long-term, fixed-rate, FHA-insured mortgage became a symbol, and perhaps a stereotype, of the American way of life."[59]

Not all Americans enjoyed access to this "American way of life." The flip side of federally subsidized suburban prosperity was urban disinvestment and the construction and expansion of racial ghettos through discriminatory lending and real estate practices. The FHA had long discriminated against "inharmonious racial or nationality groups" and thought racial segregation was vital to maintaining investment value—even to the point of recommending that racially restrictive covenants be written into property deeds. Both the FHA and private lenders compiled detailed data on black residents, mapping their present and potential locations and using these maps as bases for denying loans or elevating interest rates.[60] A 1945 population survey used by Brooklyn mortgage lenders charted a solid black crescent that stretched across north-central Brooklyn from Fort Greene through Bedford-Stuyvesant to Brownsville, hugging the neighborhood of Crown Heights—home to Ebbets Field—which was itself pockmarked by a few blocks of "new locations of Negroes."[61] The ballpark sat just ten blocks below what appeared, to mortgage lenders, to be an advancing black cancer.[62]

Suburbanization, paired with racist lending and real estate practices, provoked and channeled a shifting postwar racial geography in Brooklyn and beyond, affecting who and how many went to Ebbets Field, as well as how people perceived the stadium and its relationship with central Brooklyn. During the 1940s and 1950s, 1.2 million whites moved out of New York City, mostly to suburban New York or New Jersey. The population of Long Island exploded in these decades: Nassau County grew from 407,000 to 1.3 million, Suffolk County from 197,000 residents to 667,000. As whites moved to the suburbs, people of color increasingly moved into the city; by November 1957, New York City became the first city in the world with over one million black residents—many who had been coaxed by the promise of work from the war economy and pushed by the modernization of the southern agricultural economy and the oppression of Jim Crow. Puerto Rican migrants joined these newly arriving African Americans, driven by population growth and widespread unemployment back home. This migration increasingly consisted of women, unskilled laborers, and people from rural areas—people poorly equipped to thrive in a modern urban economy. There were just over 60,000 Puerto Ricans in the city in 1940; by 1970, there were over 800,000, more than 10 percent of the city's total population.[63]

Central Brooklyn would be the home of many of these recent arrivals, due in large part to the redlining and blockbusting practiced by lending institutions, real estate agents, and landlords. Brooklyn's black population nearly doubled from 108,263 to 208,478 in the 1940s; it was 371,405 by 1960.[64] The borough had been less racially concentrated than any other major northern city in the 1930s; however, this had changed by the 1950s.[65] Most of this growth occurred in the neighborhood of Bedford-Stuyvesant, just a mile north of Ebbets Field. Nearly 86 percent of black Brooklynites lived there and in adjacent neighborhoods like Brownsville. Residents of Bed-Stuy had the lowest median income in the borough.[66] The area, once a racially and ethnically mixed neighborhood—what one Brooklynite remembered as a "stable, integrated neighborhood"—became impoverished and almost exclusively black by the late 1950s.[67]

Thus was a racial and economic ghetto maintained and expanded to the north and east of Ebbets Field through the 1940s and 1950s. The carrot of affordable mortgages drew many white New Yorkers further south in Brooklyn or out of the borough to the suburbs. Discriminatory real estate policies defined acceptable residential zones for people of color and lumped more and more residents into those areas. Predatory landlords then contributed to the physical decline of those areas by subdividing apartments and neglecting maintenance—all while reaping above-market rents because of the residential limitations black and Latino citizens faced.[68] The policies of the New York City Housing Authority—and Robert Moses, who administered the city's Title I funds—further contributed to the expansion of the ghetto, siting nearly all postwar public housing projects in black neighborhoods like Harlem or "changing" areas like Brownsville and the South Bronx.[69] Ethnic whites ostensibly benefited from racist lending policies and assimilation into an amorphous pool of postwar "whiteness"; and yet they also had to pay for the privilege of moving to a new area, often selling at a discount to escape "changing" neighborhoods. Banks, insurance companies, realtors, and landlords typically profited on both ends of these transactions.[70] African Americans, meanwhile, were often blamed for the conditions that were thrust upon them.[71] Critics called attention to the destruction that such policies wrote on the city. They noted how FHA and private lending policies damaged inner-city neighborhoods by drawing the urban middle class to the suburbs, thus stripping the city of its middle-class taxpayers. They argued that these policies constructed and reinforced income- and race-based segregation of the suburbs and the city.[72] And yet racialized suburbanization and urban disinvestment continued in Brooklyn in the postwar era.

Ebbets Field sat in the midst of these profound changes—outside the ghetto, but too close for many people's comfort. The ballpark was in the southwest corner of Crown Heights. In 1950, the neighborhood was 89 percent white, with 50 to 60 percent of that number Jewish. Median incomes remained well above the borough average, though some African American areas near Atlantic Avenue along the neighborhood's northern edge were significantly poorer. By 1957, there were about 37,000 blacks, both African Americans and recent Afro-Caribbean migrants, in the neighborhood, or 25 percent of the total population.[73]

While the black ghetto loomed north and east of Crown Heights, there were a number of middle-class neighborhoods to the south. Prospect-Lefferts Gardens, just southwest of Ebbets Field, was becoming more racially diverse in the 1950s, a mixture of black, white, Caribbean, and Asian American residents.[74] South of Prospect-Lefferts was Flatbush—an example of "good, solid, almost suburban living," according to a *New York Times* correspondent in 1955. Apartment buildings were increasingly being constructed there, however, altering the makeup of the neighborhood.[75] East Flatbush was largely populated by Italian Americans and American-born Jews living in detached and semidetached wooden frame houses, row houses, and walk-ups that had been built over the previous three decades.[76] Aging Ebbets Field sat within arm's length of all these neighborhoods: the expanding and impoverished African American neighborhoods of Bedford-Stuyvesant and Brownsville to the north and east and the ethnic middle-class neighborhoods of Prospect-Lefferts and Flatbush to the south.

Though the area immediately around the ballpark remained largely white, many assumed that it was just a matter of time before Crown Heights was racially folded into Bed-Stuy and Brownsville. Herb Ross grew up five blocks from Ebbets Field; his family moved away from Brooklyn in 1950. Ross remembered it as a "predominantly white, Jewish neighborhood . . . a stable area, for want of better words. Meaning no blacks." However, when African Americans began moving into the area after the war, the Rosses and many of their friends moved out. He recalled, "I remember when the houses started to sell. Everyone tried to hold on in the beginning. Then one or two would go, and a couple of people would panic, and everybody was worried about real estate values, and the Jews left. We all left." Resident Bill Reddy claimed, "Many of the Jews moved away and gave in to the pressure of the blockbusters and the people trying to get the neighborhood away from them. In '57 everyone who could was running to Long Island. Long Island, Staten Island, and New Jersey, but mostly Long Island, which built up very, very quickly."[77] In truth, Crown Heights remained a white neighborhood for many years beyond the departure of the Dodgers in 1957. It was approximately 70 percent white in 1960 before becoming 70 percent black by the end of that decade.[78] Reddy's memory suggests the panic with which many looked upon the changing race of central Brooklyn and, by succumbing to blockbusting tactics, how they enabled that very process.

The perceptions and realities of spatial change occurred at a time when Brooklyn as a whole seemed to be falling apart. The Navy Yard—the largest employer in New York State during World War II, employing over 71,000 in 1944—was considerably downsized after the war.[79] Brooklyn's sugar and beer industries were in decline. The *Brooklyn Citizen*, one of the borough's two daily newspapers, closed in 1947. The Brooklyn Children's Museum, located in Brower Park in Crown Heights, unsuccessfully solicited money from the city to relocate to a safer neighborhood in 1952. The *Brooklyn Daily Eagle* shut its doors in 1955.

Money that had once maintained the city flowed to the suburbs, leaving behind a rapidly deteriorating landscape. Ebbets Field reflected the physical decline of the borough around it. Like many urban parks, it had suffered years of infrastructural neglect, through the depression and war years. Columns and trusses had corroded; water seepage and freezing had damaged the park's structural deck system.[80] It symbolized the churning spatial, racial, and economic changes of Brooklyn—changes driven by the expanded use of the private automobile, suburbanization, the outmigration of whites, the inmigration of people of color, public housing policies, and urban disinvestment. Central Brooklyn was changing, and with it perceptions of Ebbets Field.

Diversity, Anxiety, and Shifting Perceptions of the Urban Public

It is difficult to pin down precisely what the makeup of Ebbets Field crowds was and how it changed, in part because different people responded so variously to those postwar changes. Gruber remembers the ballpark, on Robinson's debut, as a "happy melting pot."[81] Doris Kearns Goodwin recalls a "sense of camaraderie" among the fans in 1949 as they wore down opposing players with their constant hectoring.[82] But not everyone seemed so enamored with the ballpark and the changes they perceived there. In 1951, one fan wrote in to *Brooklyn Eagle* columnist Tommy Holmes to complain of a drunk, "dressed as badly as a Bowery bum and smelling the same," who sat near him and his wife at a recent game. The drunk filled the first five innings with "loud nonsensical chatter," "constantly borrowed cigarettes from those about him," then "fell into a sound sleep." The writer said he had been going to games for years, "and I have noticed more and more boisterous, intoxicated people in the grandstand to spoil the occasion for those who wish to enjoy the game." Another fan, attending a Parents' Day promotion that same year, called it an "out-and-out disgrace. I was seated in the middle of two foreign language speaking families and in back of two families, including six children ranging in age from four to seven. . . . The six children in front of me were unmanageable . . . and in general made nuisances of themselves by doing everything but watch the ball game. And incidentally, I saw about 20 drunks that day . . . I continue to attend ball games but I wonder for how long."[83] Drinkers, Puerto Ricans, and children, it seems, were enough to ruin the ballpark experience for some—though drunks and children had long been fixtures at the park. But Bill Farrell Jr., who "always said I was baptized a Catholic and a Dodger fan," remembered going to the ballpark as a "family affair" in the 1950s.[84] And for Peter Levine, in tow with his father in 1956, Ebbets was "a world of Jewish men that smelled of Schaefer beer . . . Harry M. Stevens hot dogs, the sweat of a humid spring night, and the familiar, acridly sweet odor of Bering Plazas and El Productos (the cigars of choice in my father's world)."[85]

Ebbets Field was a rich and vocal site of urban unpredictability and interaction for some and a symbol of urban degeneration and degraded diversity for others.

Many visitors to the ballpark thrilled at sharing in the experience of the Dodgers and Ebbets Field—at participating in an urban public that had been more narrowly the domain of white men on the field and in the stands for so long. Roger Green, who lived in Bedford-Stuyvesant, recalled his grandfather visiting from North Carolina, "smelling of Old Spice and his leather suitcase." After a short greeting, his first question was, "When are we gonna see the Dodgers? I gotta see my man Jackie." For Green and other African Americans, Robinson's presence "gave folks the perception that there was something different about Brooklyn, that it was a special kind of place."[86] Many who grew up in Brooklyn in the 1950s recalled the thrill of seeing black players on the field. Gruber notes just how radical this new experience of blackness was in a segregated society, recalling, "We were to become Jackie Robinson fans even though the only blacks most of us knew were caricatures who visited our homes each week via the airwaves as 'Amos 'n' Andy'—and the actors on radio were white."[87] One of the remarkable aspects of Dodgers culture was that most of the players actually lived in Brooklyn, neighbors to their supporters in the stands: "You actually got to see them in uniform, on the streets, doing things ordinary people did," as one Brooklynite noted.[88] Robinson was one of those neighbors. Max Wechsler remembered encountering him outside his home:

> When school was out, I sometimes went with my father in his taxi. One summer morning, we were driving in East Flatbush, down Snyder Avenue, when he pointed out a dark red brick house with a high porch. "I think Jackie Robinson lives there," he said. He parked across the street, and I got out of the cab, stood on the sidewalk, and looked at it. Suddenly the front door opened. A black man in a short-sleeved shirt stepped out. I didn't believe it. Here we were on a quiet street on a summer morning. No one else was around. This man was not wearing the baggy, ice-cream-white uniform of the Brooklyn Dodgers that accentuated his blackness. He was dressed in regular clothes, coming out of a regular house in a regular Brooklyn neighborhood, a guy like anyone else, going to a newspaper or a bottle of milk.[89]

"Regular clothes," "regular house," "regular Brooklyn neighborhood"—black Jackie Robinson was very much a regular guy in these contexts. Many of Brooklyn's black and white residents shared a sense of pride in the Dodgers that was bound up with the club's role in desegregation and seemed wholly unbothered by the inclusion of African American spectators in the stands in the 1950s.

For others, the increasing racial diversity of the Ebbets Field stands undermined the spirit of the place. Robinson and the other black players were a great attraction for many white fans, but according to Dodgers fan Herb Ross, it fundamentally changed the essence of the ballpark. He argues, "It was the Dodgers bringing in Jackie Robinson and other blacks to the ballpark, who changed the whole element of the crowd." The addition of players like Roy Campanella in 1948, Don Newcombe in 1949, Joe Black in 1952, and Junior Gilliam in 1953, "before many teams had any blacks at all," meant that the Dodgers "were filling up the park with blacks," according to Ross. "When the blacks started coming to the game, a lot of whites stopped coming." The "allegiance" of the black fans "was only to Robinson and the black ballplayers. They didn't care about the Symphony or Hilda Chester or even the white players. They didn't have the history we had. The allegiance of the blacks was not to institutions. The allegiance was to Robinson."[90] John Belson explained the changes in similar terms, claiming, "In the '40s the crowds had been all white, but by the mid-50s, after Jackie Robinson had been there for a while, you go to a Sunday doubleheader, and the dominant smell in the ballpark was bagged fried chicken. . . . You had a different crowd. It was no longer a unified crowd."[91] Such comments explicitly connect the presence of African Americans to the degeneration of a coherent Brooklyn Dodgers public. Though the Ebbets Field crowd had long been mixed by class, ethnicity, and even sex since the late 1930s, it had remained "unified" in Belson's mind—a unification grounded in a shared whiteness (however ethnically inflected).

Sportswriter Roger Kahn explains just how overwhelmingly white baseball was at the point of Robinson's intervention:

> Robinson was the cynosure of all eyes. For a long time he shocked people seeing him for the first time simply by the fact of his color: uncompromising ebony. All the baseball heroes had been white men. . . . Every coach, every manager, every umpire, every batting practice pitcher, every human being one had ever seen in uniform on a major league field was white. Without realizing it, one had become conditioned. The grass was green, the dirt was brown and the ballplayers were white. . . . *Black*. . . . The new color jolted the consciousness, in a profound and not quite definable way.[92]

The universal whiteness of baseball had long been a given, and the erosion of that whiteness was, for some, an explicit challenge to racial privilege. While Ross's Jewishness likely deprived him of the full benefits of whiteness, just as it did to many other of Brooklyn's white ethnic residents, baseball had long been a mechanism of assimilation for European immigrants—and Ebbets Field, in the center of Brooklyn, was a stage for racial assimilation par excellence. "The Dodgers," historian Carl Prince argues, "provided a singular and critical source of positive, even aggressive, response, a validation of the class-grittiness that white natives embraced in the borough."[93] Gritty, working-class whiteness was not, however, available to Brooklyn's black population—no matter how loudly they cheered or how many tickets they purchased. For many of Brooklyn's Irish, Italians, and Jews, the presence of African Americans and Latino migrants was a threat, and not just a threat to real estate values. Major league baseball had been an implicit symbol of white exclusivity and supremacy, and Ebbets Field had been a place where ethnic Brooklynites could claim their whiteness; the inclusion of African Americans revealed this, unraveling the symbolic value of the team and ballpark and undermining it as a vehicle to mainstream, white American society for those white ethnics sometimes marginalized in their daily lives.[94]

One man's response mattered more than any other: Dodgers owner Walter O'Malley. He was one of those white Brooklyn residents who saw more black faces in the stands and was, in the words of Brooklyn historian James Rubin, "among the borough's fearful, white, middle-class residents."[95] Sportswriter Dick Young told Roger Kahn that O'Malley wanted to leave Ebbets Field "because the area is getting full of blacks and spics." O'Malley denied having said this to Kahn, but when Kahn mentioned it to Young again, the provocative Young reiterated, "O'Malley also said the trouble with Brooklyn was that the place had too many blacks and spics *and Jews*."[96] Kahn thought that while it was "excessive to accuse him of bigotry," O'Malley "did harbor stereotypes" and "certainly . . . was most comfortable with his Roman Catholic cadre, [Buzzie] Bavasi and Fresco Thompson."[97] O'Malley apologists could point to simple economics as the baseball club's core concern. Irving Rudd, promotions director for the Dodgers, argued that O'Malley's anxieties weren't racial but economic: "You know, a lot of people call O'Malley racist for leaving Brooklyn in the fifties [and relocating the club in Los Angeles], but, I say, he was just concerned about turning a profit. He did not care that the blacks were black, just that the blacks were poor."[98] Blacks may have been poor, as Rudd says, but by Ross and Belson's accounts they were paying to get in the ballpark. To whatever degree O'Malley cared that "the blacks were black," he was tactful enough not to mention race directly, though he could insinuate it, cloaking his comments in chivalric concern: "I was very much concerned about the future when my mother-in-law and my wife couldn't go to Ebbets Field unescorted because of the hoodlums and purse snatchers. I began to become concerned about a location where women, who at the time made up thirty percent of the audience, were afraid to go to the ball park."[99] Evidence suggests that women fearlessly or defiantly continued going to the ballpark in the 1950s, but their presence there likely heightened the stakes for white men who equated blackness with crime and femininity with vulnerability and dependence.

It is impossible to gauge just how ingenuous O'Malley's expressed anxieties were;

Crown Heights remained middle class and relatively prosperous in the mid-1950s, according to a reporter from the *New York Times*.[100] At the same time, the ghettoization of Bed-Stuy and Brownsville—coupled with nationwide concerns about juvenile delinquency and youth gang violence—might very well have shaped people's perceptions of the neighborhood around the ballpark.[101] Regardless of the realities on the ground, O'Malley's comments came after the Dodgers' departure for Los Angeles and were made to justify that move.[102] It is also quite clear that anxieties about crime, physical decay, and poverty were racialized in the minds of many. Herb Ross put a black face to the "hoodlums and purse snatchers" that O'Malley feared, confessing, "I don't know what it was about the blacks that was so frightening. Maybe they [white residents] felt that . . . you used to be able to walk Pitkin Avenue on a Sunday afternoon [east of Ebbets Field in Brownsville]. Some of the best clothing stores. Abe Stark of the 'Hit sign, win suit' had a store there. I guess little by little, people were afraid of getting mugged."[103]

As Brooklyn changed outside the ballpark, it is no surprise that the famously rambunctious stands took on a more sinister aspect to some of those in attendance. Stan Lomax, a baseball writer (and college fraternity brother of O'Malley), feared that there might be a violent incident at the old park: "The scene at Ebbets Field was one of riding on the crest of a volcano. If they didn't get a new park they would have had a riot or some terrible disturbance. Especially at the midweek games—there was too darn much drinking. There were narrow aisles, the seats were too close and you had a rough, tough bunch there. If somebody threw a bottle or stabbed someone—that's all that was needed—the dynamite was there . . . with too many people in too small an area."[104] "Too many people in too small an area": this was a statement that expressed a new postwar regard for spaciousness and comfort—a craving that would be satisfied in the new suburban landscape and modern stadiums of the 1960s. The intimacy of the urban ballpark had become claustrophobic. This was a cause of concern for people like Lomax and O'Malley. Irving Rudd recalled, "O'Malley complained about the deteriorating atmosphere at Ebbets Field throughout his tenure as the Dodgers' president. He always worried about the unruliness in the stands, which he viewed as a manifestation of Brooklyn's changing social scene."[105] Unruliness—long a hallmark of Ebbets Field—was increasingly viewed through the lens of race and class, what Rudd refers to as the "changing social scene," by white men of means.

One of O'Malley's top lieutenants, "Fresco" Thompson, pulled no punches in his assessment of changing Brooklyn. After the Dodgers had departed Ebbets Field and central Brooklyn, he wrote of the old situation, "There were close to 400,000 people within walking distance, in addition to two subway lines, bus lines, and half a dozen trolley car lines feeding us—yet they would continue to supply us with the same element of people, a pretty indigestible potpourri at best."[106] Thompson explained,

The loyal and substantial fan, the family man, had moved away. He was now living in Westchester County, out on Long Island, in New Jersey, or in Akron, Ohio. He was replaced by the undesirables. I brand no race, color, or creed as objectionable. They all have their scum. But unfortunately, the scum was now thick in Brooklyn. The element drifting into decaying Ebbets Field and using unprintable language in catcalling to the players or in the stands would shame women to the extent that on Ladies' Day only a handful of the most rugged and probably deafest of the distaff side could weather the string of words.[107]

Though Thompson acknowledges that "scum" comes in all colors, he appears to have a certain color in mind. Urban diversity, so central to the culture of Brooklyn and Ebbets Field, had become an "indigestible potpourri" for baseball executives like Thompson (who had reimagined the ballpark's archetypal rowdy fan, the bum, as the "family man"). They wanted ballparks that expressed the new suburban sensibility, sorting people by class and race, drawing together respectable men and women into clean, comfortable, roomy new spaces.

O'Malley, Thompson, and the Dodgers were on the front edge of these changes in postwar stadium space. Though Ebbets Field and Brooklyn were in many ways sui generis, they also exemplified how ballparks and cities were changing after World War II. Urban stadiums were typically located in areas that suffered from urban disinvestment the most. A new economy exploded in the postwar years, as white and upwardly mobile Americans shed their old identities as frugal savers and embraced a throwaway culture of consumption. They moved into brand-new suburban homes, stocked with colorful, push-button appliances; they commanded powerful new automobiles, encased in gleaming chrome, that expressed a new era of movement and freedom. The old streetcar ballparks—the realm of trolley dodgers—seemed relics of another time. Walter O'Malley realized before others that the postwar consumer with money to spend would demand more than an old stadium that smelled like stale beer, cigars, and, occasionally, urine.[108] A new Ebbets Field wouldn't be built for Brooklyn Bums but for suburbanites.

CHAPTER 2

FICTION AND FUNCTION

NEW SPACES FOR SPORT IN THE 1950S

MORE PEOPLE CROWDED INTO EBBETS FIELD IN 1947 than in any other year in its existence. The Dodgers won the National League pennant, then lost to the pinstriped Yankees—the Bums' crosstown foil—in a seven-game World Series. Jackie Robinson broke the major league color line, becoming a hero to many and a symbol of racial progress and social possibility. Ebbets Field hosted arguably one of the most diverse stadium scenes and urban publics in American history, a collection of men, women, and children of different economic classes and ethnic and racial identities. And yet, not even three months after this remarkable season had concluded, Walter O'Malley was scouting locations for a new ballpark.

"It had always been recognized that baseball was a business," sportswriter Red Smith noted, "but if you enjoyed the game you could also tell yourself that it was also a sport . . . O'Malley was the first to say out loud that it was all business—a business that he owned and could operate as he chose, and the community the team had pretended to represent for almost seventy years had no voice in the matter at all."[1] Indeed, Walter O'Malley's interest in the sport was largely, if not solely, financial.[2] The passage of the Dodgers' presidency from Branch Rickey to O'Malley in 1950 signified a broader change in the business and culture of baseball. As Rickey's biographer Murray Polner put it, "To Rickey, baseball remained a civil religion which acted out public functions organized religion was unable to perform. O'Malley's faith rested on balance sheets and dividends."[3] Even something as so-cially significant as baseball's desegregation was a matter of dollars and cents for O'Malley; he petulantly told Roger Kahn that Rickey signed Jackie Robinson to boost attendance because a clause in Rickey's contract gave him a percentage of gate receipts.[4] Though this claim partly reflected O'Malley's well-chronicled animosity toward Rickey, it also suggests his tendency to view most things through the lens of profitability—even something as socially consequential as desegregation. Kahn saw O'Malley as a master manipulator who could make money at will. Angry about the Dodgers' move to Los Angeles in 1958, Kahn would later reflect, "It amazes me to this day that once I stood in the ranks of journalists who, in the most furious words they could summon, indicted a capitalist for being moti-vated by a passion for greater profits."[5]

O'Malley was a businessman and people were profits. Embracing the logic of capital-ism, O'Malley believed that the Dodgers could only finish first or last—he would say, "The history of the Brooklyn club is that fiscally you're either first or bankrupt. There is no second place."[6] To finish first the Dodgers had to invest in the team, but finishing first was a means, not an end, for O'Malley. Finishing first had to be profitable to O'Malley to make it worth his while. As he would write in the *Brooklyn Eagle*, "My business is baseball."[7] O'Malley saw people as abstractions, wallets with legs who would either come to the sta-dium or not. He was not concerned with the role of the club in the history of the borough. He was concerned with locating a stadium at its most profitable location and using sta-dium space as profitably as possible.

For a decade after that monumental and profitable season in 1947, Walter O'Malley looked to reinvent the stadium in Brooklyn for a new audience in a new age. Famed the-ater and industrial designer Norman Bel Geddes first bent the ears of the Dodgers in 1948, attempting to sell them on a stadium-as-community-center design that anticipated both the emergent shopping centers of the later 1950s and the "mallparks" of the twenty-first century. Intrigued by the idea, but increasingly weary of Geddes's self-promotion and pricey plans, O'Malley turned to another celebrity designer, Buckminster Fuller, to build him a more affordable version of a domed sports center. Across the country, politicians and hucksters hawked extravagant new stadium proposals to grab public attention—proj-ects that shared the brash confidence and sense of excitement expressed by Geddes's de-signs. None of them would be built, though the stadiums of the 1960s and 1970s would unevenly and incompletely embody Geddes's proposed solutions to the problems of the prewar stadium in the postwar city. These designs exhibited new ways of thinking about stadium space and stadium culture—visions characterized by modernist aesthetics and visual order, the expansion of stadium consumption and entertainment, extensive auto-mation and technological display, acquiescence to the demands of the automobile, and the cultivation of a more orderly and affluent audience.

But Walter O'Malley wasn't the only agent in the shifting national geography of professional sport. Outside of Brooklyn, new stadiums were conceived, pitched, and even built in the fifteen years after World War II. Some of those stadiums were quite radical propositions but existed merely in paper form. Many of the ones that materialized—in places like Milwaukee and Baltimore—were more notable for where in the city they were built rather than how they were designed. As Geddes and Fuller sketched possibilities, O'Malley watched these cities build new stadiums to attract major league baseball and football clubs—stadiums that were, in his mind, rather ordinary. He struggled to find a site for a new stadium in Brooklyn—one easily accessible to suburbanites and Manhattan's business class. He wrestled with New York politicians and the powerful Robert Moses, who had visions of his own for a new stadium in Queens. By the end of the 1950s, a decade after Geddes had started his scheming for the Dodgers, O'Malley figured the ultimate solution to the problems of Brooklyn's Ebbets Field and the changing character of urban space and life: a new Dodger Stadium three thousand miles west in sunny, eager, politically compliant Los Angeles. With its opening in 1962, in the wake of new stadiums in San Francisco and the District of Columbia, a new era of stadium design and culture had taken a recognizable form.

Norman Bel Geddes and the Stadium Futurama

The winter after Robinson's debut with the Dodgers, O'Malley targeted a site for a new stadium in downtown Brooklyn near Borough Hall, at Jay and Tillary streets, adjacent McLaughlin Park. The area was ideal for baseball in O'Malley's estimation, for a variety of reasons. It had great access to a range of different types of transportation: subway, bus, trolley, and private automobiles via tunnel, bridge, and highway. Traffic problems would be minimized by use patterns. In a memorandum he noted that the area was "dead as a door nail" on Saturdays, when many people weren't working. Baseball traffic during the workweek was different than downtown traffic, concentrated in the midafternoon for day games and at night, after area workers had gone home. O'Malley noted that a stadium in downtown Brooklyn would be closer to Columbus Circle than the Polo Grounds on the northern edge of Harlem or Yankee Stadium in the South Bronx. The new stadium would also be near a large population of affluent men, he exclaimed, "in the shadow of Wall Street!" At that time, the site was slated for a housing development; O'Malley hoped that the development site could be swapped with the Ebbets Field lot. If that was untenable, he thought the club could build just south at Jay Street and Myrtle Avenue or directly west at Cadman Plaza. He called the war memorial at Cadman Plaza "a flop," proposing that they "call [the] new ball park Memorial Stadium or Park or What[ever]," flippantly adding, "Put up all the bronze tablets the walls will hold" to memorialize the soldiers. The architect for his new stadium would be "a man by the name of Norman Bel Geddes—who is reputed to be terrific."[8]

The reputation of Norman Bel Geddes—though perhaps unfamiliar to Walter O'Malley—was well established by the late 1940s, thanks particularly to the wildly popular Futurama exhibit at the 1939 New York World's Fair. Visitors were given buttons that read "I have seen the future" as they exited the exhibit housed in the General Motors Building. Over twenty-seven thousand saw the future each day, if the buttons were to be believed, queuing up in lines five- to fifteen-thousand-people long to get a glimpse of Geddes's vision of a 1960 American landscape in miniature and "the motorways of the world of tomorrow." Geddes boasted in 1940, "There have been hit shows and sporting events in the past which had waiting lines for a few days, but never before had there been a line as

FIGURE 16. Walter O'Malley hoped to build in downtown Brooklyn in the late 1940s, targeting the area just east of Cadman Plaza, pictured here. Brooklyn Bridge and lower Manhattan are visible beyond the plaza. BROOKLYN PUBLIC LIBRARY—BROOKLYN COLLECTION.

long as this, renewing itself continuously, month after month, as there was every day at the Fair."[9]

Visitors entered the GM Building through a notch in its massive streamlined façade. Descending switchback ramps in a dark auditorium, they finally arrived at a row of plush, high-backed seats on a rubber-tired conveyor and were taken on a simulated airplane ride over a model of the American landscape of 1960. Geddes's massive dioramas stretched over a three-level, thirty-six-thousand-square-foot area and contained a million trees, half a million buildings, and fifty thousand streamlined cars (ten thousand of them animated). Visitors wowed at a landscape of dams and hydroelectric plants, farms and glass-domed orchards, towns and suburbs, and a modern metropolis of spectacular glass towers spaced across a rationalized cityscape, its grid defined by its means of transportation. Movement by automobile appeared to be the future's defining feature. Pedestrian ways were perched above the street level, protecting walkers from streamlined cars speeding to and from their destinations—while simultaneously enabling the automobile to express itself unimpeded. Geddes and General Motors, whose eight-million-dollar investment funded the exhibit, hoped for such a future of seemingly frictionless movement pivoting on the private automobile.[10]

Through Futurama, Geddes seemingly solved the problem of the automobile in a world that wasn't designed for it. Collisions, traffic, confusion, irritation: people were "eager to find a sensible way out of this planless, suicidal mess." However, Geddes argued, "masses of people can never find a solution to a problem until they are shown the way. Each unit of the mass may have a knowledge of the problem, and each may have his own solution, but until mass opinion is crystallized, brought into focus and made articulate, it amounts to nothing but vague grumbling. One of the best ways to make a solution understandable to everybody is to make it visual, to dramatize it."[11] In Futurama, he dramatized not only how to integrate the automobile into the canvas of the American landscape but also what the new city might look like. It wouldn't look like Central Brooklyn, home of Ebbets Field. And just as he "dramatized" how to reshape the nation to accommodate the automobile—rescripting the city in the process—Geddes would dramatize solutions to the old urban ballpark in his stadium proposals for the Dodgers.

Geddes initially approached the Brooklyn Dodgers by writing to co-owner Branch Rickey in December 1947, proposing a "new stadium principle" that would increase capacity, provide better visibility, and allow expansion at the Ebbets Field site in Crown Heights. Geddes was cryptic about the solution but claimed it could be installed section by section so as to not interfere with baseball play during the season.[12] He then met with O'Malley in January 1948 to discuss his plans; he hoped to gain an audience with the Dodgers' board to present his proposals more fully and formally.[13]

Geddes got the chance in March 1948, when he presented a series of proposals to the

FIGURE 17. Spectators take a simulated airplane ride of the city of 1960 at Norman Bel Geddes's Futurama exhibit at the New York World's Fair of 1939. Manuscripts and Archives Division, The New York Public Library. "General Motors - Futurama - Visitors in moving chairs viewing exhibit," NEW YORK PUBLIC LIBRARY DIGITAL COLLECTIONS.

Dodgers—most of which addressed the deteriorating Ebbets Field. The park would require an estimated six hundred fifty thousand dollars in repairs over the following three years, much of it committed to correcting the structural problems born of water seepage and corrosion. Geddes outlined some possible approaches to the Ebbets Field conditions, including proposals that would rebuild the park on site and one plan for an entirely new stadium at a new location—a plan characteristic of the designer of Futurama.

Most of Geddes's plans, or "schemes," as he called them, would reconstruct Ebbets Field at Bedford Avenue, one section of seating at a time, converting the park from a crooked box to an egg-shaped oval. The playing field would be shifted slightly to the east, moving the western boundary westward, from McKeever Place to Franklin Avenue; the club owned the narrow strip of property between the streets. Doing this would allow Geddes to install stands encircling the entire playing field. This seemed a rational and balanced correction to the park's then lopsided shape, whereby it was squeezed up against Bedford Avenue, separated from the street not by stands of seats but only a wall.

FIGURE 18. Workers set up an urban scene in Futurama, where massive towers sprang out of a grid defined by superhighways—a new American landscape bent to the will of the automobile. Manuscripts and Archives Division, The New York Public Library. "General Motors - Futurama - Artists standing among models of buildings" NEW YORK PUBLIC LIBRARY DIGITAL COLLECTIONS.

The reconstruction schemes were differentiated solely by the amount of seating capacity they would allow in the new, on-site stadium—ranging from 60,000 to 80,400. Geddes would break up the old park's single upper deck, which hung over the lower deck and was supported by columns, into a series of smaller stacked and cantilevered decks; the support posts would be moved toward the back of the stands, not completely eliminating obstructing views but minimizing them. The scheme for maximum seating would create a stadium of four levels—a thirty-row lower level, a twenty-two-row second level, and thirteen-row third and fourth levels. Geddes claimed that three shallow tiers, instead of a single, deep upper deck, would provide 52 percent more capacity in the same area. He also promised that the vertical stacking of shallow tiers would retain "the intimacy of Ebbets Field," in spite of its greatly increased capacity—a sensitive nod to one of the existing park's signature features. Another noteworthy element of his new seating design was the elimination of the tunnels through seating decks that spectators used to get to and from their seats. Ramps in his new schemes would be buried within the sections of seats, running parallel to the rows of seating, sloping upward from a channel between the sections. All told, Geddes's reconstruction of Ebbets Field would yield higher seating capacities, larger and more comfortable seats, more row spacing, wider aisles, fewer columns in sight lines, half the average walking distance for customers, and reduced maintenance, making Brooklyn "the world's most progressive baseball club." Comfort, spaciousness, convenience, mobility, clear sight lines: these were signal qualities of the emerging modernist stadium, contrasting it with existing urban ballparks.

Geddes emphasized that the club had to move forward, past the old ballpark forms. He told the Dodgers' board, "Whether the present property is improved—or new property is developed—it is evident that the Brooklyn baseball club should have a modern plant."[14] Whereas a "conventional design" would be an improvement, the designer was clearly angling for "something entirely new in concept and utility"—a new stadium at a different, less restrictive location. A new modern stadium for the Dodgers could be designed to be more than just a baseball park, drawing new revenue streams from improved concessions, the rental of space as fireproof record storage, the staging of winter sports in the off-season (skating, tobogganing, and skiing on artificial ice and snow), boxing, and midget auto racing.[15] Geddes's new modern stadium would cost an estimated $3,320,000 or $55.32 per seat (at 60,000-seat capacity). This was a bare-bones structural estimate that didn't include items like lighting, toilets, concessions, offices, escalators, clubhouses, and field drainage. Geddes hoped to rationalize service by developing mechanical vendors "to improve service" and eliminate "low grade concessionaire labor." He envisioned a "mechanical ticket selling and admission system" to further eliminate human labor from the space. He wanted to create more sophisticated color schemes for the stadium, as well as design "an intelligent uniform" for the players more attentive to temperature, absorption, color, cleaning, comfort, style, and "popular appeal"—a plan reflecting Geddes's background in theatrical costume design and his characteristic attention to design at all scales.[16]

Finally, Geddes believed that the club should put an "emphasis on developing ideas to attract women."[17] Of course, the Dodgers had been cultivating a female audience since the club's introduction of Ladies' Days in the late 1930s, and baseball club owners had long tried to attract a certain class of women—and the respectability they signified—as a way of "civilizing" male audiences and elevating the game's cultural status (while also conveniently boosting attendance). Geddes's phrasing, however, suggests that he imagined appeals to women who weren't drawn by baseball itself—after all, new ideas would have to be developed. Geddes would have a stadium attract more casual consumers of the game in addition to the die-hards; in the process, he would further feminize a traditionally masculine space.[18]

As a salesman, Geddes seemed to have a two-pronged strategy in his dealings with the Dodgers. He got his foot in the door with more modest promises of a redesigned stadium at the Ebbets Field site, but then used this opening to pitch his more radical ideas about a new stadium altogether. He promised the club that he would implement a "public relations program" that would pique the interest of those who didn't just read the sports pages, grabbing feature space in general-interest magazines like *Life* and securing a presence in syndicated newspaper feature stories, newsreels, radio, and television. He would reach "a new public," and the attention the extravagant plans attracted would enhance the club's "top prestige."[19]

Geddes's appetite for self-promotion pulled against O'Malley's need, as a buyer of real estate, to keep plans quiet. In late February, O'Malley was busy trying to restrain his partner, Branch Rickey, from publicizing plans after an article in the *New York Journal American* scooped the Dodgers' plans for a new stadium.[20] The best strategy, O'Malley told Rickey, was to plant the seeds for a new stadium in the minds of influential figures like Robert Moses and Brooklyn borough president John Cashmore, allowing them to be "the father of the idea." Otherwise, these powerful men might resist a plan if "they thought it was being shoved down their individual or respective throats." Ironically, O'Malley cited a conversation he had with Geddes regarding this strategy, perhaps not yet appreciating what a self-promotional animal his prospective designer was; O'Malley wrote, "Mr. Geddes, with the modesty that goes with one so talented, is more interested in the consummation of something practicable along the lines we have considered than he is a publicity release that might defeat the idea."[21]

News of stadium plans were published by the press in mid-March, though details of the stadium were various and confused. The *New York Post* reported on March 15 that Geddes was working on a stadium covering ten acres in the Borough Hall area, constructed of concrete and stainless steel, with foam rubber seats, and with an eighty-thousand-seat capacity. The following day the *New York Times* reported that Geddes had submitted plans for "a streamlined Ebbets Field" to be built on the Ebbets Field site, quoting O'Malley; he denied that the club was intending to build in downtown Brooklyn. The estimated cost for the reconstructed stadium exceeded six million dollars. O'Malley told the reporter, "We appreciate that the Brooklyn fans are entitled to more seats and in a modern stadium but it just does not seem possible in the near future." The *Brooklyn Eagle* reported yet another version of the story, claiming that plans would be executed, according to Geddes, within three years. The stadium would be located either at the Ebbets Field site or in the Greenpoint neighborhood on the northern boundary of Brooklyn, adjacent the East River and Queens.[22] Geddes told the paper that the new concrete and stainless steel stadium would retain "the intimacy which is the chief attraction of Ebbets Field." It would boast "all modern improvements," including automated ticket collection. The paper reported that owners of small parcels around Ebbets Field had refused to sell to the Dodgers, undermining the possibility of expansion there. In response to this wave of attention, O'Malley made it clear that Geddes was no spokesman for the club. Calling him an "an eminent theater designer," O'Malley told the paper that Geddes had volunteered to study the expansion of Ebbets Field and had "completed his assignment." His plans would be too costly for the Dodgers. Furthermore, O'Malley clarified, "any statement that Mr. Bel Geddes has made to the press is on his own behalf. Of course, he is not talking for the Brooklyn Baseball Club."[23]

O'Malley's denials certainly didn't stop the designer's lips. Geddes called reporters into his Park Avenue office to present them with the stadium schemes he had laid out for the Dodgers. The *New York Herald Tribune* reported that Geddes "articulated on his latest enthusiasm, with presumably the same amount of zeal that produced the Futurama." The designer discussed his plans for a reconstructed Ebbets Field on the current site, oval and made of steel and aluminum (not "cement," the reporter noted explicitly). The outside would be "sheathed with gigantic venetian blinds with three-foot slats" that could be opened and closed to modulate the temperature and wind currents inside the stadium.[24]

Lester Rodney, sports editor for New York's communist paper, the *Daily Worker*, was also impressed by Geddes's vision—though he considered it a bit more critically than did the mainstream press. He recalled the "entrancingly logical slumless world" of Futurama, echoed in the new stadium plans. He made a distinction between Geddes as a "modernistic" designer, as he referred to himself, and a "futuristic" one, as Rodney branded him. Geddes's work was futuristic because "this free enterprise system of ours seems to have all kinds of trouble providing mediocre apartments for its veterans, let alone beautiful planned large communities of homes." The stadium was, by Rodney's accurate estimation, a thing of the future rather than the modern present. But Rodney also walked through, in enhanced detail, the stadium's features. He pointed out plans for elevators and escalators, wider aisles, wider seats with cushions built in, no obstructing posts, lighting incorporated into the structure (rather than perched on trussed frames above it), a sunken field to make for less climbing, lots of restrooms, and the climate-manipulating venetian blinds. He mentioned the possibility of a roof atop the whole thing—a rather significant detail that was oddly left out of other reports.[25]

Stories of Geddes's futuristic stadium plans for the Dodgers spread well beyond the boundaries of New York, as they were eagerly picked up by news syndicates. Such stories called Geddes a "futuristic designer who sees weird but wonderful things through his saucer-sized eyeglasses." He was cast as a versatile eccentric; his designs had "run the futuristic scale from streamlined yachts to a study that determined milady's kitchen should be painted white to soothe the nerves." People across the country read of the new aluminum stadium in Brooklyn that "could be painted just like an automobile." A reporter seemed skeptical that such a radical reinvention of the stadium would be realized, offering, "Chances are maybe your grandchildren will see a park like it."[26]

Geddes's well-publicized plans seemed to suggest his intentions: if the Dodgers weren't going to employ him to build a futuristic new structure, others could. His penchant for promotion pushed his stadium visions into newspapers across the country. He unveiled to sports fans, accustomed to plank bleachers and simple grandstands, what a reporter called "his handbook for the emancipation of America's baseball fans."[27] Geddes's handbook would rationalize the iconic urban space of the ballpark, making it larger, mechanized, and more comfortable, with better sight lines and lighting. It would order space logically, efficiently, and profitably. More than just a stadium, it would express and produce a new modern city—a radiant and slumless world—that planners and designers like Le Corbusier, Geddes, and Robert Moses envisioned.

The Modern Stadium Revised, 1952

The Dodgers backed away from Geddes and his stadium schemes for a few years. Attendance sagged to 1,185,896 in 1950 (down nearly 30 percent from the previous season) and recovered just marginally in 1951, to 1,282,628—and this in spite of having one of the best teams in baseball both seasons.[28] Rumors of a new stadium exploded again in 1952. In late February O'Malley announced plans for Emil Praeger and Geddes to visit the Dodgers' Vero Beach spring training complex to brainstorm a new 5,000-seat stadium there.[29] Praeger was a civil engineer who had developed a concrete breakwater used in the invasion of Normandy during World War II; he had also designed and collaborated on airports, city highways and parkways, bridges, and the United Nations complex.[30] After they arrived in Florida in early March, Geddes outlandishly suggested a "portable stadium made out of inflated rubber," which could be constructed more cheaply than one of wood and steel.[31] O'Malley didn't pursue that design.

Geddes's trip to Florida rejuvenated rumors of a new stadium in Brooklyn as well—a rearticulation of Geddes's schemes from 1948 that promised to reinvent the American stadium. When the club's deliberations leaked in late February, O'Malley told a reporter for the *Long Island Press*, "This will be a modern plant in every sense of the word. It is no longer good business to build a ball park just as a ball park. My idea is to build a park so that it can be used for many other things when it isn't being utilized for the primary reason—a baseball stadium." While baseball parks had long been used in multiple ways—most frequently as a theater for political speeches, religious revivals, and football games—O'Malley and Geddes imagined a stadium engineered precisely to convert to other uses on its central stage and host other functions under its roof.[32] More uses meant more revenue for a costly structure occupying a central location in the city. But more than just a shift in uses, O'Malley also promised a shift in the relationship between the stadium operator and the visitor; he alleged, "The prime consideration will be the fan."

He thus signaled a new attention to, and promotional rhetoric of, customer service at the stadium. In the expanding and increasingly crowded postwar entertainment landscape, the stadium visitor was no longer a fan but a consumer of a product: sports-themed entertainment.

A rash of stories followed in New York newspapers and via syndication across the country in March—as well as a Geddes visit to NBC's *Today* television show—followed by a four-page article in *Collier's* in September.[33] Syndicated reports cast the new stadium, to be built on a site outside of Crown Heights, as a much-needed corrective to the ballparks of the early 1950s. One reporter called for a new paradigm: "Outdoor stadiums haven't changed much in the last 2,000 years—same general layout, same uncomfortable seats, same susceptibility to the inhospitable elements. . . . It's time we had a change."[34] Another told readers across the country that Geddes "envisions an ultramodern baseball park which would put to shame the shabby, strictly functional parks of the present." The ultramodern would be pricey, however, costing an estimated eight million dollars.[35]

The stadium, which the *New York Times* called "grandiose" and suggested was "probably far in the future" and the *Newark Star-Ledger* branded the "ball park of the future," was highlighted by a retractable roof (an "aluminum umbrella," according to one reporter).[36] A syndicated report told readers: "There is an aluminum roof which slides out from the top of a garage next door which houses 7,000 cars. If the weather begins to rain or blow or thunder, the stadium manager simply presses a button, the roof creeps over like a hood, lights come on, and whatever is going on goes right on."[37] Other highlights of the new stadium, which distinguished it from any park in existence, were foam rubber seats that could be heated in cold weather, armrest drink holders, automatic hot dog vending machines placed throughout the grounds, a new lighting system integrated into the stadium structure, and synthetic grass that could be painted any color.[38]

Geddes explained his new structure, which represented a radical reconfiguration of the stadium and its social function:

> You have to start with an entirely different concept of a stadium's place in the community. The ballparks today are far behind the times. Now we have to think not only of today, but of what we'll want 30 years from now as we plan for a really modern stadium. It won't be just a ballpark, of course. It will have to be more of a community center, with shopping facilities, playgrounds for children, possibly a couple of small movie houses—all kinds of things. A mother will be able to go to the ball game, leave her children at the playgrounds or at the dentist's or doctor's office, leave a list of foodstuffs to be gathered and wrapped for her, and find everything ready for her when the game's over.[39]

This new stadium-as-community-center echoed other new proposals merging consumption and community spaces. Victor Gruen and Elsie Krummeck had sketched out plans for a postwar shopping center in *Architectural Forum* in 1943; it would include not only a range of retail stores but also a cafeteria, a bar, a movie theater, a service station, a nursery, a post office, a library, and an auditorium. It would be both a center for shopping and "the center of cultural activities and recreation . . . the one important meeting place of the community."[40] Geddes's plan to reinvent the stadium for women, consumption, and auxiliary entertainments channeled the vision of Gruen and Krummeck that would be materialized in postwar shopping centers. It would also be expressed, in different ways, in many of the stadiums of the 1960s. This vision for a consumption- and entertainment-oriented civic space was novel indeed, preceding the opening of the first fully enclosed shopping mall—Gruen's Southdale in suburban Edina, Minnesota—by four years and Gruen's downtown version of consumerist civic space at Midtown Plaza in Rochester, New York, by a decade. The project reflected the then unrealized visions of planners like Gruen, who would wed together consumption and community as they rewrote the postwar city and its suburbs. The Geddes proposal was different through its ideological fusion of male and female spaces—the combination of sports and shopping. Other sports entertainers, O'Malley among them, would also attempt to attract female audiences in the coming years by building non-sporting amenities—restaurants, luxury lounges, shops, and conspicuous displays of service—into new stadiums.

The stadium that Geddes planned would have fit right into his Futurama city. The entire structure was rectangular, consisting of two separate but linked squares—one a parking garage, the other the "all weather–all purpose" stadium. The flat shell of the roof split in two, one portion sliding across elevated rails onto the adjacent garage. The streamlined roof looked like the hood of an automobile; it was supported by (and decorated with) girders that stretched across the top like chrome accents. Below the displaced roof, the parking garage was boxy and horizontal, with broad openings for automobile traffic on each side, anticipating the modern blockhouse design of enclosed suburban shopping centers of the later 1950s. Its smooth symmetry, expansive scale, and technological futurism marked a striking departure from old Ebbets Field.

Through March 1952, only Geddes, his draftsmen, the Dodgers, and some reporters had seen what the futuristic stadium might look like. The general public had been forced to rely on descriptions in the press, refracted through their imaginations. Geddes preferred to "dramatize" solutions by making them visual, and he would make the modern stadium visible to a national public in the September 1952 edition of *Collier's*.[41] The *Collier's* illustration crystallized the futuristic stadium being conceived in Brooklyn for a nation of viewers, stitching together fragments of reportage and materializing the incipient modern stadium into a more coherent form for a national audience.

The stadium design published in *Collier's* was framed as a collaboration between O'Malley, Geddes, and Praeger. The illustration of the new park did not come from Geddes's office but was a rendering by Rolf Klep drawn from Geddes's blueprints. Klep was an illustrator whose art appeared in magazines like *Fortune, Collier's,* and *Life,* often depicting space-age or maritime scenes; this experience was evident in the illustration. Klep's illustration seemed part space station and part ocean liner, and its smooth, gleaming, curvilinear white surfaces and ribbon windows contrasted magnificently with the anonymous, boxy, brown and gray buildings of old Brooklyn around its perimeter. The base of the

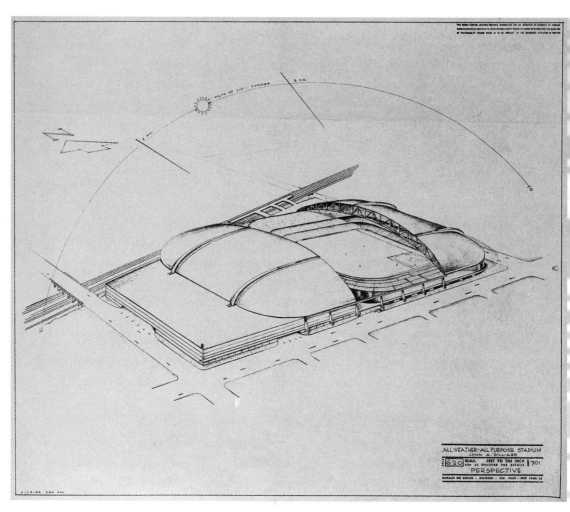

FIGURE 19. This perspective drawing of Norman Bel Geddes's sliding-roof stadium for Brooklyn (1949) was likely seen by the Dodgers and reporters but not published alongside stories describing the new stadium in March 1952. Harry Ransom Center, University of Texas at Austin. IMAGE COURTESY OF THE EDITH LUTYENS AND NORMAN BEL GEDDES FOUNDATION.

stadium was a two-story square, consuming the entirety of a large city block. A third level with rounded corners, receding from the square base, supported a domed roof. Four covered pedestrian walkways protruded from the stadium's second level like huge gangplanks, elevating the city sidewalk and privatizing it, shielding the stadium from the everyday foot traffic of the streets. Traffic lanes surrounded the stadium like a moat, each lane divided by a median that separated private cars, taxis, and buses. At each corner of the base, atop the curved third level, were two American flags—the only splash of color on what was otherwise a pristinely bleached exterior.

More remarkable than this exterior were the curiosities the cutaway revealed inside—a dollhouse of miniature activity. At the center was, of course, a baseball diamond with a symmetrical outfield surrounded by three decks of cantilevered stadium seating. Behind these seating decks were retail stores, a movie theater, storage, and a supermarket. Below the seats were decks of parking and service stations, concealed beneath the stadium and underground, reachable by seamlessly integrated ramps off the street. All of these features were marked with labels and arrows. In this miniature scene, diners and shoppers milled about wide concourses even as the stadium was full of baseball fans. Cars rested in tidy rows in the stadium's bowels; other vehicles whizzed around the outside of the structure in its meticulously managed traffic patterns.

The article explained the philosophy of the design and what O'Malley, Geddes, and Praeger hoped to achieve through it. There were a number of problems the new stadium was intended to address—problems that were already impacting business at ballparks in the early 1950s and that were certain, it seemed to baseball executives like O'Malley, to be exacerbated in the coming years. Fans were increasingly arriving at ballparks via private automobile, many of those fans having moved to the suburbs; they were faced with uncompromising traffic jams and parking problems as they tried to negotiate a dense urban landscape ill-equipped for the car. Once they arrived at the park, fans had to climb flights of stairs and travel narrow, dim, often moldy concourses to get to their seats. Seats in old parks were narrow and hard, and many of them had obstructed views due to pillars supporting upper decks. Fans watching baseball on television, of course, confronted none of this.

The article's title, "Baseball's Answer to TV," foregrounded this challenge. Baseball owners were terrified of the impact that television and the comfort of the living room would have on their attendance and income in the coming years, as television ownership rates soared with more and more people moving to the suburbs.[42] Television granted Americans who were new to a suburban neighborhood, and recently disjointed from their old social networks, instant access to a virtual community of families that were sharing the same pleasures and challenges of suburban life. Not only did television help smooth the transition to the suburbs, but it could also provide its residents with a version of urban culture without the hassle of urban living.[43] Television executives like Pat Weaver of NBC saw television as an adaptation of more traditional community experience and a mechanism for spatially transporting people from their living rooms to the world beyond. He theorized in 1951 that television didn't bring shows to people but took people "from their living rooms to other places—theaters, arenas, ball parks, movie houses, skating rinks, and so forth."[44] Not only could it broadcast baseball games, but it offered competing shows and was just one of many postwar leisure options—bowling, fishing, softball, and do-it-yourself projects around the house among them—that were much closer to home for the suburbanite than was the urban ballpark. For suburbanites, a trip to the stadium from their sofa was far more convenient than one in their car. Because baseball owners had historically received the great majority of their income from gate receipts—and had unevenly monetized the power of television through broadcast rights—this was threatening indeed. New stadiums—in the eyes of forward-thinkers like Geddes and O'Malley—would have to be easier to get to, feature some of the comforts of home, and be stocked with their own attractions that the living room couldn't match.

O'Malley was ahead of most other owners in trying to confront the challenges facing the sports business. His task for Geddes and Praeger was, according to *Collier's* writer Tom Meany, "the creation of a stadium in Brooklyn embodying the refinements of modern engineering" motivated by "the rather novel theory that baseball fans are people." It would deploy cutting-edge technical know-how in the service of convenience and comfort. The *Collier's* plan amplified all the features Geddes had been pitching in previous versions of his stadium: a weatherproofing roof that made the arena functional for events besides baseball; organized transportation in and out of the stadium in a way that exemplified Geddes's infatuation with a totally designed and coordinated "vehicular ecosystem"; padded theater seats that could be adjusted at different viewing angles for different events; wide aisles and rows; automated ticket sales and vending machines; synthetic turf that was more predictable and cost-efficient; standardized outfield dimensions, for the sake of fairness and order; and the diversified use of the building as a whole—from the events held inside to the range of commercial enterprises housed along the stadium concourses.[45]

O'Malley presented the stadium directly to Brooklynites through a column in the *Brooklyn Eagle* a month after the *Collier's* article ran. The article was part of a series titled "10-Point Program for Brooklyn," in which prominent local figures proposed ways of reviving the borough. O'Malley boldly stated in his opening line that his part of the plan was "to make baseball Brooklyn's business." Noting Brooklyn's "international reputation" for being a baseball town, he hoped the borough might "capitalize on the fact and encourage the erection of the first all-purpose, all-weather sports and convention arena." The

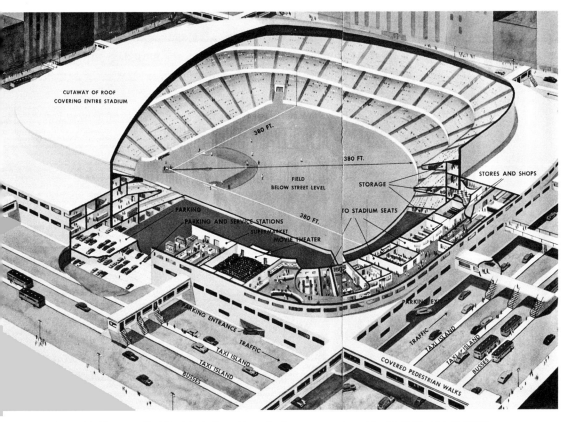

FIGURE 20. Norman Bel Geddes's Brooklyn stadium, as rendered by Rolf Klep in *Collier's*, September 1952. Rolf Klep, "Baseball's Answer to TV," ink on paper, 1987:222. JORDAN SCHNITZER MUSEUM OF ART, UNIVERSITY OF OREGON.

new six-million-dollar stadium was, he assured readers, "beyond the 'pipe-dream' stage, and past the drawing-board phase, for that matter." Geddes and Praeger had blueprints at the ready, and the club had "definite ideas" about locations that would put it closer to Wall Street, Rockefeller Center, and the Long Island Rail Road station than was either the Polo Grounds or Yankee Stadium. In unpacking the details, O'Malley prioritized transportation—and particularly the driver of the car, claiming that the new stadium would be "strategically located to give maximum convenience for rapid transit patrons, but most important—it will offer the maximum accessibility to the motorist." Another major point of emphasis, "the most revolutionary feature of the new Dodger park," would be the six-hundred-foot roof that would eliminate the rain check and allow all sorts of events, including conventions, exhibitions, and sporting events during the winter. A third significant point, highlighted in bold type, was the multifunctional use of the arena's perimeter, which would house supermarkets, shops, and storage—"making the park an intimate part of the surrounding community." O'Malley concluded by arguing that the facility would allow such a range of events that "Brooklyn datelines would appear almost daily throughout the world," a first step toward the borough's secession from New York City, second fiddle to Manhattan no more.[46]

Five months later, O'Malley tried to get Roger Kahn to write a story for the *New York Herald Tribune* publicizing the new stadium plans. O'Malley laid out his vision:

> Did you ever ask yourself why in an electronic age we play our games in a horse-and-buggy park? . . . The aisles are too narrow. The stairs are too steep. Poles obstruct the views. We can't park enough cars. We need twice as many seats. The bathrooms smell. The girders holding up the whole thing are rusting away. . . . Imagine a new park. Seventy thousand seats just like the Yankees have. No poles. You can cantilever construction now. Escalators take the fans to their seats. Plenty of parking. Restaurants and train stations right in the park. Then, to end worries about rain, we put a dome over everything.[47]

Spaciousness. Mobility. Cleanliness. Size. Automation. Amenities. Climate control. This was the modern dream—the changes that would move sport and society from a horse-and-buggy era to an electronic one. It would be a stadium that commanded metropolitan space by sitting at the nexus of rail routes and modern freeways, eliminated working human bodies, dismissed the natural and social environments beyond its walls as if they weren't even there, and filled its spaces with an affluent and well-behaved audience. Kahn wrote a piece outlining O'Malley's vision, but the paper's sports editor rejected it, telling him, "You're supposed to be writing baseball, not Walter's fantasies."[48]

For the time being, O'Malley could merely fantasize, inspired by the illustration of Geddes's domed stadium on his office wall.[49] In 1952, Ebbets Field drew just over one million fans, down 40 percent from the 1947 high, in spite of a pennant-winning team. As O'Malley struggled to find a new location in Brooklyn and justify a new stadium outlay, more and more Brooklynites moved to newer areas of the borough or out to the new suburbs of Long Island. The dense urban terrain about the park, difficult to manipulate by automobile, served as a deterrent for these migrant Dodgers supporters to return, as did the comforts and demands of their new suburban homes. But while the Dodgers faced a certain set of business challenges, increasingly evident by the end of 1952, their National League rivals, the Boston Braves, were on the brink of existential failure. Fewer than three hundred thousand came to Braves Field to see the team play in 1952. While O'Malley, Bel Geddes, and Emil Praeger theorized the new modern stadium, the Braves would have simply been happy for customers, whatever the stadium.

Milwaukee's County Stadium and the
Shifting Geographies of Baseball

Braves owner Lou Perini, upon relocating the team from Boston to Milwaukee for the 1953 season, told reporters, "There were many reasons for my decision." The most immediate factor—and the reason that the move came so abruptly, just weeks before the opener as the unsuspecting players were in Florida for spring training—was pressure from Bill Veeck, owner of the American League's St. Louis Browns. The Browns were struggling horribly for attendance in St. Louis and, like the Braves, were the second most popular team in a two-team city. Veeck hoped to move the club to Milwaukee, where a publicly financed stadium was being completed, and Milwaukee's civic leaders welcomed Veeck's overtures. Perini, because he owned the minor league Milwaukee Brewers, held the rights to the city by agreement with the other major league owners. But by refusing to sell those rights to Veeck, effectively blocking his move there, he risked alienating Milwaukee, becoming the man who barred it from major league status. Perini was interested in potentially moving his own club there, though not that season. But Veeck's interest in Milwaukee, coupled with poor preseason ticket sales in Boston, pushed Boston native Perini toward making a quick decision.[50]

Other National League owners unanimously supported the move, in spite of the inconvenient timing, as their share of the gate at Boston's Braves Field had been collapsing over the previous seasons. The Braves' attendance peaked in their pennant-winning 1948 season, when 1,455,439 came to Braves Field. That figure would drop precipitously in the following seasons, to 1,081,795 (1949), 944,391 (1950), 487,475 (1951), and then a measly 281,278 (1952) in what would be the club's final season in Boston.[51] Through the late 1940s, the Braves had recorded modest profits of between $150,000 and $300,000 per season. The club reportedly lost over $200,000 in 1951 and $600,000 to $700,000 in the disastrous season of 1952.[52]

Lester Smith of the *Sporting News* reasoned, "There is room for only one major league team in the Hub [Boston]."[53] Perini agreed with this assessment, concluding, "Since the advent of television Boston has become a one-team city."[54] That "one team" was the Red Sox of the American League. Even when the Braves were at their best, they were the second favorite in Boston. They made it to the World Series in 1948 but were outdrawn that season by the Sox. In 1952, the Sox finished nineteen games out of first place but still drew 1,115,750 (compared to the 281,278 who visited Braves Field).[55] Many agreed with Smith and Perini's assessment: Boston was a one-team city. By 1950, Boston was the tenth largest urban area in the United States, with a population of 801,444; there were 637,392 people in the Milwaukee area.[56] Cities like New York, with nearly 8 million residents, and Chicago, with over 3.5 million, were able to sustain more than one baseball club at a time

FIGURE 21. Boston's Braves Field in 1933. Commonwealth Avenue runs diagonally across the top of the image; the Boston & Albany Railroad tracks are in the foreground, between the ballpark and the Charles River. COURTESY OF THE BOSTON PUBLIC LIBRARY, LESLIE JONES COLLECTION.

when competing games and other entertainments were increasingly televised into people's living rooms; Boston could not. Neither could Philadelphia and St. Louis, both of which lost one of their two clubs over the following two years. An expanding leisure market that included televised baseball dragged down attendance at ballparks from its postwar highs in the late 1940s. When some clubs like the Braves sold their rights fees to local stations, the payback was a pittance compared to what they received through gate receipts and concessions at the game, which amounted to as much as 90 percent of a club's income. Perini had sold the Braves' TV rights in Boston for the 1951 and 1952 seasons for a paltry $40,000. This was a drop in the bucket compared to the estimated $600,000–700,000 he lost in 1952.

Braves Field did little to encourage attendance. Opened in 1915, the stadium was touted as "the world's largest ballpark ever" by owner James Gaffney. A single-deck covered grandstand, seating eighteen thousand, stretched around the diamond infield. The roof towered above the flatly pitched bank of seats, supported by long beams and trusses; the high roof made the stands seem like a barn to some commentators. Uncovered pavilions for ten thousand spectators each flanked the baselines. A small stand of bleachers seating two thousand sat in right-center field; it became known as the "Jury Box" after a reporter once noted that only twelve fans were sitting there during a game. Trees were added beyond the outfield fence in the 1940s in an unsuccessful attempt to shield the sight of smoke from the adjacent rail yard.[57]

Braves Field was located little more than a mile away from Fenway Park, but the character of each was vastly different. The stands at Braves Field were expansive, sloping, and open; Fenway Park was tight, condensed, and enclosed. Lester Smith claimed, "Chummy Fenway Park is ideal for baseball and without question that is one reason why many people preferred to see games there instead of barnlike Braves Field."[58] Baseball writer Al Hirshberg thought the park was the number one reason the Braves failed in Boston. Braves Field was shoehorned between railroad tracks and industrial buildings. It was just a block away from Commonwealth Avenue, one of Boston's major streets, but only one streetcar line served the park. The main entrance was on a dead-end street shared by trucks servicing the armory on the other side of that street. Hirshberg argued, "Except for people who lived in the vicinity, Braves Field was one of the hardest public places in Boston to reach." But location wasn't the only problem, Hirshberg wrote: "The plant itself was antiquated and barny. There was so much room on the field that fans in some sections of the stands needed field glasses to see what was going on. There was no feeling of intimacy there—no chance for kinship between players and public."[59]

The absence of intimacy in the park was counterbalanced with an excess of intimacy outside it: there simply wasn't much parking space for a population that was increasingly using automobiles. Perini owned a club in Boston that fewer and fewer people were coming to see, at a park that was difficult to get in and out of and wasn't a particularly pleasant place to watch a game. An alternative, as a reporter for the *Boston Herald* pointed out, was "the glowing prospects in Milwaukee with a stadium that will accommodate 31,000 and which can be increased to 37,000, and which has parking space for 10,000 automobiles."[60]

The Braves were urged to stay in Boston by a resolution from the Massachusetts Senate and pleas from Governor Christian Herter, Mayor John Hynes, the president of the Greater Boston Chamber of Commerce, and "the man on the street," according to Smith.[61] But many people on the street—including women—didn't care all that much. In a *Boston Herald* article headlined "Man in Street Sorry, But Most Don't Blame Owner of Braves," Daisy Clarke, a resident of nearby Back Bay, ventured, "They're gone? I think that's wonderful. I never did like the National League. This is definitely an American League town.

The park at Braves Field was no good, and the parking problem was even worse. I'll get along without them."[62]

The Braves were astonishingly successful in Milwaukee, exceeding the expectations of nearly everyone in baseball. The team attracted 1,826,397 fans in their first season there. They beat that number in 1954 (2,131,388) and topped two million fans every season through 1957.[63] In their first six years, they sold nearly twelve million tickets and won two pennants and a World Series. Milwaukee was fertile soil for Perini and made him the envy of many baseball owners.

While Perini claimed to have been beaten out of Boston by many sticks, there was one primary carrot in Milwaukee: a new stadium at the attractive cost of practically nothing. Milwaukee County Stadium, a thirty-five-thousand-seat, county-owned baseball park two miles west of downtown, was on the brink of completion when the Braves announced their move. The Milwaukee County Board had approved the construction of a new baseball park in the Story Quarry section of Milwaukee on February 24, 1947. After rejecting a 1948 bond issue, voters approved a revised version in 1950 and ground was broken on a new stadium that October. The new stadium replaced Borchert Field, an old baseball

FIGURE 22. A game crowd exits Braves Field in 1935, filing slowly past the main entrance beyond right field. COURTESY OF THE BOSTON PUBLIC LIBRARY, LESLIE JONES COLLECTION.

park located in a residential neighborhood about two miles north of downtown. The new stadium had no major league tenant but was intended to be a magnet for any relocating major league teams. City leaders planned for the Brewers, of the minor league American Association, to play there until they could attract a major league franchise.[64]

Visitors to the new County Stadium arrived via freeway, decamped in the parking lot, and navigated their way between rows of gleaming chrome, approaching what looked like an airplane hangar dropped on a suburban office park. Two stories of red brick and ribbon window wrapped around much of the first tier. Visitors filed under a long, low canopy through the ticket gates into the belly of the ballpark. A gray metal barn sat atop the brick base, rising up like a receding layer cake. Inside, the double-decked grandstand stretched from first to third base, seating 28,011. There were two banks of roll-away bleachers along the third-base line and beyond the left-center field fence that could house an additional 7,900 visitors. The total capacity was 35,911 in 1953. A wire fence outlined the boundary of the playing field, curving symmetrically around the outfield: 320 feet down the foul lines, 376 feet in the power alleys, and 404 feet in center.[65] A scoreboard, 57 feet tall and 61 feet across, sat beyond the right-field fence. Beyond the bleachers and scoreboard, a permanent green wall defined the ultimate edge of the stadium; beyond that was the expansive parking lot.[66]

The total cost of the stadium, funded by the county, was five million dollars. County leaders had expected to collect $35,000 per season in rent from the minor league Brewers but offered a discounted rental to entice the major league Braves westward. The contract called for the Braves to pay an annual rent of $1,000 for the first two years. For the following three, the county would receive 5 percent of gate receipts and most of the concessions.[67] The Braves owned the radio and television rights in Milwaukee; however, Perini banned the broadcasting of regular-season games in his new home, believing that television had seriously undermined his attendance in Boston.[68] Boosters expected the club to attract 400,000 out-of-town visitors who would spend, on average, six dollars per person in the area—theoretically reimbursing the city in lieu of the paltry rental fees.[69]

The arrival of a big-league team, as a civic status symbol, was important to many of Milwaukee's most powerful men. Fred Miller, owner of Miller Brewing Company, was at the front of this effort to attract a big-league team to the city. He was a force on the Greater Milwaukee Committee for Community Development, which planned a range of improvements for the city, including airport enhancements, new expressways, a new zoo, a new library, a museum, and a war memorial—all at an estimated cost of over two hundred million dollars. The city had already built a four-million-dollar downtown arena and the new County Stadium.

Major league baseball wasn't just a status symbol, though; the people of Milwaukee embraced the Braves unabashedly. Magazines like *Life*, *Look*, and the *Saturday Evening Post*

FIGURE 23. Milwaukee's County Stadium, home of the Braves, pictured in 1955.
WISCONSIN HISTORICAL SOCIETY, PHOTO BY MILWAUKEE JOURNAL SENTINEL, WHS-50114.

ran articles about the city's response to the new team, painting a portrait of an unaffected midwestern community showering country charm on a team spurned by easterners who couldn't be bothered. These stories were accompanied by photos of players pulling home-made sausage from gift boxes, players' wives going through piles of donated merchandise and sitting on free furniture, and community groups presenting players with gifts at the dugout steps. Articles noted free groceries and gas, and they described when the crowd regaled pitcher Max Sukront with "Happy Birthday." Manager Charlie Grimm confessed, "I've got to watch out they don't smother us with kindness, beer and sauerbraten."[70] This lovefest wasn't just a media concoction. Braves star Eddie Mathews remembered, "The way the fans treated us—I can't even describe it. We were getting cars loaned to us, free gasoline, free drycleaning, gifts of every kind. This went on throughout the fifties. We were taken into people's homes. It was just like one big happy family."[71]

Milwaukee's successful courting of the Braves became a fixation for baseball owners, the worried fans of their teams, and the civic and business leaders of cities without a major league team—places like Los Angeles, San Francisco, Montreal, Toronto, Dallas, Houston, Denver, Minneapolis-St. Paul, Kansas City, and Seattle.[72] An American city wasn't truly significant, in the eyes of many boosters, unless it was "big league," and being big league in the 1950s meant having a major league baseball franchise.[73] An executive for the *Milwaukee Journal* victoriously proclaimed, "Big League Baseball put Milwaukee on the map and brought it into national prominence more quickly and more completely than anything else

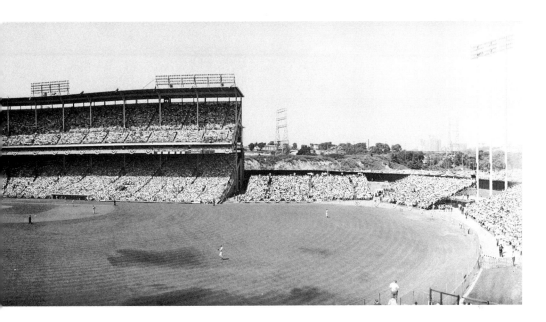

in the community's history. That includes our reputation for beer."[74] He noted the impact on community spirit: even if times were tough on the economic front, residents would be happy "as long as Mathews keeps slugging." Prominent civic figures in other cities, eager for major league status, looked to Milwaukee and used that episode to try to spur action in their communities. The proud claims of the *Milwaukee Journal* executive, for example, were republished as a foreword to a promotional magazine printed by the Minneapolis Chamber of Commerce in 1954, titled, "A Prospectus of a Metropolitan Sports Area for the Twin Cities." The group hoped to motivate support in Minnesota for a publicly funded ballpark there, to attract a major league club just as Milwaukee had; they would use a new stadium to successfully lure the Washington Senators westward in 1960.[75] In 1959, as some Houstonians tried to make their city "big league" by building a new stadium and attracting a team, a columnist for the *Houston Chronicle* celebrated the drive and gall of "the thrifty burghers of Milwaukee County [who] took a $7.5 million gamble and won." That "gamble" was building a stadium without a tenant in hopes a club would move there.[76] The writer from the *Chronicle* suggested, not so subtly, that Houston, too, should have that sort of panache and ambition (and it would, in spades, when it began building the incredible Astrodome a few years later).

Alongside that Houstonian's call for community bravado in the *Chronicle* was a photo that revealed what was, fundamentally, at the heart of the success of baseball in Milwaukee and the game's economic failure in many old major league cities. It was an aerial photo showing what was arguably the park's most distinctive feature: the massive parking lot. The lot's expanse, while visually clear, was reiterated by the caption: "Home of the

Braves—and Lots of Parking Room. Milwaukee's County Stadium Surrounded by 11,000 Cars."[77] This was not the baseball park of most people's imagination, shoehorned into an old neighborhood, like Brooklyn's Ebbets Field, New York's Polo Grounds, Washington's Griffith Stadium, St. Louis's Sportsman's Park, or Boston's Braves Field. Nor was it like Milwaukee's old grounds, Borchert Field—a bizarre, rectangular ballpark squeezed into a residential neighborhood. Bill Veeck called Borchert an "architectural monstrosity": the foul poles were just 266 feet from home plate, fans sitting along the first-base line couldn't see the right fielder, those on the third-base side couldn't see who was playing left, and no location in the stands provided a view of the entire field.[78]

County Stadium was a huge improvement over Borchert Field, but it was hardly cutting-edge; it was a simple, multitier ballpark architecturally notable only for its plainness and symmetry relative to some of the early twentieth-century urban baseball parks. Yet the stadium's situation made it the envy of many owners—Brooklyn's Walter O'Malley

FIGURE 24. Milwaukee's County Stadium, new home of the Braves—most noteworthy for the acres of parking. WISCONSIN HISTORICAL SOCIETY, WHS-54731.

in particular. The challenge of parking was particularly acute for the Dodgers at Ebbets Field. In O'Malley's mind, the Milwaukee parking lot created a competitive imbalance between the Braves and the rest of the league. He told a reporter for the *Saturday Evening Post* in 1960 that one of the reasons he would eventually leave Brooklyn for Los Angeles was that the Braves were drawing twice as many people to their games.[79] O'Malley was unimpressed by County Stadium itself, thinking it little more than a newer Ebbets Field with its vision-obstructing support poles and steep stairs to the upper deck. O'Malley was, however, clearly impressed by Milwaukee's commitment to the automobile and the advantages gained from easy access to freeways and abundant parking. This was the catalyst for the Braves' explosive attendance figures, these automotive veins to the spreading suburbs and its middle-class populations that had more money than ever before and more time to spend it. Perini himself noted, "People here can afford to support baseball."[80]

Milwaukee instantly became a symbol of future possibilities, both for owners who craved a new stadium without the heavy personal investment and for fans who feared their club's owner might head for greener pastures. Perini, along with most baseball watchers, had a sense of what the Braves' move west signified for baseball and sport more generally. He predicted, "Baseball in general will benefit. I feel that this is just the start of a realignment in baseball. California may well come into the majors within the next five years. There are going to be great changes."[81] Tim Cohane of *Look* added, "As pioneers in the redrawing of baseball's major-league map, now definitely under way, the Braves will be remembered."[82] Though the stadium site itself was nothing much to speak of, the situation profoundly impacted the sports landscape in every large American city.[83] In the coming years, major league cities reckoned with Milwaukee's example, either by losing a team, gaining one, or building a stadium to keep the team there.

The St. Louis Browns had very nearly been Milwaukee's new darling. Bill Veeck bought 80 percent of the club's shares in 1951, "knowing perfectly well that the city could support only one team." The Browns' local rivals, the National League's Cardinals, were certainly the more popular of the city's two teams, drawing nearly 1.1 million to Sportsman's Park in 1950, while the Browns couldn't even muster a quarter of a million to the same ballpark. Over the previous twenty-five seasons, no team other than the Yankees had won as many pennants as the Cardinals. The ambitious and inventive Veeck was convinced, however, that Cardinals owner Fred Saigh didn't know how to properly run a baseball club and that the Cardinals could be pushed out of town. Veeck's plans were torpedoed when Saigh, imprisoned for tax evasion, sold the club to St. Louis–based Anheuser-Busch in 1953. The Cardinals, now flush with cash, weren't going anywhere. Veeck's Browns were doomed, and he tried to plot an escape to new pastures. Thwarted by Perini's move to Milwaukee in 1953, Veeck looked to Baltimore, which had built the first level of a new stadium and was poised to top it off with a second deck. By the time the Browns moved to Baltimore for the 1954 season, however, Veeck had been squeezed out by American League owners. For them, Veeck was a headache, regularly besmirching their game with lowbrow promotional antics, and they forced him to sell his Browns shares to a group of Baltimore businessmen.[84]

Baltimore had once been a "big-league" city, if a major league baseball team was the measuring stick. The Orioles played there at the start of the century but relocated to Manhattan in 1903, where they became known as the New York Highlanders and, a decade later, the Yankees. At the end of World War II, Baltimore's business and political leaders hoped to reclaim that status. As German forces surrendered in early May 1945, industrialist Charles P. McCormick, chairman of Baltimore's mayor-appointed stadium committee, warned citizens: "Baltimore stands today at a civic crossroad." The committee had been tasked with exploring and proposing stadium options for a city with major league ambitions. According to the stadium committee's report to the mayor, the city had been "outrun by a number of younger cities in the race for national and international prominence." Once "the hub of the world's shipping," the city had seen its "progress . . . gradually [slow] down." The war had brought people together, reversing that trend. But "it is for the leaders of Baltimore and Maryland to see that the reversal is permanent." Building a new stadium, the committee concluded, "should be only the first step in a broad general program—but it would serve . . . as would no other concrete action in announcing to the nation our concerted intentions for the future."[85]

The stadium committee recommended the construction of a war memorial stadium seating up to 100,000 under an aluminum roof that stretched 900 feet across and 170 feet tall at the center, and covered 13 acres. The revolutionary roof—just one-eighth of an inch thick—would be "pumped up" from its resting position (about twenty feet above spectators' heads) to a maximum height in ninety minutes. The roof would then slowly deflate over the course of a month, before requiring reinflation.[86] Plans were for an integrated sports complex, equipped with an Olympic-sized swimming pool, a gymnasium, bowling alleys, a roller rink, handball courts, a cafeteria, a small theater, a coffee shop, a travel office, gift and sports equipment shops, and even a pistol range. Though the stadium's primary purpose would be to host baseball and football games, flexible seating arrangements would allow for non-sporting events as well, including town hall meetings, conventions, religious exercises, musical performances, circuses, and other entertainments. The stadium committee called for a site outside the city limits along two highways, with "ample" parking space to attract people from the suburbs. The stadium committee whetted the appetites of Baltimoreans by promising, "The youth who yelled his enthusiasm at a Saturday football game could easily be made to feel just as much at home applauding a symphony orchestra the following Wednesday evening. He couldn't fail to take a more personal interest in a political convention if it were held in the same place where he watched the Orioles trim Jersey City."[87] Thus the stadium might function as a threshold, initiating young sports fans into the world of high culture and democratic values. Aircraft manufacturer Glenn L. Martin, a member of the stadium committee, urged action: "Speed is essential, obviously. To the first city to begin such a project as we propose will go not only the advertising and publicity value, but the recognition accorded the pioneer in any field."[88] Much more than a building, the postwar stadium could be a material advertisement for a city's spirit and intentions. According to the stadium committee, it would also have great financial value, attracting conventions and stimulating private investment in the tourism industry, particularly the construction of new hotels. But in Baltimore, as in most cases, the funding didn't match the ambition. The estimated stadium cost of five million dollars soon grew to seven million. By August 1946, the mayor had pivoted to support reinvestment in the city's horseshoe-shaped Municipal Stadium—a structure that would be reinvented as a traditional, open-air, double-decked stadium in the 1950s. By 1947, the roofed stadium project had effectively died. One war veteran, writing in to the *Baltimore Sun*, was relieved. "Half the enjoyment of a game is freezing to death in a windy stadium, cheering for the home team," he wrote. "Perhaps we Americans are getting soft, after all."[89]

The new Memorial Stadium emerged from the shell of old Municipal Stadium. Its egg-shaped first deck was built in 1949 and 1950. The minor league Orioles played through the reconstruction, as did football's Colts—first as part of the All-America Football Conference, beginning in 1947, then as a member of the NFL in 1950. That team was dismal, winning just one game out of twelve, and its owner sold the franchise and its player contracts back to the league. Three years later, a new version of the Colts—assembled from the ashes of another failed NFL club, the Dallas Texans—began play in new Memorial Stadium. When the Colts' season started in 1953, the new concrete stadium—a work in progress— had a capacity of just 23,715. But as the season progressed, construction workers added seats and a second deck, pushing stadium capacity to over 45,000 seats in 1954. Though the Colts wouldn't enjoy a winning record until 1957, a vibrant stadium culture developed at Memorial Stadium in the 1950s, replete with a cheerleading corps, a band, majorettes, flag lines, and a pony mascot named Dixie that darted around the field after Colts' scores. By the end of the decade, the team had won back-to-back championships, as the club grew with the league itself. The 1958 championship game, played against the Giants in Yankee Stadium in the first NFL game to be telecast to a national audience, is considered by many to be "the greatest game ever played" and pivotal to the NFL's rise to national prominence. The Colts' quarterback, Johnny Unitas, sporting a crew cut and high-topped black shoes, channeled working-class grit and up-by-the-bootstraps perseverance; the Colts had signed him from the sandlots of western Pennsylvania where he was making six dollars per game. Unitas exemplified the spirit of professional football in the 1950s—this wasn't a game for college alums swelling with pageantry and school spirit but a game for skilled and tough professionals in an era of postwar prosperity that threatened to render Americans soft. When Unitas and the Colts played at Memorial Stadium it became, in the words of a writer for the *Chicago Tribune*, "the world's largest insane asylum."[90]

But in 1953, an NFL franchise didn't grant a city major league status. Baseball would make Baltimore big league again, and American League owners were convinced that Baltimore was a better bet for major league ball than cities like Los Angeles, San Francisco, Minneapolis, Kansas City, Montreal, and Toronto—thanks to the new stadium, the city's vibrant baseball history, and an ownership consortium with $2,475,000 to buy out Bill Veeck's controlling interest in the St. Louis Browns. The newly minted Orioles began play in Baltimore in 1954. A civic spectacle marked opening day. Joseph Sheehan—sent by the *New York Times* to cover Baltimore's reintroduction to the majors—noted, "This normally sedate old city was prepared to pull out all the stops in celebration of the return of major league baseball to one of the diamond sport's original hotbeds after an absence of fifty-two years."[91] Schools were closed and city workers were granted a half-day holiday, as 350,000 people lined the parade route that hailed Baltimore's return to the big leagues. It was a "spectacle of Mardi Gras proportions," Sheehan wrote, as twenty bands, thirty-two floats, and convertibles filled with baseball players and dignitaries rolled three and a half miles through streets to City Hall.[92] *Life* magazine called it the city's "biggest and most exuberant demonstration since Civil War days."[93] "The Orioles were almost overwhelmed by the frantic welcome they were given," a reporter judged. "Pretty girls tossed 5,000 orchids into the streets as Baltimore's answer to the red carpet Milwaukee laid out for its Braves last year. Everything had to be bigger and more lavish than the Milwaukee 'miracle' of 1953."[94] It wasn't enough to simply be major league: Baltimore needed to be *more* major league than Milwaukee, whose residents had famously committed themselves to their new team the preceding season.

On the approach, Memorial Stadium appeared a modern monument—orderly and geometrical in a way that mirrored its large and symmetrical outfield within. Its perimeter was cloaked in smooth swaths of red brick wall broken here and there by windows and the slanting concrete of pedestrian ramps, stacked neatly atop one another. The second deck leaped out from the brick below, perched delicately on stretching concrete supports. Steel lighting standards patrolled the air above. At night, the stadium insides glowed through the spaces in the wall and against the bottom of the concrete bowl of the upper deck. Its public face was a 116-foot-tall memorial wall of brick and cast stone, boldly marking it as "MEMORIAL STADIUM" in a custom-designed Art Deco typeface that seemed more depression era than postwar. Upon the wall were the city seal and a long dedication to veterans of the world wars that concluded, "TIME WILL NOT DIM THE GLORY OF THEIR DEEDS." But if the typeface expressed a previous era, the engineered austerity of the exposed concrete second deck suggested changes to come in American stadium design. In 1954, the stadium was largely seen as an improvement, but nothing revolutionary. Sportswriter Povich thought the city "came up with one of the better baseball parks," for the six-million-dollar cost.[95] For Sheehan of the *New York Times*, it was "a fine ball park and a worthy acquisition by the major leagues."[96]

Memorial Stadium was, in a sense, between times. Even at its opening, its brand of modernism seemed already a bit out-of-date—one writer would later claim it "looked like the worst of stark Socialist Realism."[97] This sort of modernism didn't exactly signify the future in 1953, and the city's future didn't look entirely bright. It was clear to Baltimore's business and political leaders in the early 1950s that the glow of a war-era boom fueled by the concentration of heavy industry and military in the area was fading. Middle- and

FIGURE 25. Baltimore's Memorial Stadium during the 1958 All-Star Game. Residential neighborhoods framed the parking lot. COURTESY OF THE MARYLAND HISTORICAL SOCIETY, ITEM ID #PP79.1314.

working-class whites were leaving the city for the suburbs of Baltimore County. With them went tax revenue, then companies in the service industry, and then manufacturing. Attracting a major league baseball team might stem the flow of money to the suburbs and catalyze the redevelopment of the center city. But then again, Baltimore wasn't an ideal place to relocate a major league team. The market was geographically restricted, hemmed in by Philadelphia to the north and Washington to the south—and both of those cities would shed clubs westward in the coming years. Of course, it took a club-friendly deal to get the big leagues there—the city ran an annual deficit of over two hundred thousand dollars to keep the stadium running. Though Memorial Stadium wasn't a perfect situation for the Orioles—not enough parking, too many bleachers, not enough backed chairs, too many obstructed-view seats—the club was happy with the setup. It had a new stadium in a white, middle-class area. In fact, the stadium location served as a recruitment tool for the club, whose agents would show off the neighborhoods around the stadium to potential signings, then take them to Washington's Griffith Stadium, in the heart of the District's black community, as a point of comparison.[98] Black Baltimoreans were accustomed to such racism from the city's baseball men. Many remembered how white Baltimoreans had abused Jackie Robinson when he played against the Orioles as a member of the Montreal Royals in 1946.[99] Indeed, the new major league Orioles were happy to pretend that blacks didn't exist, motivated by a mixture of prejudice, anxieties about losing racist white fans, and the possibility of racial conflict in the stadium or locker room.[100] A stadium that aspired to modernity, but didn't quite make it, seemed appropriate for such a club.

For the Philadelphia Athletics, the third major league club to change cities in consecutive years, ignoring African Americans wasn't an option. The club relocated to Kansas City for the 1955 season, moving into an area that was 99 percent black.[101] Like the Braves in Boston and the Browns in St. Louis, the Athletics had become the second club in a one-team city. And also like the Braves and many other clubs to follow, the A's moved west. But unlike other clubs, Kansas City's new team played in a stadium that was built in the black part of town. Chicago businessman Arnold Johnson bought the club from legendary owner-manager Connie Mack and his family. He then purchased Muehlebach Field, a minor league ballpark opened in 1923, that had been the home of the Kansas City Blues and the famed Negro League club, the Monarchs, employer of luminaries like Satchel Paige, Jackie Robinson, and Ernie Banks. Kansas City bought the old park from Johnson, tore it down, and replaced it in just six months with Municipal Stadium, a double-decker stadium modeled after Detroit's Briggs Stadium (a ballpark opened in 1912). Not only did the stadium seem to step out of the past but so too did its scoreboard in right-center field; it had been in Boston's Braves Field two years before.[102] Johnson's Athletics leased the new ballpark from the city at a pittance, and the city guaranteed them one million spectators for each of the first three seasons.[103] If the stadium and the setting seemed old, the deal making was not—a city aspiring to be "big league" in the 1950s paid for the privilege.

Buckminster Fuller's Brooklyn Dome

As the national sports landscape shifted, Walter O'Malley continued to explore options for a new stadium in Brooklyn. Norman Bel Geddes had given shape to what seemed a fantasy for many in New York's sporting press, but increasingly O'Malley was squeezing him out of the picture and leaning on his trusted engineer, Emil Praeger. O'Malley told Geddes in January 1954 that it was "quite unlikely that there will be a chance for you to collaborate on any phase of the proposed new stadium." Geddes continued to contact O'Malley, however, writing to him in September 1955 about the possibility of a wide-span roof and insisting that he would keep his plans under wraps in deference to their friendship. O'Malley responded, "Feel perfectly free to submit your idea to any other club. We are still far from doing anything definite. I know that Capt. Praeger has had ideas about a covered stadium and he, Buckminster Fuller and I have had several conferences."[104] Perhaps O'Malley trusted that Praeger could execute some form of Geddes's vision (and at a lower cost); perhaps O'Malley had tired of Geddes's self-promotional antics; perhaps O'Malley wanted input from another design visionary in his turn to Fuller. Without a site at which to build a new stadium, the Dodgers were certainly "far from doing anything definite." By turning to Fuller, O'Malley signaled that a roof was an absolute requirement to any stadium he would build in Brooklyn; it also suggests that he thought the publicity accompanying his flirtations with name designers might mobilize political support for his project in Brooklyn. Fuller was, after all, the master of the dome, and everyone knew it.

In the 1950s, Buckminster Fuller was largely viewed as an eccentric tinkerer on the fringes of the establishment, a figure whose visions were seductive and revolutionary but not quite generally accepted and practiced; he was an engineer of futuristic solutions but not a legitimate architect. This "white-haired, crew-cut man of 60, built along the lines of a jar of yogurt," as a writer for *Sports Illustrated* described, had "purged himself of all worldly ambitions save one: to remake the face of the earth."[105] *Time* magazine claimed in 1958, as Fuller's status as an intellectual and designer became more secure and accepted, that he had "been the gadfly, delight and despair of the technological world" for years.[106] In 1955, he would have been best known for his Dymaxion projects of the 1920s and 1930s, which attempted to maximize functionality from a minimal use of materials and energy, and the geodesic dome. In the early 1950s, the geodesic dome was a much-talked-about, but infrequently executed, building form—one that seemed poised to enjoy wide use but hadn't yet. Aline B. Louchheim of the *New York Times* wrote, "Many serious and informed persons in the field of building and architecture agree with the inventor that such geodesic domes will some day be accepted as an important solution to housing" given their light weights, relatively low costs, functional flexibility, and mass-production capabilities.[107] Fuller's most prominent dome to that point topped the rotunda at the Ford Motor Company in Dearborn, Michigan, which opened in 1953; ninety-three feet wide, it consisted of aluminum struts covered with a plastic skin.[108] He also had dipped his toes in the water of stadium design, having consulted with an interested minor league club owner in Denver and planners in Minneapolis.[109]

O'Malley contacted Buckminster Fuller in late May 1955 regarding the design of a new domed stadium for Brooklyn, voicing his interest in a roofed stadium that would not only abolish the rain check but also open the structure up to other uses besides baseball. Though a roof might be constructed of concrete or other materials, O'Malley thought that it should be translucent, and had spoken with representatives from Owens-Corning Fiberglass Corporation. Previously alarmed by Geddes's price tags, O'Malley required that Fuller's dome be more affordable. And yet O'Malley pledged his intention of building the next generation of stadium, telling Fuller, "I am not interested in building just another baseball park."[110] Fuller, who seemed up for any project, set to designing a quarter-sphere domed stadium that was seven hundred fifty feet in diameter and tall enough to cover a thirty-story office building, as many publications noted. Fuller claimed the dome—an aluminum truss structure with plastic skin—would be the largest clear-span structure in the world.[111] According to the Dodgers, New York enjoyed only sixty-five usable playing days a year for an outdoor stadium. Adding a roof would not only make weather irrelevant for baseball but also expand the stadium's suitability for other events like conventions, prizefights, and the circus. This would add, according to O'Malley, two hundred thousand dollars to his bottom line annually. The stadium would have "natural air conditioning," according to the *New York Times*, whereby "natural currents" of air would circulate under the dome. These currents could be controlled in winter to heat the structure as well. The plastic, translucent roof would diffuse sunlight, cutting down on glare and shadows. Besides diffusion of light, there would also "be diffusion of sound to prevent deafening cheers," as a reporter for the *Washington Post* noted. Another welcome feature of the stadium, according to the *New York Times*, would be the absence of support posts, thus "making the discomfort of fans seated behind columns a thing of the past." The *Washington Post* agreed: "Every fan knows what a pain those posts are."[112] Fuller claimed that the plastic skin would allow fans to get tans without being burned and eliminate troubling shadows from the playing surface. O'Malley particularly liked that the sky above would be visible, calling that feature "extremely important psychologically because baseball is traditionally an outdoor game." It would be a landmark, O'Malley promised, "big enough to enclose St. Peter's in Rome. . . . It would be one of the wonders of the world."[113]

FIGURE 26. Walter O'Malley and Buckminster Fuller stand in front of a model for a domed Dodger Stadium. O'Malley's hand rests on the shoulder of Theodore Kleinsasser, a Princeton architecture student whose design attracted the attention of the Dodger boss.
BETTMANN/GETTY IMAGES.

Fuller put some students at Princeton's School of Architecture on the job that winter, when he was a visiting lecturer there. In January 1956, they presented their studies to a panel including Fuller, Emil Praeger, and O'Malley. O'Malley particularly liked some of the ideas of Theodore W. Kleinsasser, whose design called for a 55,000-seat structure with a plastic dome 550 feet in diameter and 250 feet tall at its highest point (compared to Fuller's design that would be 750 feet in diameter, 300 feet tall). Located at the intersection of Flatbush and Atlantic, it would include seating for 2,000 in hanging box seats, a small tramway across the top for tours, and parking for 5,000 cars.[114] The estimated cost of the stadium would be $6 million, with $1.5 million going toward the dome itself.[115]

Published images of the Fuller-designed stadiums accentuated their modernity. A November 1955 article in the *New York Times* included a photo of two men lifting the lid off a large stadium model designed by Fuller, four feet tall and five feet wide—an image that would also appear in other publications. The stadium was a simple white bowl, with five peaks around its rim, connecting to a translucent dome that resembled the top of an umbrella. It smooth, white minimalism stressed the design's cool, clean modernity.[116] The trade journal *Progressive Architecture* superimposed a sketch of Lever House, the iconic modern office tower, atop an architectural sketch of Fuller's stadium. And thus a stadium—what many readers might have previously considered a mere feat of engineering—was elevated to the status of elite architecture.[117]

Another version of the Fuller dome was published in the July 1956 issue of *Mechanix Illustrated*. An illustrator for the magazine, inspired by Fuller's plans, drew a circular stadium topped with a translucent white shell. It was a "huge plastic bubble" to replace "hallowed but decaying" Ebbets Field. Like the *Collier's* illustration of Geddes's plans, a portion of the stadium was removed to reveal the human activity inside—an underground parking lot, escalators, and an interior promenade lined with shops and restaurants. As with many modern stadium illustrations staged in the city, the structure's curves contrasted notably with the boxy grids of old office buildings and street patterns depicted around it. Its sense of ordered symmetry expressed a brand of rationality at odds with the idiosyncratic ballparks in use in the 1950s. Clean, monumental, and spacious, it seemed a modern space capsule had landed in the city.[118]

And yet, this space pod never landed in Brooklyn. Only O'Malley knew how serious he was about ever constructing any of his roofed stadium projects; Kleinsasser, for one, didn't think O'Malley was committed to the design he and Fuller produced at Princeton, speculating that it was a public relations ploy.[119] This interpretation seems plausible and might also explain O'Malley's repeated dalliances with Geddes, as he indeed had to muster public support for his stadium as a means to generate political backing. Space pods required landing spots, and any new Dodgers' stadium downtown would occupy some very costly real estate—even in a period of urban decline.

O'Malley had been scouting the area in downtown Brooklyn near Borough Hall in 1947, but by the mid-1950s he coveted a site near the intersection of Atlantic and Flatbush. His new stadium would displace the Fort Greene Meat Market and multiple small businesses, while also requiring the redevelopment of the existing Long Island Rail Road depot. The stadium would then sit adjacent a two-thousand-car parking garage (down from five thousand as proposed in 1952), two major subway lines, and a publicly redeveloped Long Island Rail Road station that would give Brooklynites who had moved to the Long Island suburbs easy access to arena events.[120]

O'Malley wanted to fund stadium construction privately so that he would control stadium revenues; however, he needed public support to acquire the site and make other infrastructural improvements around the new ballpark, which would have been prohibitively expensive. An engineer's report for a stadium-centered redevelopment proposal from Brooklyn borough president John Cashmore estimated that it would cost the city upwards of twelve million dollars for this, while removing about five million dollars per year in tax revenue from the loss of the existing taxpaying properties.[121] O'Malley asked that the city employ Title I of the Federal Housing Act of 1949 to acquire the land; this would enable the city to use federal funds to secure the site and turn it over to a private developer who would construct something there for a public purpose. Unfortunately for O'Malley, Robert Moses was the chairman of the city's Committee on Slum Clearance. Moses told O'Malley in 1955, "A new ball field for the Dodgers cannot be dressed up as a Title I project."[122]

In truth, Moses used Title I funds liberally in postwar New York and could have certainly helped the Dodgers had he wanted to; he simply had no interest in supporting a stadium project in downtown Brooklyn. For one, Moses believed in the automobile, not public transportation. He built freeways and bridges, and his power emanated from the dollars that flowed through his tollbooths—much of which came from the swelling stream of cars from the Long Island suburbs. While O'Malley wanted his customers to have easier access to his new stadium by car, his plans also called for arrival by subway and commuter rail, and Moses had no interest whatsoever in improving the Long Island Rail Road terminal that would sit beneath the new stadium. This would be aiding the competition to his new freeways.[123] But Moses also had another plan for sport in the metropolis—a new modern stadium to be built in Queens's Flushing Meadows, where he had converted swampland into a home for the 1939 World's Fair and Geddes's Futurama. While Moses actively stymied O'Malley's overtures, he wasn't the only political hurdle the Dodgers needed to clear. Though Mayor Robert Wagner publicly supported helping keep the club in New York, his political support was lukewarm at best. Furthermore, politicians from the other boroughs had no interest in financing Brooklyn's team.[124] Public support for a stadium might be widespread in a minor league town like Milwaukee or Baltimore, but New York had two other major league clubs to go along with all the rest the city could offer those looking to spend their leisure dollars.[125] Moses wasn't the only one to scoff at O'Malley's plans. Arthur Daley, of the New York Times, called his domed stadiums "fanciful" and suggested that O'Malley knew as much, writing, "The Dodger president is realist enough, however, to know that Utopia Stadium was a mote too frothy for anyone but a Space Cadet to consider."[126]

One of those space cadets was Hulan Jack, borough president of Manhattan, who pitched an enormous new stadium complex to rescue the Dodgers' great rivals, the Giants, from the aging Polo Grounds. He first mentioned the possibility of a new, privately financed "stadium in the sky" in a radio interview in March 1956.[127] The 110,000-seat domed stadium would sit atop stilts sixty feet above the New York Central railroad tracks, bordered by 60th and 72nd streets, West End Avenue, and the West Side Highway.[128] By April, a thirty-five-man committee of bankers, government workers, sports businessmen, and engineers were reportedly sketching out a two-million-square-foot project that might help the city compete for the 1964 Olympic games and stage major college football contests (including a "Sky Bowl" to rival the Rose, Orange, and Sugar bowls). The dome would be similar to those envisioned for downtown Brooklyn and the Dodgers, though the complex—which would come to be known as "Stadium City Center"—would also be expanded to include a new thirty-five-story-tall office building housing a "Television City" production center and studio for networks. Project add-ons included a heliport, a subway station, a theater, a Skyline restaurant overlooking the Hudson River, and a massive 20,000-car parking garage equipped with escalators for patrons (box holders would enjoy parking spaces directly adjacent to their seats).[129] Arthur Daley noted in May that it was "almost too grandiose a scheme"—indeed, plans quickly unraveled after that.[130] Though Mayor Wagner would meet with project architects and Horace Stoneham, owner of major league baseball's Giants, by late May he had backed off the Manhattan plan, which by then was being estimated to cost seventy-five million dollars.[131] Days later, a writer for the *New York World-Telegram-Sun* claimed that the stadium was "not likely to become a reality . . . a fatal victim of its own enormous proportions."[132]

California Modern

New York had three major league teams in 1957; in 1958, only the Yankees remained. Los Angeles mayor Norris Poulson began his courtship of the Dodgers at the 1956 World Series, a few months after Fuller's Brooklyn dome was published in *Mechanix*. Poulson and other powerful Angelenos hoped to secure big-league status for what was, at the end of World War II, the nation's second largest population center and third largest center for manufacturing. The war economy had fueled this growth, with $70 billion of federal money spent regionally on shipyards, aircraft plants, and other war-related research and development between 1941 and 1945.[133] This spending was joined to federal subsidies for the construction of highways and suburban homes.[134] Atop this foundation, the area population exploded. Los Angeles County alone grew from 2,785,643 (1940) to 4,151,687 (1950) and 6,038,771 (1960)—more than doubling over two decades. Orange County, directly to the south, more than tripled in population during the 1950s alone, growing from 216,224 residents to 703,925.[135]

Los Angeles civic leaders were particularly anxious about the city's downtown. Poulson told Angelenos in 1955, "We've got to support and strengthen the downtown area. It's my notion that no city can be a great city without a strong downtown core."[136] Strengthening the downtown core meant more than just building modern corporate office towers; influential residents believed it essential that institutions like museums and opera houses culturally anchor that downtown core. The *Los Angeles Times*, one of the most prominent boosters for downtown growth, editorialized that a modern and vibrant downtown would answer "the critics of Los Angeles" who insinuate "that we have no culture, that nothing really important ever happens here, that there is no metropolitan 'feeling' to the town, that we are a mere collection of suburbs in search of a city."[137] In downtown Los Angeles, that would mean using the powers of eminent domain and Title I funds to bulldoze Bunker Hill—a racially diverse working-class community—replacing it with modernist office towers, luxury apartment buildings, and finally a new Music Center that would open in 1964. If Bunker Hill would be the new home for high culture, a new modern stadium located near the city center might be a magnet for more middlebrow tastes. Chavez Ravine, it seemed to many, would be an ideal central location—at the crux of regional freeways—to further manufacture a sense of city spirit and cohesion.[138] After his initial meeting with Poulson in autumn 1956, O'Malley sent an engineer to investigate Chavez Ravine as a possible site for a new stadium.

Chavez Ravine was a hilly area, five minutes north of downtown by car. Just a half decade before, it had been home to the Mexican American neighborhoods of Bishop, La Loma, and Palo Verde—a place with a vital street life and a strong sense of community. The houses and shops were, however, considered "substandard" by outsiders. Given its already working-class makeup, relatively low population density, and valuable location near central Los Angeles, Chavez Ravine was targeted as an ideal site for new public housing under the terms of the National Housing Act of 1949. Plans called for a massive complex to house 3,360 families—over three times the number that then lived in the area—in 24 thirteen-story towers and 163 two-story structures. By the end of 1951, most of the families that had lived there had been relocated elsewhere and their homes destroyed. However, plans for new housing had run up against a well-organized antihousing campaign—from a group including the California real estate lobby, the Home Builders Association, and the chamber of commerce, allied with the powerful mouthpiece of the *Los Angeles Times*— charging that such projects were "creeping socialism" or even communistic, and most certainly an affront to American values.[139]

After a year of court battles, city council scraps, and investigations of the California Housing Authority by anti-communist state senators, plans for public housing at Chavez Ravine were undone. Congressman Poulson—with the full backing of the *Los Angeles Times*—defeated the four-term, pro-housing mayor, Fletcher Bowron, in 1953. Poulson negotiated a series of compromises that allowed those projects already under construction to move forward in exchange for canceling plans at Rose Hill and Chavez Ravine—the two largest projects that would have accounted for more than half of the total planned units. The federal government, owners of the land, sold the parcels back to the city under the condition that it be used for public projects. The city bought Chavez Ravine for $1.28 million, $4 million less than the federal government had paid for it. Residents of Bishop,

La Loma, and Palo Verde who had resisted removal were temporarily spared their homes, as members of the Los Angeles elite tried to figure out an appropriate "public purpose" for Chavez Ravine that didn't reek of communism.

All-American baseball certainly didn't smell like communism, and for the city's powerful, a new big-league stadium was very much a "public purpose." Poulson appointed a "Blue Ribbon Commission" in November 1956 that was tasked with examining the city's park and recreation needs. The commission, unsurprisingly, recommended a new modern stadium be built in Chavez Ravine. To start the project, it also recommended a two-million-dollar item in the 1957 budget for land preparation of the site. In February, O'Malley exchanged his Fort Worth minor league franchise for the Pacific Coast League's Los Angeles Angels and their ballpark, Wrigley Field, located on a nine-acre lot about a mile south of downtown. This gave the Dodgers the major league rights to the territory, facilitating a possible move. The courtship continued at Dodgertown, the club's spring training facility in Florida, where a city delegation led by Poulson hoped to strengthen the budding relationship. O'Malley afterward visited Los Angeles, ostensibly to review his new minor league club, but he also brought along an engineer to again examine Chavez Ravine; after this visit, he was certain that this location would be the best for the Dodgers, given its access to three freeways nearby. At that time, Los Angeles was prepared to offer the Dodgers 185 acres in Chavez Ravine and the two million dollars for land preparation—money that was technically to be used, according to the 1957 budget, for building access roads to a new zoo and art gallery. And yet, on a map prepared for a May 11 city council meeting, a stadium had replaced the gallery.[140]

Later that month, National League owners cleared the Dodgers and Giants to move to California. The clubs were, according to Joseph Sheehan of the *New York Times*, "backed against the wall" because of declining attendance, "a result of obsolete facilities and metropolitan New York's saturation with televised baseball." It wasn't, however, a done deal: O'Malley was reportedly still hoping for a downtown Brooklyn stadium and Los Angeles had not yet delivered legislation meeting the Dodgers' terms there. Neither had San Francisco, and a new municipal stadium there was essential to convincing Giants owner Horace Stoneham to move.[141] While O'Malley and Stoneham were publicly noncommittal, talk in the sports pages was loud enough to prompt an investigation of antitrust laws by the House Judiciary Committee, chaired by Emmanuel Celler of Brooklyn—a probe that resulted in public declarations and political grandstanding but no action.

More threatening to O'Malley's plans for Chavez Ravine than the congressional hearing was the increasing awareness among Los Angeles officials that the restrictive clause in the land deed, which required its use for public purpose, might be a legal obstacle to turning over the site to the Dodgers. The mayor pushed forward. The city negotiated a contract with O'Malley that would give the Dodgers 315 acres in Chavez Ravine in exchange for the minor league ballpark, Wrigley Field, and its nine-acre plot. The city would kick in $4.74 million in land preparation, and O'Malley would build a youth recreation center on forty acres adjacent the new stadium; this was added to satisfy the "public purpose" stipulations of the deed (though, in the end, the public recreation center was never built).[142] O'Malley announced the Dodgers' relocation from Brooklyn to Los Angeles on October 8, and the Los Angeles city council approved the contract on October 9.

The Dodgers were on their way, but the Battle of Chavez Ravine had a few skirmishes in it yet. Opponents of the contract—objecting to the donation of public land to a private enterprise—collected signatures to trigger a referendum, Proposition B, for the following June. A massive campaign to vote "yes on B," which would approve the contract, was highlighted by a televised "Dodgerthon," featuring star power like Jack Benny, Lucille Ball, George Burns, Groucho Marx, Debbie Reynolds, and Ronald Reagan. The measure passed narrowly, but the opposition took its cause to Los Angeles County Superior Court in July. There the voters were overturned, as the judge ruled that land purchased with public monies and specifically deeded for public purpose couldn't be transferred to a private business. The California Supreme Court unanimously overturned this decision in January 1959. After this decision was appealed, the United States Supreme Court validated the city's contract with the Dodgers in October 1959.[143] By then, the Dodgers had already played their second season in Los Angeles, drawing over two million fans to their temporary home at the Coliseum, an athletics and football oval that had been awkwardly rigged to host baseball.[144] With the Supreme Court decision, Walter O'Malley could finally start building

FIGURE 27. Walter O'Malley discusses plans for a new stadium at a Los Angeles press conference in June 1958. AP PHOTO.

FIGURE 28. New Dodgers fans watch the team in the third game of the 1959 World Series. The playing field was shoehorned into the Los Angeles Coliseum from 1958 to 1961, as Dodger Stadium was planned, adjudicated, and constructed. An enormous mesh fence bracketed off left field in order to cut down on cheap home runs. AP PHOTO.

his new stadium. Poulson celebrated victory by asserting, "Progress must not be stopped in Los Angeles."[145] The *Los Angeles Times*, once so adamantly against public development, deemed the stadium "one of those mixed public and private enterprises which end happily if they are properly planned. . . . Although it would never be designated as such by the bureaucrats the Chavez Ravine stadium is an excellent example of urban renewal and development." Councilman Edward Roybal disagreed, arguing, "It is not morally or legally right for a government agency to condemn private land, take it away from the property owner through Eminent Domain proceedings, then turn around and give it to a private person or corporation for private gain."[146]

San Francisco's power brokers also had big-league aspirations, and the realization of those ambitions was indelibly intertwined with those of their rivals to the south. In 1953, a coalition led by Mayor Elmer Robinson and city businessmen began pitching citizens on the need to draw a major league baseball team there, believing it would benefit the city economically and culturally. As was so often the case, local newspapers championed a cause that would also make them "big league": sportswriter Curley Grieve was a major advocate for the plan, writing regularly about the city's need for a major league team in his column for the *San Francisco Examiner*. At Robinson's request, the Board of Supervisors approved a $5 million bond proposition for a new stadium. City supervisor Francis McCarty argued that if Los Angeles was going to build a stadium to attract a major league baseball team, San Franciscans "must keep pace. We don't want that city to get the jump on us." Voters seemed to agree, approving a $5 million stadium bond in November 1954, provided the city bring a major league team to San Francisco within five years.[147]

The pursuit of a major league club gained traction in 1957, when Mayor George Christopher visited New York to pitch Horace Stoneham on relocating to the West Coast. Stoneham's Giants played at the Polo Grounds, a stadium that was "unconventional, illogical, absurd, and a lovely place to watch a ball game," according to a writer for the *New York Times*.[148] It was certainly distinctive, for better or worse, with its peculiar pinched horseshoe shape and memorable location, wedged between the Harlem River to the east, an escarpment known as Coogan's Bluff to the west, and 155th Street to the south. Like most major league clubs, the Giants had enjoyed an attendance boom in the immediate postwar years followed by a 1950s decline; attendance peaked at just over 1.6 million in 1947, but by 1952 it had dropped below one million.[149] The decline—as in Brooklyn—was attributed to a combination of the suburbanization of many of the club's fans, shortages of parking around the stadium, the relative convenience of watching games on television, the physical deterioration of the ballpark, and suburban perceptions of the area around it. The Polo Grounds, built in 1911, adjoined the neighborhoods of Harlem and Washington Heights. Harlem had, of course, been famous for decades as a center of African American cultural, economic, and political life. But like Central Brooklyn, it suffered from the economic and social effects of racial segregation. Washington Heights hovered above the Polo Grounds atop the bluff, a distinctive physical and psychological boundary. As had happened in central Brooklyn, many white ethnics—particularly Irish and Jews—left Washington Heights in the 1950s, often replaced by new African American, Puerto Rican, and Cuban residents.[150]

Talk of a Giants departure began to circulate in the early 1950s. In a September 1953 article in *Sport* magazine, Jack Orr noted rumors that the Giants would leave the Polo Grounds, after their 1962 lease was up, to become tenants across the Harlem River at Yankee Stadium. Robert Moses, the gatekeeper for the city's Title I funds, suggested that the

FIGURE 29. A view from the Polo Grounds grandstand in the late 1930s, obstructed by second-deck support posts, illustrates the sense of compact intimacy—and absurdity—of watching sport there. WPA FEDERAL WRITERS PROJECT, NEW YORK CITY MUNICIPAL ARCHIVES. COURTESY NYC MUNICIPAL ARCHIVES.

FIGURE 30. The Polo Grounds were squeezed by Coogan's Bluff to the west, the Harlem River to the east, and a new housing development to the north. Directly south of the parking lot was 155th Street, the northern edge of Harlem. This aerial view is from April 1963. AP PHOTO.

Giants abandon the Polo Grounds before then so that the stadium could be torn down and replaced with public housing.[151] The Yankees seemed unlikely, however, to assist their National League rival with an affordable lease. The Giants remained profitable in the 1950s, but tenuously so. The club relied on radio and television; in a market like New York, television both gave and took away, driving down stadium attendance but compensating in rights payments. Stoneham rented out the park for events like football games, boxing matches, and religious revivals. The eleven home games with the archrival Dodgers each season were also crucial to the Giants' bottom line.[152] That bottom line, though, took a major hit when the NFL's Giants moved to Yankee Stadium after the 1955 season, following thirty years at the Polo Grounds. They had worried about the future of the Polo Grounds given the rumors about the baseball team's possible departure; they were also attracted by the larger seating capacity, better parking facilities, and better transit service at the sta-

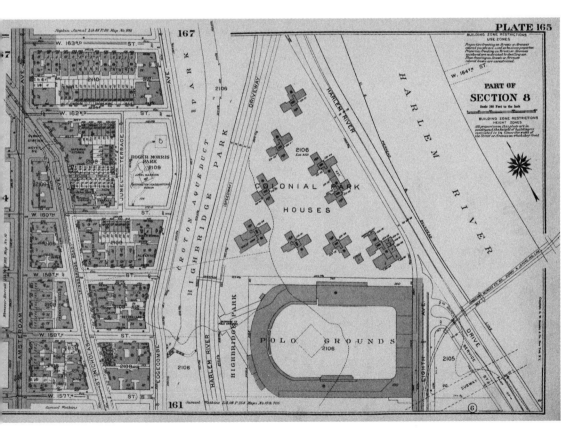

FIGURE 31. A 1955 land map suggests the shifting modes of urban space—from the dense cityscape of Washington Heights atop Coogan's Bluff to the west of the Polo Grounds, to the new, modern, space-positive Colonial Park Houses to the north. LIONEL PINCUS AND PRINCESS FIRYAL MAP DIVISION, THE NEW YORK PUBLIC LIBRARY. "PLATE 165, PART OF SECTION 8," NEW YORK PUBLIC LIBRARY DIGITAL COLLECTIONS.

dium just across the Harlem River in the Bronx. The departure of the football Giants cost Stoneham's baseball business approximately seventy-five thousand dollars per season in rental and concessions revenue.[153] It was clear to most that the Polo Grounds was nearing its end and that the Giants—known as the Gothams at their inception in 1883—might not be in New York much longer, particularly once the Dodgers began contemplating a move to Los Angeles.

Though the future of the Giants in Harlem seemed uncertain, even unlikely, Stoneham reportedly scoffed at San Francisco's initial $5 million proposal, saying "any figure other than 10 or 11 million dollars shouldn't even be discussed." Mayor Christopher returned to San Francisco, needing to convince his stadium allies to up the city's ante. Publicly, Christopher claimed that a major league team would "give San Francisco a dateline in almost every daily newspaper in the country" and economically benefit the city. But privately, stadium advocates worried that another proposition doubling the bond issue might not get past the voters, and so Christopher and his partners created a nonprofit corporation called Stadium, Inc.[154] This instrument allowed stadium advocates to issue city-backed bonds without a vote. It also shrouded stadium dealings in secrecy, as the corporation could

FIGURE 32. The Giants, led by Bobby Thompson, race toward the center-field clubhouse at the end of the club's final home game at the Polo Grounds in September 1957, outpacing pursuing fans. Apartment buildings of Washington Heights, perched atop Coogan's Bluff, are visible in the background. BETTMANN/GETTY IMAGES.

evade the city charter and assign contracts without competitive bidding and open books. Stadium, Inc., floated an additional $5.5 million bond issue, dodging the vote required of the first bond. On the first board of directors for Stadium, Inc., was area contractor and multimillionaire Charles Harney—who would play a key and controversial role in the stadium's construction—along with two of his employees.[155]

As Stoneham considered his options in New York, San Franciscans debated potential stadium sites over the summer of 1957. Candlestick Point, on the southern edge of the city, became the favorite spot of Christopher. It offered the open acreage that might fit a 50,000-seat stadium and 10,000-car parking lot. A reporter called it a "breezy track of wild grass, red rocks, chaparral and torn trees . . . all strewn with whiskey bottles and beer cans." That "breeziness" concerned some, but Christopher dismissed these complaints. After engineers tested it one morning, the mayor reported that the wind never exceeded fourteen miles per hour, not "enough to blow a peanut sack from first to second." The city had owned the targeted forty-one-acre plot just four years earlier but had sold it to Charles Harney for $2,100 per acre. In 1957, Harney sold it back to the city for $65,853 per acre—over thirty times the original price. At the time of the sale, the city bought land adjacent Harney's plot for just $6,540 per acre. Harney was paid $2.7 million for the land; he was also given a construction contract for $2 million and another $2 million for grading and filling—all in a privately negotiated deal with Stadium, Inc.[156]

The Giants' move seemed increasingly inevitable, though it wasn't quite official. In an article titled "San Francisco or Bust," John Drebinger of the *New York Times* claimed that the Giants were as good as gone. He pointed out that the drop in attendance didn't correlate to a decline in quality on the field, as the 1951 and 1954 versions of the club were pennant winners. He figured, "When, in the thick of a sizzling pennant race, the top contenders pass in review and draw 3,000 in the afternoon and 9,000 at night, brother, you've had it. . . . The Polo Grounds is dead."[157] On August 19, 1957, Stoneham's board of directors voted 8–1 to move to San Francisco.[158]

There were 11,606 at the Giants' last game at the Polo Grounds, a 9–1 loss to the Pittsburgh Pirates on September 30. As the final out was being recorded, many fans were already pouring over the walls and onto the playing field. The players, expecting this, began running across the field toward the center-field clubhouse. The fans chased them there, a "mass pursuit . . . touched off by affection, excitement, nostalgia, curiosity and annoyance at the fact the team next year will represent San Francisco," according to *New York Times* reporter Milton Bracker. Most of the players and coaches made it safely to their clubhouse; Bracker observed, "The players having eluded them, the fans went to work on the field."[159]

Over the next thirty minutes, many of the crowd unharnessed a fit of destruction. They tore out the regular and warm-up home plates, the wooden base beneath the main plate, two other bases, and the foam rubber protection for outfielders on the center-field fences. They broke the bullpen sun-shelter. They stole signs and telephones. Some even ripped a memorial plaque off the center-field wall. Others looking for a souvenir turned to the field itself, pulling up scalps of turf and handfuls of infield dirt. Four boys took the pitcher's rubber onto the subway. Home plate was dragged away by a small woman who claimed to be a teacher from Queens. She embodied the pervasive sense of abandon, as people seemed to momentarily lose their minds in a baseball riot.[160]

Onlookers were variously somber, bitter, and angry at the Giants' departure. One reporter interviewed an ensemble of horn players blowing the "Giant Victory March," which had historically been played at special events and after wins. The interviewees—a barber from the Bronx, a steamfitter from Brooklyn, a cab driver from Manhattan, and a seventy-four-year-old housewife from Staten Island—weren't pleased. One suggested that they should have played a funeral march. Another said, "I came here to attend a wake."[161] As some silently mourned and some pillaged, others congregated outside the center-field clubhouse. They called for their idol, Willie Mays, hoping that he would emerge on the steps as so many Giants had over the years, to receive the fans. He didn't. They called for the head of Giants owner Stoneham, chanting, "We want Stoneham! We want Stoneham! We want Stoneham—with a rope around his neck!"[162]

Perhaps the spirit of the day, the mixture of nostalgia, of anger, of attachment, of resentment that seemed to overwhelm the fans, was best captured in one of the group's final songs as the stadium darkened. To the tune of "The Farmer in the Dell," they sang:

> We hate to see you go,
> We hate to see you go,
> We hope to hell you never come back—
> We hate to see you go.[163]

Though the Giants were on their way, stadium construction in California had still not begun by February 1958. Harney announced in July 1958 that the stadium would not be ready for next season's opening day. The following month, a grand jury began investigating the financial dealings, focusing particularly on Harney's land deals with the city. The stadium foundation was finally poured at the end of October 1958—an event met with protests by area residents. At year's end, the grand jury submitted its report, which found that the price paid to Harney for the land at Candlestick Point was "exorbitant"—between $650,000 and $1 million too much—and that Mayor Christopher had acted "hastily" to draw Harney into the project. The report stated that voters had been misled; San Franciscans had approved a $5 million stadium construction bond in 1954 but now faced costs of over $15 million.[164]

The grand jury report made waves, but the stadium project limped forward—thanks in part to favorable coverage from the major local papers.[165] Even so, the ballpark wasn't ready for 1959, and by the end of the season, costs had reached $17 million. Harney's construction company remained in charge of the project, though Harney was reportedly miffed when San Franciscans voted in March to name the stadium Candlestick Park and not Harney Stadium. While some speculated that a resentful Harney then dragged his feet on construction, it is also true that this was the first stadium he had ever built—just as it was the first stadium that architect John Bolles had ever designed.[166] They built a stadium that was visually striking, auguring a new age of engineered stadium, but also tragically flawed.

As the Giants waited for their new stadium in San Francisco, they made do with pleasant Seals Stadium, where the Pacific Coast League's San Francisco Seals had played for a quarter century.[167] The Art Deco park, opened in 1931, had a single-decked, roofless grandstand that looked out across the recently constructed James Lick Freeway toward Potrero Hill, crawling with homes and apartments in the distance. A Hamm's brewery towered behind the grandstand; a three-dimensional, thirteen-foot-tall goblet of beer sat atop its roof. While charming, Seals Stadium was a minor league park designed for a different era. It had been expanded twice over the years and yet still only held 22,900 at its peak. A second deck couldn't be added, as the existing structure could not support the weight. Even without expanded capacity, there wasn't enough space adjacent the ballpark to install the parking lots that George Christopher had promised Horace Stoneham. Furthermore, the area around the park was becoming increasingly Latino and working class. Sixteenth Street, just over the right-field wall, reflected these changes; by the late 1940s, it featured Latin restaurants, bakeries, and other specialty shops. As more people moved in, housing was subdivided and deteriorated; it soon had a reputation as a poor neighborhood.[168] Densely textured, working class, and non-white—this was the sort of area most ball clubs would try to escape in the coming years.

Candlestick Park was finally completed, after two years of delay, in April 1960. *Sports Illustrated*'s Robert Boyle wrote that the occasion stamped the city as "major league once and for all." Seals Stadium, he allowed, "was a charming little park, but in San Francisco, where appearances count for a lot, it was a reminder of the times when the town was minor league." *San Francisco Chronicle* columnist Charles McCabe concurred, writing that the games at Seals Stadium "always looked rather as if a major league team was playing in the high school field . . . for some terribly worthy cause." Candlestick Park, by the looks of it, was no high school park.[169] "With its soaring wind baffle, immense but seemingly fragile," a writer for the city's *News-Call Bulletin* suggested, "the stadium was like some great conch shell, settled on the shores of the Candlestick Cove."[170] Candlestick Park's signature feature was the baffle, sitting atop the main grandstand—a concrete piecrust around the stadium rim. The upper deck rested on a series of inverted V-shaped concrete columns that loomed over fans making their way into the ballpark. Part boomerang, part swept wing, part tail fin, these iconic supports almost seemed in motion—an understated cousin to Southern California's Googie modernism of the roadside strip.[171] Inside, the double-deck grandstand curved, cool and collected, around a lightbulb-shaped playing field with symmetrical outfield distances—from 335 feet at the foul poles to 420 in dead center. As in New York, the Giants' home sat between hill and water. At the stadium's back was Morvey's Hill, peeking over its left shoulder; beyond the outfield was San Francisco Bay. Whereas Seals Stadium fit snugly into the diverse cityscape of North Mission, Candlestick Park sat solitary in a 9,000-car parking lot—an engineered sculpture fully on display. Upon its opening, J. G. Taylor Spink, publisher of the *Sporting News*, celebrated the park as "simply wonderful, marvelous, unbelievable," adding, "Baseball has never known anything like it."[172] Horace Stoneham boasted, "The new stadium is a beautiful structure—I like to think

FIGURE 33. Seals Stadium in 1957, months before the Giants committed to San Francisco.
AP PHOTO.

it is the finest sports arena anywhere . . . all San Franciscans have reason to be very proud of it as one more expression of civic enterprise and progress."[173]

Visually striking and a symbol of civic progress, it was also designed to improve the comfort of the stadium experience. Red Smith noted, "Every seat commands an unimpeded view. The seats are broad, of comforting contour design, with ample leg room. The wide aisles should eliminate congestion."[174] A writer for *Baseball Digest* assured readers that the modern fan would be "considerably more comfortable than his grandfather, or even his father, was." The Candlestick seats represented "the peak of the engineer's art," with their "form-fitting curves" and "all-weather finish" that guaranteed "a splinterless existence" for visitors.[175] One of his colleagues called the park a "fat man's paradise" because the seats were two inches wider than those in any other stadium.[176] Not only were the seats wide, but many were supposed to be heated as well. As the park was being constructed, reporters were particularly interested in the installation of heating pipes throughout the concrete terraces—thirty-five-thousand-feet worth that channeled hot water beneath fans to battle the nighttime chill of the bay.[177]

Creature comforts were amplified in some of the stadium's more exclusive spaces. John Drebinger of the *New York Times* remarked on the "sumptuous club offices" and "plush stadium club, patterned after the one in the Yankees' abode but with far more polish."[178] The Stadium Club housed a restaurant and bar where dues-paying members could eat dishes like brook trout "fresh from Springfield Rocky Mountain Waters" for $4 or filet mignon "selected for tenderness" at $5.95.[179] A writer for the *Los Angeles Times* ran readers through the catalogue of stadium features: the heated floors, the seats with backs and armrests, the deluxe loge boxes, the members-only Stadium Club with a bar and restaurant, the twenty-two bathrooms, and—significantly—"Oh, yes, and usherettes yet!"[180] The all-female usher staff caught the eye of visiting reporters and players alike; Yankee icon Mickey Mantle called Candlestick "a beautiful park," adding, "The ushers are also very nice."[181]

At first glance, Candlestick Park seemed a portrait of modernist functionality—an orderly and sculptural home for sport, near the city but not fully in it, with its spacious parking lots liberated from urban gridlock and updated amenities catering to an affluent postwar society. In practice, however, the stadium was a notorious failure. Robert Lipsyte of the *New York Times* told New Yorkers, "There is no joy . . . in Candlestick Park in San Francisco. It is a masculine stadium of strong, bleak lines, a fortress on a hill silhouetted against a sky that can suddenly turn as dark as turtle soup. The wind whips in from everywhere carrying portents of tragedy: It is here that Oedipus could tear out his eyes; here that a little fearful governess could knock on a door thrown open by a mad and violent Rochester."[182] A stadium full of enchanting female ushers couldn't soften the stadium's "masculine" concrete austerity—what one architectural critic has called its "muscular,

FIGURE 34. The cool, engineered modernism of Candlestick Park is accented by precast concrete supports that boomerang around the stadium's iconic "wind baffle." SAN FRANCISCO HISTORY CENTER, SAN FRANCISCO PUBLIC LIBRARY.

tense energy."[183] Nor could they outcharm the weather that regularly turned Candlestick into a scene of sporting madness. The *New Yorker*'s Roger Angell, an aficionado of the old, boxy ballparks, thought that Candlestick looked "like an outbuilding of Alcatraz" with its "raw concrete ramps and walkways and its high, curving grandstand barrier."[184] No doubt many visitors—and the Giants themselves—would come to feel like prisoners there.[185]

Candlestick Park was a powerful argument for the type of roofed stadium many had been imagining over the previous decade. Its cold and windy setting became its defining characteristic, outrageous even for San Francisco, where fans were used to sitting through winds and evening chills at Seals Stadium. Candlestick quickly became known as the "cave of winds." Sportswriters from sunny Los Angeles particularly enjoyed mocking the grounds of the Dodgers' relocated rivals to the north. Al Wolf referred to it as "cyclonic Candlestick Park . . . where the icy winds blow." Visitors, according to Art Rosenbaum, were forced to "dress for an Alaskan costume party." Frank Finch joked, "It's been written before but we'll write it again: Compared to Candlestick Park, the late Admiral Byrd could have disported in his undies with impunity at Little America." Giants pitcher Stu Miller, who would be blown off the mound by wind gusts during the 1961 World Series, complained, "You just don't like to say this is a lousy ball park, but it is." His teammate Ed Bressoud agreed: "This is a joke. This is the worst ball park I ever played in, and I'm not alone in my sentiments. Ask the other guys."[186] Giants' fans, at least according to Roy Terrell, had it better than the players; "the weather does not faze the natives," he wrote in *Sports Illustrated*, "who simply wrap up in parkas and blankets and Martinis and sit there as if shivering were fun."[187]

Architect John Bolles was often blamed for the stadium's inability to cope with the wind and cold, though perhaps unfairly. He was familiar with the location: he was in fact born not far from there and had designed a number of structures nearby during World War II. His preliminary designs for the stadium had called for a roof covering both decks and wrapping almost fully around the playing field to protect it from powerful and swirling afternoon winds. Cost concerns forced a redesign and reduction of the wind baffle. Bolles also wanted to landscape Morvey's Hill with eucalyptus and pine trees to use as windbreaks. But these plans were also scotched.[188] The Giants hadn't realized the problems the wind would cause until the stadium was well under construction. Chub Feeney, Giants vice president and nephew of Horace Stoneham, typically visited the architect at the site in the morning. Then, one day, he visited in the afternoon and could barely stand up to the winds. When he asked a worker if it was always like that, the worker replied, "No sir. It only blows like this between the hours of one and five." Feeney, knowing that this was when the Giants typically played their games, realized he was stuck with what Arthur Daley of the *New York Times* called "a $15,000,000 lemon." Daley mused, "Candlestick Park will be with us for a long time to come unless—happy thought—the wind blows it into the bay. It's the one hope for saving real baseball for San Francisco."[189]

Arctic conditions weren't the only problem fans and players faced, and once again the siting of the stadium was blameworthy. Moving out of North Mission would have, presumably, made a stadium more automobile friendly. In this case, it made it worse. One Giant official admitted, "We don't anticipate any three or four hour trips to the ballpark, but we know it's going to be rugged."[190] Motorists could arrive via the Bayshore Freeway—a major thruway for city commuters—or take busy Third Street. Narrow access streets clotted up as cars tried to enter the expansive parking lot. The bus service to the stadium—there were two regular and three express routes—might save one from driving but not the traffic. Only the well-popularized pier that received water traffic would allow patrons to avoid the cramped automobile arteries.[191]

Once inside, blanketed, and properly martini'd, fans had to battle other obstacles.[192] One headline announced, "Giants' Park Not 'Intimate'"; the reporter noted the need for binoculars.[193] Some referred to the stadium as "Candlestink Park"; a nearby lagoon received raw sewage and waste dumping.[194] Those sitting below the upper deck had to watch for dripping water, as the pipes from the seat-heating system leaked. Business manager Jerry Donovan said of the celebrated heating system, "I'd have to call it a total loss."[195] During the planning phases, John Bolles had referred to the ballpark as "an old man's stadium" because there would be no long flights of stairs, just a simple ten-foot ramp to the upper level from the parking lot. In practice, some thought the stadium was actually killing its customers. Just six weeks after the stadium opened, the long walk from the parking lot had been blamed for six fatal heart attacks. The police department announced plans to build a new parking facility just fifty feet from the stadium entrance for patrons with heart problems. Incredibly, coroner Henry W. Turkel suffered a slight heart attack while studying the problem.[196] The parking lot itself, which had been partly built on bay fill, was already sinking into San Francisco Bay that same month, according to the director of public works in San Francisco. This would require $15,000 immediately to fix and $5,000 to maintain each year.[197]

Nevertheless Giants fans endured. Attendance climbed from 1.4 million at Seals Stadium in 1959 to 1.8 million at Candlestick in its first season. This far exceeded the numbers at the Polo Grounds, where just 1.3 million fans came through the gates in the final two years combined. Attendance would remain well above the levels in New York, averaging about 1.5 million through 1966, but by 1972, the Giants were drawing fewer fans than they had in their final season in Harlem. Candlestick Park had never been a place to draw fans on its own merits; by the 1962 World Series, columnist Wells Twombly would write, "Candlestick was already starting to look like the world's oldest new stadium."[198] It was modern and had plenty of parking, and yet San Francisco had clearly got it wrong—a point that other stadium builders were well aware of. Emil Praeger would design Shea Stadium in Queens, future home to the New York Mets—the new club that would replace the Giants and Dodgers back east. He provided his assessment of Candlestick in a letter to Robert Moses in May 1960, writing, "I inspected Candlestick Park shortly before it was complete and while it is better than many old stadia, I do not think we have a great deal to learn from it."[199] Praeger also designed the Dodgers' new stadium in Los Angeles. When planning that park, Walter O'Malley reportedly told him to look closely at the plans for Candlestick. "Study these," O'Malley instructed, "and learn what not to do."[200]

As San Franciscans battled nature, Dodger Stadium was celebrated as a symbol of man's ability to tame it. On its opening in 1962, Walter Bingham told readers of *Sports Illustrated*, "Walter O'Malley had turned a goat pasture called Chavez Ravine into the finest baseball stadium in the world."[201] This turn of phrase echoed the way many had been talking about the 315-acre plot over the previous years. Dodger boosters—including club officials, politicians, and the *Los Angeles Times*—often made a point of describing the area's desolation. O'Malley called it "210 taxable acres of hilly ground that would be of interest only to goats."[202] An editorial in the *Los Angeles Times* pronounced it "a sort of half-forgotten wilderness" that was "nearly empty and requires little displacement of anything except irregularities of terrain."[203] Charles Detoy, a former president of the chamber of commerce, claimed, "The property has no market value today. . . . The city is fortunate to be getting someone to develop this problem property."[204] For Frank Finch of the *Los Angeles Times*, Chavez Ravine was "300 acres of steep hills, eroded gullies, weeds, stunted trees and a few ramshackle dwellings, including an abandoned schoolhouse. The area was densely populated by possums, skunks, jackrabbits, gophers, rusty tin cans, rotting tires, moribund mattresses and broken beer bottles."[205] Dodgers vice president Fresco Thompson's first impression was "of Hades without the River Styx. The topography featured a series of crisscrossing gullies, all trying to escape each other. I couldn't visualize any game being played there except tag by the gophers." Chavez Ravine, he continued, "had always been a haven for possums, jackrabbits, skunks, and squatters."[206]

It was a disingenuous portrait of Chavez Ravine. The land was extremely valuable as the largest undeveloped parcel in the center city; an outside consultant hired by the city council in 1958 appraised the "commercial value" of the land at up to eighteen million dollars, were it to be leveled. It also remained the home to more than four-legged wildlife in 1959.[207] Dodger Stadium construction could only begin once area residents had been forcibly removed from the land by the police—an eviction that was captured on television and horrified many Angelenos who saw it as a violation of the country's first principles.[208] One of those evicted was Abrana Arechiga, who had settled in Chavez Ravine with her husband, Manuel, in the 1920s, raising four children there. As her family home was being bulldozed, she pointedly shouted in Spanish, "Why don't they play ball in Poulson's backyard—not in ours!"[209] Arechiga understood the uneven burden of postwar redevelopment and growth far better than most.

But the spectacle of eviction and possession was one that stadium advocates, even in McCarthyite Los Angeles, preferred to erase. Charlie Park of the *Los Angeles Times* told readers—as O'Malley already had and *Sports Illustrated* would—that the stadium occupied a space that "only a short time ago was a mountainous goat pasture." The primitive had been replaced by progress—"an artistic and engineering marvel." To make wilderness productive required massive effort—the moving of 8 million cubic yards of dirt; the assembling of staggering amounts of steel (13 million pounds), concrete (40,000 cubic yards), wood (375,000 board feet), cast iron (550 tons), and asphalt (80,000 tons).[210] The numbers were astonishing—and worked as expressions of modern progress in their enormous scale. The Dodgers' *1962 Souvenir Yearbook*, which fans would have bought for fifty cents upon arriving at the new stadium, celebrated the *process* of construction—and the men who made it possible—more than the stadium itself. Photo after photo portrayed the reshaping of this seemingly vacant frontier. A photo caption textually anchored this visual

FIGURE 35. Chavez Ravine is excavated to make way for Dodger Stadium in May 1960. Downtown Los Angeles is visible to the south. AP PHOTO.

story, telling readers that there were "mountains to be leveled; ravines to be filled." Judging by the stadium program, the act of building was more exhilarating than the building it produced.

But what a stadium it was. The eighteen-million-dollar Dodger Stadium opened in April 1962 and instantly became the gold standard in baseball venues.[211] It was, according to local writers, a "mammoth, multicolored mansion," a "gorgeous triumph of high-rise architecture in living Technicolor with levels of ocher, aqua, coral and skyblue," the "Taj Mahal of Sport," an "elegant edifice of which every Angeleno can be justly proud," and the "Taj O'Malley."[212] Pastel decks of sweeping, cantilevered stands hugged a symmetrical playing field cleansed of the dimensional oddities back at Ebbets. Fifty-six thousand fans enjoyed open views of the field and verdant Elysian Park beyond; there were none of the pesky structural posts that obstructed fans' views at old ballparks. Clean and orderly, it seemed a rebuke to Brooklyn. Even more, it projected the glamour of Hollywood through its "swank" members-only Stadium Club where the elite could sip scotch at linened tables.[213] Ushers, with uniforms designed by a Beverly Hills fashion house, orchestrated crowd movement.[214] Young and attractive usherettes patrolled the dugout boxes at field level—what a sportswriter called "your own little private domain, far from the maddening throng high above you."[215] Four terraced parking lots—each for a different seating level—rationalized entry and exit, minimizing the stairs that had to be climbed. A five-lane drive circled the stadium, with traffic lights to manage the swarm of cars entering and exiting. Dodger Stadium's exterior was painted a light blue, with silver and gold accents. Made of concrete, steel, and plastic, the stadium's bright modernism echoed the new corporate skyscrapers and civic structures being erected in Los Angeles's reinvented downtown.[216] This was a long way from Crown Heights, Brooklyn.

From above, Dodger Stadium resembled the stylized boomerang or parabola emblazoned on postwar consumer products from Chryslers to butterfly chairs to cigarette lighters. This was "the shape of motion," as design historian Thomas Hine has noted.[217] And while the Dodgers' *1962 Souvenir Yearbook* privileged the Faustian process of carving out a stadium spot in Chavez Ravine, the program's cover told car-crazy Angelenos that this was a stadium designed for the driver. It featured an enlarged and colorful Dodger Stadium upon a black-and-white map of the Los Angeles area, with different communities clearly labeled—from San Fernando to Huntington Beach, Malibu to Pomona. Massive pastel arteries stretched outward from the stadium through these communities like veins, suggesting just how easy it would be to traverse this cluttered landscape.[218] All roads, it seemed, met at Dodger Stadium—great comfort for a population that used automobiles for 95 percent of their trips around the city.[219]

Even as the 1962 program cover advertised the stadium's automobile accessibility, it also proposed the stadium as a centerpiece to a sprawling collection of communities—a point that many stadium advocates had made over the years. Days before O'Malley announced the club's departure from Brooklyn, a *Los Angeles Times* editorial argued, "The major league baseball team might be expected to bind the neighborhoods together with a sort of communal glue." The Dodgers "will sow a new seed of civic consciousness and pride," the editor promised, adding, "Consider what happened to Milwaukee."[220] Upon the stadium opening almost five years later, the newspaper editorialized, "It will be the most easily accessible gathering place in the community, literally at the crossroads of the freeway network." It would be both geographically and spiritually central to a city some thought was spread too thinly: "Dodger Stadium is another of those things that help to give the city a living heart. It is additional insurance that the central city will not wither. It is a show place built on an ancient enclave of dinginess which, 10 years ago, seemed to have no future except as an institutionalized slum of low-rent public housing."[221]

Ebbets Field had also functioned as a sort of community center for Brooklyn. In Los Angeles, however, a great deal was made of the "wholesome" character of baseball and the

FIGURE 36. Visitors to Dodger Stadium in 1962 might have bought this program, which highlighted above all else the ballpark's connectedness to freeways. A. BARTLETT GIAMATTI RESEARCH CENTER, NATIONAL BASEBALL HALL OF FAME.

new Dodger Stadium.[222] Those eager to build the stadium and draw the Dodgers westward often made this point. O'Malley promised "everything here [Dodger Stadium] will be in keeping with the high family standards in Southern California."[223] This emphasis on wholesome family values led many to compare the stadium to nearby Disneyland. Pro-Dodgers forces made this connection explicit during the Proposition B campaign. The similarities weren't lost on outsiders; Bob Addie of the *Washington Post* referred to O'Malley's "own type of Disneyland out in Chavez Ravine."[224] Just as Disneyland cleansed the carnival experience of another Brooklyn icon, Coney Island, Dodger Stadium tamed the disorderly ballpark experience of Ebbets Field for the suburban middle-class family. As historian Eric Avila argues, Dodger Stadium could function—like Disneyland—as a postwar town square for a sprawling suburban metropolis. Each brought the appearance of public space under the eye of private, commercial interests—a simulated public, narrower than those to be found at the old ballparks.[225]

Roger Angell compared the new stadium to another component of the postwar landscape after visiting in 1962. He figured that Dodger Stadium must have been designed by an admirer of suburban supermarkets, with its pastel color scheme; electronic message board that functioned like a grocer's placard; "superfluous decorative touches," like the rickrack roofs over the outfield bleacher pavilions; and the "same preoccupation with easy access and with total use of interior space." The dugout boxes behind home plate, where "movie and television stars, ballplayers' wives, and transient millionaires" were stocked, seemed to Angell "a special shelf for high-priced goods."[226]

Angell revisited Dodger Stadium in 1965. In spite of his affection for the old boxy ballparks, he admired this one, calling it "the finest plant in baseball—a model of efficiency and attractiveness." He seemed less impressed by the crowd; the scene he sketched might have come straight from Disneyland's Main Street, U.S.A.—hardly the crowd of committed rooters Angell valued. Fans wore "green stretch pants and russet golf cardigans." Men in the upper decks sported "long bellies and golf caps," sitting by their wives and their "elaborately waved white or dyed hair, their mahogany hands crossed in their laps." Angell noted the ubiquity of transistor radios in the crowd—announcer Vin Scully's voice floated over the stands like an opium cloud, seeming to pacify the audience; he suspected the Dodger fan carried it "in order to be told what he is seeing," as "fans here seem to require electronic reassurance."[227] When the Dodgers were winning, victory was "a source of continuous and uncritical self-congratulation" and accompanied by "a nonstop high-decibel babble of joy"—"Marvelous! Oh, marvie, marvie, marvie!" one woman cried after Dodger hits, Angell recorded. On one visit, he said, he had the feeling he "had wandered into a radio breakfast show for moms" with mass sing-alongs. When the Dodgers were losing, however, fans "sat there, inning after inning, in polite, unhappy silence, like parents at a rock concert."[228]

Fellow New Yorker Robert Lipsyte didn't bother to hide his contempt for the sort of crowd Dodger Stadium cultivated. Writing for the *New York Times*, he called it "Lollipop Park," noting its Hollywood atmosphere. It seemed to Lipsyte that it was more important to be seen at the park than to see the Dodgers; he claimed, "Only in Lollipop could Doris Day throw licorice bits into [player] Frank Thomas's mouth during batting practice and leave in the seventh inning of a no-hitter. No one watches the game, for the stands are alive with long-legged cupcakes." Like Angell, Lipsyte was continually aware of the buzz of the radio, noting, "Sometimes the play-by-play announcers stopped talking long enough for the crowd to hear itself not cheering wildly." "Round and jolly, painted in pastel," he wrote, "there is nothing but joy in Los Angeles's Chavez Ravine. Brooklyn Bums, they weren't."[229]

Doris Day had replaced Hilda Chester. The transistor radio had replaced the Sym-Phony. Where there was once the street life of Bishop, La Loma, and Palo Verde, now there was what Angell called "O'Malley's Safeway," packed with suburbanites in golf shirts and stretch pants. The shift from Brooklyn to Los Angeles, Ebbets Field to Dodger Stadium, the old city to the new suburban metropolis, marked radical changes in what the stadium was and what it might be. In just over a decade, the stadium had gone from private business to public investment. The rusting industrial Northeast was giving way to a booming Sun Belt, where status was marked by becoming "big league." Sports space was being untangled from dense urban neighborhoods and plopped into enormous parking fields. And a new modernist idiom—a visual marker of progress itself—had been adopted by designers. The growing suburban middle classes were the target now, as new stadiums would have to compete with television for their dollars. In the end, Walter O'Malley's replacement for Ebbets Field resembled Geddes's futuristic "pleasure dome" not in form but in spirit. And the man who had thwarted Geddes's dome in Brooklyn, Robert Moses, would soon build a new stadium that he thought suitable to the automobile age. But first, New York's baseball purists—like Roger Angell and Robert Lipsyte—would see old stadium culture get a brief reprieve.

CHAPTER 3

FROM TENEMENTS TO SUBURBS

THE DOMESTICATION OF THE MODERN STADIUM

FREDERICK EXLEY, IN THE AUTOBIOGRAPHICAL *A Fan's Notes*, described a season of visits to the Polo Grounds in Harlem in the mid-1950s to see the New York Giants football club. This was a few years before football became explosively popular nationwide, before the Giants moved across the Harlem River to the imposing Yankee Stadium, and before the team adopted a "formal navy blue" jersey and added "a snooty N.Y. emblem" to their helmets, as Exley put it. It was before the team played in front of "sell-out crowds of Chesterfield-coated corporation executives and their elegant-legged, mink-draped wives." "The Polo Grounds," he wrote, "was never sold out." Exley got into the stadium by purchasing a one-dollar bleacher seat, then bribing ushers to place him in seats between the 40-yard lines. He waited at the backs of the stands through the first quarter, as the ushers identified the unused seats, with a group of other men doing the same thing. His compatriots were

> an Italian bread-truck driver, an Irish patrolman, a fat garage mechanic, two or three burly longshoremen, and some others whose occupations I forget—we were a motley, a memorable picture. Dressed as often as not in skimpy jackets, without gloves, we were never dressed warmly enough. Our noses ran. To keep warm we smoked one cigarette after another, drank much beer, and jogged up and down on the concrete. The Brooklyn guys talked all during the game, as much as Brooklyn

guys ever talk, which is to say hardly at all. Brooklyn guys issue statements. There is a unity of tone that forbids disagreement. "Take duh fucking bum outa deah!" or "Dat guy is a *pro*"—that designation being the highest accolade they allowed a player for making some superb play. Hollow-chested, their frigid hands stuffed deep into their pockets, their eyes and noses running, they looked about as fit to judge the relative merits of athletes as Ronald Firbank. Still, because of their cocksure, irrefutable tones in which they issued their judgments, I was certain they knew everything about football, and I enjoyed being with them immensely.

As the season progressed, the men tacitly agreed to stop moving to seats, lest they have to split up, choosing instead to stand together at the back of the stands. "We were," Exley wrote, "wops and Polacks and Irishmen out of Flatbush." They banded together each week, first as strangers, then as something more, in the "murderously damp, bitingly cold stadium"—a self-selected medley of city men in a masculine space at a time when more and more men were leaving the city for its suburbs and more and more women were spending leisure time with men.[1]

The football Giants moved to the Bronx. The baseball Giants left for San Francisco. But the Polo Grounds endured longer than many expected. The old stadium even resisted Robert Moses for a few years, as he looked covetously at the land it sat on, imagining modern housing slabs shooting up from the soggy soil.[2] Under the poised blade of the guillotine, the idiosyncratic Polo Grounds lived on to hatch two new professional clubs in its final years: the American Football League's Titans and baseball's National League Mets. For many of the city's old baseball fans, the Mets at the Polo Grounds would be a final encore for the old, urban stadium culture, in kind with that of Ebbets Field and Exley's motley crew of football watchers. But the encore didn't last long. Robert Moses would get his land for another housing project beneath Coogan's Bluff; he would also get the stadium he had long craved, Shea Stadium in Flushing Meadows Park. It wouldn't be a stadium for fat garage mechanics and burly longshoremen, wops or Polacks out of Flatbush; it would be built at the gateway to the suburbs, cast in the image of those suburbs, for the white and affluent Americans of the suburban middle classes.

A Polo Grounds Revival

The Polo Grounds enjoyed a new lease on life in the early 1960s. The Giants had left for San Francisco after the 1957 season. But the National Exhibition Company, the corporate face of Horace Stoneham's club, still owned the stadium at Coogan's Bluff; and while it didn't own the land the stadium sat atop, its lease with the landowners—the Coogan family—ran through April 1962. Between 1957 and 1961, Stoneham's stadium hosted various

FIGURE 37. Kyle Rote of the Giants reaches fruitlessly for a pass during a game at the Polo Grounds in 1955. Men stand at the back row of the thin, elevated banks of seats that run along the sidelines—just as Exley and his fellow supporters did. BETTMANN/GETTY IMAGES.

entertainments and gatherings, including Catholic masses, a ten-year anniversary of Israel's existence, hurling and Gaelic football, a Billy Graham revival, a meeting of Jehovah's Witnesses, soccer, ice skating, and rodeo. The Polo Grounds gained a new tenant in 1960, when the Titans of the upstart American Football League, a challenger to the National Football League, began play. The club had signed a two-year lease, paying rent equal to 13 percent of its gross revenue, at a minimum of $7,500 per game. The National Exhibition Corporation received all revenue from parking and concessions.[3]

The Titans arrived to a broken, old structure that seemed to be grafted together from spare building parts—an uneven assemblage of walls, windows, grilles, crossing cables, and slanting ramps. The center-field clubhouse and offices faced east, across the 8th Avenue elevated train. The stadium's west side burrowed up against the Harlem River Speedway and the bluff behind it, the parallel flanks of the stadium linked with a half circle of dark, gradually pitched roof resembling a railroad roundhouse. To the north were the Colonial Park Houses, eight 14-story middle-income apartment buildings built by the New York City Housing Authority and opened in 1951; to the south was a narrow strip of parking for 1,400 cars.[4] When he had designed the Polo Grounds in 1911, New York City architect Henry B. Herts had called it "utilitarian," though he was likely comparing it to the many theaters he had designed around Times Square in the preceding years.[5] A writer for *Baseball Magazine* had disagreed, celebrating it as "the mightiest temple ever erected to the goddess of sport."[6] But nearly fifty years later, the Polo Grounds most certainly lived up to its father's stern assessment. Long gone were ornamental touches like the decorative friezes lining the second deck. Time had taken its toll, and the National Exhibition Company had looked on disinterestedly.

The stadium was barely habitable by the time the Titans took up residence. Titans coach Sammy Baugh recalled, "It was the dirtiest damn place you ever stepped in." Seats were broken and covered with grime. Reporters found the press box full of pigeon feces. After moving in, players claimed that rats had gnawed off the edges of their shoulder pads in the locker room. The playing field was equally inadequate, beset by poor drainage and a high water table.[7] The National Exhibition Company performed little maintenance on the stands or the field itself. Playing at the Polo Grounds, according to Titans player Don Maynard, was akin to "playing in a vacant lot." The grass was uneven—barren in some places, overgrown in others. There were holes and divots throughout, and even a ravine between the 40-yard lines, which Maynard called "Wismer's Gully" for the Titans' blowhard owner Harry Wismer.[8] Another player claimed, "It was like the Marines in Guadalcanal. You felt, 'I served my time in hell.'" Weeb Ewbank, who took over as coach of the club in 1963, its final season at the Polo Grounds, said of the stadium, "It was simply the world's worst."[9]

The Titans consoled themselves with the knowledge that the Polo Grounds was destined for demolition. The New York City Board of Estimate decided, in March 1961, to raze the stadium and replace it with low-income housing. The federally subsidized project would erect four 30-story towers for more than 1,600 families at a cost of nearly $30 million. The Titans' lease only ran through 1961. However, the needs of New York's new National League baseball team, the Metropolitans, stayed the stadium's execution.[10] Formed in October 1960, the club was set to begin play in 1962. Plans called for them to play at either the Polo Grounds or Yankee Stadium until a new 55,000-seat municipal stadium could be constructed in Flushing Meadows, Queens.[11] The Yankees had no interest in helping a competing business get a foothold in its market, and so the Mets turned to the old baseball grounds in Harlem. Befitting its new ballpark, the club quickly became remarkable for its ineptitude.

The Mets moved in with the Titans at the Polo Grounds in 1962, and both clubs played there through 1963, as delays in the construction of a new publicly funded stadium in Queens pushed its opening back a year. While the presence of the Titans at the Polo Grounds hardly registered for most New Yorkers—after all, the able-bodied and beloved football Giants played just across the river—the birth of the Mets stirred the emotions of many who had spent countless hours in the old park as National League baseball fans and had mournfully witnessed the departure of the baseball Giants and Dodgers years before. Though still the same old stadium, the Polo Grounds was given what a writer called a "herculean" $300,000 facelift by the Mets—improvements a new and sparsely funded sports club like the Titans couldn't afford but certainly benefited from—including a comprehensive repainting, the regrading and resodding of the playing field, the installation of new reflectors and lamps in the lighting towers, the unveiling of a new electronic scoreboard in center field, and the creation of the Met Lounge, an exclusive cocktail lounge for box-seat holders.[12] The Polo Grounds hadn't conjured up much sentiment for old football fans when the Titans moved in—Frederick Exley aside, professional football spectators seemed less sensitive to, sentimental about, or contemplative regarding stadiums and their cultures. But for many New York baseball fans, the Polo Grounds was "an old friend, so long unvisited you'd almost forgotten its once familiar, comfortable old face," in the words of sportswriter Leonard Shecter—"a place uncounted thousands of us remember going to as boys."[13]

Sportswriter George Vecsey noted the reopening of the Polo Grounds for baseball as a rebirth for many old New Yorkers, men in particular. Many visitors crossed the bridge from the Bronx, where they had parked or exited the subway. Strangers chatted as they walked to the grounds, embodying "a feeling of community . . . the kind of closeness that New Yorkers usually permit themselves only in a severe snowstorm or a blackout." He mused, "There was an air of surprise, of unexpected good fortune, as if something precious from the past had been born again. It was as if all these men in their heavy early-spring jackets had suddenly grown five years younger. Or it was as if a married man, now living in the suburbs, had visited his favorite old tavern in the old neighborhood and found all his buddies still drinking there."[14]

The Polo Grounds experience started across the Harlem River in the Bronx in Shecter's imagination as well. Old-timers piled out of the subway or automobiles they had parked near Yankee Stadium then walked past "the monolithic Yankee Stadium, which never seemed so warm, so friendly, and so comfortably dilapidated as the Polo Grounds." As they crossed the bridge, the Polo Grounds came into view, "green and ugly, scrunched into Coogan's Bluff as though trying to hide its ugliness." When one neared the park, "there was the delicious odor of roasting peanuts and the cheerful whistling of the vendors' ovens."[15] Shecter painted a vivid portrait of the stadium itself, as an icon of a previous age and a perfectly imperfect vessel full of people's experiences.

> It was a ball park of an old and vanishing school, the Polo Grounds, wood rather than concrete, a fortune wasted in obstructed views, yet there was an unmatched intimacy with the game on the field for all of that. Ebbets Field in Brooklyn had

it and Griffith Stadium in Washington and the St. Louis ball park. . . . The Polo Grounds was a lovable freak. . . . The charm of the Polo Grounds, as it was for all the old, angular, billboard-decorated baseball parks, was that its shape was a factor in baseball games. . . . It had been five years since a baseball was hit in anger at the Polo Grounds when the Mets got there. It was old and crumbling. Yet there was a style to the old place, and a feeling. This feeling was a mixture of joy and despair, just the ingredients that made up the new team that had come to give the Polo Grounds its brief respite from inevitable doom. From the very first day the Mets got there till they left it forever after two seasons, that was the emotional mixture at the Polo Grounds, joy and despair.[16]

Others found no joy, but only despair. Bobby Bragan of the Milwaukee Braves called the Polo Grounds "a chamber of horrors."[17] Arthur Daley of the *New York Times* rated it a "diamond slum," just a way station before the Mets moved into the "glittering . . . palace" of their new stadium.[18] But sportswriter Robert Creamer was arguably the old ballpark's most aggressive and bitter critic. In the national platform of *Sports Illustrated*, Creamer called the Polo Grounds "ancient," without a hint of sympathy or feeling. He marveled at the number of people actually attending games there, given the stadium makeup. Among its many vices: the top row of bleachers was almost six hundred feet from home plate; the peculiar shape of the stands blocked people in the upper-right or upper-left stands from seeing the outfielders nearest to them; and the support posts, "of which the Polo Grounds has a splendid supply," regularly obstructed fans' views. Creamer complained, "Some seats in the Polo Grounds are behind several posts simultaneously. . . . Watching a game there is like watching it through a picket fence, and the people who sit there sway back and forth continuously during a game, first one way to get a glimpse of the pitcher winding up—as the batter disappears behind the post—and then the other way, abruptly dismissing the pitcher, to watch the batter swing." As a sports theater, Creamer summarized, "The Polo Grounds is a terrible place to watch a ball game." Its failure as a stage was matched by the difficulties in arrival: "The Polo Grounds is also a terrible place to get to." The stadium was "stuck in between a cliff . . . and a river." It had only one parking lot with one gate, meaning that fans would have to arrive hours before a popular game to get a spot there, while taking nearly an hour to get the car out of the lot at the game's conclusion.[19]

Creamer attributed the early popularity of the Mets, in part, to the Polo Grounds and its idiosyncrasies that had engendered deep identification with fans over the years. As "wretched" as the park was, it was equally "beloved," he acknowledged. Creamer argued, "Grown men brainwash their children with its legends; generations of stale cigar smoke linger in the memory like a lovely, elusive perfume; realization that the new Shea Stadium out in Queens will soon be ready for the Mets and that the Polo Grounds will then be torn down and laid waste to make room for a housing project brings tears to the eyes of men sitting behind posts, or those in the upper right-field stands who are wondering what the right fielder is doing. Perversity is a form of love."[20]

This "perversity," as Creamer argued, had its roots in the long traditions of baseball in New York, which had formed distinct fan identities for each club, ballpark, and borough. The Giants were the city's oldest major league club, having joined the National League as the Gothams in 1883. A juggernaut in the early 1900s, winning ten NL pennants from 1904 to 1924, the club was then associated with "the glamour of Broadway and Wall Street," as Leonard Koppett put it. By the 1950s, however, the club had settled into less successful times and was seen as the team of the middle classes, the small businessmen, who wore shirts and ties to the game and passed their box-seat season tickets down from father to son.[21] The Yankees, once the upstarts to John McGraw's great Giants teams, had usurped the throne by the late 1920s, becoming the most successful franchise in American sports. They soon were the team of Wall Street, of the tourist, of the casual fan—too successful to be charismatic, their pinstripes signifying their aloof and conservative single-mindedness, reflected in their predictable successes on the field. At the bottom of New York's baseball hierarchy were the Brooks—loud, antagonistic, and famously eccentric with their "bum" identity and Coney Island ballpark atmosphere. Dodgers fans were relentlessly loyal but continually stymied by their teams—seemingly underdogs even when successful in the 1950s.[22] Giants outfielder Monte Irvin described the difference between Giants and Dodgers supporters this way: "We had good fans and the fans the Dodgers had we didn't want anyway. They might have been loyal, but they were not that classy. Around the league, the borough of Brooklyn and its fans were looked down upon—they were considered second-class fans."[23]

Koppett speculated that the different fan identities played a significant role in the racial composition of the clubs. Brooklyn desegregated the major leagues in the late 1940s, and the Giants quickly followed by signing players like Irvin and Willie Mays. The Yankees, on the other hand, would not field a black player until the mid-1950s. Compared to the Dodgers and Giants, the Yankees, "from their pinnacle of nobility, moved cautiously and reluctantly and—since they were winning—without urgency. They acquired, quickly, a patina of conservatism that actually helped them with some of their immediate customers but cut them off permanently from any universally warm acceptance by a city of New York's outlook."[24] George Weiss, general manager of the Yankees, told sportswriter Roger Kahn in 1954 that they feared the signing of African American players would attract an African American audience—something their fans from Westchester County wouldn't abide. According to Kahn, Yankee owners Dan Topping and Del Webb "had no discernible social conscience" and Weiss, who would become president of the Mets at their inception, simply didn't like blacks.[25]

The image of the Yankees as lily-white, privileged, pinstriped automatons contributed to the hatred many New Yorkers felt for the team in the Bronx. Robert Lipsyte observed, "Yankee-hating was always a kind of perverse pleasure in New York." The Yankees were the team "for the tourists," the Giants were "for the sophisticated fan," and the Dodgers were "for the rabble." Then, noted Lipsyte, "in came the Mets, and Mrs. Joan Payson became a Statue of Liberty for all the huddled masses yearning to see National League baseball again."[26]

The "New Breed" of the Polo Grounds

Joan Payson was the primary owner of the new club, leading the ownership group and putting up most of the money for the club's entry fee in the National League. A lifelong Giants fan, she had been a regular at the Polo Grounds over the years and attempted to purchase the club from Horace Stoneham to prevent its move to San Francisco. Payson's money came from inheritance—one hundred million dollars on the death of her father, Payne Whitney, in the 1920s. Her brother, John Hay "Jock" Whitney, was ambassador to Britain and the publisher of the *New York Herald Tribune*.[27] Joan, Jock, and their mother, Helen, ran the family-owned Greentree Stable—a major thoroughbred stable and breeding farm—upon Payne's death.

Some commentators seemed unsure what to make of a female owner in a man's game—the first to own a team she hadn't inherited. Vecsey joked, "People wanted to know if she had bought the team with Green Stamps or scrimped on the family budget or what."[28] Payson seemed to utterly confound *Sports Illustrated*'s Alfred Wright, who profiled her upon the Mets' debut. Wright began, "The beautiful Lena Horne sings a song in which the lyrics go, 'Can't stand baseball. The game's insane.' Therein she speaks for virtually her entire gender. Women go to baseball games with their men rather than stay home alone, and some even follow the results in the press so they can appear interested. But few really enjoy the game for its own sake." But Payson's sporting credentials were unassailable. Her "addiction" to baseball had been cultivated in her childhood by her mother, who used to take her to the Polo Grounds. Helen had once played baseball herself. Wright struggles to re-feminize Payson, calling her a "grandmother" with the "approximate proportions of a Wagnerian soprano" who was "not athletic in her own right." He notes that many of her memories of sports events were "mingled with the usual milestones in a woman's life"—a reference to her being pregnant. Indeed, Payson was a pregnant onlooker of the first and famous Jack Dempsey versus Gene Tunney heavyweight boxing fight. For Payson, this was normal; she told Wright, "I've seen just about every heavyweight championship fight."[29]

Portrayals of Payson in local media were generally much less concerned with puzzling out Payson's status as a sports fan and a woman—perhaps accustomed to the game's popularity among New York's women, or perhaps just more familiar with Payson herself. Yet Payson's gender remained a subject of curiosity for many—just another feature of the Mets that pushed the club off-center and distinguished it from the straight-laced and traditional Yankees. Payson seemed an appropriate co-conspirator to Casey Stengel, the "Old Perfessor," who was in his seventies by the time he took over as field manager of the Mets and whose ballpark philosophizing and clowning provided a perfect voice-over to the club's tragic performances on the field. The cover of a Mets 1964 stadium program illustrated these two eccentric heads of state. A broad-chested opposing player, about to step on a "welcome" mat, is distracted by a vision of the new Shea Stadium. Hiding behind the image, cartoon versions of Stengel and Payson, outfitted in Mets uniforms, wait with string in hand, attached to the mat, poised to pull it out from under the burly opponent.[30]

Lipsyte's "huddled masses," those drawn together by the figure of Payson as Statue of Liberty, quickly became known as the "New Breed." The identification of a peculiar Mets fan began almost instantly. Robert Teague of the *New York Times* wrote an article in June 1962 (just three months into the club's inaugural season) unpacking the figure, which he described as a "warm-hearted mixed-breed. . . . His natural habitat is the Polo Grounds, where he cheerfully and regularly pays from 75 cents to $3.50 to suffer the exquisite tortures involved in watching the objects of his unbounded affection battle valiantly but vainly against clearly superior forces."[31] Leonard Shecter—taking a shot at the Yankee crowds—observed that the Mets fans were not another "collection of bankers on a day off who didn't know or care about the game. This crowd made noise on every pitch, cheered called balls when the Mets were up, booed strikes."[32] Mets fans at the Polo Grounds were so loud that some Yankee fans incorrectly thought the club was using canned noise when they broadcast the games over the radio.[33] Mets pitcher Jay Hook claimed, "These people are the real fans. They can't afford a big night out but they'll pay to get into the park and have their fun cheering. They enjoy themselves. They aren't tourists, like you see in some ball parks. I've never seen fans like this. When I get knocked out early, I sit in the stands and listen to them. We can be down, 9–0, but they'll be cheering for a rally. They know the game, too. We've really got the best of the old Bums and Giants, don't we?"[34]

Many observers echoed Hook's observation—that the Mets fused the old fan traditions of the Dodgers and the Giants, seemingly in a quirky alliance against the hyperachieving Yankees. Mets supporters came from all over the city, taking subways and buses from Brooklyn, Manhattan, Queens, and the Bronx or walking to the park from Harlem and Washington Heights. White suburban fans stayed away at first, discouraged by the lack of parking, fearful of Harlem and "whatever it was that had driven them out of the city in the first place," as Vecsey put it. But even some of these white, middle-class suburban fans began returning to the stadium over the course of the Mets' two years at the Polo Grounds.

FIGURE 38. Mets' 1964 *Revised Year Book* cover featuring manager Casey Stengel and owner Joan Payson. A. BARTLETT GIAMATTI RESEARCH CENTER, NATIONAL BASEBALL HALL OF FAME.

As Ebbets Field played an important role in constituting Brooklyn's sporting public, so too was the Polo Grounds essential to developing an idiosyncratic stadium culture around the hapless Mets. While the uncomfortable and aged stadium didn't "encourage new fans, particularly women," as Vecsey noted, it did bring together New York's refugee baseball supporters who had been rejected by the relocation of the Dodgers and Giants in 1957. The old stadium had been made the "private Guernica" of Harlem's pigeons, the seats were too small, and narrow corridors often led to dead ends; however, the intimacy and history of the Polo Grounds sprouted a distinct fan culture.[35]

Understanding and interpreting the emergence of the New Breed became something of a parlor game. Leonard Koppett theorized that the New Breed shared a spirit with the Kennedy era, "hopeful, forward-looking, sophisticated, humorous, and exciting." Both Kennedy and the Mets appealed to the young. Intellectuals could pass the Mets off "as camp" or embrace them in a gesture of solidarity with the have-nots. And those have-nots might have recognized the sort of structural machinations that conspired against the underclasses, in sport and in life. In joining the league, the Mets were forced to build much of their roster by taking on players from existing National League clubs—typically marginal players or those on overly generous contracts. The system was rigged against the Mets: something many city-dwellers could identify with. Koppett concluded, "For the black, the poor, the henpecked, and the underage, this was strong material for identification."[36] A New York psychologist argued that Mets fans were the types of people who couldn't bear success because of their unconscious fears of displacing their fathers.[37] Another drew the distinction with the Yankees as the Establishment, whose symbol was a top hat and whose name conjured images of "founding fathers and New England aristocracy." Contrasted with this, the Mets' symbol, Mr. Met, a baseball with a face, was a "kind of John Q. Public caricature" and the club's name signified a "polyglot melting pot." Others simply viewed the Mets craze as the "defiance of authority."[38]

Within this broader category of the New Breed, Robert Lipsyte identified a subgenre that he called the "Metophile." The Mets and their Metophiles together, according to a "shabby-eyed old man" Lipsyte found in the Polo Grounds bleachers, were "just folks, like me. They go out every day, they get knocked around, pushed down. They have to get up and come back for more." The Metophile was, according to Lipsyte, "5 feet 8 inches tall, weighs 166 pounds, was 43 years old on his last birthday and has lost considerable hair." A skilled laborer with a family, he lived in a small apartment and owned one good suit. On hot August days at the park, "he is likely to take his shirt off in the bleachers." The Metophile was the man who hoped that "one day he will punch that arrogant foreman at the plant square on his fat nose; that he will get in the last word with his wife; that he will win the Irish Sweepstakes; that the Mets will start a winning streak." Yankee fans, of course, looked down on the Mets as "laughable, disgraceful—an essence of rabble." To the Metophile, these Yankee fans were "that stuffed-shirt at the bank who refused his loan application, the haughty maitre d' who seemed to sneer at everything he ordered: all those men who seem to be winners, to be in complete and supercilious control, who make people feel inferior and less intelligent." Lipsyte pegged these contrasting personalities to their built environments. He asserted, "The Stadium is large, well-groomed, handsome and forbidding. It has the intimacy of a bank. The Polo Grounds is warm, ramshackle and as clubby as a tenement stoop." Policemen who had worked at both stadiums called the Yankee Stadium crowd "quiet, orderly and inoffensive," whereas the "Polo Grounders are loud, often rowdy, more hostile to the authority of a uniform, and are seemingly perched along the edges of hysteria." Lipsyte figured that the "pure Metophile" would be gone from the stadium in a few years, replaced by "more ordinary people" as the Mets progressed from "incompetency to mediocrity," success became more important, and the "psychological pull" of the ragtag underdogs dissipated.[39]

Many found the New Breed mania obnoxious. The Mets new general manager, George Weiss, was one of them. Another was cynical Robert Creamer, who called the Mets fans a "quaint cult," writing, "In New York there is no question but that rooting for the Mets is the right thing to do; it is smart, it is right, it is In. The boys in the advertising dodge, always alert to trends (narrow brims, vodka Martinis, pro football), are Met fans almost to a man and are up on all the latest deprecatory gags. Intellectuals who still confess an ignorance of TV ('I really don't get a chance to watch it') rally around the Mets."[40] Others, too, resented what Creamer called "the carnival." For player Richie Ashburn, "a Goldwater Republican from Nebraska," as described by Vecsey, "the Met mystique sounded like a creeping socialism." Ashburn offered, "I don't think it's a moral victory to get the tying run to second base against the Dodgers. What good is that. Winning is the only thing. They shouldn't settle for losing good."[41]

Ashburn couldn't stomach moral victories, but the New Breed lived on them. In its short time at the Polo Grounds, the Mets fan culture quickly developed its own tics, habits, and symbols recalling the quirks of the Ebbets Field denizens. Whereas Ebbets had Hilda Chester, the rotund, cowbell-wielding icon, the Polo Grounds had the "Mother of the Mets," described by Vecsey as a "big-boned Negro woman who had spent her years working for a wealthy family."[42] Bumbling first baseman Marv Throneberry, or "Marvelous Marv," became an ironic icon for the club, symbolic of the team's broader ineptitude.[43] After games, fans at the Polo Grounds would walk across the field to the clubhouse in center field, stand at the bottom of the stairs, and call for one of the day's heroes (mostly tragic heroes in losses), and the player would have to dress and come back out to the top of the stairs to wave, as Shecter put it, "like Il Duce from a Roman balcony."[44] But certainly the most visible accent of New Breed culture—both visually evident and widely discussed—was the banner.

The homemade banners initially displayed by Mets fans at the Polo Grounds were, in the words of Koppett, "to become the life blood of Metdom." They were first seen in the home series against the Giants and Dodgers in late May 1962. At first park police and ushers tried to stop the use of banners, made of old sheets or towels, handwritten and often misspelled.[45] George Weiss thought them undignified, or as Vecsey put it, "unbecoming in such a holy place as a ball park." They also obstructed other spectators' views. Fans were ejected, but newspapermen treated their plight sympathetically, particularly the influential Dick Young. Bolstered by the press, fans returned with more banners, and Weiss was forced to either take a stand or relax his standards. Met management relented, and fans became more inventive. The banners were sometimes self-deprecating ("We Love Our Mets—Run Sheep Run"), sometimes intellectual ("Eamus Metropoli"), and almost always playful ("METS SI, YANKEES NO").[46] Weiss was slow to realize how effective the banners were in creating a sense of atmosphere and franchise identity, but even he began to catch on with time.[47] By the club's second year, the Mets were hosting an official Banner Day. Even then, Weiss, ever the traditionalist of the Yankee Stadium pedigree, was reported to survey the scene and mutter, "These people . . . these noisy people with their bedsheets. . . . Where do they come from? . . . Why don't they keep quiet?"[48]

The Polo Grounds became a temporary reincarnation of Ebbets Field—ironic given the long history of antagonism between the Dodgers and the stadium's longtime occupants, the Giants—and yet the park was always just a way station as the new municipal stadium was constructed, with ample delay, in Queens. Those thumbing through the club's 1962 *Year Book* at the ballpark were regaled with visions of the new stadium being built in Flushing Meadows, the "most convenient, comfortable and attractive public arena on the eastern seaboard," promised to open in April 1963. The program included a brief note on the Polo Grounds, where the reader likely sat as he or she read, describing it as "the scene of many an historic moment" in baseball, football, and boxing over the previous half century. It was "fitting," the club claimed, that the Mets should "pause here before moving on to the fabulous new Flushing Meadows Stadium, for a great deal of National League history was made in this very park." The volume also acknowledged another of New York's historic stadiums, Ebbets Field, a place renowned for its "moments of greatness and . . . moments of zaniness. It well could be that the latter outbalanced the former but all were equally enjoyable to the Dodger fan." This gesture toward the history of Brooklyn—and attempt to unite the existing (and antagonistic) fan traditions of the Giants and Dodgers (as signified by the Polo Grounds and Ebbets Field)—was characteristic of broader narratives explaining the Mets and the New Breed, through which the Mets fans were psychoanalyzed as successors to an eccentric, heterogeneous, and urban identity to be contrasted not only with the staid, conservative success of the Yankees but also the clean-cut affluence of the new suburban classes.[49]

Beautifully Functional Shea Stadium

Shea Stadium opened in April 1964, and many agreed, it was a "beauty." New York City mayor Robert Wagner called the stadium "one of the most modern and beautiful sports facilities in the world." Commissioner of the Department of Parks Newbold Morris noted the "symmetrical beauty and color of the facade and the interior" and the "beauty, the efficiency and the comfort" of the structure. Stan Isaacs of *Newsday* branded it "beautiful," as did Leonard Shecter of the *New York Post*, who added, "It's the nicest thing you can say about a woman or a ball park." A reporter for the *Long Island Star Journal* called it "beauteous." Leonard Koppett of the *New York Times* termed it "sturdy and beautiful." Jack Mann of the *New York Herald Tribune* called it "a beautifully functional thing." "Shea Stadium is beautiful," the *Washington Post*'s Bob Addie informed his readers, "and, as we sidewalk architects are fond of saying, it is also functional."[50] In the eyes of its beholders, beauty could mean many things—modernity, symmetry, efficiency, comfort, functionality. In other words, the Polo Grounds it was not.

Shea Stadium in truth looked like a fortress, with a soaring one-hundred-forty-foot-tall frame; the squishy soil of the meadow prevented the field from being built below

FIGURE 39. Well-heeled fans enjoy the Shea Stadium opener from the box seats. NEW YORK CITY PARKS PHOTO ARCHIVE.

grade.[51] Robert Moses intended it to resemble the Colosseum in Rome; in case anyone had missed the imperial connection, he remarked on its completion, "When the Emperor Titus opened the Colosseum in 80 A.D. he could have felt no happier."[52] Stacked pedestrian ramps defined the exterior, banks slanting this way and that. Thin wires ran perpendicular to the ground around the outside; upon them were hung ornamental aluminum squares colored blue or orange. The ground level, below the banks, was faced with brick, the wall punched through with both single doorways and garage-door openings that served as entrances and exits for the crowds. A rim rounded the top, the back end of a small roof that would protect the very highest seats from the weather. The stadium innards were committed to pedestrian movement to and from seats, consisting of gradually sloping ramps, steeply climbing escalators, elevators, and concourses at the various seating levels. Concession stands ringed the concourses, occupying the spaces below the seating deck. Once beyond this network of passageways, visitors entered the stadium interior itself— the smooth, sweeping, symmetrical decks of seats, each colored differently in shades of yellow, orange, brown, and green. Spectators could look out through the huge gap in the stadium, opening to the northwest—beyond an enormous scoreboard, over row upon row of parked automobiles, junkyards, more freeways and a tidal bay, the sign atop the old Serval Zippers building, and into downtown Flushing in the distance.[53]

Shea Stadium was flanked on one side by the elevated Interborough Rapid Transit line (IRT) and on the other by freeways. To the south of the elevated train ran the Long Island Railroad, and to the south of that was Flushing Meadows Park, site of the 1964– 65 World's Fair.[54] To the north of the stadium, just across the intersecting freeways, was Flushing Bay and LaGuardia Airport. In the early 1960s, downtown Flushing—just east of the stadium—was home to Jewish, Irish, Italian, and German American communities.[55] The area had acquired a distinctively middle-class image, having become a destination for many relocating from denser parts of Brooklyn, Manhattan, and the Bronx after the war. A subway ride from downtown Flushing to Grand Central Station took about forty-five minutes. Its tree-lined streets, private homes, and new apartment buildings were joined with local shopping and "respectable" schools.[56] Corona, to the west of the stadium, was an African American community of middle- and lower-middle-income residents, made up of two- and four-family dwellings. Its most famous resident was Louis Armstrong, who had moved there in 1943 and whose home was less than a half mile from the stadium site.[57] This neighborhood was largely disconnected from the stadium, however; Shea Stadium turned its back to Corona—opening, instead, toward downtown Flushing—and was physically separated from the neighborhood by a multilane freeway. Indeed, the stadium—and Flushing Meadows Park as a whole—was neatly circumscribed by Moses's roads. It was "a landscape by Moses," historian Robert Caro argues, "bearing his signature as plainly as if he had scrawled it into the concrete in giant letters."[58]

FIGURE 40. Aerial view of Shea Stadium, from the north. The elevated Interborough Rapid Transit Line runs along its south side, separating the stadium from the World's Fair grounds. AP PHOTO/NEW YORK TIMES/LIEBOWITZ.

FIGURE 41. The view from the New York State Pavilion Observation Deck at the 1964 World's Fair. Shea Stadium is visible at the top of the scene. NEW YORK CITY PARKS PHOTO ARCHIVE.

Flushing Meadows had once been a salt meadow, connected via Flushing Creek to Flushing Bay. In 1907, a contractor had begun buying land along the creek, hoping to construct a port there for large cargo ships facing the bay. To provide a foundation for the construction, garbage and ashes were heaped in the meadow—a setting made famous by F. Scott Fitzgerald's reference to the area as the "Valley of the Ashes" in *The Great Gatsby*. Construction plans fells through, and it remained little more than a dump until 1937, when Robert Moses began to prepare the site to host the 1939 World's Fair. The first proposal for a stadium there was made in November 1940, when the Chamber of Commerce of the Rockaways in Queens and chamber president Andrew J. Kenny began to petition the City of New York to build a stadium for sports and entertainment.[59] Another was proposed in 1956, when Moses suggested the city build a stadium there that could be used by the Dodgers. Walter O'Malley was as opposed to this plan as Moses was to the building of a new stadium in downtown Brooklyn. Moses had fancied Flushing Meadows Park as an automobile-age replacement to Central Park—it was, in a phrase often used by Moses and his marketers, "at the very geographical and population center of New York." Moses and his armies had turned the area, "the scene of a notorious ash dump," as he called it, into "one of the very great municipal parks of our country."[60] His new stadium put an exclamation point on Moses's achievement.

Moses had initially laid out plans for a $15 million, 55,000-seat stadium in Flushing Meadows Park in a letter to the Board of Estimate in September 1959. It would be "designed to support a movable roof," to be added after the stadium's initial opening. The new stadium would be used for "public exhibitions and particularly by the proposed third big league baseball association," a reference to the planned Continental League being organized by former Dodgers co-owner Branch Rickey and William Shea to compete with the existing major leagues.[61] A month after Moses's letter, the Board of Estimate appropriated $170,000 for preliminary engineering plans for a Flushing Meadows Park stadium. It anticipated a completion date of April 1, 1961, to be ready for the opening day of the Continental League's inaugural season in 1961.[62] Shea made his dreams of a retractable roof public in November 1959, a feature that would make the stadium useful during inclement weather. The cost of the roof, according to Shea, would be around $1.75 million. An illustration in the *New York Times* presented one possibility. In it the stadium was expressively modern: a smooth-faced oval structure sat precisely in the center of a circular, symmetrical parking lot bordered by trees. A parabolic arch soared 210 feet over the stadium's outfield. A series of evenly spaced cables, which would support a retractable plastic covering, stretched down connecting to the roof below. With the cityscape in the background, it seemed a clean, modern oasis, protected by a green belt of forest, far from the city.[63]

By April, estimates on the cost of a roof had doubled to $3.5 million, but Mayor Wagner assured New Yorkers that a stadium would be built. Shea remained optimistic that the stadium would get a dome—financed by private capital—though the anticipated opening had been pushed back to 1962. It wasn't until March 22, 1961, that the Board of Estimate formally approved contracts and financing on what was by then an $18.3 million project. Controller Lawrence E. Gerosa objected to the plans, arguing that the Parks Department vastly overestimated the incoming revenue that would pay off stadium debt. Even so, the project was pushed forward. The Metropolitan Baseball Club—which had shifted its allegiance from the planned but unrealized Continental League to the established National League in late 1960—signed a thirty-year lease with the city on October 6, 1961.[64] Ground was broken on the new stadium three weeks later.

The groundbreaking was marked by speeches from John T. Clancy, borough president of Queens, Mayor Robert Wagner, and Robert Moses, who was then president of the upcoming World's Fair. Moses bloviated in typical fashion, citing Titus's opening of the Colosseum; invoking Rabelaisian taverns, the Rape of the Sabines, and *The Great Gatsby*; taking contentious sportswriters to task; goring Walter O'Malley; and concluding that because of the stadium's groundbreaking, "my faith in the ultimate triumph of the democratic process has been restored." Shea would be like the "playing fields of Eton" that had, according to the Duke of Wellington, prepared the British to win the Battle of

FIGURE 42. This illustration depicts one possible design for a movable roof for Shea Stadium, to be added after opening. Sections shaped like pie pieces would stack atop each other when retracted, as pictured here. NEW YORK CITY PARKS PHOTO ARCHIVE.

Waterloo; Moses promised, "Many a future American triumph will have its origin in the Flushing Meadows Stadium."[65] A program for the groundbreaking, enhanced with architectural renderings of the stadium and its exterior, advertised the stadium's accessibility via private automobile, subway, or railroad, the rotatable seating banks that could shift the field between baseball and football formats, the column-less views of fans, and the ease of movement inside via ramps, escalators, and elevators. "Every consideration," writers from the Parks Department assured officials, "has been given to the safety, convenience, comfort and pleasure of visitors."[66] Though considered and often trumpeted, a costly roof was not included in the stadium plans; many hoped it would be added to the stadium after its opening.

Most writers seemed to accept the stadium as a necessary replacement for the out-of-date Polo Grounds, while others advocated openly for it and some loudly opposed it. A major proponent was Dick Young of the *New York Daily News*.[67] Other writers critiqued the plans. Joe Williams of the *New York World-Telegram-Sun* looked at the rising costs of the stadium and the lack of transparency from Moses and the city and feared New Yorkers would "wind up with the biggest white elephant this side of the Caspian Sea . . . and traditionally, the big town has always cherished the biggest in all things." He cited councilman Stanley Isaacs, another vocal opponent, who said, "If there were even a remote chance that the stadium would pay off, private capital would have financed it." Williams and others weren't necessarily opposed to any stadium, but they were opposed to the stadium as it was being designed and executed.[68]

Opponents of the project may have watched with some disgust (or cynical satisfaction) as the stadium's opening date was continually pushed back and the cost of the project climbed over twenty-five million dollars. Originally pegged for 1961, the opening of Shea Stadium—named for William Shea, who had played such a central role in securing a major league club for the city—was rescheduled for 1962, then 1963, and finally April 1964. But for many, it was well worth the wait. New Yorkers could finally lay the old Polo Grounds to rest—a stadium built before World War I, for the streetcar city. Shea, on the other hand, was designed for an era of automobiles and suburbs.

From Tenement Slums to Suburban Split-Levels

As it became clear that the Polo Grounds was in its final year, Roger Angell reimagined the old ballpark for readers of the *New Yorker*:

> The dirt, the noise, the chatter, the bursting life of the Met grandstands are as rich
> and deplorable and heartwarming as Rivington Street. The Polo Grounds, which
> is in the last few months of its disreputable life, is a vast assemblage of front stoops

and fire escapes. On a hot summer evening, everyone here is touching someone else; there are no strangers, no one is private. The air is alive with shouts, gossip, flying rubbish. Old-timers know and love every corner of the crazy, crowded, proud old neighborhood: the last-row walkup flats in the outermost lower grandstands . . . the outfield bullpens, each with its slanting shanty roof . . . the good box seats just on the curve of the upper deck in short right and short left—front windows on the street, where one can watch the arching fall of a weak fly ball and know in advance, like one who sees a street accident in the making, that it will collide with that ridiculous, dangerous upper tier for another home run.[69]

It was a scene that might have warmed the heart of activist and author Jane Jacobs, whose book *The Death and Life of Great American Cities* had been published two years previously. Jacobs channeled the sentiments of a growing movement of activist urbanites protecting an older vision of the city—a city of row houses, walk-up apartments, and neighborhoods, where visual and functional diversity was prized, not bulldozed.[70] Housing activist and Columbia professor of planning Charles Abrams anticipated a new era in urban planning—and the unraveling of Robert Moses's regime—at a panel discussion at the New School organized by urban activists in June 1958. In a call to arms against Moses's plans to ram Fifth Avenue through Washington Square Park, Abrams celebrated "the rumblings of a new social revolution in America . . . a reaction against . . . conformity and for the preservation of diversity. It is . . . the first rediscovery of what is good in our cities and the first concerted stand against the heedless destruction that has been the theme of the slide-rule era." Prefiguring Jacobs, Abrams claimed, "A city and a nation are as strong or as weak as the neighborhood units which compose it." Angell's interpretation of the Polo Grounds—a stadium that many New York newspapermen would refer to as a "slum" and "tenement" in its dying days—clearly owed much to the well-publicized urban portraiture of activists like Jacobs and Abrams.[71]

That Angell chose Rivington Street as the setting for his Polo Grounds scene—and not Jacobs's traditional stomping grounds in the West Village—was telling. Rivington ran across Manhattan's Lower East Side—arguably the city's most convenient geographical symbol of dense, diverse, immigrant-fueled urbanity, the home of the "huddled masses yearning to breathe free." It was, in succession, a seat of German, Irish, Jewish, Italian, African American, Puerto Rican, and Chinese settlement in the city. Kleindeutschland, Little Italy, Chinatown, Loisida: they were all on New York's Lower East Side. It was where Jacob Riis examined "how the other half lives." It had been the first neighborhood in the city to be racially integrated after World War II.[72] Dirty and loud. Deplorable and heartwarming. Crazy, crowded, and utterly public. Angell's analogue for the Polo Grounds exemplified New York's urban life and history over the previous century.

The Lower East Side was another of many battlegrounds for Moses—and one that suggested his waning power. "Bob the Builder" had long dreamed of sending three elevated expressways across Manhattan. His Lower Manhattan Expressway (LME) would have perched thirty to forty feet above Broome Street, two blocks south of Rivington, connecting the Holland Tunnel in the west and the Williamsburg and Manhattan bridges in the east. Drivers would have enjoyed a straight shot across Manhattan, but the LME would have split neighborhoods apart and required the eviction of nearly two thousand households and over eight hundred businesses. Buoyed by the successful protest campaigns at Washington Square Park in 1958, local property owners, tenants, and civic and religious leaders petitioned, lobbied, and wrote letters. Assemblyman Louis DeSalvio, with six hundred of his constituents from Little Italy at his back, told the Board of Estimate in December 1962, just months before Angell's article, "Except for one old man, I have been unable to find anyone of technical competence who is for this so-called expressway, and this old man is a cantankerous, stubborn old man . . . [and] the time has come for the stubborn old man to realize that too many of his technicians' dreams turn out to be nightmares for the city."[73]

If the LME was one of Robert Moses's final defeats, Shea Stadium was one of Moses's final victories. He had stonewalled O'Malley's attempts to build a new stadium in downtown Brooklyn. He pushed for the destruction of the Polo Grounds to make way for new public housing towers—which, at the time of Angell's writing, was inevitable. And he saw a new stadium built at Flushing Meadows—long a dream of his, located at a new geographical center of the metropolis's sprawling population. Moses was increasingly stymied in places like Greenwich Village and the Lower East Side, but Shea Stadium was a late triumph for Moses, in which he took a traditionally urban form and rebuilt it to the tune of the automobile and in the spirit of the suburbs.

Moses, Angell, and others knew that replacing the Polo Grounds with Shea meant more than just swapping playing fields and spectators' seats. It marked profound changes in the American city and public life. Many writers expressed the move from old stadium to new in terms such as Angell's, using residential metonyms to make sense of it. And in doing so, they framed and channeled public interpretations of the new stadium, squaring the moves of the Mets and Titans with postwar aspirations for the suburban "good life."[74] Milton Gross of the *New York Post* confessed some affection for the old stadium, and yet he wrote of "the slum of the Polo Grounds," "the tenement atmosphere of the Polo Grounds," and "the slum on the Harlem." He also called it a "shanty" and a "junk heap." Conversely, Shea Stadium was a "palace" and "the Versailles on the Meadow."[75] *Newsday*'s Stan Isaacs claimed he would miss the Polo Grounds, where he had as much fun as he had ever had watching baseball, although it was, in his words, "outmoded, outsized, dilapidated, dirty, [and] old." He likened the new Shea to a "split-level palace," gesturing toward the popular suburban split-level ranch houses of the time.[76] Writing in the *Saturday Evening Post*, Jimmy Breslin called Ebbets Field, the Polo Grounds' Brooklyn cousin, "a broken-down place that seemed like a small apartment with the in-laws staying over." On the other hand, Shea Stadium "climbs out of a parking lot . . . in Flushing Meadow, which always was considered the start of the suburbs. It climbs five levels high and is spread out like a big split-level."[77]

Angell and Robert Lipsyte of the *New York Times* plumbed this urban-suburban figure more deeply than others. Lipsyte introduced the housing metaphor in April 1963, a full year before Shea opened (and thus a year before anyone started actually using the facility). He claimed the Polo Grounds to be "warm, ramshackle and as clubby as a tenement stoop."[78] Two months later, he wrote again of "the rickety, six-to-a-bedroom, tenement-stoop clubbiness" of the Polo Grounds. It was a place where, Lipsyte argued, "a man can relax, strip down to his mental undershirt and let his stomach sag. . . . After all, man, you've got family around." He glumly anticipated the move of the Mets into Shea Stadium, with its modern comforts and conveniences, worrying, "It will be different in Queens, that smug borough of bourgeois achievement with its nouveau riche stadium."[79]

In a full-throated rant published just days after Shea's opening in April 1964, Lipsyte continued to sound the warning he had prefigured the year before: that the move to Shea Stadium would fundamentally alter the nature (and meaning) of the Mets, in fact ending what he called "the Era of the Mets." Shea would be an oasis for suburban values, with the New Breed giving way to the "antiseptic suburban Met fans." Lipsyte claimed that Shea Stadium was built in Queens "because it's the gateway to the suburbs, to all the neatness and conformity and togetherness and bourgeois values." He predicted that the team on the field would improve, "as befitting their clean, modern, character-less new home." The crowds would grow and Shea would be "THE PLACE" to be. The Polo Grounds–era Met fans, Lipsyte wrote, would have to "crawl back into the rooming houses and doorways and lofts and tenements [sic] whence they came." Those fans, the men who liked to take off their shirts and "loose the aggressions and invective," would have no other option than to go to the Bronx and, according to Lipsyte, "join 2,000 other members of the Old New Breed at old, clubby, friendly, urban Yankee Stadium."[80] This is, of course, the same Yankee Stadium that Lipsyte had claimed, just one year earlier, had all the intimacy of a bank: to call Yankee Stadium "clubby" in relation to Shea Stadium was, coming from Lipsyte, an insult of considerable order.

Angell, like Lipsyte, anticipated that the move from the Polo Grounds would initiate broad changes in the consumption and meaning of the Mets. In his May 1963 essay for the *New Yorker*, he speculated,

Next year, or perhaps late this summer, all this will vanish. The Mets are moving up in the world, heading towards the suburbs. Their new home, Shea Stadium, in

Flushing Meadow Park, will be cleaner and airier—a better place for the children. Most of the people there will travel by car rather than by subway; the commute will be long, but the residents will be more respectable. There will be broad ramps, no crowding, more privacy. All the accommodations will be desirable—close to the shopping centers, and set in perfect, identical curves, with equally good views of the neat lawns. Indeed, a man who leaves his place will have to make an effort to remember exactly where it is, so he won't get mixed up on his way back and forget where he lives. It will be several years, probably, before the members of the family, older and heavier and at last sure of their place in the world, indulge themselves in some moments of foolish reminiscence: "Funny, I was thinking of the old place today. Remember how jammed we used to be back there? Remember how hot and noisy it was? I wouldn't move back there for anything, and anyway it's all torn down now, but, you know, we sure were happy in those days."[81]

Angell's laundry list of suburban characteristics—cleanliness, airiness, consumerism, privacy, spaciousness, symmetry, and respectability—is not so different from Lipsyte's. Less bitter than Lipsyte, Angell seems to accept the move to Shea as a necessary accommodation to the times. And as much as he values the Polo Grounds and the memories forged there over many years, he acknowledges that no place is timeless, even tentatively allowing that the Mets' suburban move, like that of other New Yorkers, might be best given the circumstances.

Angell revisited the Polo Grounds a year later, as the Mets moved into Shea Stadium. He listed the small things he would miss about the old park: the flights of pigeons; the "plock" of a line drive against the wooden wall in deep left field; the rusty chains, warmed by the sun, that cradled one's arm in the boxed seats. On the brink of departure, Angell seemed less comfortable with the physical destruction of urban landscapes than he had been the year before. Now, the death of the Polo Grounds "constitutes the death of still another neighborhood—a small landscape of distinctive and reassuring familiarity." "Demolition and alteration is a painful city commonplace," he acknowledges, "but as our surroundings become more undistinguished and indistinguishable, we sense, at last, that we may not possess the scorecards and record books to help us remember who we are and what we have seen and loved."[82]

Angell's departing words anticipated the most common complaint of the modernist stadium—"undistinguished and indistinguishable"—an image that would become increasingly fixed in the coming years and decades (cohering particularly in the early 1970s). In 1964, Shea Stadium was not just another example of an engineered behemoth in a parking lot on the highway—it was one of the first of this type. Yet the ethos of the modern stadium—as identified by Lipsyte and Angell—was that of a clean-sweep modernist planning, which would substitute the big for the small, the new for the old. For both Angell and Lipsyte, this move from the Polo Grounds to Shea more than just aped the move that many had made from Brooklyn or Manhattan to Long Island, from tenement apartments and dense neighborhoods to modern suburban installations. For Lipsyte it was the marginalization of an urban, largely masculine subculture of the rambunctious and shirtless that existed prior to and in opposition of the "antiseptic" world of suburbia. For Angell, it revealed the rush to move forward without fully considering the consequences of severance from landscapes that shaped who people are in the first place.

As readers moved from page to place, to experience the stadium firsthand, they found a stadium that was genetically cousin to postwar suburbia.

The Suburban Virtues of Shea Stadium

In the imaginations of New York's sportswriters, the move from the Polo Grounds to Shea was akin to relocating from a run-down tenement to a new suburban split-level. Upon visiting Shea, many New Yorkers must been struck—consciously or not—by just how suburban the stadium seemed.[83] Spatially and materially, Shea Stadium embodied many of the celebrated qualities of postwar suburbia. Built to accommodate the automobile as much as the human being, celebrated as a symbol of American affluence, and bursting with color and gadgetry, the postwar stadium broadcast suburban aspirations at monumental scale.

Ease of movement—or at least the illusion of it—was a core virtue of Shea and suburbia. Problems of transportation and parking were proposed as the core reason the city's National League clubs had departed for California. The 1964 stadium dedication magazine explained that the Giants and Dodgers had left "because they considered the Polo Grounds and Ebbets Field inadequate and obsolete. The ball parks were not centrally located, had almost no parking space and poor public transportation facilities . . . New York needed a modern sports stadium."[84] Transportational convenience, the magazine suggested, was a measure of modernity. According to a 1964 ticket application brochure, the "pioneer" Mets fans who had "endured through two seasons" at the Polo Grounds would "be joined by new ones who formerly did not choose to grapple with the middle-of-the-city traffic and the ensuing, often-fruitless search for parking space." Problems of traffic and parking would be "erased by subway, railway and multi-million dollar highway arteries which converge from all directions on the heart of the stadium and its vast surrounding parking acreage," resulting in the "dawn of a new era . . . for the team and its fans."[85]

As the new era dawned, publications and press releases from the Mets and the Department of Parks emphasized that the stadium was at the "geographic and population center of New York City."[86] They boasted that the stadium was reachable by car, subway, train, bus, taxi, and boat. This combination would make it "the most convenient-to-reach stadium in history." Local and national press echoed these talking points. *Popular Science* magazine informed readers that Shea would be "one of the most convenient sports arenas in the world" and that "acres of parking and direct ramps from train stations make getting into the stadium easy." Vincent Butler of the *Chicago Tribune* wrote of Shea's geographical centeredness and echoed the architects' claims that the stadium would be "the most convenient" in the country. Bob Addie of the *Washington Post* located Shea at the center of a whir of transportational activity: "La Guardia Airport is nearby and planes and helicopters are forever circling the stadium. . . . There is an elevated track next to the ball park and a maze of new freeways. . . . The effect sometimes is startling with planes, trains and cars buzzing, chugging and whizzing by."[87] Though the IRT reported that 34,000 visitors took the elevated train to the game on opening day in 1964, the most obvious form of transportation to the game was private automobile; after all, Shea sat in more than forty-five acres of parking, connected to a new $110 million expressway program.[88] This was the stadium's primary reason for being, one of the main reasons that Robert Moses blocked Walter O'Malley's overtures to build in downtown Brooklyn. As sportswriter Leonard Koppett put it, "The right way to go to Shea Stadium would be by car."[89]

An illustration used in club publications helped readers visualize precisely how heavenly the arrival by automobile would be, painting an idyllic scene at one of the entrances northeast of the stadium. A row of nine small ticket booths awaited arrivals. For a game-day crowd, the traffic was improbably sparse: cars approached the booths unimpeded.

FIGURE 43. An idyllic rendering of the approach from the stadium's northeast entrance suggests an automobile pastoral. NEW YORK CITY PARKS PHOTO ARCHIVE.

Though many fans had already arrived, plenty of parking spaces remained. Trees accented a tranquil scene—a far cry from the condensed streets and packed lot of the Polo Grounds. Unlike Harlem, there were no other buildings in sight here. Instead there were cars, but without competition—a harmonious automobile utopia.[90]

Maps abounded in club and city publications and city newspapers as the stadium was planned, constructed, and opened. The stadium became the focus of the city, linked to its population through a swarm of expressways and parkways, as well as train lines running out from Manhattan and in from Long Island. A newspaper map headline promised readers, "All Roads Lead to Shea Stadium."[91] Traffic plan maps, marked with directional arrows, steered would-be drivers into the parking lot's three entrances as cars arrived from the network of roads and highways that coursed past the stadium site. Accompanying articles informed readers that games would be monitored by Traffic Commissioner Henry A. Barnes from a helicopter; from there he would use a two-way radio to direct "engineers" on the ground.[92] And yet, in spite of all the promises that Flushing's Shea Stadium, with its engineered traffic patterns and accessible new freeways, would be a modern corrective to Harlem's Polo Grounds, one of the dominant stories of the stadium's opening was the horrific traffic jams. The *New York Times* cover-page aerial photo of the stadium's pregnant parking lots was topped with the headline "Shea Stadium Opens with Big Traffic Jam" and included the subhead "Motorists and Mets Are the Losers."[93]

The preoccupation with movement didn't end at the stadium parking lot. The 1964 *Dedication* magazine boasted, "You are now sitting in a sports stadium which has been designed specifically for your comfort and pleasure. William A. Shea is unique in the rapidity with which spectators may reach their seats, regardless of the level on which they are located. No other sports arena approaches Shea Stadium in vertical circulation. By means of ramps, elevators and escalators you can go from one level to another in a matter of seconds."[94] This celebrated mobility was structurally achieved through twenty-four pedestrian ramps (which the Department of Parks called "wide, gently sloped ramps"), twenty-one escalators, and two elevators.[95]

The ramps themselves were arguably the most visually conspicuous feature of the stadium. Six banks of sloping ramps, layered six high, encircled the exterior of the structure. Shea Stadium wore its sense of movement on its sleeve as the ramps animated the outside, calling attention to the easy, airy slopes and demanding comparison to the dark and narrow concourses and banks of steps in old parks. They seemed cousins of the expressway ramps—miniature, engineered, concrete freeways for people. But while the ramps were visually privileged, writers were certainly more excited about the escalators.

There were plans for escalators from the start; designer Richard Praeger (son of engineer Emil) didn't want people having to climb flights of stairs to get to their seats.[96] There would have been plenty of climbing without the escalators, as the stadium peaked out at one hundred forty feet tall. Otis Elevator designed the escalator system—twenty-one in all—that serviced different stadium levels. Each four-foot-wide escalator was color-coded to match the specific tier of seating it served and could carry eight thousand people per hour. At the end of each game, the direction was reversed so fans could leave. The *New York Times* branded it "the largest escalator installation in any stadium in the world . . . a system of 21 local and express color-coded stairways to the stars."[97] Print coverage of Shea, both local and national, rarely failed to mention the escalators.[98] The Mets 1963 *Year Book* boasted that the escalators meant there would be "no more Alpine climb, no jamming before or after ball games."[99] A reporter argued that it would "take the toil out of grandstand climbing if not out of grandstand living."[100] At the dedication ceremony, Mets manager Casey Stengel assured the team's supporters: "You can have your health for many years by following my Mets. Just see the escalators and elevators they put in for the old folks."[101] Robert Lipsyte winked, "Its 21 escalators will make leg muscles obsolete."[102]

Just as suburban spatiality promised transportational ease and autonomy, so too did it provide more room to maneuver in. After riding effortlessly up the banks of escalators and making the short walk to their seating sections, visitors found seats that were "contoured" and "extra-wide," according to the Parks Department.[103] The Mets proclaimed, "Never before had a baseball fan been offered the conveniences such as those offered by Shea Stadium. You may reach your seat by escalator or elevator. In your seat you will find more room than in any seat at any sporting event you ever attended."[104] Stadium visitors enjoyed seats, rows, and aisles that were broader than they had been accustomed to at the old parks. But not only did they enjoy more personal space, the stadium itself seemed much more spacious and open than its predecessors—both materially and psychologically.

Unlike those at Ebbets Field, the Polo Grounds, and Yankee Stadium, the upper decks of Shea Stadium weren't supported by view-obstructing pillars; they were instead cantilevered, ensuring that no visitors would have to crane their necks around posts to see the action on the field—a major concern for stadium designers and sports executives accustomed to the stacked-deck stadiums of the previous generation. Club publications and reporters alike celebrated this feature.

The upper decks of the old prewar stadiums crouched over their lower levels, drawing inhabitants closer to the field and vertically enclosing the space more tightly. But in a cantilevered stadium like Shea, the upper decks were pushed away from the playing field, relieving the intimacy—or claustrophobia—that old stacked-deck stadiums encouraged. As he designed the stadium, Richard Praeger promised "a clean and airy stadium" with an "open feeling."[105] The project's resident engineer, Robert Schoenfeld, claimed, "This should be a lovely structure. It will stand about 130 feet high. It will cover about eight city blocks. It will be airy. It will breathe."[106] The openness of the modern stadium was not only structural but psychological as well, contrasting considerably with the compact intimacy of the old grounds—a spatial and ideological analogue to the plazas that fronted modern corporate office towers, the Corbusian green spaces between new public housing slabs, and particularly the private lawns and yards distinguishing postwar suburban ranch and split-level houses. Open floor plans and picture windows gave homes a sense of spaciousness—certainly in comparison to old city apartments. Patios outside sliding glass doors seemed to extend living space beyond a home's walls.[107] Just as city-dwellers evacuated dense residential spaces for the openness of suburban developments, the sports fan moved from physically and visually constricted stadiums to modern and expansive ones.

Many noted explicitly how enhanced cantilevering impacted the experience of watching games—and almost always compared it to the fan experience at the Polo Grounds and Ebbets Field. While acknowledging the advantages of extra legroom and unobstructed views, Isaacs also noted that "the upper-deck spectator is far away from the field. There isn't that closeness to the action that made the Polo Grounds—and Ebbets Field particularly—intimate areas."[108] Vecsey claimed, "The $1.50 seats in the top of the upper deck might as well have been in Connecticut or New Jersey because nobody up there would ever see the twinkle in Casey's eye. In the Polo Grounds, the overhanging grandstands would often encourage connections between players and fans. The roundness of Shea Stadium discouraged that intimacy."[109] Angell, too, wrote of the loss of "intimacy" at the new stadium as compared to the old grounds. The banked seats, he wrote, "sweep around in a lovely circle, offering everyone a splendid and unobstructed view of the action. Unobstructed and, I should add, too distant. . . . This imposed geometry keeps the elevated fan forever distant from the doings within the contained square of the infield." Angell blamed this arrangement on the need for the stadium to double as a home equally adaptable to football—not a baseball-first orientation, as was the case in the old parks where football teams played second fiddle. Though impressed by the engineering that would automatically pivot seating sections to accommodate the layouts of both sports, Angell lamented the need regardless, claiming,

> It has been achieved at the expense of the baseball fan, for the best ballparks— Ebbets Field, say, or Comiskey Park—have all been boxes. Many of the games I saw this spring [1964] were thickly attended, but again and again I had the impression that I had lost company with the audience. In the broad, sky-filled circle of the new stadium, the shouts, the clapping, the trumpet blasts, and the brave old cries of "Let's go, Mets!" climbed thinly into the air and vanished; the place seemed without echoes, angles, and reassurance. No longer snug in a shoebox, my companions and I were ants perched on the sloping lip of a vast, shiny soup plate, and we were lonelier than we liked.[110]

FIGURE 44. A stadium illustration highlights the sense of spaciousness designers hoped to achieve—an openness that contrasted profoundly with the tight intimacy of the Polo Grounds. IRMA AND PAUL MILSTEIN DIVISION OF UNITED STATES HISTORY, LOCAL HISTORY AND GENEALOGY, THE NEW YORK PUBLIC LIBRARY. "FLUSHING MEADOW PARK," NEW YORK PUBLIC LIBRARY DIGITAL COLLECTIONS.

Like Isaacs, Vecsey, and many other sensitive witnesses, Angell was particularly aware of the fundamental changes in the game wrought by its new environment.

The attention paid to personal mobility and spaciousness had a profound effect on postwar stadium design and reflected postwar tensions between individual autonomy and the realities of living and moving among others in urban landscapes.[111] Catering to private transportation required moving stadiums from dense urban areas to more open spaces, readily accessible to freeways. The movement of the individual from home to parking lot, and then from parking lot to spacious seat, was a central concern for stadium designers, to the point that consciously or not, the revealed pedestrian ramp, an expression of easy mobility, became a visual cliché of the modern stadium—first with D.C. Stadium in Washington, then in Shea, and in many other stadiums that would follow. The fascination with personal movement and space, however, was not the only way that the stadium overlapped with a postwar suburban ethos. The socioeconomic segregation of the suburbs was echoed in the exclusionary spatial character of Shea Stadium.

In his 1959 polemic, *The Status Seekers*, Vance Packard said of his fellow Americans, "Whatever else we are, we certainly are the world's most self-proclaimed equalitarian people." Those proclamations, Packard asserted, papered over social stratification that was becoming more pronounced and permanent. He wrote, "All in all, we are in the process of becoming a many-layered society. Status is crystallizing. The boundaries between the various layers are becoming more rigid." Indeed, Packard wrote at a time when suburbs were becoming increasingly more hierarchical socioeconomically.[112] Historian Lizabeth Cohen argues that this stratification was driven in large part by the postwar belief that the home was a consumer product—a commodity that could be traded in for an upgrade as one ascended the various economic rungs of suburban communities. Homogeneity became a privileged quality in a neighborhood—it made the market values of homes and attached status predictable, thus protecting residents' investments and image. Philadelphia-area developer Ralph Bodek and University of Pennsylvania marketing professor William T. Kelley argued in a 1955 study, "It is interesting to note that people prefer to live near others as much like themselves as possible—they do not seem interested in the possibility of new stimulating associations with people different than themselves."[113] Homogeneity was predictable; it was also conflict free. Peaceful consensus was a virtue in and of itself in the suburbs of the 1950s.[114]

Postwar America was the site of these two ideas at tension: equality and distinction. Many celebrated a classless society of democratic abundance and consumption, against the realities of socioeconomic segmentation and stratification. Shea Stadium embodied both. Class difference was denied, or elided, through the stadium's conspicuous absence of bleacher seats and inscribed, less visibly, through the stadium clubs and restaurants.

A major difference between Shea Stadium and the old grounds was the absence of bleachers—the simple benched seating typically encircling ballpark outfields. An often-made claim of Shea Stadium promoters was that 96 percent of the seats were between the foul lines, thus eliminating the traditional site of the bleachers in the outfield.[115] Bleacher seats were typically the cheapest tickets in the stadium—seventy-five cents at the Polo Grounds—and thus historically the home of the working class and the young. For many writers, these were the places occupied by the purists. George Vecsey called them "the traditional 75-cent haven for the tired, the hungry, the poor," noting that in 1964, "even Yankee Stadium still had its 75-cent bleachers where fans could drink a beer and take a nap in the sun."[116]

From one angle, the elimination of bleacher seats seems to express materially the common canard that the United States had become a classless society in the lap of postwar prosperity. By this logic, every Mets fan deserved a comfortable, spacious, contoured seat and no one should sit on the primitive bleacher bench.[117] And yet the absence of bleacher seats materially crowded out the working class and thus many of the city's more eccentric fanatics who had once populated Ebbets Field and then the Polo Grounds as early Mets supporters. This was how many baseball watchers interpreted the change. Stan Isaacs of *Newsday* lamented the omission, writing of the bleachers: "It's baseball's open-air forum. The bleachers stand for cheap seats and the masses." He understood the move away from bleachers as a symbol of baseball's reorientation toward the more affluent, writing, "Maybe that's one of the things wrong with baseball, the so-called national pastime. Owners are too interested in the carriage trade and the television revenue. They put down the fan who would like to be able to come to a game on the spur of the moment and still have a chance to get within breathing distance of the field." He pointed out the irony of the blue-blood Yankees still offering 75-cent bleacher seats: "Puerto Rican fans flock to the Yankee Stadium bleachers, so there must be some people left who like to get the cheap seats. The Yankees are supposedly the rich man's team, yet they have bleachers. The Mets are the underdogs' team and they don't have bleachers."[118]

Roger Angell also noted the impact of the new stadium on seating for the traditional bleacher-seat patrons. He pointed to the "acres of box seats" throughout the field level, loge circle, and at the front of the mezzanine and upper stands, which he reckoned were "probably a valid tribute to our affluent times," though he wished "that unmoneyed fans, who usually make up a team's true loyalists, didn't have to climb to the top ten rows of the upper level to find an unreserved seat."[119] The box seats at Shea cost the same as those at the Polo Grounds: $3.50; however, there were over 21,000 box seats at the new stadium, compared to just 3,814 at the old park. General admission seats remained $1.30, but whereas there were over 34,000 general admission seats at the Polo Grounds (including the bleachers), there was a mere fraction of them at Shea, whose highest deck combined 4,020 upper box seats with 16,356 reserved and general admission seats.[120] Bleacher seats were, of course, nonexistent. Changes in the distribution and segmentation of seats thus allowed sports businesses to reshape the makeup of stadium populations without directly raising ticket prices—important when publics, not the teams themselves, were increasingly footing the bills for stadium construction and maintenance.

Even as the poorest customers were squeezed out—while the general stadium population became more affluent—new exclusive spaces were being built into new stadiums. The private club was, in the postwar years, an increasingly popular way for the privileged to reassert class difference in the face of democratic consumption. Vance Packard remarked, "With the rise of national opulence permitting plumbers to drive limousines and foot doctors to buy mansions, the private club has looked more and more attractive to status-minded people as a place to draw lines. In the private club, you can sit, as in a fortress, in judgment of pretender-applicants."[121] The Yankees had built what sportswriter Arthur Daley called "an exclusive Stadium Club" in 1945—"two swank taverns under the stands where thirsty holders of season tickets can quaff a stray beaker safe from the vulgar gaze of the hoi-polloi."[122] Candlestick Park and Dodgers Stadium both had private clubs. Even the poor old Polo Grounds had one—a cocktail lounge installed by the Mets in 1962. Shea Stadium featured two such private subscription clubs, the Combo Room and the suggestively named Diamond Club.

Fans who purchased the "Combination" ticket plan—a set of forty-four games in the box or reserved sections at regular game prices—could also apply to be a member of the Combo Room at the cost of ten dollars per seat per year. The Combo Room Escalator took visitors directly to a restaurant and bar where subscribers could "enjoy a quick snack or hot meal depending upon their mood," as a membership application stated. The club sat 244 diners in a room paneled with synthetic wood walls and decorated with murals of players. Illustrations in a ticket brochure depicted men and women in casual clothing, suggesting the ideal crowd would be informal, middle class, and even domestic—the suburban ranch-house resident, perhaps. Though the Combo Room offered some respite from the masses, it wasn't exactly Packard's "fortress" for the status minded; they drank their scotch and ate their meat in the more exclusive Diamond Club.

"For magnificence and elegance in dining," a Mets ticket brochure boasted, "the Diamond Club is on par with any restaurant in the country." Those buying season box tickets for all eighty-one home games could apply for the Diamond Club at the cost of twenty dollars per seat per season. "Spacious modern elevators" took subscribers directly to the club, which consisted of a lobby and gift shop, the Diamond Club Restaurant, the Diamond Club Bar, and the Charcoal Room. The wood-paneled restaurant could seat 372; its members dined atop white tablecloths, their shoes buried in plush carpeting. The Diamond Club Bar, a cocktail lounge, was "a thing of beauty—spacious, and luxuriously appointed, with the accent on ease and comfort." The Charcoal Room featured wood floors, brick walls, exposed timber frames, and a grill pit—a more rugged, masculine setting for the sporting playboy. "Meat always seems tastier and juicier when cooked over an open fire," the brochure promised. Sketches of the Diamond Club rooms, nine in all, largely portrayed a be-suited clientele, giving the potential applicant the impression this was a club geared toward the business class.[123]

Some commentators thought the Diamond Club was a fitting symbol of changing stadium standards. Milton Gross of the *New York Post* used the Diamond Club to mark differences between the Polo Grounds and Shea Stadium. He compared the "tenement atmosphere" of the Polo Grounds and its fans, with their homemade banners drawn on bedsheets, to the "monument to modernism" of Shea, exemplified through its "diamond clubs, Mrs. Payson's posh executive lounge and season ticket plans for the corporations that can write off the cost as a tax deduction." He termed the contrast "obscene." Concerning the move of the Polo Grounds crowd to Shea, he figured, "A bunch of kids with crayons and cardboard will be as much at home as finger painters in the Louvre. Gradually their artistic sense must be beaten out of them by the architecture, conformism and the Brooks Brothers types who will take their places and push them back to the uppermost rows of pure fandom."[124]

The Diamond Club also expressed, to many, how the rich and powerful protected and extended their privilege. Vecsey wrote, "In a classic example of letting its patrons eat cake, Shea Stadium did have the plush Diamond Club for its season ticket holders, a restaurant in the upper right-field section where fans could eat, drink, and watch the game through the cigar haze, win or lose."[125] Jimmy Breslin facetiously referred to the clubs as "the saloons inside the ball park," adding, "Mrs. Payson does not like her friends drinking in dingy places."[126] The *New York Herald Tribune*'s Jack Mann reported that Moses kept his speech short at the stadium dedication, saying, "This is no time for oratory. Let's get to lunch." Mann quipped, "And they did, in the 'Diamond Club' that was readier than any part of the plant." Mann's insinuation, that those at the top of the social order made sure they were taken care of first, was evidenced in the fact that the private club was ready before the field itself.[127]

Shea Stadium's location and spatiality catered to suburban ideals of mobility and spaciousness. Its spatial segregation was fraught with postwar anxieties about both classlessness and distinction. And in some ways Shea Stadium primitively aped the suburban home itself. The use of color to brighten the space and the celebration of gadgetry within reflected those same characteristics in the stocked Cape Cods, split-levels, and ranch-style houses of Long Island—expressions of the postwar good life and triumph of American capitalism and consumerist democracy. As significantly, the stadium was both openly and subtly advertised as a place for women; its promoters embraced a new domestic orientation in line with postwar gender ideals that distinguished Shea from the old, rough-and-tumble Polo Grounds.

In spite of its plain, engineered concrete frame, Shea Stadium was outfitted with colorful decoration. Orange and blue aluminum panels of various sizes were suspended from vertical cables at the edges of the banks of ramps. These aluminum squares gave the exterior a sense of whimsy, partially concealing the severe geometry of the ramps. Some praised the panels, likening them to the ceiling of Lincoln Center or an abstract painting.[128] Others were less complimentary; one thought the aluminum panels looked like "Navajo blankets displayed for Albuquerque tourists."[129] Mets employee Bob Mandt recalled that stadium workers called the plates "the laundry" because "they just hung up there like the laundry and rattled when the wind blew."[130]

The blue and orange panels of the stadium's perimeter were outdone by a riot of color inside. The most obvious characteristic of the interior was the range of seating colors, each horizontal section a different color and shade. The lowest seats were bright yellow. The loge seats, behind them, were dark orange in the boxes, mustard colored in the sections behind the boxes. The mezzanine was royal blue at the front, sky blue in the rear. The up-per deck was dark green in front, pea green in the back.[131] The intense coloration of the stadium prompted sportswriter Dick Young to call it a "pastel beauty."[132] Roger Angell was less enthusiastic and noted that others might share his reserve: "The bright colors of the different stands are cheerful, I guess, but women in the field boxes are not going to be pleased with their complexions during night games, when the floodlights bouncing off those yellow seats make the section look like a hepatitis ward."[133]

The colors of the stadium echoed the range of colors, the abundance of choices, con-sumers enjoyed in postwar product lines. Pastel colors, curving contours, and techno-logical referents were characteristics of a postwar decorative style historian Thomas Hine termed "populuxe." Populuxe items, as the name implies, combined the image of luxury and the accessibility of the popular. They expressed postwar abundance and the widely held belief that consumption choices reflected participation in the good life. The futuris-tic affectations of populuxe items—tail fins indicating speed, handles suggesting mobility, push-buttons signifying automation—implied that the fruits of modernity were available to all. Shea Stadium was in many ways a populuxe stadium, striking for its extravagant color scheme and the display value of "technology" within.[134]

The lowest level of seats, Angell's "hepatitis ward," was noteworthy for its role in mak-ing the stadium "convertible"—a characteristic rhetorically celebrated and analogous to the push-button automation of populuxe styling. These two banks of five-thousand-seat stands sat atop tracks that allowed them to pivot—powered by four electrical motors—in order to accommodate both baseball and football. For baseball, the seats were drawn together at one end to form a V, hugging the diamond, so that fans were angled toward second base; for football, the seats were shifted so that they faced one another, framing the rectangular field and aligning fans toward the 50-yard line. Shea Stadium was the second stadium to feature moving banks of seats like this; the first was D.C. Stadium in Washing-ton, in which the movable section was also designed by Praeger-Kavanaugh-Waterbury.[135] Shea was the first to use motors to automate the process, as stadium propaganda would enthusiastically point out.[136]

The massive Stadiarama Scoreboard injected more color and whiz-bang technology into the setting. It filled in part of the gaping space between stands, curving around the baseball outfield. The scoreboard was 175 feet long, rose 86 feet above the ground, and weighed over 60 tons. It was backed by a huge, white "cycloramic shell," which displayed color light shows choreographed to music. An eighteen-by-twenty-four-foot rear projec-tion screen, the Photorama, sat atop the scoreboard and displayed player photos and color motion pictures. Put in terms a suburban audience could grasp, the program informed readers, "Electrical power to operate the scoreboard complex is sufficient to provide full electrical service for fifty homes."[137] The 1964 *Dedication* magazine instructed visitors that they were experiencing "the most modern scoreboard in the country." It was "unlike any in the country" and "as tall as a seven-story building."[138] The midseason team yearbook devoted almost half its content to the scoreboard and its "enormous electronic brain."[139] This artificially cerebral scoreboard, it boasted, would connect fans to information more fully than ever before. The Play-O-Gram feature could explain confusing plays. Score-O-Gram would help fans keep score. The board would, of course, track the scores of the day's other baseball games, as scoreboards always had. But surely the most mesmerizing element sat atop the board—the "living color 'television'" as one reporter called it, or the "Giant Movie Screen," according to a headline.[140] This screen would show still photos of players at bat but could also broadcast video replays of key moments via kinescope, or even movies in the case of rain delays. An illustration of the new scoreboard ran in the *New York World-Telegram-Sun* and *New York Times*, a rendering that was often used in club publications as

FIGURE 45. The Stadiarama Scoreboard in 1964. AP PHOTO/JOHN J. LENT.

well. The black board was lit up with information: statistics, scores from other games, and information about players. The gleaming white screen seemed to hug it, leaning forward as though in motion—befitting a scoreboard for a populuxe stadium.[141]

The Stadiarama Scoreboard was designed, so the club claimed, to address a basic need of both serious and novice watchers of baseball: to illuminate the unclear play. Baseball writer Ed Rumill of *Baseball Digest* noted that this was a real flaw of earlier parks—the paying fan often knew less about the game than the one listening to the radio or watching a television, who benefited from the explanations of broadcasters.[142] In practice, however, the board was used less to enmesh fans more fully in game action than to distract and entice them. Angell complained in May 1964 that the board wasn't being used to relate game information, such as relief pitchers warming up, but instead "the gargantuan scoreboard" with its "huge central message center . . . has been largely employed to boost souvenir and tickets sales and (very unsuccessfully) song lyrics for between-innings and sing alongs."[143] Animated scoreboards like the Stadiarama interjected themselves into the game experience—pitching products and directing fan cheers. Serious sports fans needed no such entertainment or direction; the natural lulls in action were moments for conversation and strategic contemplation, and experienced supporters knew when and how to support (or chastise) their teams. The scoreboard as entertainment was an appeal to the casual consumers of the game who, executives figured, were more likely to be suburban and affluent—not Roger Angell's screaming sans-culottes or Robert Lipsyte's shirtless tenement dwellers.[144] Shea's Stadiarama Scoreboard represented an early escalation in the stadium scoreboard arms race. Bob Addie, of the *Washington Post*, wrote of the new Shea Stadium scoreboard as though it was another consumerist status symbol of postwar America, like a new car or home: "Perhaps the piece de resistance is the new scoreboard. For some reason, the baseball people have gone daft over scoreboards in the past few stadiums. The scoreboard must be the new status symbol. The bigger your scoreboard, the more prestige."[145]

The stadium was rewritten in the spirit of the suburbs through the use and celebration of color and gadgetry; it was further suburbanized—and domesticated—by actively inviting women as labor and customers. The New York Mets, taking a cue from the relocated Dodgers and Giants, employed young women as greeters to evoke a sense of dignity and manners—to "civilize" the traditionally masculine stadium space. Many New Yorkers were introduced to the new corps of female ushers—"chic usherettes in tailored suits," according to the *New York Times*—a month before the stadium opened. An illustration featured an improbably svelte and sophisticated woman outfitted in the equestrian-wear "women once used when they went riding side saddle," readers were told.[146] Upon the stadium's opening, Larry Van Gelder of the *New York World-Telegram* wrote, "In matters sartorial the Met management was right up there in first place." A visitor to the new stadium claimed, according to Van Gelder, "It's tremendous—the color, the atmosphere! It's stylish—high sophistication with a lot of class."[147] Robert Lipsyte noted that the ushers, officially known as "female directors," were "installed by the Met management to add 'class' to the ball park and create a warm first impression on newcomers."[148]

By installing women as labor, the Mets tried to influence the culture of the stadium in multiple ways. For many men in the crowd, the usherette might have seemed a cross between a secretary and a stewardess; young, attractive, and seemingly single, these women were pieces of eye candy to stroke the male ego between parking lot and seat. But many also assumed that well-dressed and attractive young women naturally injected a sense of class and distinction into a space, and they were used as service employees in many industries for this very reason. When airlines were legally challenged for hiring almost only women for their in-flight service positions, industry responses revealed some of the widespread cultural assumptions about men and women that gendered certain service positions as female. United Airlines claimed in 1966, as a defense of its practice of hiring women only: "Men can carry trays, and hang up coats and assist in the rare event of an emergency—they cannot convey the charm, the tact, the grace, the liveliness that young girls can. . . . [Men] cannot create for the passenger the psychological impression of a memorable occasion . . . add to the pleasure of the trip, the loveliness of the environment or the ego of the male passenger."[149] These "uses" of femininity in the air were equally exploitable on the ground. Furthermore, the presence of young women didn't just work on men. These charms no doubt also worked on women, who, after playing the service role within the walls of their own homes, surely enjoyed being catered to in the stadium.

A trip to the stadium could be a welcome escape from the domestic constraints of suburban women's everyday lives, whether they were battling what Betty Friedan famously called "the problem that has no name" or trying to balance the expectations of homemaking and child-rearing with a part-time job or other professional aspirations and public service.[150] The Mets quite openly tried to attract and develop female fans by organizing the Met Women's Booster Club.[151] But to draw "respectable," middle-class women to the stadium required changing the stadium, imaginatively and in practice. While women had long been regulars at the ballpark, it had remained a masculine space, dominated by men tossing peanut shells under their feet, downing tepid beers, and puffing on cigars. This image needed to change. The Mets used female ushers to add "class." They also appealed to potential female customers in other ways.

Visual representations of women in stadium spaces could prescribe a domestic audience, suggesting to readers that Shea Stadium was a space appropriate for respectable female attendance. A rendering of the stadium and parking lot that often appeared in club and city publications staged just such a scene. Visitors approached from the stadium's west side. Pairs of fans—almost all male-female couplings, men in sweaters and slacks, women in long skirts or dresses—strolled toward the stadium across the lot. It seemed a pleasant, sunny scene—a lovely day for a drive out to the stadium and a game with the wife or husband. This was, certainly, how the image was to be read and understood, a point made clear by the staging. Realistically, most of these couples would have parked their cars much nearer the stadium—alongside those who had already arrived—not at the far reaches of the parking lot. But the display value of domestic companionship trumped realism, suggesting the deliberateness of this rhetorical gesture and the conscious effort of designers to insert women into the frame.[152]

Colorful, mechanized, and domesticated, Shea Stadium was loaded with referents to suburban homes and lifestyles. In a sense it was constructed in the image of the living room, its suburban crowds lounging in comfortable seats, looking onto a massive television screen atop the scoreboard. This was a response not just to the old ballparks but also to the challenge of televised baseball and the comforts of home. When designing the stadium, Richard Praeger suggested as much: "We are competing with the stay-at-home, the garden puterer [sic]. We want to get him out of there. . . . There are no columns in front of his TV set, and he doesn't have to climb three tiers to get there, either."[153] But if the stadium was part living room, it was also part suburban kitchen—a much-celebrated site of color and gadgetry. Vice President Richard Nixon had famously sparred with Soviet

FIGURE 46. Rendering of Shea Stadium parking lot from the west, published in multiple club and stadium publications. IRMA AND PAUL MILSTEIN DIVISION OF UNITED STATES HISTORY, LOCAL HISTORY AND GENEALOGY, THE NEW YORK PUBLIC LIBRARY. "FLUSHING MEADOW PARK," NEW YORK PUBLIC LIBRARY DIGITAL COLLECTIONS.

premier Nikita Khrushchev in the "kitchen debate" in 1959 at the opening of the American National Exhibition in Moscow. For Nixon, the model ranch-style home loaded with appliances was tangible proof of the superiority of the American capitalist way of life over the Soviet communist model. The realization of the American Dream, in the mind of Nixon and many others, was "successful breadwinners supporting attractive homemakers in affluent suburban homes," as historian Elaine Tyler May puts it.[154] Shea Stadium expressed this dream at gigantic scale, designed to be the equivalent of affluent suburbia, stocked with successful breadwinners and attractive homemakers. Massive, modern, and engineered, Shea hardly seemed to have much in common with a suburban ranch house. But beneath its soaring verticality, it embraced and embodied a suburban ethos grounded in spaciousness and mobility, spatial segregation and distinction, color and gadgetry, and affluent domestication.

The Suburban New Breed

In spite of nearly two decades of postwar suburbanization, the spirit of old Brooklyn remained in New York. At least, Jimmy Breslin claimed as much in the *Saturday Evening Post*, after witnessing the Mets and the New Breed set up shop at Shea in April 1964. On opening day, Breslin recounted, "a wall of noise fell out of the stands in one piece and crashed all over the field. . . . There were 53,000 people in the stands, and they were all shouting and shaking fists, and you knew they would be doing it all afternoon long and that it will be like this for the rest of the season, too."[155]

The enthusiasm was generated, as always, by the club's legendary incompetence. It was a team "so bad at playing baseball that it has stepped out of sports and has become, along with the Guggenheim Museum, a driving force in the city's culture." In a city of winners, as Breslin framed it, "filled with people who are successes and others who are in search of success," it was the ineptitude of the Mets that gave them their charisma. Winning would "spoil everything. . . . Anybody can root for a winner"—this final remark a jab at the fan base of New York's other major league baseball team, the Yankees.

This exuberance was the evidence Breslin needed to argue that Brooklyn still existed, though it was "Brooklyn-in-1964." Brooklyn used to be "trolley cars or the Brighton Beach subway line or crowds of people in shirt sleeves walking through traffic to get to the park," but then it moved to places like Levittown, Long Island, and Tenafly, New Jersey. The Giants and Dodgers left town because they thought the suburban exodus would make the city dead to any baseball beyond the Yankees, "who draw all the bankers and all the out-of-towners." Yet, Breslin claimed, "this view was wrong. There always has been a spirit to New York, and just because you put a lot of the spirit onto something called the Long Island Rail Road every night does not mean you are losing it. Lose? Hell, this city hasn't lost a thing." New Yorkers, then spread out among the suburbs, tapped into the spirit of the Mets—a vacuum created by the departure of the Giants and Dodgers. These people "turned everything into Brooklyn, 1964." For Breslin, Shea Stadium seemed a jar of formaldehyde preserving the city and its eccentric minions in the face of that city's supposed erosion.[156]

The spirit of Brooklyn seemed to be present at Jets games as well. The former Titans—renamed the Jets for the 1963 season, in anticipation of the opening of the new modern stadium—stormed new Shea Stadium, channeling some of the offbeat qualities of the old New Breed and Frederick Exley's blue-collar football buddies. The opening night crowd in September was 52,663—beating the previous attendance record for any AFL game by over 14,000. Like their baseball cousins, Jets fans made quirky banners: one on opening night read, "Lima, Peru. Loves the Jets." The first new football hero of Shea was the hard-hitting linebacker "Wahoo" McDaniel, a Choctaw Indian who moonlighted as a professional wrestler. He explained his professional motivation in terms that the old New Breed could have identified with: "There's an incentive being an Indian, part of a people that's always been pushed around."[157]

The Jets and Mets fans were certainly loud—particularly in Shea Stadium's early days—but other commentators began to poke holes in Breslin's early (and perhaps wishful) claims that the stadium was the second coming of Ebbets Field or even the Polo Grounds. Roger Angell, also writing in the stadium's early days, saw some carryover of the fan culture from the Polo Grounds—more than he had expected even. He had feared that "the move from the banks of the Harlem River to the shores of Flushing Bay might civilize the Met fans, transforming then into a cautious, handclapping audience of suburban lawn-tenders," but that transformation wasn't immediate. He noted, "There are more well-dressed, unexcitable, merely pleasant onlookers visible in the gleaming new stands," though he thought some of them might be visitors from the adjacent World's Fair. Angell seemed pleased to report that some of that old urban, masculine culture remained, evidenced when "a dozen or so of the New Breed—the *old* New Breed—staged a rousing fistfight in the lower right-field stands, attracting roars of encouragement and subsequent boos for the fuzz." Clearly Shea Stadium wasn't wholly civilized early on, as some of the old guard took the subway out to the stadium.[158]

Writers like Leonard Koppett, George Vecsey, and Leonard Shecter also testified that those early Shea Stadium fans remained noisy but were constituted differently. Koppett thought that the crowds "combined some of the features of past and present. Although they were distinctly more orderly, and undoubtedly more prosperous, than Polo Grounds regulars, they were just as diligent about cheering and making signs."[159] Vecsey noted, "The makeup of the fans seemed to change a little." Notable Polo Grounds eccentrics like Louie Kleppel and Mother of the Mets stopped going to games "because there was no forum for their lectures, no bleachers where they could express their freedom of speech." There were "somewhat fewer black and Latin fans now that the club had moved from uptown. But if the Met fan turned a lighter shade of pale in 1964, his noise level remained constant—hysterical and zonked out."[160] Koppett thought the opening day crowd was "noticeably different in character from the Polo Grounds variety"—a notably well-dressed group, even for an opening day crowd. He thought the fans "somehow less passionate even though they were just as noisy." Part of this was due to the stadium itself—the games could be expected to be less "bizarre" because Shea was "a symmetrical and roomy park," unlike the curious dimensions of the Polo Grounds. "In this, as in the crowd," he concluded, "an element of respectability had been introduced."[161] Robert Lipsyte, on the other hand, minced no words, claiming that the "bourgeois smugness" of Shea almost instantly changed its residents. "One doesn't have to be a materialistic dialectician to see what this all adds up to," he wrote in May 1965. "The Mets are not representatives of the proletariat any more."[162]

Many commentators connected crowd makeup and behavior to the prospects of winning and losing. Central to the "old New Breed" identity was this ironic sense of regeneration through failure; the team's loser status begged its support, and the drama of losing in creative and extravagant ways only fueled the club's legend and fan attachment. Theoretically success would unravel New Breed identity. This formulation was complicated by a move to the achievement-oriented suburbs as well, where losing, many speculated, would be less tolerable. Shecter introduced this idea by noting "a different flavor" to the crowds at the two stadiums. At the Polo Grounds, "the fans were raunchier, somehow. They seemed to drink more beer and spill more of it on themselves and in the stands. They laughed a lot more, too, and seemed to have a better time—even when the Mets were losing." He observed, "The fans at Shea have a good time, too, these days. But winning seems more important to them."[163] Vecsey believed this as well, writing, "The Mets were up against a different crowd now—theoretically. They were appealing to a suburban, success-oriented crowd. Would a father with a high-paying job pack up his 2.3 children and drive all the way in from Split Level Land to watch a team that could not win?"[164]

Increasingly—and rapidly—the rambunctious stadium culture of the old city was being institutionalized. In Shea's opening season, Angell had sensed that some Mets supporters, fueled by media fascination, were becoming aware of themselves as performers of a New Breed identity. He reasoned, "As must befall all fanatical movements, self-consciousness and formalization have overtaken the Met religion." Of course, a shift in venue partially explains this observation: behavior deemed organic and honest in the shabby confines of the Polo Grounds might well have seemed orchestrated and artificial in the modern suburban cleanliness of Shea. But television, too, played a role, particularly in the formalization of the Mets' banner culture. Banner makers increasingly hoped to catch the eye of the camera, and the banners provided broadcasters with engaging content beyond the game on the field. Angell noted that many of the banners at Shea seemed to have "been created by art students or advertising men . . . made for the television cameras rather than for the team; mostly they are unfurled when a foul ball, with its attendant TV eye, comes into the stands, instead of when the Mets desperately need a run."[165] Koppett saw evidence of the institutionalization of the Mets in the promotions put on by the club, like Banner Day, Fan Appreciation Day, and Senior Citizens Day. These were "sound, progressive business practice," he admitted, "but they made official things that had been unplanned, spontaneous, fan-initiated, and that meant a different kind of environment."[166]

Four years after the move to Shea, the Mets fans had unquestionably changed. Koppett eulogized the New Breed in 1968, noting, "Shea Stadium customers now were predominantly suburban, middle-class, running heavily to family groups." The young and rebellious of the Polo Grounds years had been "good-natured rebels"; those of recent vintage "had turned their attention to far more serious things than baseball, and the young people at Shea Stadium were very much Establishment." They still made banners, but by then this was "an expression of conformity—to Met tradition—instead of a spontaneous flowering of irrepressible expression." Mets fans were "stoic" in defeat; they didn't masochistically luxuriate in it. "They came more and more from Long Island and Queens and Brooklyn, and less from the inner city," he suggested, "more by car than by subway." They often arrived as organized groups, their presence then acknowledged by the Mets' marketing team on the Stadiarama scoreboard. They were still loyal, but much had changed: "the Met Mystique had long since become institutionalized."[167]

Professional football had also become institutionalized by the mid-1960s, as television contracts plowed money into the game and teams were increasingly the beneficiaries of new municipal stadiums designed to suit both major sports. Just a decade before, professional football was largely followed by working-class men; when Shea was opened, professional football's audience tended to be college educated, professional, affluent, and suburban.[168] The staid Giants, playing in Yankee Stadium, remained a defender of conservative, old-school football—a game of toughness and discipline. But the Jets were decidedly new-school, and their quarterback—electrically charismatic Joe Namath—seemed the most rebellious of professional football players. In a game famous for its selfless warriors in black shoes, Namath played in sleek white cleats. Richly talented on the field, he was as well known for what he did off it—chasing "foxes" in New York's hippest clubs, while outfitted in a Fu Manchu moustache and a full-length mink coat.[169] Sonny Werblin, the managing partner of the Jets, had come to the team after thirty years working for the largest talent agency in show business. "I believe in the star system," Werblin said. "It's the only thing that sells tickets."[170] When the AFL signed a massive new television contract with NBC in 1965—paying five times the league's previous contract with ABC—Werblin splashed some of that cash out for Namath, signing him to a $427,000 contract at a time when most NFL stars made about $25,000 per season. "I don't know how to define star quality," Werblin said, "but Joe Namath has it. Few do."[171] Namath's star qualities polarized the press; some celebrated his devil-may-care attitude, others excoriated him for violating the codes of the game. But really, he was an iconoclast in style, not substance. According to cultural historian Michael Oriard, "Joe Namath had everything the Youth could want—Youth not marching for civil rights or against the war, that is. Namath's hedonism belonged more to an older era than the 1960s—booze and broads, not dope and hippie chicks—but set against the ascetic and violent image of professional football, it seemed not just rebellious but revolutionary." In other words, Namath was a rebel in the stadium, but not within the contexts of the countercultural 1960s. His brand of "hair and hedonism," as Oriard notes, was already being mainstreamed by the end of the decade. This was the *image* of rebellion—one that certainly sold tickets to men and women alike.[172]

By 1969, Shea Stadium had become, according to the *New York Times*, "one of the best spots in town to find a date"—a claim that was surely never made about the Polo Grounds in the early 1960s. As the team made its improbable pennant run in 1969, Shea Stadium officials estimated that one-quarter of attendees that season were women, a number that was escalating as the club moved closer to first place. Reporter Nancy Moran, after noting the great surge in female interest, described the stadium as a site not for female fans of baseball but for female fans of men. Marilyn Marcus, a twenty-eight-year-old "blonde-model" in attendance, explained the phenomenon: "Women like winners. Successful men, whether they're ballplayers or businessmen, are sexy. Right now, the Mets are very successful." Moran noted that twenty-three of twenty-seven Mets players were married, and those who weren't had "been flooded with offers of marriage and home-cooked meals" since they had started winning. The odds of landing a Mets player were thus pretty slim, though she added, "If the girls don't marry a Met, they may still find a doctor or lawyer or salesman at Shea." Another attendee, eighteen-year-old Jane Nagel, used this strategy, informing Moran, "I used to write letters to Ron Swoboda, but all I got back were pictures of Wes Westrum. Then I started paying attention to the boys in the stands. I haven't had to ride home alone on the subway all summer."[173]

The New Breed might not have been dead, but it no longer seemed at home at Shea. If it had a home, it was in the streets. After the Mets improbably won the World Series in 1969, some of the *old* New Breed poured onto Manhattan streets to celebrate. George Vecsey recounted one scene that illustrated the tension between the production of fan culture at Shea and the joyful artlessness of the New Breed at the old Polo Grounds:

On East Forty-fourth Street, between Third and Lexington avenues, it was like V-E Day, like Lindbergh's homecoming, like New Year's Eve used to be. But it was even better because it was spontaneous. No Commissioner of Civic Celebrations engi-

neered this display. It just happened, and the streets belonged to the people. . . .
In one circle, holding hands, there was a Chinese man with sleek black hair, a
young man with a razor haircut and turtleneck shirt, a chunky Puerto Rican girl
with smoked glasses, a Negro man in a jacket and bow tie, a very tall girl in a very
short skirt, a short black girl in an Afro haircut, a husky middle-aged salesman with
floppy cuffed trousers. They had come together in an outpouring of happiness. It
was the kind of afternoon when anything was possible. The Mets had delivered a
miracle to the fans who had kept the faith.[174]

Here was the urban diversity that New York was famous for—an accidental and spontaneous public like those who had taken to the Mets of the Polo Grounds. If Ebbets Field had
seemed to defy geography, stretching from Greenpoint to Coney Island, the Polo Grounds,
if only briefly, defied time—reincarnated in Midtown. But by the end of the 1960s, much
of the old city had been rebuilt. As his reputation plunged and his power began to wane,
Robert Moses had succeeded in erecting a new stadium for the postwar era—a stadium
built for the automobile, organized around a modernist sense of spaciousness, echoing the
design of a new suburban landscape. Battles over urban space reached a head as the 1960s
unfolded—as did questions of what it meant to be American. Increasingly, as the world
around it seemed to fall apart, the stadium became a safe space for many Americans who
had been invited into the suburban middle classes after World War II. The ballpark, a hallmark of old urban life just years before, had been reinvented in the image of the suburbs
and made home to a new sporting public.

CHAPTER 4

PAST TO FUTURE

THE STADIUM AND MODERN PROGRESS

IN JANUARY 1962 A GROUP OF Houston politicians in cowboy hats broke ground for the Harris County Domed Stadium by firing Colt .45 pistols into the dirt at their feet. In retrospect it seems a peculiar image—suited civic leaders playacting cowboys to initiate construction on the most revolutionary stadium in American history. But in fact, the charade perfectly captured the self-perception of many Houstonians who figured themselves a unique blend of the wild western frontier and the space age. The iconic Texan was, in the minds of many writers, defined by his adaptability—a character at ease with the dazzling pace of modern change. Author Mary Lasswell reckoned, "The more a Texan changes, the more he truly becomes himself. . . . The country itself is suddenly and violently changeable, often in clashing conflict with itself . . . like a Texan's conflict between his pioneer past and his urban present."[1] The Texan—in his own mind at least—might have been the perfect agent to drag sport from its dusty past into a plastic future, pistols blazing. In the early 1960s, Houston indeed seemed a city for a new age. One year after the stadium groundbreaking, the Manned Spacecraft Center opened twenty-five miles south of downtown Houston. Two years after that, the Astrodome debuted, drawing attention from around the globe, much of it fixating on the stadium as an expression of the future. Observers claimed it was like a spaceship, recently arrived from another planet.[2] Buddy Diliberto of the *New Orleans Times-Picayune* promised readers, "When the first astronaut (Uncle

Sam's) climbs out of his space capsule and sets foot on the moon five, 10 or 20 years from now he won't be any more awed by the sight than you'll be the first time you step inside the Astrodome. The place is unbelievable. Just unbelievable. It takes your breath away on first look. It's like stepping out of the real world into a land of make-believe—only it's not make-believe."[3]

Celebrated as the "Eighth Wonder of the World" by boosters, the Astrodome was the modern world's first completely enclosed, roofed stadium.[4] Sited seven miles southwest of downtown, adjacent to Houston's new freeway loop encircling the city, the massive structure rose 218 feet above a 30,000-space parking lot. Its roof spanned 642 feet—twice the size of any other roofed expanse.[5] It was built to attract a major league baseball team but would also host a wide range of mass gatherings. Athletes, fans, conventioneers, religious revivalists, and circus animals alike escaped oppressive Houston summers to a cool 74 degrees and 50 percent humidity, prompting an observer to quip, "Texas has just discovered a new frontier—the Great Indoors."[6] The stadium was notable for a number of other features as well. The animated scoreboard, four stories high and nearly 500 feet long, was

FIGURE 47. Judge Roy Hofheinz, the central figure in promoting and shaping the Astrodome, addresses the crowd at the stadium's groundbreaking. MSS 0114-1170, HOUSTON PUBLIC LIBRARY, HOUSTON METROPOLITAN RESEARCH CENTER.

an object of great attention and envy from other cities. The facility boasted six different restaurants, each catering to a different economic slice of society. Around the top, the stadium was ringed with fifty-three private luxury boxes for its highest-paying customers. The suites, exotically themed with names like "Bangkok" and "Old Mexico," were outfitted with many of the luxuries of the suburban home of the 1950s and 1960s: pile carpeting, plush sofas, telephones, radios, televisions, toilets, ice makers, and bars.[7] These stadium features prompted the *New Yorker*'s Roger Angell to call the stadium a "giant living room—complete with manmade weather, wall-to-wall carpeting, clean floors, and unrelenting TV shows."[8] The Astrodome had one-upped Shea Stadium, making the stadium even more like the suburban home than its counterpart in Queens.

Shea Stadium modernized stadium space by suburbanizing it, shifting mass spectator sport from the crowded streets of Manhattan to the presumably flowing freeways of Queens, housing sport in a stadium that "breathed" at the edge of Flushing Meadow Park while bestowing precious elbow room on its suburban patrons, making them feel at home through its populuxe accents. In material and spatial terms, the Astrodome resembled Shea—it, too, seemed a stadium analogue to the suburban landscape by privileging mobility, spaciousness, color, and push-button technology. But in Houston, features like enormous parking lots, escalators, and automated scoreboards registered differently. Unlike New Yorkers, Houstonians were accustomed to spaciousness, living in a sprawling city organized around the individualized freedom of the automobile. While Shea expressed a new modern and suburban spatiality, Houston's Astrodome demonstrated a dogged faith in modern progress. It functioned as a new marker of civilization to rival ancient empires, a material embodiment of the benefits of science and free-market capitalism in the midst of the Cold War. For Houstonians, anxious about their status in the pecking order of American cities—worries that postwar New Yorkers didn't share—the modern stadium was a symbol of civic progress, a utopian megastructure that venerated a particular version of American postwar life (while also revealing some of its major fissures and blind spots). The worldview materialized by the Astrodome was articulated time and again by stadium advocates and their allies in the press.

The most coherent expressions of the stadium's "official" meanings were assembled in *Inside the Astrodome*, a thick, glossy-paged, color souvenir guidebook published by the Houston Sports Association (HSA), the stadium's operators, and purchased by visitors for a dollar. Readers—typically sitting there under the stadium's revolutionary roof, in its padded theater seats, cooling off in its air-conditioned climate—were introduced to the dome in the volume's opening pages with the following proclamation:

> Sparkling like a rare jewel on a one-time Houston swamp, the ASTRODOME is the
> Taj Mahal of all stadiums from Rome's Colosseum on down to this day. It is beyond

compare because nothing like it has ever been built before. It is big, beautiful and
something to behold. It rises from the flat Texas plain like some dazzling new
creation out of the Space Age. From the outside, the gently, curving blister-bubble
roof resembles nothing so much as a lunar landscape. When workmen are on
the roof, they look like spacemen crawling on a planet in outer space. Inside, the
stadium is a bright picture of color and symmetry giving the spectator a warm glow
of intimacy.[9]

The passage collapses time and space, placing the Astrodome among some of the most
iconic human creations, before denying its comparability. It is otherworldly. And yet its
interior color and intimate warmth reanchor its space-age cool in recognizable domestic
security. Promoters for the Astrodome, like the HSA and local business and political leaders, never tired of celebrating the stadium as the pinnacle of human creation. But they
weren't the only ones: hyperbole was the accepted mode of expression when it came to
the Astrodome—and understandably so. It may not have been beyond people's *imaginations*; in many ways, it realized Norman Bel Geddes's schemes for Brooklyn in the early
1950s that had received national attention. But it was certainly the most remarkable building most of its visitors had ever experienced and probably ever would. Advocates and
skeptics alike, from Houston's boosters and reporters to regular citizens, registered their
understandings of the Astrodome in epic terms, often comparing it to the works of other
"civilizations." The suggestion was clear: the Astrodome represented the pinnacle of human
achievement, an end point on the steady climb of human progress. The magic of science
had produced a utopia whose residents, in varying degrees, luxuriated in the consumer
comforts of the greatest civilization the earth had ever hosted. And yet, viewed from a different angle, the Astrodome was not an Eden but an escape pod, not just an expression of
national hubris but also a manifestation of deep anxiety that denied the realities of social
dysfunction that haunted Houston and the nation outside this miniature world.

Postwar Houston

The Astrodome was, in many ways, the perfect expression of postwar Houston—a brash,
modern, expansive structure befitting a city of the same qualities. The *London Times*
predicted in the 1950s that the postwar United States would soon be organized around
four major cities: New York, Chicago, Los Angeles, and Houston. By the 1960s, it was
clear that this prediction held some merit. Houston's explosive growth and increasing
national significance rested on the oil, gas, and petrochemical industries so vital to the
postwar economy. The city's population grew by 51 percent between 1950 and 1960, from
947,500 to 1,430,394. It grew by nearly 40 percent between 1960 and 1970, from 1,430,394

FIGURE 48. The Astrodome was seven miles southwest of Houston's central business district. A new freeway loop runs just south of the stadium site. MSS 0287-002, HOUSTON PUBLIC LIBRARY, HOUSTON METROPOLITAN RESEARCH CENTER.

to 1,999,316. A significant expansion in residential and commercial construction in the 1950s accommodated this booming population. Over 99,000 new homes were built in that decade, expanding the city's suburban footprint. This residential growth was joined by the new commercial and office buildings outside the city center—unrestrained construction as a result of the city's lack of zoning laws.[10] Houston thus grew haphazardly, without any substantive central planning. It spread outward, annexing adjacent communities into a widespread, sprawling, and uneven cityscape.[11] French journalist Pierre Voisin said of the city in 1962: "There is no plan. I am horrified. Everyone is just doing as he pleases, building here and there. . . . Houston is spreading like a spilled bucket of water. If something isn't done about it quickly, it will be horrible, horrible."[12]

Few Houstonians in power shared Voisin's revulsion. Instead, the city buzzed with excitement and anticipation. A writer for the *Dallas News* wrote in 1962 of the city's continuing and anticipated growth: "It is likely that even many Houstonians have no conception of what is happening and what it may mean to their community."[13] Houston journalist George Fuermann wrote of the city's youthful enthusiasm and sense of hope. He claimed in 1962 that the median age of the city was 27.5 years, making it the youngest of America's big cities. Fuermann thought the youthfulness of the population a natural fit for a city so forward-looking and unbothered by history: "The city seems younger than it is, for since the 1920s Houston has given the impression of being always new. Few structures stand long enough to become old. When the lovely patina of age does get a chance to form, it is scrubbed away as though it were an embarrassment . . . Houstonians have shown little compassion for their city's past."[14]

Major construction throughout Houston reflected this disregard for the past and embrace of the future. The $100 million Manned Spacecraft Center opened twenty-five miles south of downtown Houston in 1963. The $125 million Jetero Airport was under construction by 1964, designed to relieve the pressure on Houston International.[15] Houston's downtown skyline—dominated by an assortment of new office towers—reflected a modern contempt for history. Ten new downtown buildings opened in 1963 alone, increasing office space by 41 percent.[16] By 1964, half of Houston's downtown core floor space was in office buildings—455 percent more footage than in 1950—and several new buildings were being planned.[17] As in many American cities, new and old, the central business district (CBD) in Houston was largely given over to big business in the 1960s. Most professionals had left, along with retailers. Three large regional suburban shopping centers, each over fifty acres in size, had opened since 1950. There was little housing in the center city, and what remained was increasingly being torn down and replaced by surface parking lots to support the influx of daily commuters.[18]

A traffic expert told the Houston City Council in 1961 that Houstonians, more than any other Americans, preferred private cars to public transportation.[19] By 1960, 95 percent of Houstonians were using private cars to get around, up from 86 percent in 1953; bus use, the only other significant form of transportation, dropped from 13.7 to 4.5 percent over that same period.[20] A spate of new postwar freeways enabled Houstonians' driving habits. A four-lane expressway to Galveston, the Gulf Freeway, was completed in 1952. The cost was $28 million, paid largely by the state and federal governments. In 1953, the Texas Highway Department announced plans for a $2.5 million freeway interchange as part of a larger $100 million highway system encircling downtown Houston.[21] Highway construction became a constant and visible feature around the city for the remainder of the decade and into the 1960s. By then, the city had become a core of sleek office towers and a wide ring of over five hundred square miles of suburbia, all strung together by massive freeway arteries, coursing through and around the city, linking the suburbs and region to the downtown and the Astrodome site seven miles to the southwest. Writer Kirkpatrick Sale suggested, "The spirit which infuses all this is, as it has been since the founding of Houston, the making of money. The business of Houston, as its functional character would suggest, is business."[22]

Oil-rich Texans figured prominently in the national imagination in the 1960s. "Cowboy" was an epithet used by those on Wall Street who encountered the newly powerful Texas entrepreneurs of the late 1950s and early 1960s. Their power stemmed from their roles in the petroleum industry, which was physically centered in Texas—first emanating from the East Texas field in the 1930s, then the Permian Basin in the 1950s, and then the Gulf of Mexico in the 1960s. Houston was the oil capital of the United States and increasingly was an energy center for the world over. The incredible amounts of wealth spawned countless legends and caricatures of the spend-happy Texan, in cowboy hat and tooled-leather boots. Sale noted the "infinitude of tales about Texans with four ranches, one for each season, or right- and left-wheel Rolls-Royces so both arms get tanned."[23]

The popular conception that the business of Houston was business led many to assume that the city and its power brokers were politically and economically laissez-faire, opposing interventionist government—an image these men cultivated rhetorically. But the image of laissez-faire Houston belied its reality on the ground. Houston, historically, had been a city profoundly and repeatedly shaped by the decisions of business leaders in major industries in consort with state intervention, whereby government was "the instrument of the local business community," according to sociologist Joe R. Feagin. Houston's growth throughout the twentieth century relied on the largess of public funding that supported private industry, from state and federal support to dredge the Houston Ship Channel beginning in the late 1800s, to federal money for highways and bridges, to post–World War II federal home loan policies, to the substantial military-industrial aid for the petrochemical industry during World War II and later for the Manned Spacecraft Center of the 1960s. Government officials working with business leaders—or, more accurately, installed by business leaders in office—funded business endeavors through the use of special bonds while maintaining weak regulatory mechanisms. While Houston's elite often supported governmental intervention for their profit-making projects, they typically opposed state involvement in other types of projects like the development of neighborhood infrastructure, the regulation of development via zoning or planning, increased taxes to fund public services, or the assistance of poor residents through social welfare programs. Free-market advocates celebrated Houston as an example of the extensive benefits of private development and markets blessed with a low-tax, business-friendly government geared toward creating a "good business climate." On the other hand, the intense resistance to taxation and spending on public services and other infrastructure produced a city that was enormously stratified socioeconomically and beset consistently by major flooding, water pollution, toxic waste, sewage, and street maintenance problems.[24]

In many cities, politicians emerged from machines or unions; in Houston, most top city politicians were either members of or sponsored by the business elite. Business leaders in Houston not only received the support of government; they effectively controlled it. From the late 1930s into the 1970s, much of the business of Houston's government was channeled through the "Suite 8F crowd"—so named for the hotel suite where these powerful men met regularly to lunch and plot the city's future.[25] R. E. "Bob" Smith was one of Houston's more influential oil entrepreneurs and played a major role in city real estate and politics. By virtue of his wealth and holdings, he was part of, though not central to, the 8F crowd. Smith would become arguably the second most important player in the construction of the domed stadium in Houston as the most prominent private financier of the project. He was a strong man with a powerful build at the age of seventy—called "Croesus with a mane of white hair and a mania for physical fitness" by one writer.[26] A *Texas Sunday Magazine* article featured a seven-photo spread of Smith lifting weights. The accompanying profile cast him as a winner, a man of few words, a Christian, and an advocate for desegregation—at least within churches.[27] Smith was an influential oilman and owner of much land around the fringes of Houston—including the land that the Astrodome was built on. He had a public reputation: Kirkpatrick Sale put him in the ranks of those "great names of oil . . . the old-timers who bring faraway looks to the eyes of modern oilmen as the evening waxes moister," a group that included J. Paul Getty, H. L. Hunt, Sid Richardson, Clint Murchison, D. H. "Dry Hole" Byrd, John Mecom, and Glenn McCarthy.[28]

Smith was the economic brawn behind the domed stadium; Judge Roy Hofheinz was the brain. The Suite 8F clique had installed Hofheinz as mayor in 1953, only to switch its support away from him in 1955 when he became too centrist for their extremely conservative tastes. Hofheinz had been a pro–economic growth mayor, but his support of a property reassessment drive downtown, which would have increased taxes there, and his opinions on some social issues, regarding civil rights for example, alienated him from some of Houston's elite.[29] But Hofheinz's public image was defined by much more than this short period as mayor. Hofheinz was a classic Texan "rags-to-riches" story: he had become a lawyer at age nineteen, a member of the Texas legislature at twenty-two, a four-term county judge in Houston's Harris County beginning at age twenty-four, and mayor from 1953 to 1955. Just fifty-three years old when the Astrodome opened, Hofheinz had become a multimillionaire through a range of business interests in radio, real estate, television, law, and oil.[30]

Hofheinz was, without a doubt, the star of the show—a magnet for attention from reporters and citizens who treated him with a mixture of bemusement and revulsion but were largely incapable of resisting his ebullient personality. A reporter from the *San Antonio Express* captured Hofheinz's essence effectively when he wrote, "Perhaps the only thing in Houston more amazing than The Dome is the stadium's father, Roy Hofheinz. Tuesday he stood on the stadium's fourth level and talked to newsmen for over an hour—without once repeating."[31] This was the most obvious of Hofheinz's skills—the ability to talk and talk, pitch and promote, convincing people that building a domed stadium was not only possible but also a good investment. Jack Valenti claimed that he was the best platform speaker around outside of Hubert Humphrey. A director of marketing for the Houston club compared his oratory powers to those of Franklin D. Roosevelt and Adolf Hitler.[32] Hofheinz was described by writers as a "far-seeing Texas tycoon," a "biscuit-bodied dynamo, a Texas operator," and a "futuristic genius."[33] Roy Terrell of *Sports Illustrated* provided a fuller portrait: "Roy Hofheinz is a large man with an even larger stomach, a theatrical flair and a mind as quick as a cash register. He smokes a box of cigars a day, sleeps only when there is nothing else to do and would, if charged with the U.S. space program, have had John Glenn in orbit by the astronaut's third birthday. He is considered unusual even in Texas."[34] Many introductions to Hofheinz noted his pear-shaped physique and his standard accents: the heavy, black-rimmed glasses that gave him the "look of an enormous owl"; his lank, black hair; the ever-present cigar, a signifier of masculine power; and the telephone, a symbol of deal making, Hofheinz's specialty.[35] *Sports Illustrated*'s Liz Smith called him "a shrewd and sophisticated operator in the Lyndon B. Johnson genre—country-boy geniality mixed with a gimlet-eyed grasp of the realities."[36] Robert Lipsyte of the *New York Times* compared him to Sam Houston, Lyndon Johnson, P. T. Barnum, and the fraudulent Texan wheeler-dealer Billie Sol Estes.[37] "This guy Hofheinz is the most refreshing mind to come into baseball in years," a New York television executive said of him, adding, "You watch him. He'll out-O'Malley O'Malley and out-Veeck Veeck. I just hope he doesn't decide to change the rules of the game."[38]

Planning and Building the Astrodome

Houston's postwar boom made some citizens long for the "big-league" status a major league baseball team would grant the city. George Kirksey, a former sportswriter who moved to Houston in 1946 and owned a small public relations firm, tried to entice existing clubs to the city in the 1950s. His attempts to put together an investor group to either purchase another club or lure a discontented owner south were unsuccessful until the late 1950s, when he joined forces with Texaco heir Craig Cullinan to form the Houston Sports Association (HSA), a syndicate of twenty-eight investors. In their bid to attract a major league franchise to Houston, the HSA faced a common problem for aspiring cities: local leaders were afraid to support the construction of a new stadium until the city was promised a team, but no major league team would move to a new city unless a new stadium was secured. Milwaukee had taken a leap of faith in the early 1950s, approving a new stadium, and was rewarded when the Boston Braves moved there in 1953. The Harris County Board of Park Commissioners was created to assemble a proposal for a new stadium that might, like Milwaukee's County Stadium, attract a major league team. Houston voters bought this logic, approving a $20 million bond issue on July 25, 1958, that would finance a sports center and exhibition park, including a $6 million air-conditioned coliseum.[39]

With stadium financing in hand, the HSA applied for membership in both the American and National leagues in 1958, to no avail. The group then joined other sports entrepreneurs—like Branch Rickey and William Shea in New York—to start a third major league, the Continental League. At first, National and American League owners were unbothered by the prospect of a new competitor; however, they were soon spooked by congressional action. Senator Estes Kefauver of Tennessee chaired a subcommittee that investigated the application of antitrust laws to professional sports leagues. Kefauver was a close friend of Senator Lyndon B. Johnson of Texas; Johnson, in turn, was close to Roy Hofheinz, who had administered his senatorial campaign in Texas. Kefauver's subcommittee unsurprisingly produced Bill 3843, which clearly stated that obstructing the creation and operation of a new major league baseball club was an antitrust violation. Johnson pushed for an early vote on the bill, which nearly saw it passed. The near-victory was victory enough for Houston. Major league owners, fearful that the Continental League might actually become a reality, negotiated with some of the most attractive ownership groups to forestall the creation of a third major league. On October 17, 1960, the National League awarded Houston and New York franchises to begin play in 1962. The public face of the HSA at this point consisted of Cullinan, Hofheinz, Smith, Kirksey, and K. S. "Bud" Adams, who was a cofounder of the fledgling American Football League and owner of that league's Oilers. The American League added teams in Los Angeles and Washington, D.C. (to replace the club that had relocated to Minneapolis in 1960), to begin play in 1961. The potential challenger, the Continental League, was thus successfully gutted by baseball's major league incumbents.[40]

Hofheinz set to regaling Houstonians and anyone else in earshot with his vision of a new domed stadium, lugging a $35,000 model around the city and its satellite communities. He received the support of local media, which actively endorsed new stadium plans before and after the National League awarded a team to the HSA. In 1959 the *Houston Chronicle* ran a series on how other minor league cities had tried to attract major league clubs. One such article chronicled how Milwaukee had rolled the dice on a stadium and won. "Without even a prospect of acquiring a major league baseball team at the time," the reporter wrote, "Milwaukee County built one of the finest stadiums in the United States on the chance that a big league club might someday move in. The gamble paid off in a hurry."[41] Newspapers published drawings of planned domed stadiums that would be tall enough to cover the famed Shamrock Hotel; one such plan was a geodesic structure from Buckminster Fuller's Synergetics firm.[42] These well-publicized arguments and proposals, joined with Hofheinz's salesmanship and well-funded promotional campaigns, helped convince Harris County voters. They approved Propositions One and Two on January 31, 1961. Proposition One provided $18 million in bonds to acquire a site and construct the stadium; it passed by a vote of 62,033 to 54,204. Proposition Two approved $4 million in bonds to build access roads and bridges to the site; it passed by a vote of 64,041 to 48,292. It was the largest voter turnout for a bond election in the city's history. Support for the propositions came from the city's more affluent southern and western areas; northern and eastern Houston was largely opposed or narrowly in favor. Black precincts supported the project enthusiastically.[43]

Houston's African American population played a pivotal role in the stadium's construction as a voting bloc. It also leveraged its support to reshape the makeup of Houston's public spaces. Quentin Mease, a Houston activist, threatened to organize black votes against the project if the stadium wasn't fully desegregated. Other city leaders soon realized that more than just the stadium would have to be racially integrated; a television producer asked Hofheinz, "Have you thought what will happen when the Giants come to Houston? You can't have Willie Mays and the other ballplayers staying at a segregated hotel." More interested in big-league status than Jim Crow, many business leaders collaborated with local media to desegregate the city's downtown stores and restaurants quietly, without immediate news coverage. This averted organized resistance to the changes. John T. Jones, publisher of the *Houston Chronicle*, nephew to the powerful Jesse Jones and administrator of the Houston Endowment, ended segregation in many of the city's major hotels—the Rice, Lamar, and McKinney hotels were all owned by the Endowment—on April 1, 1962, just days before the Houston team began play.[44]

Ground was broken for the domed stadium on January 3, 1962. By the end of May, Harris County commissioners determined that the stadium couldn't be built for the remaining $13.4 million from the original $15 million bond issue dedicated to construction costs. As costs rose, powerful Houstonians weighed in with their support for the project in an attempt to head off any budding public restlessness. Chamber of commerce president George T. Morse Jr. told the Houston Rotary Club that the stadium was vital to the attraction of tourists and industry to the city: "County Stadium must be built . . . first class in every respect and air conditioned. We must provide whatever funds are needed."[45] The case was made on the grounds of civic pride. A *Houston Chronicle* editorial stated: "The domed stadium has already become known world-wide. It is a symbol, outside of Texas, of the way Texans do things—with flair, imagination, comfort, class. We either wind up with the equivalent of 'an Eiffel Tower' for Houston, or a costly international black eye. We're for the stadium instead of the black eye."[46]

A new set of construction bids released November 1, 1962, produced a low bid of $19.44 million, $6.64 million more than the original estimated cost. The *Houston Press, Houston*

Post, and *Houston Chronicle* all supported new funding. Commissioners voted to propose an additional $9.6 million bond issue for voters to decide.[47] Houston voters approved the additional bonds on December 22, 1962, by a vote of 42,911 to 36,110. As the HSA turned to the county for more funding, it also underwent dramatic changes. Cullinan, convinced that Hofheinz's involvement and influence over the project were undermining the future of baseball in Houston, dropped out, asking Smith to buy his shares. Smith obliged, and with Hofheinz the two fully controlled the HSA. Only three of the original shareholders still owned a stake. Hofheinz, backed by Smith's money, strengthened his grip over the stadium and the club.[48]

Construction was begun on the stadium in early 1963; it opened in April 1965. The final cost of the total project was $45,350,000. Most of this, $31.6 million, was financed through county bonds approved by referendum and spent on construction, architectural and engineering fees, land acquisition, and parking lot and access road pavement. Hofheinz and the HSA dropped $6 million dollars to outfit the stadium with luxury skyboxes, restaurants, elaborate scoreboards, and other concessions. City and state agencies and property owners spent the rest on road development around the stadium.[49] The HSA signed a forty-year lease that would theoretically amortize the bonds and pay the stadium's operating expenses.[50]

The stadium aggravated many locals with its rising costs and construction delays. Opposition, however, was relatively anemic and well contained by stadium advocates. Former councilman Gail Reeves argued before the voting on Propositions One and Two in January 1961 that the public shouldn't take on debt to support a private corporation. After the vote, he acknowledged the impossibility of battling with the well-financed promotional campaign supporting the stadium: "It's hard to stop a panzer division with a cap pistol, but we tried. It's hard to fight dollars with sense."[51] A resident of Baytown, a satellite community of Houston, complained to the *Houston Post* that the Dome was "sickening. Imperial Rome had nothing on us. . . . We have overcrowded hospitals. We have a populace of questionable morality which voted money by the millions for the unneeded stadium, but voted down a . . . tax for the relief of our unfortunates who are ill, and in dire need of adequate medical care."[52] A high school teacher suggested, "The voters should have air conditioned the schools instead of the stadium."[53] Larry McMurtry, writing for the progressive *Texas Observer* after the stadium opening, likely reflected the opinions of a silent minority in Houston:

> Pallid though the argument may appear, it seemed a bit conscienceless for a city with leprous slums, an inadequate charity hospital, a mediocre public library, a needy symphony, and other cultural and humanitarian deficiencies to sink more than $31 million in public funds into a ballpark. (Conscienceless, but not surprising.

Houston is the kind of boom city that will endorse almost any amount of municipal vulgarity so long as it has a chance of making money. Here, it is customary to build in order to steal, and however questionable the motive, it means that all sorts of public marvels do get built.)[54]

The stadium was certainly a marvel—a concession made by its harshest critics. But as it was being built, the Houston Colt .45s would have to make do with something rather less marvelous: the short-lived Colt Stadium.

Colt Stadium, Baseball's "Old Wild West"

Colt Stadium, the first home of major league baseball in Houston, was constructed in a corner of the future Astrodome's parking lot. The 33,000-seat stadium was originally estimated to cost just $800,000, it being little more than an assortment of simple, uncovered banks of seats. Hofheinz's peculiar and extravagant demands, however, drove the bill to $2 million. Gabe Paul, Houston's initial general manager, had wanted the team to play at Buff Stadium (renamed Busch Stadium in 1953, in acknowledgment of the brewery that owned its parent club, the St. Louis Cardinals). It had been the home of Houston's minor league teams from 1928 to 1961. The 12,000-seat park—featuring a Spanish revival, tiled-roof stucco main entry—sat atop an eighteen-acre site adjacent railroad tracks and the Gulf Freeway, about one mile southeast of downtown Houston. Buff Stadium sat directly atop one of Houston's lines of racial division, nestled up to areas to the southwest and northwest that were almost entirely African American. A predominantly Latino census tract reached to just a few blocks north of the park, while the area east was almost entirely white.[55] Paul reasoned that the city's baseball fans would be so excited about having a major league team that they'd gladly go to the old grounds. Hofheinz was less interested in baseball die-hards; he hoped to draw those casual customers who might be put off by driving to an old ballpark situated as it was. Paul's interest in putting together a good baseball product was at odds with Hofheinz's commitment to putting on a show, or as Hofheinz would later put it, "I guess I scared the hell out of Paul. Paul had been in business too long to have the imagination required for the job we needed done here."[56]

Hofheinz's "imagination" hatched a western-themed ballpark bordering on the surreal. A writer for the *New York Daily News* called Colt Stadium "the damndest [stadium] you ever saw . . . its atmosphere is a blend of Disneyland and the old wild west."[57] A visit to Colt Stadium began in the thirteen-thousand-car parking lot branded with names like "Matt Dillon Territory" and "Wyatt Earp Territory"—heroes of the western frontier both real and fictional. Parking attendants wore white overalls, orange Stetsons, and blue neckerchiefs. At the stadium gates, customers encountered turnstile attendants in 1880s pillbox-

FIGURE 49. Colt Stadium (bottom) was home to the major league Houston Colt .45s from 1962 to 1964. The simple, single-deck structure was built quickly, though expensively (costing two million dollars thanks to some of Hofheinz's add-ons). It was built in the future parking lot of the Astrodome; the foundation of that stadium is visible here (top). RGD 0006-0362, HOUSTON PUBLIC LIBRARY, HOUSTON METROPOLITAN RESEARCH CENTER.

style baseball caps, blue-and-white blazers, and orange pants. The Triggerettes, the Colts' female ushers, wore pinstriped blouses and skirts—blue stripes on white, with orange piping—as well as blue-and-orange pillbox baseball caps.

The Triggerettes escorted fans to extravagantly colored seats: chartreuse, turquoise, burnt orange, or flamingo, depending on the section. Many of these seats were located behind seventy-five-foot dugouts, which were intentionally made much longer than standard dugouts because, according to Hofheinz, "everybody wants a box seat behind the dugout." As people made their way to the seats, they heard a Dixieland band made up of banjo, clarinet, trumpet, and trombone honking out southern tunes as the players warmed up. On the field, the grounds crew wore fluorescent orange coveralls, blue cowboy boots with orange trim, and blue cowboy hats. If fans got tired of watching the poor play of the Colts on the field, they could retreat to the brightly colored umbrellas in the picnic area behind the right-field stands or stop by the concession stands that reminded a reporter of "a carnival, each booth decorated with strings of pennants and splashes of vivid colors."[58] Stadium programs boasted that visitors were "pleasantly surprised by the appearance of colorful Colt Stadium, which provided an appealing eyeful to fans used to the drab green of most major league baseball parks."[59] Certainly, all that color made an impression. Multiple sportswriters referred to the stadium as "a riot of color."[60] Players called it "the rainbow sherbet."[61]

The Wild Western pantomime was enhanced for the stadium's high rollers in the Fast Draw Club, a private bar and restaurant for season ticket holders willing to pony up the yearly $150 membership fee. It seemed to be a saloon straight out of the television series *Gunsmoke*, housed in a temporary building near the main gate. Bartenders—in straw hats, striped shirts, vests, and stiff cuffs and collars, sporting handlebar moustaches—manned an eighty-foot-long, brass-trimmed mahogany bar accented with spittoons. Chandeliers hung from the ceiling, as did a saloon girl balancing on a swing high above the bar. The walls were decorated with prints of old baseball players and, according to Joseph Sheehan of the *New York Times*, "Rubens-like paintings, including one of a reclining nude mischievously retitled [*sic*] 'Safe at Home.'" If not perched atop a bar stool, patrons sat in tavern

FIGURE 50. Buff Stadium (later renamed Busch Stadium) was Houston's old minor league baseball park, pictured here in 1960. RGD 5-7493, HOUSTON PUBLIC LIBRARY, HOUSTON METROPOLITAN RESEARCH CENTER.

chairs at sturdy oaken tables. Waitresses in low-cut ruffled gowns, net stockings, and lacy garters (equipped with toy pistols) patrolled the dining hall, along with a chef astride a small wagon, dishing out "Braggin' Beans," "Cow Country Corn Pones," "Hell Fire Stew," "Branding Iron Sourdough Bread," and "Cow Puncher Coffee." A player piano rocked the hall with songs from the 1890s. Sheehan was moved to claim, "[It] outshines in lavish splendor the most ornate eating and drinking parlor of Denver's gold-rush days."[62]

The team's western identity was accentuated through publications and souvenirs. Most Houston Colt game programs in the franchise's first three seasons of play featured a western theme. Pistols, wood grains, knobby decorative typeface that recalled frontier newspapers, cowboys, and buxom saloon belles in fishnet stockings marked club publications during its occupation of Colt Stadium. The Colt .45 handgun was central to the club's identity in its early years—an easy signifier of a western frontier attitude that Houston's leaders often celebrated. The gun was so important to team identity that it not only was part of the club's logo but even made it onto the home uniforms—a six-shooter stretched across player chests, underlining "Colts." Fans could buy a stake in this image by purchasing a range of Colt .45 souvenirs at the stadium and through the mail—T-shirts, replica uniforms, head scarves, pajamas, jackets, key chains, and cigarette lighters, all adorned with the iconic six-shooters.[63] The western charade even extended off the field; Hofheinz employed fashion designers to produce cowboy ensembles for players to wear on road trips—outfits that "would make Gene Autry's fancy $300 duds look drab by comparison," according to Frank Finch of the *Los Angeles Times*.[64] Team members objected to the circus-like atmosphere that the powder-blue outfits seemed to invite, and the dress code was scrapped halfway through the 1962 season.[65]

All this Disneyfied fantasy and color was an elaborate bait and switch—compensation for what was a Spartan stadium in the most trying of climates. Stadium programs claimed that the stadium was "comfortable" in addition to being colorful, but few would have agreed.[66] Structurally the stadium was little more than "a glorified assemblage of wooden steps with folding chairs atop them," as Ray Sons of the *Chicago Daily News* put it.[67] A reporter from the *New York World-Telegram* called it "a wooden plant resembling a vast bleacher" and claimed that if the fans continued their coordinated stamping of feet, he could imagine "the whole she-bang collapsing and everybody drowning in an oil field."[68] But worse—much worse—than the amateurish banks of stands was the physical reality of watching and playing baseball in Houston—a city of unrelenting heat, unwavering humidity, and plagues of mosquitoes. Robert Lipsyte of the *New York Times* was as unimpressed with the stadium as he was with the mediocre team, writing: "The Houston Colts are as interesting as a swamp. Their field is hot and fetid and damp, and it is said that the mosquitos are big enough to take infield practice with the regulars."[69] The heat and humidity, which prompted broadcaster Harry Caray to announce a game in his under-

FIGURE 51. The Wild West was central to the early identity of Houston's baseball club; stadium programs celebrated gun-slinging frontiersmanship when the team was known as the Colt .45s in its first few years of existence. A. BARTLETT GIAMATTI RESEARCH CENTER, NATIONAL BASEBALL HALL OF FAME.

wear, was made all the more miserable by rigorous swarms of insects.[70] Concession stands sold insect repellent along with the traditional ballpark fare, and outfielders carried small cans of it onto the field when playing defense. Player Carl Warwick claimed, "It wasn't much more than a swamp to start with, and when they dug that huge hole in the ground for the dome it seemed like every mosquito in town found it."[71] Mosquitoes coupled with the heat and humidity made the park a truly dismal place at times. Player Rusty Staub recalled, "I don't care what ballpark they ever talk about being the hottest place on the face of the earth, Colt Stadium was it. There was just no relief, no place to hide. It was the hottest stadium that's ever existed."[72] In a game with the Dodgers in June 1962, seventy-eight fans were treated for heat exhaustion. During that series, one starting pitcher lost fifteen pounds pitching just four innings. An umpire had to retire from a game, faint from the heat. A *Los Angeles Times* headline captured the spirit most visiting clubs surely felt after a series at Colt Stadium: "Dodgers Happy to Leave Town After Summer Roasts Houston."[73] Houston's baseball fans, however, didn't enjoy their opponents' luxury of leaving town. They counted the days to when the domed stadium, being constructed just a few hundred feet away from Colt Stadium, would provide them relief from the heat, humidity, and mosquitoes.

The move from Colt Stadium to the Astrodome was a remarkable one for spectators and players alike. The team was rebranded as the Astros, as the HSA put aside the old Wild West signifiers of the Colt .45s and embraced a modern, progressive image resonant with the new NASA Manned Space Program headquarters just south of the city. It replaced its old six-shooter logo for an atomically themed one, featuring an image of the Dome as a nucleus being orbited by baseballs. Customers followed the team into a new stadium that was no dusty old saloon from an imagined frontier past but the most modern of buildings—a structure "like a giant space ship that came in from another planet," according to a reporter, a stadium that another writer thought "belongs on Mars instead of on Earth."[74]

The Astrodome, Progress, and Modern Masculinity

Larry McMurtry, having arrived early on his first visit to the stadium, spent an hour or so before game time in his seat, "perusing a fascinating compendium called *Inside the Astrodome*, a book I would love to review." *Inside the Astrodome* was the definitive stadium guidebook, published by the HSA. The glossy magazine, 260 pages in length and one dollar in cost, was "a book you will want to preserve in your home library," according to its introductory address to readers. McMurtry captured the essence of the text in his brief description: "It contained a letter from the President, another from the governor, a quote from Coleridge (guess which), a detailed comparison of the Astrodome and the Roman Colosseum, and page after page of Staggering Statistics on the Dome. The stadium's ice plant can produce 18 tons of ice a day, for example—no one in this climate can fail to be impressed with such a figure."[75]

The guidebook—a back-slapping combination of self-congratulatory celebration, explanation, and advertisements—was the most coherent source of information on the stadium, presenting a unified message about what the operators and designers hoped to accomplish there. McMurtry's précis hinted at the book's dominant messages: the Astrodome was the product of great men and their visions (befitting of presidential letters), a monument for the ages (on par with the Colosseum), and a marvel on a scale hitherto unknown (comprehensible only through page after page of measurements and figures).

Though the stadium had many critics who opposed it on a range of issues from its financing to its impact on stadium culture, virtually no one disagreed with the guidebook's central points: that it emanated from the effort, savvy, and vision of scientists, engineers, and civic leaders, particularly Hofheinz, and that it was a structure without parallel, not only within the sporting world but beyond it. *Inside the Astrodome* crystallized this version of the stadium in a single volume; it was an interpretive device for visitors like McMurtry sitting in the stadium's air-conditioned comfort, settled into its cushioned theater seats after dining in its restaurants, entranced by its mesmerizing scoreboard, perhaps even watching the game on the field. The book comprehensively proposed the stadium as a symbol of human progress at the apex of modern know-how—an exercise in masculine expertise at a time when masculinity seemed feminized and society seemed soft, given over to comfort and consumption rather than big ideas and national purpose.

Many of the book's opening pages were platforms for expressions of stadium support from political celebrities and the self-congratulations of many of Houston's leaders. These commendations crystallized the stadium as an example of the vision and doggedness of humankind generally and Houstonians specifically. On reproduced White House letterhead, President Lyndon Johnson told R. E. Smith and Roy Hofheinz of the HSA, "You and the people of Houston and Harris County have shown the World what men can accomplish when imagination, energy and sheer determination are combined in one tremendous project. The Astrodome will stand as a deserved tribute to the genius of its planners, to be welcomed by all those who respect industry and dedication." Texas governor John B. Connally agreed: "The Astrodome is truly one of the great marvels of our time and a wonder of the world. . . . This edifice is a tribute to the imagination, ingenuity, courage and abilities of all who have made it possible."[76]

Houston's civic leaders took up this symbolism and linked it to the material prosperity and comfort of area citizens. Mayor Louie Welch mused, "Through the transparent dome of this stadium, visitors to our city will be able, at night, to see the stars. This will serve to remind them that we in this city and county are always reaching for the stars. We are constantly searching for new and striking ways of adding to the prosperity, culture and

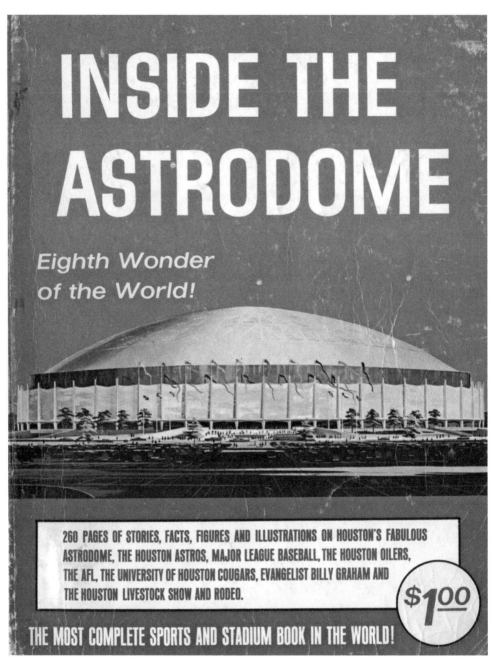

FIGURE 52. *Inside the Astrodome*, the definitive guide to the stadium, published by the Houston Sports Association. A. BARTLETT GIAMATTI RESEARCH CENTER, NATIONAL BASEBALL HALL OF FAME.

contentment of our teeming and progressive population." As Johnson and Connally suggested, the stadium epitomized human endeavor, but Welch tied this endeavor to specific goals—prosperity foremost among them.[77] Gail Whitcomb, president of the chamber of commerce, stated this local commitment to material prosperity more flatly, calling the stadium "a civic and commercial asset" whose value rested in its attraction of spenders and their "massive purchasing power" to the area for events. This led him to the conclusion, "The citizens of Harris County displayed far-reaching vision when they approved the bond issues which made this Stadium a reality." For Whitcomb and other Houston business leaders, vision and imagination were driven by consumption, business, and the growth of both in the city.[78]

The Astrodome symbolized progress, and not just to those "great men" who had the political pull to get their pictures and words into the program's early pages. Advertisers wagered on this trope as well, borrowing a bit of the stadium's visionary glamour by affiliation. An advertisement for a financial company quoted Daniel Webster: "Let us, in this, our day and generation, perform something to be remembered." Below this, the company celebrated the stadium, what it stood for, and the men who delivered it: "We have the deepest admiration for Messrs. Smith, Hofheinz, Judge Elliott and the Harris County Commissioners Court, as men of foresight who brought into reality a vision, for Houston and the nation, in creating 'something which will be remembered for generations.'"[79]

Hofheinz was the star of the Astrodome. Most agreed that the stadium would likely have not been constructed without his commitment and acumen. But Hofheinz was also a magnet for reporters—particularly those from outside Texas—who were mesmerized by his style. He was a huckster and promoter extraordinaire, a persuasive salesman of ideas who was charismatic to many, gratingly alienating to others. A walking caricature of himself, he would have been absurd had he been less effective. *Inside the Astrodome* cast Hofheinz as the inventor of the entire concept of a roofed stadium, a building shaped by his dreams of constructing an enormous covered shopping center, his observation of plant growth in an air-conditioned room in his house, and a visit to the Colosseum in Rome in the mid-1950s. Hofheinz supposedly began thinking about covering a stadium when he learned of the velarium used at the Colosseum, pulled over the stadium in inclement weather. Buckminster Fuller convinced him that with a large enough budget he could cover any size space. After he added a room onto his house and noticed how quickly plants grew in it, Hofheinz claimed, "It looked to me like the plants grew three times as fast in the air-conditioned room as they did out-of-doors. This fact along with what I had learned from Buckminster Fuller stuck in my mind, and later was to form the basis for pioneering the Domed Stadium."[80]

This "official" origin story, featuring Hofheinz's ingenuity, disregarded recent stadium proposals across the country and even in Houston—extravagant designs that prefigured

FIGURE 53. Roy Hofheinz, signature cigar in hand, surveys his creation from a luxury suite high above the Astrodome playing field. RGD 0006-1086, HOUSTON PUBLIC LIBRARY, HOUSTON METROPOLITAN RESEARCH CENTER.

a monumental stadium like the Astrodome. Famously eccentric oilman Glenn McCarthy had publicized plans for a covered stadium, which would have a retractable aluminum roof, in Houston in 1950. It would have seated one hundred ten thousand, with potential expansion to one hundred eighty thousand, and be constructed within blocks of McCarthy's Shamrock Hotel—which was, incidentally, blocks from the Astrodome site (and where Hofheinz spent much of his time, in Suite 18A, as the Dome was constructed).[81] *Inside the Astrodome*'s article on the stadium's origins noted O'Malley's attempts to build a covered stadium in Brooklyn in the early 1950s—though this acknowledgment didn't seem to complicate, in the writer's mind, Hofheinz's claims to originality. His plan for a domed stadium was hardly unique in the 1950s; and yet Hofheinz's version of an origin story trumped all other accounts and was widely circulated in public discourse, particularly among Houstonians.[82]

Photographs accompanying the *Inside the Astrodome* story on Hofheinz and appearing in magazine and newspapers profiles reinforced his intellectual and political ownership of the project; these engaged visual clichés common to stadium publications in Houston and elsewhere. Photos often posed civic leaders, sports club executives, and engineers as men of action and authority. In *Inside the Astrodome*, Hofheinz was staged with a miniature model of the Dome, removing its roof as though he were Zeus checking in on a tractable human population below. He was pictured at groundbreaking ceremonies, commanding the attention of well-dressed dignitaries—Houston's rich and powerful. In another, he held a cigar and looked pensively into the distance, seeming to contemplate his next revolutionary project for the people of Houston. He was pictured in a hard hat, under the stadium's incomplete frame, pointing, directing, explaining—another photographic cliché that signified authority, technical expertise, and control.[83] Such photographs appeared throughout club publications, as well as in newspapers and magazines—sometimes featuring Hofheinz and sometimes not, but always positioning men (and men alone) as directors, as commanders, as helmsmen of the engineered and technological.[84]

Men like Hofheinz controlled a project that was staggering in scale—a structure regularly referred to as a "wonder of the world." Photographs provided evidence of that human control by breaking down the construction process into a series of steps, producing large-scale "how-to" manuals for readers—many of whom were no doubt tinkerers and model-builders back at home, as was the postwar fashion for suburban men.[85] *Inside the Astrodome* featured a nine-page spread of twenty-three photos of the construction process itself, visually laying out the monumentality of the task. There were photos of the massive foundational hole, the ferro-concrete support walls, the placing of massive support towers (that looked like familiar Texas oil derricks) for the roof, the raising of the circular steel frame, and the laying of lamella trusses across the towers in a gigantic metal spider web. Captions let readers in on the inside dope of construction specifications, wowing them with figures; for example, they were told, "The key to the dome is the 300-ton tension ring, one continuous band of steel which circles the stadium and rests on 72 steel columns, each capable of supporting 220,000 pounds, or a total of 16,000,000 pounds." Text emphasized the engineered precision of the stadium and linked it to aerospace technologies, telling readers, "Wind-tunnel tests were made on a 1/16th inch model by McDonnell Aircraft Corp., to determine wind pressures, uplift pressures and various other computations." The difficulties and dangers of putting together such a monumental structure were outlined in detail surely beyond the comprehension of most. Together, these photographs and texts highlighted the accomplishment by revealing a process that united brains and brawn—one that was painstaking, deliberate, and guided at every step by scientific expertise.[86]

The massive superstructure of the Astrodome was matched to an interior stocked with automated devices and modern comforts, tangible evidence of the "magic" of science. Visitors were told, "The sports fan who comes to the ASTRODOME will, without actually knowing it, step right into the middle of the Age of Automation."[87] Of course, every visitor to the Astrodome would have been fully aware of the stadium's automated character, as it was promoted so roundly in HSA materials and circulated so widely in stadium discourse.

The most obvious of the stadium's modern comforts and signifiers of automation was its climate control. Promoters crowed, "Houston and Harris County have provided 'the world's largest room air conditioner' to give patrons of the Astrodome solid comfort the like of which earth man has never before experienced at an athletic contest." Numbers and figures tried to relate the monumentality of the accomplishment: the forty-one million cubic feet of space in the Dome required "four centrifugal refrigeration machines supplying 6,600 tons of cooling capacity" to regulate the temperature. These figures were also translated into layman's terms as "approximately the amount of cooling given off by the daily melting of enough ice to cover a football field to a depth of nearly five feet."[88]

The air-conditioning was controlled by a "modern, revolutionary Control Center, nicknamed 'The Brain.'" Readers were told that this was the "biggest advance in customer comfort in sports annals." The Brain was monitored and manipulated at a seventeen-foot-long console, combining "the most modern system of electronic and mechanical gadgets, gauges, scanners, testers and instruments of its type ever put together on one operation." Its sensory reach was so complete that it replaced the labor equivalent of 280 men. The Brain cost $333,000 (though reportedly much more in development by Honeywell), required 8 miles of instrument tubing, and consisted of 150 miles of wiring. As if the reader could make any sense of it, he or she was told that the Brain controlled more than 200 valves that ranged in size from half an inch to 14 inches, that the device operation was enabled by "more than 2,000 relays mounted in 50 individual fan room panels," that the 400 remote weather measuring devices had a "display accuracy of up to one part in 1/1000th," and that the system could scan "400 data input points periodically at a speed of three points per second." This technical nonsense undoubtedly impressed many who valued numbers and measurements out of hand as an expression of scientific expertise and precision. All this centralized automation made the system more responsive and less error prone than human-run operations, according to the program. However, men were still in control of the magical device: to illustrate the point, operators were photographed punching buttons on machines, reading computer screens, and checking power readings.[89]

Climate control required a roof, and the roof was designed to be less a barrier to the outside than a filter—allowing in sunlight, keeping out Houston's tropical humidity, mosquitoes, and torrential downpours. One of the most celebrated technologies in the stadium was the Lucite paneling of the roof. These translucent panels would allow an indoor space to remain connected to the outdoors. The stadium needed light; architects thought there would be "something oppressive about sitting under the [light] arcs in mid-afternoon." Lucite solved the problem. It was, readers were informed, a substance both "beautiful" and "rugged." Initially introduced in 1939 as a synthetic crystal, this DuPont acrylic resin was applied to gunner cockpits of World War II—a quality advertised by stadium promoters, giving it the technological credibility of advanced weaponry, a salient association in the midst of the Cold War. Its use in the Astrodome was presented as just another milestone in this miracle material's early life. Lucite was, readers were told, "one of the most beautiful of the plastics. It comes close to realizing the chemist's dream of organic glass."[90]

The stadium as a whole was viewed as a victory for chemical invention—of mankind's ability to artificially improve on the natural world. An article in *Chemical Week*, an industry trade journal, called the stadium "a monument to imaginative application of chemical products in construction."[91] Readers of *Inside the Astrodome*—many of whom worked in Houston oil, gas, and petrochemical industries—were instructed, "The great dome itself started life as hydrocarbons imprisoned in oil and gas deposits under Gulf Coast farmlands. Freed and transformed by the modern magic of petrochemistry in one or more of the refining and processing complexes dotting the coastal landscape, some became the methacrylate base for the 4,596 'Lucite' plastic skylights and others provided the raw material for the waterproof synthetic rubber skin over the solid portions of the span." The foam cushioning of the seats relied on the work of petrochemists who "whip up nylon from ammonia, cyclohexane and benzene," all based in natural gas. The polyurethane likewise was derived from natural gas. Natural gas powered the air-conditioning, it heated the water for the hot dogs and steaks found in the range of food stands and restaurants, and it even greened the grass as a base for fertilizers. "Thus it is," the writer concluded, "that the great Gulf Coast community of oil and gas people—from roughnecks to research scientists—can point to the ASTRODOME as something very special indeed. . . . Examples of an industry's impact just don't come this big very often."[92]

Even the grass, "the green velvet floor . . . the most pampered grass in the nation," was intricately engineered. Its scientific and official name, Tifway 419 Bermuda, distinguished it from a pedestrian suburban lawn. This grass "was not merely grown" but "conceived, developed and nurtured." Dr. M. H. Ferguson, a Texas A&M agronomist, directed this development. Tifway 419 Bermuda combined African Bermuda, common Bermuda, Merion bluegrass, Pennlawn Red Fescue (which had been developed by breeders at Penn State University), and Poa Trivialis. In preparation for the seeding, the Astrodome's topsoil "was thoroughly cleaned and sterilized before the seed was even sown." The Davidson Grass Farm took a truckload of soil from the inside of the stadium and brought it to its plant, where it was "purified" and fumigated with methyl bromide—eighteen hundred pounds in all. Readers learned that increased carbon dioxide levels, due to spectator exhalation, actually helped the grass grow by increasing photosynthesis. Thus the Dome provided a closed ecosystem for its grass that improved upon nature's design.[93] The following year, Hofheinz would replace this grass with an even more unnatural replacement, installing a fully synthetic surface branded "AstroTurf."[94]

Central to stadium discourse was the notion that the Dome had made weather irrelevant through the wonders of man-made technology. The HSA told visitors, "The searing Texas sun will still beat down, the angry Gulf Coast winds will still howl and the tropical rains will still fall, but NOT on the spectators in the ASTRODOME." Companies inserted their products into this narrative of scientific control. A DuPont advertisement asserted, "Skylights of acrylic sheet cast from Du Pont LUCITE help Harris County Domed Stadium conquer the Texas climate." The Buffalo Forge Company, which made some of the Dome's fans and air-conditioning units, claimed, "This beautiful Texas weather . . . was made in Buffalo!"[95] Climate could be conquered and weather "made"—commentators readily embraced the stadium as a symbol of human victory over the natural. Wells Twombly, writing for the *Houston Chronicle*, announced, "Man has triumphed over nature."[96] Syndicated sportswriter Red Smith noted that the person who coined the saying "Everybody talks about the weather but nobody does anything about it" didn't live to see "the revolutionary all-weather, temperature-controlled, bubble-topped, science-fiction hothouse which will shelter, but not conceal, Houston's Astros."[97] A syndicated story called it a "monument to man's war with nature."[98] A year later, Mickey Herskowitz borrowed that line, claiming, "What the Domed Stadium will really be is a monument to man's war with nature."[99]

The Astrodome was a prominent expression of what cultural historian Michael L. Smith has called a "global engineering ethos" that stretched from the 1930s into the mid-1960s. Central to this ethos was the rhetoric of conquest, particularly humankind's conquest of nature. Natural environments were portrayed as challenges to or sites for large-scale projects. Gigantism was central to this vision—dams, nuclear plants, space stations, all in their massive scale, signified human triumph over the natural. Though critiques of this ethos were increasingly vocal in the 1960s—Jane Jacobs's battle with the "master builder" Robert Moses in New York being a prominent example—these ideologies of engineered conquest remained salient for many mainstream Americans. Exhibits like Futurama II at the 1964 World's Fair depicted what Smith called "technocolonial" projects, locating people in futuristic communities on the moon, under the sea, in the jungle, and in the desert.[100]

In Houston, Texas, where everything was presumably bigger, this ethos thrived: Exhibit A was the Dome. It was so big that "a small neighborhood village could be put underneath the vast caverns of the Astrodome." Stadium lighting was "powerful enough to light a city of 20,000 persons." It housed 14,000 square feet of HSA offices, "enough for seven medium sized homes." It included clubhouses, dressing rooms, equipment storage, showers, interview rooms, loading docks, ticket rooms, and other offices. A reporter from Dallas thought the Astrodome was "almost like a city in itself."[101] The stadium was pitched as an enclosed world, a utopian space of consumption, entertainment, and functionality—a pitch that would have resonated with other technocolonial propositions of the time, demonstrating a thorough faith in the products of science.[102]

Steering all these techno-utopian projects was man—the engineer, the scientist, the politician, or the businessman of progressive vision. The "helmsman" has been a prominent figure throughout American cultural history, a loaded signifier in a society that had historically associated physical mobility with not only individual autonomy but also national destiny. Helmsmen like sea captains and aviators mastered their environments with technological instruments. This mastery made them useful icons for advertisers; the image of masculine expertise exhibited by the helmsman could be transferred to products—most often automobiles in the 1950s and 1960s. A consumer could purchase the car and, with it, the helmsman's expertise. The utility of the helmsman figure was salient in part because of the ambiguous relationship of humankind to mechanization, which had historically been understood as both a source of power and a threat to autonomy. The helmsman fused man and technology together in a powerful alliance, mastering the threat of the mechanical and channeling its promise. The appeal of this masculinized, mechanized power was particularly resonant in the postwar era, in a period of the "organization man," when bureaucratic values of cooperation and security were also characteristics of an ideal woman. The helmsman in control of the machine helped counter anxieties that postwar men were becoming womanly.[103] While the Astrodome was not operable or pilot-able in the way of a car, airplane, or boat, it was a highly technologized object and experience—something that promoters and reporters never ceased noting. The Astrodome celebrated a brand of masculinity grounded in technological mastery, scientific expertise, and progressive ambition at a time when the seeming cohesiveness of the postwar era appeared weakened and the "national purpose" was being thoroughly and publicly questioned.

In the late 1950s and early 1960s, many Americans fretted over the "flabbiness" of what seemed a materialistic, satisfied, directionless public that was indifferent to the threats of the Cold War and insensible of any national mission. A national space program addressed this problem, as did a series of studies intended to reinvigorate a sense of national purpose. President Eisenhower appointed a Commission on National Goals in 1960. A Rockefeller-funded project studied national purpose, and Henry Luce ran a series of essays on the topic in *Life*.[104] Kennedy's New Frontier and Johnson's Great Society were sweeping national projects that coalesced individual goals into a national program. Arguably, the Astrodome project itself symbolized the "problem," as it was an elaborate vehicle for entertainment and consumption; however, the rhetoric of the Astrodome project resonated with high-minded calls for an invigorated national purpose and the grand social endeavors of the 1960s intended to aggregate and realize a national purpose—and in doing so, perhaps quelled Houstonians' anxieties about their considerable public investment in what seemed a clear expression of social decadence. For in the end, that was where all this masculine endeavor and technical ingenuity led: a democracy of comfort for men of all classes and, crucially, their wives.

The Modern Spectator and a Democracy of Comfort

Houston mayor Louis Welch suggested the stadium's earthbound progressiveness in the opening pages of *Inside the Astrodome*, when he linked the stargazing aspirations of Houstonians to "prosperity, culture, and contentment."[105] The stadium on one hand could be a symbol of the technological mind and masculine control; on the other it was a material entity that satisfied and validated Houstonians' mundane desires for comfort and entertainment. Alongside celebrations of technological progressiveness were tributes to the stadium's many comforts and luxuries that set it apart from stadiums of the past, recasting it as an upscale space where not only Houston's jet set and oil barons could see, be seen, and seal their big-money deals with firm handshakes but also Houston's hoi polloi could enjoy a "democracy of goods" and partake in the consumable prosperity of postwar progress.

Hofheinz, the HSA, and like-minded newspapermen embraced the seemingly contradictory notion that the Astrodome was a site of both equality and distinction, a place where everyone enjoyed the material fruits of modern progress—though, presumably, some more "equally" than others. Hofheinz bragged to a *New York Times* reporter: "Now let's talk about real grandeur, about the guy who spends $1.50 to see a ball game, and can sit on a foam rubber [seat], and have a reasonable meal without having to eat hot dogs. If we've established grandeur we've done it for the bleacher fan and the country club member."[106] *Inside the Astrodome* proclaimed, "Sit down sports fan! Your day is here. A ticket to the Astrodome makes you a king . . . for the first time in sports history you can watch a baseball game from deep-cushioned, foam-padded, nylon-upholstered chairs. You will be able to sit in a chair as comfortable as any found in the world's finest theatres and opera houses."[107] Visitors were told that the days of hard bleachers were over, as there was "a seat for everyone from pavilion to luxury boxes." Gary Cartwright, of the *Dallas News*, alleged curiously, "This is EVERY MAN'S STADIUM—from the cushioned center field section at $1.50 to the upper rim of blue suites which can be grabbed for $18,000 a year"—a claim that was reprinted in the souvenir guide.[108] Cartwright's formulation at once appropriated the democratic suggestiveness of the "every man" and gutted it of this meaning; for him, "every man" didn't signify the typical or the ordinary but rather each person's socioeconomic distinctiveness and ability to pay. This wasn't a democracy of equality but merely the right to consume at whatever level one could afford.[109]

This conflation of equality and hierarchy—the idea that equality meant access to elevated, though still differentiated, degrees of comfort and luxury—was shot through the stadium's interior spaces and discourse, most obviously in the presentation of stadium restaurants available (and unavailable) to customers. The stadium featured five separate restaurants, ranging from the elite Skydome Club, restricted to occupants of the luxury boxes and featuring a view of downtown Houston from its 210-foot-long glass window, to the plebeian Domeskeller, located on the stadium's bottom level and featuring a view of part of the playing field through mesh wire. Descriptions of the restaurants in *Inside the Astrodome* attempted a delicate balancing act, on the one hand denoting the relative advantages of each space, on the other hand hedging these distinctions by pointing out similarities. In the Skydome, Japanese women prepared food at the patron's table; each owner was given a gold spatula to serve himself or herself. Five-course meals were served in the Astrodome Club, a private membership club for season ticket holders. The Trailblazer, open to the public, dished up its pre-prepared entrées (three to choose from) on molded trays; nonetheless, readers were reassured, "the food is comparable to that served in the ASTRODOME Club." Another spot down the totem pole was the Countdown Cafeteria. While the means of distribution—"two super-speed lines" that "make it possible to feed more than 1,000 persons in a reasonable length of time"—might have suggested a decline in food quality, and although "the menu is limited to five or six basic items," program readers were told the offerings remained "comparable to [those of] the clubs." The restaurants were thus simultaneously different and equal, as stadium promoters tried to convince patrons that "every taste and every appetite is catered to with a variety of food and speed of service never attempted before at a baseball park, football field, race track or convention center."[110] They were most certainly correct in the latter claim and were often successful in convincing patrons that difference and equality were two sides of the same

FIGURE 54. Even those in the far reaches of the upper deck enjoyed cushioned seating in air-conditioned comfort—chairs "as comfortable as any found in the world's finest theatres and opera houses," according to promoters. RGD 0006-0001, HOUSTON PUBLIC LIBRARY, HOUSTON METROPOLITAN RESEARCH CENTER.

coin. As writer Larry McMurtry put it after visiting the stadium: "Everyone who comes to the Astrodome considers they have escaped the lower class."[111]

The most genuinely democratic form of comfort in the stadium was the air-conditioning—a comfort and technology that all enjoyed and that allowed the stadium to behave in very un-stadium-like ways. The roof that made the stadium "all weather" and air-conditioned was, at the bottom of it, the stadium's reason for being. It made events possible on the hottest and wettest of days, it allowed for the installation of cushioned theater seats, and it enabled people to dress up in ways appropriate to the stadium's more upscale spaces. The roof inverted the stadium, turning it from an outpost for sporting die-hards into an oasis for sporting illiterates; Hofheinz told Red Smith, "Up to now baseball has been a fair-weather game. We expect to do our biggest business on weekends when the weather is bad." A stadium visitor added, "And on a nice night when it's too stinkin' hot to breathe, people will say, 'Let's go out to the ball park and cool off.'"[112] Once there, the climate control provided, according to *Inside the Astrodome*, "comfort the like of which earth man has never before experienced at an athletic contest."[113]

Houstonians loved their air-conditioning, so much so that the technology became a core component of the city's image. Author James Street called the city an "air conditioned Tower of Babel."[114] The chamber of commerce claimed that Houston was "the most air-conditioned city in the nation.[115] One of the first movie theater air-conditioning installations in the South was Houston's eighteen-hundred-seat Texan Theater, where climate control was installed in 1926. Air-conditioning was a central appeal of the movie palaces of the 1920s and 1930s, not only making the spaces more comfortable but also making them seem more modern, progressive, and luxurious—sites where the lower-middle classes could fantasize about upper-class luxury. After World War II, air-conditioning began to seem less a modern novelty than a middle-class necessity—an attitude driven in large part by the air-conditioning industry, which targeted the single-family home as a ripe market in the postwar years. Air-conditioning makers claimed that their products guaranteed comfort, or were even synonymous with it. Ads often spoke directly to women, suggesting that air-conditioning would enhance family togetherness and reduce cleaning. Like household appliances, air-conditioning increasingly seemed an essential part of the suburban ideal of a clean home, healthy and well-behaved children, and happier husbands.[116] Indeed, the Astrodome—even more than Shea Stadium—seemed a postwar suburban home exploded in scale.

It was unapologetically populuxe, celebrating technological and futuristic affectations at every turn. Liz Smith of *Sports Illustrated* noted that the stadium was "full of mechanical marvels."[117] *Inside the Astrodome* celebrated the stadium's automated maintenance and cleaning devices, using language that called to mind the housekeeper's chores in the suburban home. The stadium would be kept "spic and span and shiny new" by a maintenance

FIGURE 55. A table in one of the Astrodome's five restaurants overlooks the field. PHOTO BY MARK KAUFFMAN/TIME & LIFE PICTURES/GETTY IMAGES.

crew of over one hundred for capacity crowds. A "permanent house keeping crew" of twenty-seven was backed up by contracted labor. The "foam-rubber cushioned seats are vacuumed on a continuous basis." The cleaning crew used "24 litter vacuums, 10 vacuum cleaners for seats, automatic scrubbing machines, floor scrubbing and polishing machines, power sweepers and power riding sweepers for the parking lots." Altogether, the HSA estimated the "yearly housekeeping tab" at $250,000–300,000—an amount of "housekeeping" that would have surely impressed many homemakers.[118]

The scoreboard challenged climate control as the stadium's most treasured feature. The HSA called it an "electronic marvel" and boasted, "The $2,000,000 Scoreboard Puts the Aurora Borealis to Shame."[119] The complete board was 474 feet long and over four stories high, and it stretched across the entire outfield above the pavilion seats. It weighed 300 tons, consisted of 1,200 miles of wiring, was lit by over 50,000 bulbs, and was controlled by a 25-foot console board in the press box manned by six technicians and a producer. At either end of the massive board were two illuminated advertising medallions, for which Gulf Oil paid one million dollars for five years.[120] Most of what was called the scoreboard was actually an expansive dark screen pocked with 14,000 fixed lightbulbs that, when illuminated in a pre-orchestrated, animated routine, rendered the celebrated "home run spectacular." At the center of the massive installation was "the world's largest 100 line television screen," which covered 1,800 square feet and was capable of displaying animated or still pictures and messages. This screen was flanked by two 141-by-21-foot electronic boards that provided game statistics and information, plus written messages.

The "home run spectacular" consumed most of the scoreboard's space and mesmerized audiences. After the Astros hit a home run, the forty-five-second routine would begin. The show included images of a baseball exploding from the roof of the stadium and soaring across the screen; two agitated cowboys, kicking their heels and freely discharging their six-shooters (their bullets ricocheted around the board, incredibly missing the two gunmen but filling the screen with streams of light); two fire-snorting steer, with Texan and American flags sprouted from their horns; and a cowboy on horseback wielding a lariat, trying to rope a steer that had appeared on the other side of the board. This spectacular fusion of forward-looking whiz-bang gadgetry and backward-looking Texan iconography then concluded with a multicolored fireworks display, backed with exploding sound effects, covering the entirety of the 474-foot board. In a September 1964 tour of the yet unfinished Astrodome, a guide promised Jerome Holtzman of the *Chicago Sun-Times*, "It's going to be worth the price of admission just to see that scoreboard go off."[121] The 1965 stadium souvenir guidebook dubiously reported, "It has been said that the scoreboard pyrotechnics are so spectacular that some fans will now say: 'Let's go to the Scoreboard tonight,' instead of the tried and true 'Let's go to the ball game.'"[122] Other scoreboard routines, displayed on the video screen, included a player retiring to the shower when an opponent's pitcher was

FIGURE 56. The Astrodome scoreboard lights up after the Astros' Jim Beauchamp hits the stadium's first home run. AP PHOTO.

pulled, the exclamation "Tilt!" when an opponent hit a home run, and the urging, "Go! Go! Go!" If an opponent made it to second base, the television board showed an Astro fall out of the sky and land on that player, followed by the word "WHOA!" The fans then responded, "Whoa!" in unison. A common conceit was a small cavalryman riding across the screen followed by the instruction "CHARGE!" Sometimes a small bull burst across the screen followed by "OLE!" Larry McMurtry, speculating on the relationship between the screen and the game, asserted, "What the game did was provide material for the man who operated the screen"—a subjugation of the game on the field to the entertainment around it. He wondered if fans would have even endured a game between the feeble Mets and the Astros without this artificial stimulation from the "big electronic screen in center field."[123]

The *New Yorker*'s Roger Angell was also reluctantly infatuated with the scoreboard. He confessed, "The giant set is impossible not to look at, and there is no 'off' switch." Although a baseball purist, wholly intent on watching the game on the field, Angell "found that I was giving the game only half my attention; along with everyone else, I kept lifting my eyes to that immense, waiting presence above the players." Multiple times during Angell's visit to Houston, fans started cheering organically (for example, starting to clap rhythmically, in unison) only to be overwhelmed by commands from the board to yell "Charge!" which stifled the fan-generated cheering. When he was leaving a game, he noticed that others weren't discussing the game itself but an episode in the second inning, when the scoreboard controller had accidentally set off the home run spectacular in response to a mere double off the top of the outfield wall. Angell concluded, "The board had been the big hit of the evening."[124]

HSA president Roy Hofheinz would have been pleased by those words. When Angell told Hofheinz that he had seen few fans keeping score manually at an Astrodome game—one of Angell's signifiers of true baseball fandom and engagement—Hofheinz responded, "This park keeps 'em interested enough that they don't *have* to keep busy with a pencil and a scorecard. Why, in most other parks you got nothing to do but watch the game, keep score, and sit on a hard wooden seat. This place was built to keep the fans happy. They've got our good seats, fine restaurants, and our scoreboard to look at, and they don't have to make a personal sacrifice to like baseball."[125] This idea—that baseball was something to be endured rather than enjoyed—suggested that stadiums required a range of carrots to get customers to the ballpark. For Hofheinz, this was progress in the realm of sports entertainment. He told Angell, "We have removed baseball from the rough-and-tumble era. . . . Baseball isn't a game to which your individuals come alone just to watch the game. They come for social enjoyment. They like to entertain and *be* entertained at the ballpark." After describing his conception of the modern baseball consumer, Hofheinz added, "We make a big effort to bring out the ladies."[126] The ideal Astrodome patron was not really there for the baseball, according to Hofheinz; the ideal visitor was there to socialize, entertain, and be entertained. For the men designing the postwar stadium experience, women were essential participants in and markers of such an environment.

Bringing Out the Ladies

Air-conditioning and other entertainments were the precondition, in the minds of many, for attracting women to the stadium. But these new stadium features were not enough. To attract women to the stadium, promoters needed to help women imagine themselves there. The types of "ladies" Hofheinz wanted to draw to the Astrodome, women who would give the stadium a sense of decorum if not prestige, were not the die-hards willing to endure hot and dusty Buff Stadium to satisfy their love of sport—women like "Grandma Brown," who attended nearly every game at the old park in the 1930s and 1940s.[127] This was, after all, a city of predominantly conservative conceptions of womanhood, a city where, according to *Houston Post* reporter George Fuermann, it was "against the law . . . for women to wear slacks."[128] Hofheinz was obsessed with attracting women to the stadium, and Astrodome publications reflected this obsession. While Shea Stadium's promoters subtly inserted women into illustrations in team publications, the HSA relentlessly displayed images of women in stadium space—as users of its luxury suites, as diners in its restaurants and clubs, as curiously arbitrary decorative devices in photos of stadium features. But such imagery didn't just appear in HSA publications like programs, scorecards, and ticket applications; photos staging women in the stadium were also circulated to print media, appearing in newspapers, magazines, and trade journals. The Astrodome was widely advertised—both visually and textually—as a space for women to wear the latest fashions, to enjoy fine foods, and to mingle with others doing the same.[129]

The HSA's efforts to display women in the stadium could produce some rather puzzling images. In many, women were staged without any narrative context in stadium spaces—in front of the scoreboard, inside the baseball dugouts, and riding escalators. Women in these images merely existed in the spaces themselves (and, in the case of the dugouts, in spaces they would never actually populate in the course of a stadium event). Other, more logical scenes staged women in the array of stadium clubs and restaurants. These tableaux, and others like them that appeared in newspapers, often shared certain qualities. Women were prominently featured in the foreground and always paired with men. These couples were always the best-dressed characters in the scene. Patrons in the background tended to be more casually dressed and often male pairings. All the fans depicted were unquestionably white. The desires of the stadium's promoters seemed clear: the ideal patrons of the Astrodome's clubs were white and affluent. Men could come with their old baseball-loving buddies, but these were really spaces to either bring a woman or be one on the arm of a man.

These images of women and men in the Astrodome advanced a new vision of how stadium space should be used and who should use it—one in line with postwar domestic ideals. Women could wordlessly signify class, civility, and respectability, marking the space as female friendly (even female centered at times), elevating it above stereotypical stadium space remembered as male, dirty, hot, and a bit uncivilized. Visual imagery was a subtler accompaniment to Roy Hofheinz's clear and colorful claims. The Astrodome allowed Hofheinz to promise extravagantly, "Women will go to the ball game now because there will be no wind to whip their hairdos, no rain to ruin their dress and no sun to turn them red. The Astrodome will get a promenade of the best-gowned, best-looking and most-influential women ever collected."[130] The HSA's vice president, George Kirksey, agreed, asserting, "Women will take a different view of sports events. Think of it; they can have their hair done, wear a new dress, and come to a ball game as easy and as comfortable as going to the opera."[131]

The interior color was an essential selling point for Hofheinz and the HSA. Shea Stadium was noteworthy for its interior rainbow of seats; Hofheinz one-upped it. Prominent New York sportswriter Dick Young noted "the eye-blinking vividness of the color. . . . The

Shea Stadium pastels are drab by comparison to the color explosion of Houston's seat-spectrum."[132] As at Shea, the seating sections of the Astrodome were a conspicuous source of this color explosion, making it "aflame with color," according to the HSA, and thus "the most eye-appealing stadium in the world." Starting at the bottom, seating levels were lipstick red, coral, burnt orange, terra cotta, black, purple, gold, bronze, and royal blue.[133] Considering the colorful layers of seats, Angell joked, "I had the momentary sensation that I was sinking slowly through the blackberry-brandy layer of a pousse-café."[134] Lou Maysel of the *Austin American* called the Astrodome "an orgy of color" and imagined Hofheinz walking into a paint store, grabbing the color book, and saying, "Give me 500 gallons of each of these colors." Then, Maysel figured, he walked into a fabric shop and "bought up every bolt of eye-dazzling material they had" and told the clerk to rush him "a few thousand yards of 'this, this and that.'"[135] The Astrodome's color extravaganza produced a synesthetic moment for Mickey Herskowitz, who called the color at the stadium opening "deafening." It wasn't just the stadium that was colorful; the people were as well. Herskowitz wrote, "There were the vendors in irredescent [sic] blue coveralls, of the type worn by airplane mechanics; the grounds crew in burnt orange spacesuits and helmets . . . and finally there were the spectators themselves, the men in dress suits and neckties, their ladies in evening wear, as though attending the opera, rather than a baseball game."[136]

If Hofheinz was to be believed, the colors were a tactic for attracting women to the stadium, which in turn was part of a broader strategy to culturally elevate stadium space. He often spoke of the two—color and women—in relation to one another. He told *Sports Illustrated*'s Liz Smith, "I studied up on color psychology and I also studied crowd psychology" and chose colors "designed to get people in the right mood for different things." He continued: "On the blue level, where our most expensive boxes are, we experimented for a week to determine what light looked best on ladies' makeup and clothes. Listen, every day here will be ladies' day."[137] Hofheinz told another reporter, "The domed Stadium was designed for beautiful women. . . . We did a lot of research before choosing the colors. We made sure that each color complemented the complexion and cosmetics and clothing of women. Believe me, it is quite a job when you have to come up with 53 different color schemes [for each of the skybox suites], trying to make each club unique. It took us two weeks alone to get the right color of blue. Many blues would give ladies a pasty-looking complexion."[138] Hofheinz definitely didn't want his ladies looking pasty—especially the elegant women of the stadium's luxury-box blue level.

Hofheinz had allies in Houston newspapers, who helped him make his pitch to the city's women. A photo of local model Elsa Rosborough, family in tow, appeared in "Chic," the fashion insert for the *Houston Post* two months before the stadium opening. The paper branded Rosborough as "one of Houston's most famous and most beautiful models [who] wore the ideal costume for a spectator, whether in the stands or a private box." Another photo featured a young couple, he wearing a madras sport coat, she sporting a two-tone dress. Rosborough's son appeared dressed in a seersucker jacket. The *Houston Post* fashion editor, Virginia Drane McCallon, wrote an accompanying article that promised readers, "The Harris County Domed Stadium should change our ideas on what to wear to a baseball game." She doubted that women would be as dressy as those at English horse races but suggested outfits something more in line with those worn at the Kentucky Derby. That is, unless one would be a guest in what she called "the prestige space boxes," where "covered cocktail clothes" would be appropriate. The private Skydome Club would be, after all, "as elegant as any club."[139]

Rosborough's photo also appeared in the stadium guide, *Inside the Astrodome*, alongside a full-page article titled "Fashion Under the Astrodome." Author Judy Ward, a fashion consultant for Battelstein's department store, previewed how the Astrodome would impact women's dress at sporting events, liberating them to wear all the latest fashions, season to season. "Houston has long been noted for its fashion conscious women," she wrote; however, the heat and sun had impeded their ability to fully express themselves. The Astrodome's air-conditioning would allow "Milady to dress in style, from the tip of her head to the tip of her toe." Ward concluded with the fabulous claim: "It has long been rumored by the male population that the majority of women attend sports events 'to be seen' rather than to view the event, and although this is hotly denied by women, let's admit the ASTRODOME will make history as the most fashionable 'RUNWAY' in America."[140] Ward's closing remark both challenged and conceded the point that a woman's primary function at the stadium was to look stylish. Her reconfiguration of the stadium as a fashion show runway may have been hyperbole, and yet it suggested that well-dressed women would most certainly elevate the stadium's status. It might not be a high-fashion runway, but it would be many notches above a dusty, old baseball park.

The feminization of stadium space was also encouraged by the use of young women as service workers. As evidenced in Shea Stadium and other modern stadiums of the early 1960s, young, attractive workers accented the Astrodome with what seemed a distinctively feminine charm. Female ushers, much like airline stewardesses or retail clerks in suburban shopping centers, marked the space with a feminine allure and sophistication that appealed to men and women alike.

Houston's baseball club hired female ushers at its inception in 1962, in the temporary and western-themed Colt Stadium adjacent the Dome construction site. Ray Sons of the *Chicago Daily News* called attention to these female ushers, comparing them to those who were employed by Andy Frain, whose ushering service oversaw fifty million people per year at sporting events and conventions: "The ushers are girls, called Triggerettes. They

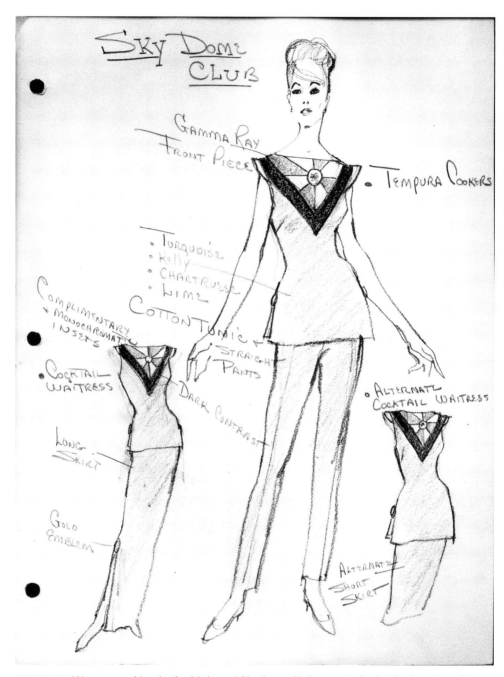

FIGURE 57. Women working in the high-end Skydome Club were to be both elegant and futuristic. Evelyn Norton Anderson, a Houston-based designer, sketched these uniforms featuring "Gamma Ray Front Pieces" for the club's tempura cooks and cocktail waitresses.

MSS 1465-B002F011-001, HOUSTON PUBLIC LIBRARY, HOUSTON METROPOLITAN RESEARCH CENTER.

haven't been in business as long as Andy Frain, but they're prettier." The Triggerettes wore blue-and-white-striped blouses with orange piping on the collars, skirts, and caps of blue and orange. They were "picked for their looks and their manners," according to Hofheinz biographer Edgar Ray; in spite of their loud outfits, their behavior was to suggest modesty and respectability.[141]

When the Houston club moved into the domed stadium in 1965, it was rebranded. The Colt .45s were a western outfit; the Astros were a space-age one. Accordingly, the female ushers were repackaged as Spacettes. At a typical game, 216 Spacettes—monitored by ten Chief Spacettes—guided fans to seats or steered them toward the stadium's restaurants, restrooms, and exits. Spacettes were eighteen to thirty years old.[142] They wore quilted gold lamé suits with blue velvet accents, gloves, and boots. Their orange pillbox hats replicated the Dome itself. Triggerettes had suffered the brutal Houston summers; Spacettes enjoyed the Astrodome's climate control. Sharon Wilhoit, head Spacette, looked forward to her new work environment: "Working conditions in the stadium should be a lot better. We had trouble with our hairdos before in the humidity. Our hairdos will stay now, and our appearances in general should be much improved."[143]

A Spacette's value derived not only from her appearance but also from the way she conducted herself. Teddye Clayton, a staff writer for the *Houston Post* women's section, introduced readers to the Spacettes' training regimen just days before the Astrodome opened. "A 10-Hour course from the John Robert Powers School insures the girls will be as charming as they are helpful," she promised. Spacettes were taught "speech and personality, poise and grooming." Instructors from the Powers School typically worked with models and actresses, helping them fine-tune their social etiquette. The school also trained airline stewardesses; Continental Airlines sent its stewardesses there in the early 1960s.[144]

Clayton's words resonated with those of American Airlines, which told recruits in 1961, "At the Stewardess College, a staff of professionals is on hand to help you learn the proper hair-styling, tricks of good grooming, make-up and figure improvement. You'll learn to walk, talk, and think with new poise."[145] The similarities are telling: Astrodome operators certainly strived to project the sense of glamour and customer service of jet travel.[146] A photo accompanying Clayton's article dramatized such refinement, as a Powers School instructor demonstrates proper posture for young Spacettes. The scene is staged field-side in some of the stadium's priciest seats, subtly weaving together many of the stadium's professed virtues: beauty, domesticity, comfort, and luxury.[147]

Women, the use of women, and the use of cultural conceptions of femininity played central roles in the design, promotion, and experience of the Astrodome and other postwar modern stadiums. They could recast the image of the stadium from urban, masculine, dirty, and uncomfortable to suburban, modern, domesticated, and luxurious. They

FIGURE 58. Astrodome ushers—the Spacette and the Spaceman—pose for photographers.
BETTMANN/GETTY IMAGES.

marked stadium space as classy and an appropriate entertainment for the affluent—a space akin to upscale restaurants and clubs, theaters, and museums. A female-friendly consumer space—an analogue to postwar shopping malls and Disneyland—resonated with moneyed, suburban, white, middle-class America. Crucially, women also made comfort and consumption acceptable for men, who could pass off the need for such frivolity onto their wives and girlfriends while enjoying them all the same.[148]

This economic upscaling of the stadium was, like the Astrodome's technologies and engineered monumentality, a symbol of progress. The Dome was a giant leap in stadium design and execution—a point agreed upon by both its proponents and detractors. One of Hofheinz's advisors remembered attending World Series games with his boss, who "saw how dirty the stadiums were, and he said his stadium was never going to be that way. . . . He said he was going to have the best dressed people in town, in neckties and coats, with air conditioning, and he was right. He got people out to baseball games that wouldn't go in other cities."[149] Hofheinz boasted to Roger Angell, "Our fans are more like the ones they have out in California. We don't have any of those rowdies or semi-delinquents who follow the [New York] Mets. We have by far a higher percentage of fans in the upper economic brackets than you'll find in any other park. . . . We make a big effort to bring out the ladies."[150] This was what progress looked like to Hofheinz and others—the business of sport modernizing itself, rejecting a rough-and-tumble past and launching itself into a clean and lucrative future. As Walt Disney had done with Disneyland, opened a decade before, Hofheinz sanitized an old form of entertainment for the middle classes, projecting a postwar sense of comfort, order, cleanliness, and safety. And like Disneyland, the Astrodome collapsed themed environments from the past and future into a present entertainment utopia.[151] It was important for Hofheinz and others waving the banner of "progress" to keep the past around, in some form or another; after all, certain versions of the past persuasively illustrated the futuristic progressiveness of the present.

From Roy Rogers to Buck Rogers

The space-age futurism of the Astrodome constantly comingled with visual, material, and rhetorical references to the past—the Texan past, the human past, and the premodern global present of Texan imagination. These representations positioned the Dome as an equal to the monumental accomplishments of humankind, the "great wonders of the world"; these representations also simultaneously located the stadium at the end of a historical arc of progress. Users, commentators, and promoters were constantly reveling in how the stadium—through the material evidence of its technological gadgetry and universal comforts—represented the pinnacle of human accomplishment. Progress was objectified through the material environment of the Astrodome; progress was not a human process of increased discovery, understanding, and social justice but rather an enhancement of automation, control, convenience, and prosperity. References to the past and seemingly premodern, exoticized present proposed and ratified this ideology, pointing to the material fruits of modernity, inviting visitors into a collective club of frontiersmen and adventurers, showing them that the Astrodome in Houston, Texas, America, 1965 was *the* time and place to be in human history.

Countless observers classified the Astrodome as a "wonder of the world"—a claim central to stadium discourse, engaged by promoters and observers alike.[152] The cover of *Inside the Astrodome* exclaimed, "Eighth Wonder of the World!" An article within, titled "And Now There Are Eight!" catalogued the Dome with the other man-made wonders of the world. Readers were told, "From the dawn of time man has built many almost unbelievable structures. In ancient times there were the seven wonders of the world, some of which defied the imagination and were awe-inspiring. Since then, man has continued to build many magnificent structures—giant dams, great bridges spanning angry rivers, and tall buildings reaching far into the sky."[153] The Astrodome seemed to exceed them all: none of the dams, bridges, and tall buildings had made the list, whereas the ancient human expressions seemed quaint in relation to the new stadium. Structures like the Egyptian Pyramids, the Hanging Gardens of Babylon, and the Temple of Artemis were built with old materials—stone, bronze, marble—and with old methods. Alongside the modern Astrodome they were curiosities of ancient times, equals in its monumentality but naive as expressions of human genius. The HSA cited a visitor from the relatively old world of Berlin to corroborate its transhistorical claims; Gerhard Kalks declared, "Without a doubt the domed Stadium will be entered in annals as one of the wonders of the western hemisphere."[154]

The Astrodome was linked to a variety of iconic world structures outside of these "wonders." A press release from the HSA asked,

> What single edifice is the world's greatest attraction?
> The Eiffel Tower? The Empire State Building? The Rome Colosseum? The Statue of Liberty? The Washington Monument? The UN Building? Rockefeller Center? McCormick Place? The Museum of Science and Industry? Smithsonian Institute? Dodger Stadium? The Louvre?[155]

The answer, of course, was the Astrodome. Writers almost unerringly compared the stadium to the world's most identifiable man-made landmarks. It was the "Taj Mahal of all sports palaces" and an "Eiffel Tower in its field."[156] One writer promised, "Your first glimpse of the Golden Gate, Washington Monument or 100-floor skyscraper pales in comparison."[157] Hofheinz boasted, "The Astrodome will become to Houston what the Leaning Tower is to Pisa, what the Eiffel Tower is to Paris."[158] The Dome's rightful competitors, for some, came from the realm of fantasy. The stadium was often compared to Kubla Khan's "stately pleasure dome" in Xanadu, the famous invention of British poet Samuel Taylor Coleridge. "It defies description," Joe Reichler of the Associated Press claimed. "It looks like it might have been built by Jules Verne in his most fantastic dream."[159] But the most common comparison was made, understandably, with the ur-stadium, Rome's Flavian Amphitheater, the Colosseum. A reporter from San Antonio called it "the most celebrated palace of play since the Romans' Coliseum opened its doors to the public."[160] A multipage spread in *Inside the Astrodome* made the comparison explicit and, unsurprisingly, deemed the Houston stadium the better of the two. An illustration of the Colosseum faced a photograph of the Dome. The interiors resembled one another—each with swooping, symmetrical arcs of seats, each with covers protecting the interiors from the weather. The velarium of the Colosseum seemed paneled, with a circular gap in the middle where the sections of cloth covering were pulled together; the roof of the Astrodome, too, was geometrical, the lamella framing intersected with the rectangular panels and a circular gondola hung from the stadium roof, echoing the velarium gap. The most distinctive visual difference was that the Colosseum was shown in use, its stands packed with hordes of faceless people, its floor the scene of a war game, populated by man-made hills, plants, and armored men fighting with animals. The Astrodome, on the other hand, was a pristinely modern landscape, clean, ordered, and uncluttered by people. Accompanying text concluded, "The ASTRODOME is bigger, brighter, and has a multiplicity of conveniences and appointments far beyond the Colosseum but, after all, Texans had almost 1,900 years to improve on the Rome masterpiece." A Galveston reporter agreed, writing, "Man, those shows in the old Roman Colosseum were back alley crap games compared to this one."[161]

Comparisons between the Dome and older stadiums were constantly made in print, but Houstonians needed to look no further than their own experiences of stadiums in Houston to understand the difference between the traditional and the modern, the historical and the futuristic. Baseball watchers in particular would have remembered the traditional ballparks of Buff Stadium, where the city's minor league teams had played for decades, and Colt Stadium, the major league club's temporary field in the Astrodome's parking lot, used from 1962 to 1964. Colt Stadium in particular would offer a marked contrast to the Astrodome, for it too was a themed space—though it was outfitted in Wild Western duds, a considerable contrast to the futurism of the Dome. The move from Colt Stadium to the Astrodome was thus an occasion to reflect on Houston's two versions of itself, caricatured as those were—the rough-and-tumble, no-holds-barred frontier cowboy and the space-age, progressive, modern, sophisticated entrepreneur. Houston sportswriter Mickey Herskowitz called attention to this shift, noting "a break with the past as dramatic as the difference between Roy Rogers and Buck Rogers" upon the opening of the new stadium.[162] While the opening of the Astrodome ushered visitors out of the Disneyfied Wild West of Colt Stadium and into a self-consciously space-age environment, Houstonians didn't fully escape representations of the past. Though the dominant theme of the Astrodome was space age, designers incorporated numerous references to a shared human past that located the new stadium at the end of a long line of human accomplishment.

The stadium restaurants provided a range of imaginative geographical and historical safaris for diners. The Astrodome Club was "reminiscent of San Francisco's old Hippodrome Theatre at the height of its turn-of-the-century opulence," according to a full-page advertisement for an interior decorating contractor in the *Houston Post*. A large illustration dominated the page, depicting what looked like the lobby of an extravagant casino or, perhaps, an upscale brothel—a gaudy, crimson setting accented with globe lights, a massive mahogany bar backed by a nude portrait, and stained glass windows. Couples in suits and minks populated the setting—one that seemed as distant from a sporting event as a trip to the opera.[163] Among the Astrodome Club's distinctively Hofheinzian oddities were a mural in the style of Toulouse-Lautrec (depicting Hofheinz examining the French can-can dancer La Goulue), mottoes such as "All That Glitters Is Not Gold" etched onto the bar, and a meat-carving chef who wore snap-on velvet sleeves with ermine tails.[164]

The other restaurants too offered visitors thematized departures from the present. The Domeskeller was a mid-nineteenth-century, Austrian-themed beer garden. Support columns were "converted into artificial trees," and the walls were decorated with crests and banners.[165] The décor of the Countdown Cafeteria depicted the history of sports from ancient Greece to the Astrodome, complete with "uniformed Blastoff Girls to serve you under anachronistic murals of Cretan bull dancers, stubby Trojan warriors and other ancient sportsmen," as Liz Smith of *Sports Illustrated* saw it. "Full-course meals comparable to those in the private clubs will be available in the Trailblazer restaurant," Smith reported, "where the murals depict man's struggle for a better life and where the judge wants the customer to feel he has achieved it."[166]

A visitor's sense of achievement was no doubt most gratifying in the celebrated luxury suites—one of the stadium's most iconic and original features.[167] Ann Valentine of the *Houston Post* speculated, "Most of the world has already heard about the wonders of Houston's unique Domed Stadium but we wonder if Vance Packard has gotten word of the latest Texas status symbol: A deluxe, private box clubroom towering 550 feet up on the royal blue level of the new stadium!"[168] There were fifty-three boxes in all. Boxes of twenty-four seats cost $15,000 per season; boxes of thirty seats sold for $18,600. Both required five-year commitments. Each box of seats was adjoined to a club room with "wall-to-wall thick pile carpeting," telephone, radio, television, ice maker, bar, furniture, Dow-Jones ticker, and closed-circuit TV broadcasting the game and other information from the field. Special elevators took the box holders to their ninth-level seats from the ground, lest they have to climb or mingle with non–box holders. Box customers could use the exclusive Skydome Club—a space-themed Japanese steak house complete with waitresses from Japan and gold spatulas. They could also order room service to their clubrooms or seats.[169]

Each private clubroom was decorated in a different style, so that, as Valentine reported, "as you open the door of each box it is like raising a stage curtain on a setting. Each box has a completely different and striking décor."[170] The Petroleum Room, for example, featured a mural of an oil refinery—a design that allowed some of Houston's elite to muse on the source of their wealth. Across the room another wall was decorated with a wire sculpture of an oil derrick that provided "a bold accent for this room with a décor that captures the zestful character of oil pioneers, past and present," Valentine claimed.[171] Pioneering rich Houstonians could alternately choose to drink their game-time scotch in the Las Vegas box, which sported massive dice for coffee tables, or in the New Yorker or Metropolitan, if they wanted a taste of urban cosmopolitanism. Many of the rooms enabled temporary journeys into the distant past: Parthenon, Classical Mediterranea, Spanish Armada, and the Aztec. Others provided a more proximate departure, like Old Mexico, Old South, and Southern Plantation—themes that might have been troubling to some civil rights advocates who were still laboring to desegregate the city's public spaces; such imagery reasserted symbols of white domination when that power seemed to be on the wane. The most popular theme tapped into a fascination with Eastern civilizations and engaged an Orientalist discourse; separate boxes were named Imperial Orient, Bangkok, Far Eastern, Panjim Emerald, Egyptian Autumn, The Red Dragon, Tahitian Holiday, Ramayana, and Pagoda Den. When placed in the context of the futuristic Astrodome, the seemingly mystical and exotic premodern qualities of the East were only accentuated, providing visitors a safely sensual counterpart to the Western hyperrationalism of the Dome, while also underscoring Houstonians' roles as pioneers in the march of human progress.[172]

These Eastern themes seemed a fetish of Hofheinz's, evidenced by his extensive use of Asian decorations in the sumptuous (and, most would note, garish) private offices at the stadium. Hofheinz's office was "of such comically voluptuous and sybaritic furnishings," Angell wrote, "that I was half convinced it had been designed by, say, John Lennon."[173] The boardroom, called "the throne room," was outfitted with velvet upholstery, Mexican onyx panels, spongy royal blue rugs, and a twelve-foot-long boomerang desk made of rosewood with an inlaid black marble top. A gold phone for deal making and dictionary for wordsmithing sat atop the desk. At each side of the desk were six-foot-tall oriental lions, fangs bared, carved of teak with wide gold collars and curling gilt goatees. Hofheinz decorated the offices himself, shipping items—like a wall-mounted, jewel-scaled dragon—back from a trip to Thailand. Upon visiting the offices, comedian Bob Hope termed the style "early Farouk."[174]

While some were impressed by Hofheinz's gilded touch, many found it hilariously gauche—Liz Smith called the Hofheinz style "fu Manchu." Others were appalled.[175] Vivian Smith, wife of Bob Smith, recalled visiting the Dome with her daughter and a friend from New York. During the tour, Fred Hofheinz, son of Roy, told them that the throne room was Bob Smith's office, as he was chairman of the board. Smith remembered: "I was horrified. I had never seen it. It was one of those garish-looking rooms with red velvet and a woman's breast exposed on the arms of the chairs. I told Fred right then, and I told [Roy Hofheinz's assistant] Mary Frances: 'Don't you dare tell anyone that this is Mr. Smith's office. He doesn't go for things like that and I think it's an insult to Mr. Smith to call it his office. Call it whatever you will, but don't you call it Mr. Smith's office.'"[176] Vivian Smith's tastes contrasted starkly with those of Hofheinz, regarding not only the decorative use of breasts but also the production of a baseball game itself; she was dismissive of the distractions and luxuries, ditching the skyboxes to sit behind home plate so she could "fuss" at the umpires.[177] Other visitors to the Astrodome shared her distaste for some of the extravagances and auxiliary entertainments that seemed to shift attention from events on the field to the socializing and consumption off it. But most found this display mesmerizing, and totally unlike any stadium ever before constructed.

People in Houston, across the United States, and even abroad listened to Hofheinz's hucksterism, and they heard it echoed in newspapers, magazines, and television coverage. Locals read claims like this one from Finger Contract, which installed the stadium interiors: "Past, present and future, near and far meet here. Under the great span of the Astrodome, the romance of foreign lands mixes and mingles with the vital pulse of America. Like a giant kaleidoscope, the picture changes, ever more colorful and exciting wherever you look."[178] The Dome exemplified for many the fruits and potential of a progressive, rationalist, consumerist modernism that used the vision and genius of man to produce a more comfortable and convenient world. It was the end point in millennia-long pursuits, a reflection of the pioneering impulse of the westerner made modern. Visitors to the Astrodome merely had to look around to witness how the present had improved on the past and how the future was now.

This narrative of historical progress was staged in a Dome that sealed off its population within, physically and imaginatively, from the social realities of mid-1960s United States.

The Astrodome was one of many midcentury escape pods for the white middle and afflu-ent classes of the time. Stocked and sealed bomb shelters in suburban backyards might offer a lifeline out of nuclear apocalypse; more mundane were the suburban housing and shopping centers that enabled an escape from urban disinvestment and crisis.

In a March 1965 address to the Houston Philosophical Society, F. Talbott Wilson, a partner in one of the Astrodome's architectural firms, delivered a speech about the ugli-ness of cities and the dangers of ignoring them. Citing shopping center designer Victor Gruen, Wilson claimed that the "Home Beautiful in the City Terrible" was "an unworkable paradox." Though he subscribed to the idea of the home as a castle, he couldn't support the notion of the home as a fortress. Wilson continued,

> To live in esthetically pleasing fortresses, defended against the outside world, with
> filters in the air-conditioning system to keep out the poisoned air, heavy curtains at
> the windows to keep out views into neighboring slums, sound-proofing to defend
> us from the nerve-racking noise of mechanized traffic, surrounded by precious
> objects to keep our minds off the vulgarity of the outside world, is a hopeless task.
> The prettier and more protected our shelter becomes, the more we suffer at every
> sortie and foray into the outside world: and inasmuch as these sorties are necessary
> in order for us to gain a livelihood and to participate in the social and cultural life
> of the community in which we live, our return to the fortress finds us physically and
> psychologically maimed and exhausted.[179]

The Astrodome embodied this turn inward; it created an engineered, utopian world that needn't bother with the conditions outside. While a reflection of nuclear-age escapism, it also articulated that other great technological infatuation of the postwar period: the space race. As residents of Space City, U.S.A., home of the Manned Spacecraft Center, some Houstonians no doubt fancied themselves as modern pioneers, the winners in a Darwin-ian race—an identity that intersected conveniently with the cowboy and boom-or-bust oilman imaginaries of Texans who took risks and won big. The Astrodome allowed every-one—from those paying $1.50 for a pavilion seat to those forking over $18,600 for a luxury box—to enjoy the fruits of modern progress. Harris County residents, who funded the structure, could pat themselves on their backs, retreating into the sealed Dome and forget-ting those impoverished residents who were left behind materially in the march of prog-ress, those whose basic civil rights remained insecure, and the city's failure to adequately fund infrastructure to stave off problems of flooding, water pollution, toxic waste, sewage, and street maintenance. In all its glory, the Astrodome revealed Houston's identity as a free-enterprise city, as opposed to a free-market city—that is, one that claimed an aversion to governmental influence but was more than willing to mobilize an activist government and its public money to support projects that would benefit the elite, both materially and ideologically.[180]

Houston was not alone. Business and political leaders in St. Louis united the power of government to the profits of private investment and ownership in the 1960s. As in New York, St. Louis replaced an old and idiosyncratic urban ballpark with a stadium embodying the qualities of suburbia. But unlike in New York and Houston, this "suburbanized" stadium was planted in the heart of the city. The modern stadium there anchored a larger project, both racial and economic in nature—the reclamation of downtown, by those who had abandoned it in the preceding decades, and a "whitening" of the black city.

CHAPTER 5

DOWNTOWN PLAYGROUND

THE STADIUM AS URBAN RENEWAL

ST. LOUIS CELEBRATED THE OFFICIAL RELOCATION of major league sport from old Sportsman's Park to new and modern Busch Stadium with a parade in May 1966. Called "St. Louis Through the Years," it consisted of twenty-three floats, costing seventy-five hundred dollars each, populated with "many pretty girls," in the words of a reporter. Most of the floats were sponsored by St. Louis–based corporations and depicted local events and icons like the 1904 World's Fair and the recently completed Gateway Arch. One float celebrated the founding of the city; another proposed the city of the future. It was an appropriate way to mark the transition from the city's home of baseball since the 1860s to a gleaming new modern stadium that seemed a harbinger for tomorrow.[1]

Though the theme attempted to connect the two stadiums across time, the parade route did not link them across space. The parade didn't start at Sportsman's Park but rather a mile and a half south, at Grand Boulevard and Washington, along the northern edge of what was once the Mill Creek Valley neighborhood. Mill Creek had been the heart of St. Louis's "Negro District" for decades, one of the few areas of the city where African Americans were allowed to live owing to the machinations of white politicians, white real estate organizations, and white neighborhood associations. Crowding, unemployment, and disinvestment rendered a deteriorating built environment. In the mid-1950s, City

Hall, with the backing of Civic Progress, Inc.—a powerful group of St. Louis's business elite—targeted Mill Creek Valley for urban renewal. It was the largest urban renewal project nationwide to that time. Slum clearance at Mill Creek displaced 20,000 working-class African Americans and demolished 5,630 dwelling units, as politicians and developers hatched plans to turn the area into a "vast and modern suburb within a city."[2] What advocates called "urban renewal" became known as "Negro Removal" to critics. Most of the "removed" relocated north, toward Sportsman's Park.

A parade route from the old ballpark to the new stadium would have taken the twenty-three floats through St. Louis's north side, where nearly all black St. Louisans lived. The most direct path would have marched past Pruitt-Igoe, a 2,700-unit public housing project that was home to many African Americans displaced by slum clearance; though it had opened barely a decade earlier, the massive complex was already suffering from a chronic level of underfunding, maintenance neglect, vandalism, and violence.[3] By either road, the

FIGURE 59. Busch Stadium sits amid models of corporate modernism—a portrait of visual order—in a newly reinvented St. Louis in 1969. RALPH D'OENCH COLLECTION, MISSOURI HISTORY MUSEUM, ST. LOUIS.

one taken or the one not, "St. Louis Through the Years" would have steered celebrants through the dramatic effects of urban renewal—on one hand, newly open spaces produced by slum clearance, and on the other, the old urban neighborhoods where so many of the displaced had relocated, perpetuating the same cycles of material deterioration that had previously beset Mill Creek Valley.

The path from Sportsman's Park to Busch Stadium was officially one of renewal and reinvention—a journey from a past marked by dirty industry and deteriorating tenements to a future of glass-walled skyscrapers, downtown luxury apartments, the stainless steel Gateway Arch, and a gleaming new modern stadium. A new kind of city would emerge from the dust of slum clearance—one befitting the downtown business elite and their property values. Busch Stadium and other renewal projects downtown were indeed tools for claiming urban space and a new urban identity grounded in corporate command, cultural consumption, and upscale living.

But like any spatial project in St. Louis, this was *also* a racial project—though one advanced under the guise of neutrality, as racial projects often are.[4] Advocates for a new stadium could celebrate the role it would play in the rebirth of the city as an instrument of "progress." They could wrest sport from an area that went from exclusively white in 1950 to nearly all black by 1970. As in so many other cities, the increasing blackness of stadium neighborhoods was almost always accompanied by cries of "obsolescence" and demands for new stadiums located elsewhere in the city. In many cities—St. Louis in particular—urban renewal projects had already been deployed for the maintenance of residential segregation.[5] Tools that had been used to preserve segregation where people lived could also be used to erect bulkheads around where they played, defining center cities and the experience of sport in the process. Altogether, the reinvention of the stadium in St. Louis symbolized and materialized ideas about the past and future, race and space, the character of the city, and who had the rights to it.

Sportsman's Park

The home of field sport in St. Louis was located for most of a century on the same patch of grass, bordered by North Grand Boulevard, Dodier Street, North Spring Avenue, and Sullivan Avenue. The ballpark around that field had been built, rebuilt, and expanded many times over the years. Old Grand Avenue Park—wooden stands that occupied the same lot as Sportsman's Park later would—was on a horse-drawn trolley line, just beyond the city's denser settlement and blocks south of the city's fairgrounds.[6] It was home to St. Louis's first professional team in 1875. Seventy years later, two major league teams plied their trade there—the National League Cardinals and the American League Browns—in a double-decker, concrete-and-steel ballpark that had been built in 1909 and extensively re-modeled in 1925. The two teams met in the 1944 World Series, won by the Cardinals. It was a rare season in which the Browns outdrew the Cardinals, attracting just over 500,000 fans and turning a profit of $285,034. Two years later, 526,435 paid to see the Browns; one million came to see the title-winning Cardinals. In 1949, 1.4 million fans visited Sportsman's Park to watch the Cards; barely a quarter million came for the Browns.[7] St. Louis was a baseball town riding baseball's postwar attendance boom, and the Cardinals were its club.

The Cardinals were St. Louis's favorite, but the club's second-place finish in 1949 would be its best for fifteen years. In the 1950s, the team's developmental system, once so produc-tive under the steerage of Branch Rickey, had become less fruitful. Rickey had moved to Brooklyn; his Dodgers, who broke the color line in 1947, employed a number of excellent black players beginning in the late 1940s and replaced the Cardinals as the NL's dominant club. The arrival of players like Jackie Robinson on the field came just years after Sports-man's Park had officially desegregated its stands in 1944. It had been the last park in the big leagues with a Jim Crow section—the right-field pavilion. The official desegregation of the stands certainly didn't make the space race-blind in the late 1940s—or even neces-sarily desegregated. Dodgers player Don Newcombe, whose major league debut came at Sportsman's Park in 1949, later recalled an episode there in which black fans were tempo-rarily barred from entering the stadium after the three-thousand-seat "colored" section had been filled. Jackie Robinson told Dodgers manager Burt Shotton that he, Newcombe, and Roy Campanella—the Dodgers' three African American players—refused to take the field unless the fifteen thousand fans outside the park were allowed in.[8] This exclusion of black fans may have been motivated not only by race but tactics as well. Game reports of the 1949 season repeatedly noted the support the Dodgers enjoyed at Sportsman's Park, suggesting that many black fans had indeed made it in to cheer for Robinson, Campanella, Newcombe, and the racially integrated Dodgers.[9]

The Browns, hoping to capitalize on black attendance to save them from bankruptcy, signed black players after Jackie Robinson's debut with the Dodgers. In 1947 the club signed Willard Brown and Henry Thompson from the Negro League's Kansas City Monarchs, the first black teammates in the major leagues, and also inked Piper Davis of the Birmingham Black Barons to a thirty-day option.[10] Richard Muckerman, one of the Browns' primary owners, hoped it might increase turnstile numbers, just as Robinson and the Dodgers attracted black fans during Cardinals games. General manager Bill DeWitt suggested, "It seems in order that this large Negro population should have some representation on their city's baseball team."[11] None of the trio of players would last through the summer with the club, however, as they struggled mightily for hits. The Browns enjoyed no attendance spike from black St. Louisans—most of whom lived directly south and southwest of Sportsman's Park—who seemed to prefer Robinson's Dodgers.

The Cardinals, meanwhile, remained an all-white club—though they certainly accept-ed payment from the city's Brooklyn supporters. Owner Fred Saigh, who was of Syrian de-scent, refused to sign black or Latino players, claiming the Cardinals were "a team for the South." Southerners indeed flocked to St. Louis games from Texas, Oklahoma, Arkansas, Louisiana, and elsewhere; the growth of radio broadcasts after World War II, and absence of a southern major league team, had fueled a regional fan base. In the late 1940s and early 1950s, the St. Louis Cardinals network included one hundred twenty stations spread over nine states. Buses of fans from hundreds of miles away would arrive on weekends, testi-fying to the scope of the radio community.[12] The club's regional support, however, didn't seem to wane after the club relented and signed black players in the 1950s, beginning with first baseman Tom Alston in 1954.

Saigh's reign at the helm of the Cardinals was short-lived, lasting from just 1949 to 1953. He had amassed his wealth from real estate ventures that attracted an IRS investiga-tion, which then resulted in a fifteen-month prison sentence for income-tax evasion. Bill Veeck had been part of an ownership group that bought the Browns in 1951. He suspected that St. Louis could support only one major league team and thought that the Cardinals, weakened by Saigh's ownership, might be run out of town—this in spite of the fact that the Browns had outdrawn the Cardinals only once in the previous twenty-five years, during the 1944 championship season.

Veeck was characteristically undaunted and put his promotional imagination to work with the Browns. To boost attendance, he sponsored jazz days, Bat Days, Grandstand Man-ager's Night, and performances from clowns and acrobats. He signed three-foot seven-inch Eddie Gaedel to pinch hit and draw a walk on August 19, 1951; Gaedel's strike zone was so small that the opposing pitcher walked him on four pitches.[13] The Browns drew 518,795 in 1952, up over 75 percent from the previous year (though the Cardinals attracted 913,113). Veeck's plans to wrest the St. Louis public from the grip of the Cardinals, however, soon hit an iceberg.

The Cardinals passed from the distressed hands of the soon-to-be-imprisoned Saigh to the welcome arms of the St. Louis–based Anheuser-Busch Brewing Association on Febru-ary 20, 1953. August "Gussie" Busch, the president and chief operating officer at Anheuser-Busch, took control of the Cardinals with $3.75 million of company funds. Veeck knew he couldn't compete with the brewery's resources and looked to move the Browns. He first hoped to relocate to Milwaukee; however, Lou Perini beat him to it, moving his Boston Braves there. Other owners prevented a possible move to Baltimore. Veeck was thus forced to return to Sportsman's Park for the 1953 season, and he sold the grounds to Anheuser-Busch for $1.1 million. Furious fans—cognizant of Veeck's overtures to other cities—can-celed their season tickets and even burned him in effigy. Just 297,238 came out to Sports-man's Park to see the Browns in 1953—fewer than 4,000 per game. Veeck was not just the

FIGURE 60. Aerial view of Sportsman's Park from the 1940s. MISSOURI HISTORY MUSEUM, ST. LOUIS. CREATED BY P. R. PAPIN AERIAL SURVEYS.

enemy of Browns fans, however; owners resented his promotional irreverence and were intent to squeeze him out of the game. Temporarily blocking the club's relocation from St. Louis—which would require their approval—baseball's club owners forced him to sell the Browns to an investor group in Baltimore, where the team moved for the 1954 season.[14]

With the Browns out of the way, Gussie Busch invested an additional $1.5 million of company money in Sportsman's Park, redesigning and renaming it. When Busch bought the property, he remarked, "The way it is now, I'd rather play in Forest Park" (the city's large municipal park and site of the 1904 World's Fair). Busch replaced or repaired every seat, removed the advertising from outfield walls, planted shrubbery in the center-field bleachers, installed new loge seating, erected a new scoreboard, and remodeled the dugouts and clubhouses.[15] He had hoped to call his new park "Budweiser Stadium," but the league vetoed this plan, not wanting a ballpark named after a beer. Instead he renamed it Busch Stadium, then introduced Busch Bavarian Beer as a work-around to the league's promotional hurdles. Many St. Louisans continued calling the stadium Sportsman's Park, nonetheless— a title that had endured since saloon owner Chris Von der Ahe and the *Sporting News* publisher Alfred H. Spink had opened a ballpark by that name at Grand and Dodier in 1881.[16]

Newly named but decades old, the ballpark had a double-decked, winged grandstand that seemed to clamp the playing field in place. The outfield was surrounded with open bleachers and a towering scoreboard in left field, along Sullivan Avenue; a small, seat-less section filled with shrubbery in dead center field, at the corner of Sullivan and Grand Boulevard; and a roofed pavilion in right field, along Grand. The park shared the block with a thin strip of surface parking just south of the grandstand's first-base side, with cars parked ten deep off of Dodier Street.

The grandstands soared upward, thin erector-set banks held up by two series of support posts. These stands seemed nearly as open at the back as they were in front, releasing the pressure of the small lot. Two press boxes, one on the roof and another hanging from it, curved around home plate. Four banks of lights sat atop the grandstand roof, two on each side. Two lighting standards towered over the right-field pavilion; two more flanked the massive scoreboard hovering over the left-field bleachers. The board, hung on a wall of trusses, was topped by a massive Budweiser logo—an eagle in an "A" that flapped its wings when the Cardinals hit home runs.

Looking in from the outfield, the tall grandstand frames, colored in red and green and topped with pennants, boxed the field in. Looking out from the grandstand—and particularly from the second deck, the park opened out to the cityscape just beyond. Over the shrubs in center was the North Side YMCA, which had sat across from the park since 1919. A Busch Bavarian Beer billboard clung to the top of a building across Sullivan Avenue, though it seemed so close as to be a part of the park itself; sometimes it teased fans with snow-skiing motifs, sometimes it presented them with the friendly face of Cardinals broadcaster Harry Caray. The scene beyond the walls was largely composed of the single- and double-unit houses making up most of the neighborhood. On game day, cars were rammed into every vacant lot, driveway, and street space. Scattered among the houses were eighteenth-century Catholic and Lutheran churches, the north side's first high school, and an Egyptian-styled Masonic Hall.[17] The massive Carter Carburetor plant loomed directly south, behind the first-base grandstand, across Dodier Street. Three stories high and over three hundred feet long, it filled up the equivalent of an entire city block. Grand Boulevard, the main artery running to and from the park, was a commercial strip defining right field.

If Brooklyn's Ebbets Field seemed connected to the entire borough, the geography of the Cardinals stretched from Sportsman's Park, across the roofs of St. Louis's north side, throughout the city, and to places all across the South. When the 1964 World Series pitted the St. Louis Cardinals against the New York Yankees, Roger Angell surveyed the scene for the *New Yorker*:

On the first two days of the Series, Busch Stadium—a seamed, rusty, steep-sided box that will be replaced within two years by a new ballpark on St. Louis's river-

FIGURE 61. The view from the upper deck of Sportsman's Park in 1946. ARTHUR WITMAN, S0717, ID
733.111, STATE HISTORICAL SOCIETY OF MISSOURI/RESEARCH CENTER–ST. LOUIS.

front—reminded me of an old down-on-her-luck dowager who has been given a
surprise party by the local settlement house; she was startled by the occasion but
still able to accept it as no less than her due. The Cardinal fans around me were
plainly and noisily delighted, but I detected none of the unbelieving hysteria with
which San Francisco greeted its first pennant in 1962. These were veteran city and
country loyalists. The parked cars around the stadium bore license plates from
Iowa, Kentucky, Oklahoma, and Louisiana, and their occupants, approaching the
gates, had to wade through a moat of trash, broken glass, and old beer cans left by
the urbanites who had camped outside the park for two cold nights while waiting

for the bleachers to open. Inside, I noticed many spectators (and two young ushers) keeping score in their programs. Clearly, that new pennant would be at home here.[18]

This was an iconic baseball setting, filled with many of Angell's markers of an authentic baseball culture—from the boxiness of the park to the fans keeping score. The aged stadium had a personality all its own, the old dowager, seemingly a human participant in the event. It drew together people from all over into a single urban public—a messy and committed public at that, willing to sleep on sidewalks among their own growing piles of garbage. It was fitting for the world's oldest baseball lot, where the game had been played since the 1860s.

In many ways Sportsman's Park seemed timeless, enduring year after year in spite of its age. Unlike Ebbets Field and the Polo Grounds, where attendance dropped continuously throughout the 1950s in spite of good teams, the attendance levels at Sportsman's Park remained relatively constant throughout the decade—fluctuating between eleven and fifteen thousand fans per game, even as the Cardinals fielded mediocre squads. Mary Ott, a

FIGURE 62. Cardinals bleacherites soak in the sun during a pause in the action at the 1964 World Series. ARTHUR WITMAN, S0733, ID 733.129, STATE HISTORICAL SOCIETY OF MISSOURI/RESEARCH CENTER-ST. LOUIS.

midwestern version of Brooklyn's famous rooter Hilda Chester, remained a park fixture into her seventies, her famously loud farm-animal calls a feature there since 1920.[19]

Complaints about old Sportsman's Park were measured and muted when compared to those about other old ballparks that were more regularly criticized for their shortcomings. The stadium certainly faced many of the challenges that beset parks like Boston's Braves Field, Brooklyn's Ebbets Field, Harlem's Polo Grounds, and Washington's Griffith Stadium. Transportation in and out of the neighborhood required patience, as the park was lodged into the grid of the old city. Street parking demanded arriving up to ninety minutes early for a game. There was room for only about four thousand cars on homeowners' property or in small individually owned lots around the edges of the park, but these spots were unpredictable and it would generally take drivers twenty to thirty minutes to get out of the lot after the game.[20]

Thus the Sportsman's experience was much more than what happened inside the ball-park's walls—visitors driving to the game could spend nearly as much time navigating the streets outside as they would in their seats. The changing face of the neighborhood—and the city in general—might have convinced many that it was time for the Cardinals to leave the old park. City officials had deemed the entire area around the park "blighted" by 1947. Most of the near north side was an "area of decadence"; planners warned, "This cancerous growth may engulf the entire city if steps are not taken to prevent it."[21] Such assessments became, as in many cities, a form of self-fulfilling prophecy, discouraging private and public investment. A mid-1960s door-to-door survey of the stadium's neigh-borhood, Jeff-Vander-Lou—which stretched south toward Mill Creek Valley—found that 50 percent of the housing was substandard, 70 percent had incomplete plumbing, and nearly all of it was poorly maintained. The report posited that the neighborhood was site of the worst health conditions, the highest crime rates, and "the most unattractive and over-crowded living and working conditions anywhere in the city." City officials estimated that 75 percent of the housing was "unfit for human habitation" according to city codes. Sixty-seven percent of residents were unemployed. The income of 71 percent was below the poverty level.[22]

Sportsman's Park was located at the northern end of the neighborhood, and the area di-rectly around the ballpark hadn't suffered the same trials as points further south. The most obvious change had been its racial makeup. The ballpark's census tract had been nearly all white in 1950—97.8 percent (compared to .2 percent black, just 13 people out of 6,739). By 1960, 48.1 percent of the area's 6,591 residents were white, 51.7 percent black. And by 1970, 92.3 percent of tract residents were black (6,392 out of 6,923).[23] St. Louis's racial geography was, indeed, quite legible and seemingly irreversible. The city's white residents—racially progressive or not—would have understood that the line of racial segregation was coming, a self-fulfilling tide, toward Sportsman's Park. And in St. Louis, blackness meant "blight."[24]

Urban Renewal and the Corporate City

The racial and economic landscape of St. Louis—as in many other American cities— changed profoundly from the 1940s through the mid-1960s, when Sportsman's Park was leveled and replaced by downtown Busch Stadium. White residents decamped for the sub- urbs, taking advantage of home loan policies that prioritized new single-family suburban housing over the renovation of existing urban units and federal highways that subsidized commuter costs and enabled more dispersed settlement patterns. The population of St. Louis city grew from 816,048 to 856,796 between 1940 and 1950, before plummeting to 750,026 (1960) and 622,236 (1970). At the same time, St. Louis County, surrounding the city, grew explosively from 274,230 (1940) to 406,349 (1950) to 703,532 (1960) to 951,353 (1970). The city shed nearly 200,000 residents over that period; the suburban county gained almost 700,000. Adjacent counties, many hosting suburban bedroom communities, grew consid- erably as well.[25] African Americans had been concentrated in the areas just west and north of downtown but increasingly moved into adjacent areas, further north and west, left va- cant by suburbanized whites. As the city's white population shrank, the number of black St. Louisans increased dramatically—typically migrants from the South—from 108,765 (1940) to 153,766 (1950) to 214,377 (1960) to 254,191 (1970). African Americans accounted for just 13 percent of the city's total population in 1940 but 41 percent by 1970.[26]

Suburbanization both undermined the urban tax base and diverted state and federal funds from the city to the suburbs, which required new infrastructure. Downtowns were suffocated as the economic oxygen—in the form of jobs and retail—was sucked into the suburbs.[27] City officials and executives eyed the slums around the city, fearing the impact these areas might have on nearby property values downtown. Together, they hatched a comprehensive reinvention of the center city.[28] It would boost manufacturing in some areas, cultivate research and development in others, draw high-income residents back downtown, and encourage urban tourism, making the central business district a regional center of economic growth.[29]

Civic Progress, Inc., was one of the key players driving redevelopment in St. Louis throughout the 1950s and 1960s. Its members were the city's business elite, and this pow- erful group of insiders worked with City Hall and other local officials to use urban re- newal to stoke economic growth that would benefit local corporations and, presumably, the city as a whole. Applied downtown, it could allow for corporate expansion or new development; it also could enhance surrounding property values. The addition of ameni- ties—like shopping, sports entertainment, and even potentially an amusement park—to the downtown area would not only attract more affluent suburban shoppers and their dollars to the city but also help businesses compete with other cities in attracting execu- tive talent.[30]

August A. Busch Jr. and Sidney Maestre of Mercantile Trust both joined Civic Progress early on. Busch and Maestre were powerful enough corporate figures that they could commit their companies to urban renewal projects without fear of being reversed by their boards.[31] They would also both be key figures in the planning and construction of Busch Stadium—Gussie Busch as owner of the Cardinals and Maestre as one of three leaders of the urban redevelopment corporation that organized and executed the stadium plans. Gussie Busch led a Civic Progress delegation to Pittsburgh in 1953 to consider the work of the Allegheny Conference there. He was enthusiastic about what he saw, reporting, "The great thing we saw up there are the city, state, and federal government funds being spent for the good of Pittsburgh."[32]

Pittsburgh's Allegheny Conference had been formed in 1943. Led by financier Richard K. Mellon, it sought to reinvent downtown Pittsburgh through an ambitious slum clearance plan and development of office towers, parks, and garages. Groups like the Allegheny Conference marked a new role for businessmen in the shaping of the city. In the contexts of the Cold War, they played an important part in making broad and comprehensive interventions palatable to an American citizenry that might otherwise be suspicious of statist solutions to urban problems. Redevelopment authorities in New York and Pittsburgh took early advantage of federally supported slum clearance projects in the late 1940s and through the 1950s—projects that often displaced poor urban residents, who were frequently African American. The business elite thus played a pivotal role in transforming American cities along capitalist, postindustrial lines, as postwar planning fused the idealism and comprehensive planning of socialists with capitalist interests. New highways, affluent housing, parks and plazas, corporate towers, and cultural amenities like Pittsburgh's Civic Auditorium—built atop what had once been the African American Lower Hill District—increasingly served as evidence of how capital could remake the broken city.[33]

The logic of urban renewal in the mid-1950s was this: in a troubled urban area, the economic risk was too great for private investors. They needed assurance that their projects would be accompanied by neighboring development, infrastructural upkeep, and maintenance of public safety. To satisfy these needs, the renewal of slum areas required that relatively large parcels of land be assembled, cleared, and then redeveloped as part of broader renewal plans. There were, however, legal and political barriers to this. While local governments *could* designate private property for public use through the power of eminent domain, they didn't typically have the compensatory money to acquire and assemble these large parcels of blighted property. In Missouri, the state government controlled the city's taxing and political powers—another complicating factor. Furthermore, using large-scale public efforts to develop land—in spite of assurances from local executives—invited complaints of "socialization" at the expense of small-scale private industry. Finally, it was difficult to transfer property from one private owner to a developer under any legal understanding of "public use"—a requirement for the use of eminent domain.[34]

Urban renewal in St. Louis and elsewhere thus relied on a complicated dance of laws and procedures. *Theoretically*, a project started when federal and municipal money was secured to assemble and clear blighted land. A state law was exercised that allowed municipal governments to designate an area as blighted, and the city made the property acquirable through eminent domain. A private redevelopment corporation was then created to develop the area, having used public funding to acquire and clear the plot. *In practice*, urban renewal in St. Louis typically followed a different process. A private developer identified a property he was interested in, local authorities designated it as blighted, and state and federal monies were then used to assemble and clear the blighted area.[35]

This practice relied on state and federal legislation, particularly Chapters 353 and 99 in Missouri and the National Housing Acts of 1949 and 1954. The Chapter 353 Urban Redevelopment Act, passed in 1945, specified the form and function of development corporations. These development corporations were the private entities that would, with the power of the city's claims of eminent domain, redevelop urban areas. St. Louis developers successfully lobbied for the act to include a schedule of tax abatements for property owners in renewal areas and allow for out-of-state investments in redevelopment corporations. This latter revision was advocated by insurance companies headquartered in New York City that hoped to take advantage of the executive reclamation of downtown St. Louis. The 1947 City Plan for St. Louis anticipated a rebuilding of the central city using Chapter 353, transforming an "obsolete" area into one with an upscale residential neighborhood, open areas, shopping centers, and park and recreation space. And yet, while Chapter 353 laid the groundwork for developing corporations, it didn't provide the necessary financial resources for acquiring and clearing the land that was to be developed.[36]

The National Housing Act of 1949 began to provide those resources. Under that law, the federal government advanced money to redevelopment agencies to survey areas and plan new developments. With federal approval of those plans, redevelopment agencies could then use federal funds to assemble and clear land, provided they also partially match the federal contribution with some local dollars and partially repay the federal money when the land was sold to private investors. The 1951 Land Clearance and Redevelopment Act (Chapter 99) facilitated this practice in Missouri. The 1954 National Housing Act then appropriated more funds for cities and loosened restrictions on residential focus. It allowed up to 10 percent of federal housing funds to be used on nonresidential projects. This was increased to 35 percent in 1965.[37]

These were the tools of the urban renewal trade in St. Louis.[38] Under the steerage of Civic Progress and political leaders, the city was physically redefined through the clearance of hundreds of acres of residential, commercial, and industrial structures; the construction of new expressways in and out of downtown; and the reinvention of downtown as a space for affluent residents and visitors, drawn by shopping, tourism, and sports entertainment.

Voters of St. Louis expressed their enthusiasm for massive reconstruction when they overwhelmingly approved twenty-three propositions, by an average margin of six-to-one, on May 26, 1955. The total cost of the measures was $110.6 million. The most expensive outlay was for three major expressways, approximately eight miles each, connecting downtown to the suburban areas to the north, west, and south at a total cost of $18 million to the city. The federal and state governments contributed $75 million to fund half of the right-of-way costs and all of the construction. The propositions also set aside $16.4 million for schools, $11.6 million for streets, $11.4 million for bridges and viaducts, $11 million for parks and playgrounds, $10 million for slum clearance, $7.5 million for hospitals, $7.5 million for flood control (matched by an $112.5 million federal appropriation for eleven miles of waterfront improvement), $6 million for street lighting, $5.2 million for juvenile and other correctional centers, and $22.3 million for neighborhood rehabilitation—including street resurfacing, voting machines, fire stations, public building improvements, garbage facilities, a planetarium, a children's zoo, new library branches, air-conditioning for the Art Museum, municipal docks, and other items. The least popular issues, for the planetarium and the museum air-conditioning, still passed at a rate of better than three-to-one. The *St. Louis Post-Dispatch* celebrated the voting in language that would capture the tone of urban renewal discourse going forward. St. Louisans "voted for the new and clean—and against the outmoded and dirty. They voted for a moving, growing, advancing future—and against a blighting, killing past."[39] New versus outmoded, clean versus dirty, growing versus killing—this sort of language framed the urban changes that occurred in the city over the next decade.

The vitality of the new relied on the erasure of the "blighting past," and the 1955 propositions included ten million dollars for slum clearance—a measure receiving overwhelming support from primarily black wards.[40] This bond issue enabled massive land assembly and clearance in two of the city's major industrial areas: Mill Creek Valley and Kosciusko. Mill Creek Valley consisted of about four hundred fifty acres, just west of the downtown. Kosciusko occupied about two hundred acres along Broadway, running south from downtown. Renewal plans for both areas were proposed in the late 1940s but didn't go anywhere until federal laws were expanded to include commercial and industrial projects in 1954. Both areas were designated blighted in 1958.

Advocates for redevelopment at Mill Creek and Kosciusko publicly promised an expansion in jobs, but the plans were primarily geared toward making these areas, which consumed city services and paid little in taxes, more fiscally solvent. The poor were dislocated from both areas without being properly relocated in modern housing; funding for clearance, it seemed, was more readily available than funding for redevelopment. Plans for Kosciusko called for the rehabilitation of existing commercial and industrial areas, along with the excising of "misplaced" residential pockets of working-class whites. Planners hoped that established industries—the Anheuser-Busch brewery, for example, at the southern end of the renewal area—would expand. At Mill Creek, a quarter of the land was reserved for the extension of the Daniel Boone Expressway development, a quarter was reserved for light industrial redevelopment, and the rest was designated for residential, public, and commercial use. At least twenty thousand people were displaced from the neighborhood, almost all of whom were African American and poor, but only a small number were actually placed in public housing. A 1964 federal audit found that more than half weren't meaningfully assisted and that most of the people redevelopment officials claimed had been relocated had ended up in substandard housing elsewhere in the city—in many cases choosing inexpen-

FIGURE 63. An aerial photograph of St. Louis is marked with projected freeways in "A Plan for Downtown St. Louis," prepared by the City Plan Commission, published in 1960, and reprinted in 1962. The central business district—"the shopping business and financial center, the hard core that we generally call 'Downtown St. Louis'"—is in the center. Busch Stadium would be located in the lower left corner of downtown, near the path of Highway-40, the city's first expressway, which ran east to the suburbs. The towers of the Pruitt-Igoe housing project are visible directly above downtown, as is Sportsman's Park just beyond that.
TWA COLLECTIONS OF THE ST. LOUIS MERCANTILE LIBRARY AT THE UNIVERSITY OF MISSOURI-ST. LOUIS.

sive private housing instead of underfunded and underserved public housing projects like Pruitt-Igoe.[41] Mill Creek's leveled and undeveloped expanses, which seemed victims of a protracted war, became known as "Hiroshima Flats."[42]

A series of plans were hatched—some realized, some not—to reinvent the downtown. An area around City Hall at Twelfth and Market Street, four blocks west of the future stadium site, was targeted for renewal. Plans were devised for a Gateway Mall running westward about one mile from the planned site of the Arch to Union Station, between Chestnut and Market. These plans were eventually downscaled to the Plaza Square area, from Fourteenth to Eighteenth, between Market and Olive. In 1959, an area three blocks north of the stadium site and adjacent the planned Arch was designated blighted under Chapter 353. Three 28-story apartment complexes opened there in 1966—part of a broader strategy to attract high-income residents downtown.[43]

FIGURE 64. The new stadium and Gateway Arch are highlights of a glowing and verdant downtown St. Louis. City Plan Commission, "A Plan for Downtown St. Louis" (1960).
TWA COLLECTIONS OF THE ST. LOUIS MERCANTILE LIBRARY AT THE UNIVERSITY OF MISSOURI–ST. LOUIS.

These plans, however, were minor compared to the two most conspicuous facets of renewal in the city. The Gateway Arch and Busch Stadium epitomized the optimistic spirit of planners and citizens in the early 1960s. Also known as the Jefferson National Expansion Memorial, the Arch was begun in 1963 and completed in 1965. It memorialized the city's past significance as the nineteenth-century jumping-off point to the American West. St. Louis, once so important as the midwestern transportation and industrial hub, had long since ceded its significance to cities like Chicago, and more recently ones like Houston. The memorial argued for the city's historical importance. And yet the Arch would be the ultimate modern icon—an abstract, monumental steel parabola—shorthand for the mathematical, the scientific, the planetary projectile in motion.[44] It yoked nineteenth-century ideas about Manifest Destiny to their twentieth-century counterpart: an unwavering faith in modern "progress." And so, as a monument, the Arch looked forward and backward, straddling the city's past and its hopeful modern future, just as it straddled its lot along the Mississippi River. The stadium would work symbolically in a similar vein, drawing an old pastoral landscape—the sporting grounds—into a city that seemed from another era, while signifying the economic and physical rebirth of a center city that many saw as dead and rotten.

Building Busch Stadium

Early proposals for a downtown stadium in St. Louis envisioned a football structure. The first pitch was made in October 1935, by the football coach at Washington University, who was trying to enhance the program's status by scheduling games against more illustrious competition. Mayor Bernard F. Dickmann proposed a 60,000-seat stadium three years later, as part of the Jefferson National Expansion Memorial.[45] World War II ended planning of the memorial, but Washington University alumni pushed for the plan again after the war. Opponents of the plan thought the memorial should be a more meaningful structure than a sports stadium.[46]

An elaborate roofed stadium proposal made its way through the St. Louis Chamber of Commerce and Missouri Senate in 1958, before being vetoed by the governor in July 1959. Supporters published an illustrated advertisement in the *St. Louis Post-Dispatch* to try to revive the dreamy project. The incredible plan called for a 115,000-seat stadium, with air-conditioning and heat, that could accommodate baseball, track, football, swimming and high diving, tennis, and conventions. It would feature a restaurant seating 1,500 on three floors, to be suspended 385 feet above the playing field, accessible by "moving sidewalks 600 feet long from the perimeter of the roof to the restaurant center." Plans called for an office building connected to the stadium, "which could boast the reference of being across the hall from all these activities." The building would house 2.5 million square feet of "international shopping facilities," providing $9 million in yearly revenue. A 27,000-car parking area would sit underneath the stadium, keeping drivers and their cars "protected from all the elements of weather." Should Cold War catastrophe strike, the compound could double as a fallout shelter for 600,000 people "with pure water to drink, pure food to eat, fresh air to breathe, forty-two acres of recreational areas under roof and the privacy of individual family cubicles." It would be a futuristic city unto itself. The entire project, the advertisement claimed, would be funded through revenue bonds paid off by rentals; no county or state bond issues were even necessary.[47]

A different, and much more plausible, stadium plan was being cultivated by the city's power brokers in 1958. Charles L. Farris, executive director of the Land Clearance for Redevelopment Authority (LCRA), presented a plan for a $30 million downtown stadium to the chamber of commerce on December 9, 1958. The peculiar-looking structure—whose upturned corners reminded some of a pagoda—was to be located on eighteen blocks near the Arch (though Eero Saarinen, the Arch's designer, had warned that a stadium might "disbalance" the skyline and undermine the memorial). The chamber put "some of its most progressive members" to work on the project, as a local reporter phrased it. James P. Hickok, president of the First National Bank in St. Louis, was named chairman of a committee to investigate the proposal. An editorial supported the project, though it was skeptical that the stadium would revitalize downtown, remarking, "Of course, some of the boosters always wanted somebody else to put up a stadium for them to move into"—a reference to Busch's prominence as both Cardinals owner and voice in redevelopment.[48]

The stadium took a giant step forward the following September, when the chamber of commerce voted to proceed with an $89 million downtown redevelopment project anchored by a 50,000-seat stadium. Hickok's committee recommended constructing a semi-bowl, double-decked, multipurpose stadium that could be expanded, if necessary, from 50,000 seats to 72,000. Construction costs would be close to $15 million; other costs would run the total project to over $22 million. The stadium would be built on a ten-block site at Fourth, Market, Seventh, and Spruce. The broader redevelopment area consisted of twenty-seven blocks bounded by Third Street Highway, Pine, Eighth, and Poplar. The committee claimed that the stadium project would attract private investors only if they were given developmental control of the area around the stadium, where they could invest in other schemes to offset stadium losses. The stadium alone, the committee estimated, would lose about $750,000 per year. To compensate for these losses, private developers could create parking for 7,200 cars in four garages, an underground location, and surface lots; a 32-lane bowling alley with a cocktail lounge and restaurant for 250; a 750-room motel; two 20-story office towers; and three commercial areas for shops and filling stations. These additional developments were deemed essential, allowing investors to generate profits of at least $350,000 per year—considered a baseline incentive.

Hickok's committee recommended that the development be run through an urban redevelopment corporation headed by Hickock, Sidney Maestre, and Preston Estep, president of Transit Casualty Company.[49] It would be called the Civic Center Redevelopment Corporation (CCRC), and it was formed one day after Anheuser-Busch pledged $5 million of the initial $20 million needed as equity to obtain a stadium loan. By February 1960, the CCRC had received capital pledges of $17 million, much of that from banks and insurance companies.[50]

The first major opposition to the Civic Center redevelopment came in late January 1960, when a spokesman for thirty-six businesses in the renewal area argued that it couldn't reasonably be designated blighted. At an aldermanic hearing, opponents of the plan pointed out that there were already businesses there. A coffee company had paid $2.5 million in 1958 for a seven-story building, invested $750,000 for equipment specifically designed for the building, did $12 million in business in 1959, and planned to do $20 million more in 1962. The owner of a printing firm noted that his business had paid $70,000 in taxes the previous year. A speaker pointed out that there were thirty-two parking lots in the area; removing them would aggravate downtown parking problems in the short term and then give the stadium corporation a monopoly on downtown parking after that.

Proponents of the plan—at least as reported by the *St. Louis Post-Dispatch*—seemed to speak past these complaints rather than engage them. They insisted that the stadium and related development would restore the area to productivity. Hickok claimed, "There is no question about the fact that there is no future—and there can be no future for this area—except through its becoming a site of the proposed $89,000,000 Stadium and Civic Center." Maestre, who also served as chairman of Downtown St. Louis, Inc., a promotional association for the city center that shared many members with Civic Progress, stated that the project would "require no financial aid from federal, state or city governments"—a disingenuous statement, given the CCRC's reliance on the use of eminent domain to make the real estate available. Aloys P. Kaufmann, president of the chamber of commerce, said that the project would produce increased economic activity and tax revenues—a proposition that, too, seemed dubious, given the tax abatements that would accompany the redevelopment of blighted areas.[51]

Backed by the city's powerful business leaders, the project pushed on. The Civic Center/Stadium Redevelopment Area, nearly ninety acres in size, was designated blighted in 1960 under Chapter 353. It was again designated blighted under Chapter 99.[52] Equitable Life Assurance Society approved a $31 million loan for the project in June 1961; that company had $900 million invested in the city and would soon relocate its new corporate headquarters within the tax-sheltered redevelopment zone in downtown St. Louis.[53] A $6 million bond issue to fund improvements around the stadium, like sidewalks, streets, and lighting, was approved by a two-to-one vote in March 1962, just two months after being defeated. A reporter would later recall that the "Civic Center and its friends" put together a persuasive "public education campaign" to change people's minds. Architect Edward Durell Stone presented his stadium plans to the chamber of commerce in March 1963, accompanied by a $12,000 plastic model. In May 1964, ground was broken.[54]

Amid the buzz of urban reinvention was a serious, but ultimately unexecuted, plan for a midwestern Disneyland across the street from the stadium. Planners for Downtown St. Louis, Inc., had sketched out a one-block area of theaters, restaurants, and stores—limited to pedestrian access—for the block bounded by Broadway, Walnut, Market, and Seventh, immediately north of the stadium site and west of the Gateway Arch. It was to be called "Riverfront Square." The CCRC was enamored with the plans, and Raymond Witcoff, president of Downtown St. Louis, Inc., consulted with Walt Disney, a Missouri native, for advice. Disney suggested his company was interested in taking over the development and received a delegation from St. Louis in March 1963, which included Witcoff, Mayor Raymond Tucker, and Preston Estep of the CCRC, at his studios in California. Walt returned a visit to St. Louis in November.[55]

Disney draftsmen drew up plans in early 1964 for a multistory, indoor entertainment center filling the block—a miniature, indoor version of Anaheim's Disneyland. The vision called for a main entrance like that of Disneyland's Town Square, featuring an Old St. Louis district opposite an Old New Orleans one (similar to New Orleans Square, which opened a few years later at Disneyland). The park would feature a "Caribbean Pirate's Lair" and "Blue Bayou" boat ride—plans that later evolved into the popular Pirates of the Caribbean ride at Disneyland. The facility would also include an Audio-Animatronics show, like that at the New York World's Fair, a "Western Riverboat" ride, a haunted house, two 360-degree Circarama theaters, shops, a large banquet room, a restaurant, a bar, and a lounge with a view of the Mississippi River. The interior atrium would stage artificial lighting and weather conditions to manipulate the time of day and compensate for the seasonal changes of the Midwest.[56]

The project ran aground when it came to financing. Disney thought that the city should finance building costs—between thirty and fifty million dollars—that would then be reimbursed by profits from the facility. Once repaid, Disney would own it. This arrangement was unworkable for the CCRC. As Disney pondered the possibility of an urban theme park, the company was offered thousands of inexpensive acres in Florida—a clean slate for a Disneyland East. This development, coupled with the only marginal profitability predicted by consultants in St. Louis (no more than 5 percent return on investment), squelched project momentum. By July 1965, the deal was dead.[57]

Disneyland St. Louis never materialized, but the CCRC proceeded enthusiastically with stadium construction and area redevelopment. It spun off three subsidiary urban redevelopment corporations to organize and manage the construction of the stadium, stadium parking garages, a Stouffer Hotel, and a series of corporate structures (Pet Milk, Equitable Life, First National, General American Life), as well as the relocation of the Spanish Pavilion from the New York World's Fair—to be used as an exhibition and performing arts space.[58] Once the stadium was constructed, the LCRA, which was a tax-exempt public body, retained the title on the land, leasing it to developers and tenants, who made payments to the LCRA in lieu of taxes to the city.[59] The CCRC facilitated the replacement of urban industry with corporate headquarters and a new stadium that was a boon to Busch, his Cardinals, and his brewery. It increased the value of the franchise, which could host more fans and sell more beer. Because the club didn't own the stadium, it avoided the costs of construction. By purchasing five million dollars in CCRC stock, the Cardinals enjoyed access to a brand-new, modern, downtown stadium at a fraction of its actual cost.[60]

The Cardinals moved into a nearly circular structure with an outside diameter of eight hundred feet, sitting on twelve sloping acres. The stadium's distinguished exterior identified it as more "architectural" than its modern predecessors, as did its designer, Edward Durell Stone. Reflecting on his work, Stone argued, "The stadium's near-round design has an elegant symmetry lacking in the horseshoe-shaped sports arenas found in most U.S. cities."[61] Upon the unveiling of Stone's plans, an editorial in the *St. Louis Post-Dispatch* agreed, favorably comparing the future stadium to existing ones and assigning credit to the city as a whole: "Considering the basic ugliness of such structures, the community may well congratulate itself on the designers' achievement."[62] Like many of Stone's other projects, Busch Stadium employed thin columns, simple geometric shapes, and an overall sense of visual order (standard features of midcentury modern architecture); however, it was also accented with minor decorative details (a departure Stone often made from modernist orthodoxy). A thin band of roof pinched inward around the stadium's top, like a rim, supported by a series of small arches that echoed Eero Saarinen's ur-Arch of the Expansion Memorial. From above, the series of arches looked like a ring of seashells or a toothed gear; from the ground, they bulged over the edge of the roof like little bubbles, sitting atop a curving colonnade of thin concrete pillars, each just two feet wide. Slanting pedestrian ramps ran between exterior and interior series of columns, undulating around the face of the structure. Though massive and monumental, these features made the stadium seem airy and light.

Besides its elevated architectural pedigree and downtown location, Busch Stadium was essentially an elaboration of the postwar modern stadium type being developed across the country in various cities: from San Francisco to Washington, Los Angeles to New York to Houston. It embodied many of those same characteristics that this series of stadiums usually shared in some form or another. Its size and footprint were markedly increased over those of the previous generations of stadium. It was more spacious and physically comfortable. Operators championed enhanced customer service, particularly to the more

FIGURE 65. An aerial view of Busch Stadium during the 1967 World Series.
ARTHUR WITMAN, S0665, ID 665.181, STATE HISTORICAL SOCIETY OF MISSOURI/RESEARCH CENTER–ST. LOUIS.

affluent. It catered to the private automobile. It was designed to be more adaptable to uses other than baseball, though the baseball club was its primary tenant.

Like many other modern stadiums, the most notable initial quality of Busch was its size relative to the stadium it replaced. The stadium "overwhelmed most of the customers with its size, simplicity and spaciousness," according to a reporter.[63] Another wrote, "What impressed first-nighters most were the massiveness and spaciousness of the stadium."[64] A local television station congratulated the fans of St. Louis for their new stadium and its "beauty, convenience, size and comfort."[65] The stadium seemed so large to some that they experienced vertigo when they arrived at the upper decks—prompting complaints that the structure featured no escalators.[66] Cardinal vice president and legendary player Stan Musial, who was also director of the national fitness program, was reportedly pleased with "the fact that the new park requires much more walking than the old one."[67] Like Musial, Ray Blades, a former player-manager for the baseball Cardinals, tried to put a happy face on the elevation of the top levels, joking, "Fifteen more feet up and I'd be in heaven."[68]

The size of the stadium cultivated a sense of spaciousness—a standard modern stadium virtue. A headline for the *Sporting News* foregrounded this quality: "Something

New in St. Louis—Spacious Stadium."[69] The interior was a great sweeping enclosure of red seats—49,453 in all, perched on three major levels—each with "plenty of extra elbow room."[70] Roger Angell registered his standard complaint of the modern stadium; he "admired everything about this open-face mine except its shape," which put the fans in the upper deck too far from the field below, "a dismaying distance from the infielders within the right angles of the diamond."[71] A reporter for the *Sporting News* noted the distance as well, though visitors quickly adjusted. "Obviously, quite a few fans have to sit farther from the playing field than they did at the much-smaller old Busch Stadium," he wrote, adding, "but many were well prepared with binoculars."[72]

Busch visually advertised its pedestrian traffic routes, like Shea Stadium and many other modern structures. The ramps around the exterior were one of its most visible characteristics, as were the distinct and tidy aisles and rows throughout the seating sections. Visitors noted the "wide outside concourse and the wide ramps inside," and many used them as observation decks to look out across the cityscape.[73] More than one and a half miles of ramps, according to architect Stone, "speed the flow of spectators" to the stadium's mezzanine and upper levels.[74]

Automobility was a primary concern for designers, as it was in all American cities. While many stadiums were moved outside of the city, toward a targeted suburban and affluent audience, the St. Louis stadium was notable for moving from a congested residential neighborhood to an equally dense downtown. Vital to the project was the complementary construction of parking garages adjacent the site—particularly because stadium development had wiped out many area surface lots. The location also relied on the development of $93 million worth of new expressways—north, south, and east from downtown—that had been voted into existence in the mid-1950s and were being constructed through the 1960s. Civic leaders hoped to revitalize downtown with the construction of the stadium and associated development—a new approach in the stadium game—but not everyone was convinced the new expressways and multilayered parking garages would properly accommodate visitors. A resident of suburban Florissant wondered in a letter to the editor why so much development was focused downtown, complaining, "How about asking them to ease up a little and to give the motorist a fighting chance?"[75]

When the suburban consumer braved the traffic and made it inside new Busch, she found a stadium space that by the mid-1960s was fairly standard. The cantilevered design removed view-obstructing support posts. The sunken playing field was adaptable to football through rotating stands like those used in D.C. Stadium, Shea Stadium, and the Astrodome; the National Football League's Chicago Cardinals had moved to Sportsman's Park in 1960 and would join the baseball team at new Busch. As at other modern stadiums, customer service was a celebrated feature. A large usher corps, over three hundred on opening day (one hundred more than had worked the old Sportsman's Park on its busiest days), attended to customers. This included the debut of a forty-two-member female usher corps of "attractive young women" who worked in the stadium's more expensive box-seat areas, charming the stadium's more moneyed patrons. Ushers wore bright red blazers, straw hats with red bands, black trousers, white shirts, and bow ties, as though they were riverboat attendants.[76] Also like other modern stadiums, Busch boasted a Stadium Club to separate the economic wheat from the chaff—a club "spacious and splendid," according to Red Smith. The split-level facility on the stadium's northeast side was outfitted with wall-to-wall carpeting, paintings and photographs depicting sports scenes, a massive U-shaped bar offering "a commanding view of the field," and "lavishly decorated" dining tables with "posh" leather swivel chairs.[77] Reporters for the *St. Louis Post-Dispatch* called it "a private retreat," and its inhabitants were "the jet set of the swank Stadium Club."[78]

The scoreboard, of course, was another cause for celebration for visitors and writers; one called it "the new St. Louis 'super-star.'" Officially named the "St. Louis Color Informatic Display," the Busch scoreboard cost $1.5 million and consisted of panels in left and right field. Powered by 492 miles of wiring and a load of 180,000 watts, it provided "enough electricity to light 450 homes"—a comparison combining the mesmerizing power of quantification with a scalability that would resonate with a suburban homeowner. The right-field panel displayed game information and trivia and advertised future home dates. The board in left field, however, was the main attraction, a 15-foot-tall, 54-foot-long panel that featured color display.[79]

The left-field scoreboard was St. Louis's answer to the Astrodome's scoreboard extravaganza. The message board could display images of a cardinal, a paddleboat, a banjo, and the salutation "howdy." What set this board apart from the others was its ability to not only flash messages but display them in color—capabilities the boards at Shea and Dodger Stadium lacked. The stadium thus added "living color" to the scene, though on opening night the board displayed only Anheuser-Busch ads (free advertising was another of the brewery's perks—along with a new stadium—for contributing five million dollars to the CCRC's coffers). Boosters praised the scoreboard's modest use, in comparison to its well-publicized predecessor at the Astrodome. Dave Lipman of the *St. Louis Post-Dispatch* claimed it took "the bull out of the scoreboard business." "The Houston scoreboard," he explained, "much to the disgust of baseball men across the country, takes an active part in the game, waging psychological warfare against the foe and actually entering into the game." Baseball had traditionally "had an understanding" that such artificial forms of partisanship would be off-limits during play. Major league baseball, as Lipman saw it, had condoned the Houston scoreboard. But, he argued, "such antics will not be the case here." To wit, scoreboard technicians in Busch Stadium would display an image of a cardinal flapping its wings and broadcast chirping noises on the public address system even when the opponent scored.[80] But even as Lipman defended the "Informatic," many visitors were disappointed that it didn't seem to measure up to the one in Houston. One reporter noted at an early game, "Once in their seats, most persons marveled at the size of the two scoreboards above the outfield walls and wondered what electronic gimmicks they could expect to see. Most were disappointed, however, because the boards displayed little of the ingenuity and entertainment of the famous scoreboard in the domed stadium in Houston."[81] This sense of civic inadequacy may have been amplified by reports that a scoreboard gag, an "electronic gimmick," went awry on opening day. When a helicopter lowered an American flag to the field for the national anthem, the scoreboard was supposed to taunt, "Let's see the dome match this." The board wasn't properly functioning, however—an ironic commentary on its relative shortcomings.[82] And yet this failure didn't quell all boosterism. Sportswriter Bob Broeg boasted, "If things get dull this summer downtown at the new stadium, a guy will have only himself to blame for the boredom, not the ball players. After all, between the colorful advertising designs on the scoreboard in left-center and the trivia, minutiae and messages of [the] moment on the board in right-center, a spectator wouldn't have to know General Eckert from General Motors to find baseball appealing."[83] It was a claim that could have come from the mouth of Roy Hofheinz in Houston. The scoreboard, a metonym for the modern stadium, could make baseball "appealing"—an assertion that revealed a remarkable lack of faith in a sport that had been one of the country's most popular forms of entertainment for over sixty years.

Many Cardinals supporters would have certainly disagreed with Broeg's suggestion that baseball required Color Informatic scoreboard entertainment. In 1964, Roger Angell had called St. Louis "perhaps the most dedicated baseball town in the country"—no mean compliment coming from such a perceptive and well-traveled observer.[84] Baseball in St. Louis was serious business, and had been for a very long time. Though the stadium experience was becoming increasingly standardized across the country by the mid-1960s—new modern structures had opened in San Francisco, Washington, D.C., Los Angeles, New York, Anaheim, and Atlanta since 1960—the modern stadium experience was a drastic departure for most St. Louis sports fans. They were accustomed to watching baseball, football, and soccer at grounds that had been used for that purpose for a full century, in a ballpark that, aside from some modifications, had been constructed over fifty years before. For them, the modern Busch Stadium was something totally new.

For many in St. Louis, encouraged by the promises of Civic Progress, the stadium was also a symbol of the city's future, embodying dreams for a new downtown that was a clean, sparsely populated center for commerce, business, and entertainment. Downtown St. Louis, Inc., extolled the virtues of a deindustrialized, modern St. Louis, claiming that "all great cities have in common two characteristics, an exciting Downtown filled with a great variety of shops, theatres, museums, and other attractions" and "a large middle class population residing near downtown possessing the purchasing power and tastes to help sustain its activities."[85] The modern, chamber-of-commerce vision for the downtown contrasted dramatically with a genuinely old Sportsman's Park.[86] That stadium, repeatedly called "ancient" by writers across the country, was a structure from another time, in a geography of mixed uses, classes, and races—not a new and modern downtown pitched to affluent white-collar bureaucrats and their suburban wives out for a night on the town. The transition from one place to the other, the old city to the new one, was narrated by two overlapping discourses— one employing rhetorical and visual representations of death and life, the other engaging conceptions of "progress," together illustrating the stakes of a new stadium and the new city.

Decay and Rejuvenation

To call an old baseball park "ancient" was unremarkable in the 1950s and 1960s. Writers used the term to describe Brooklyn's Ebbets Field, Harlem's Polo Grounds, Boston's Fenway Park, Cincinnati's Crosley Field, and no doubt many other stadiums of that type.[87] The term "ancient" bore different meanings, depending on the user. Sometimes it was a simple pejorative—sportswriters like Robert Creamer of *Sports Illustrated* and John Hall of the *Los Angeles Times* used "ancient" to dismiss the Polo Grounds in 1963 and Fenway Park in 1967 as obsolete and inappropriate to modern times.[88] But "ancient" could also suggest something more than just age and obsolescence. It was sometimes instilled with reverence and deference to the authority and accrued wisdom of a park loaded with human experience and memory. Easily the most common descriptor of Sportsman's Park (old Busch Stadium), even as early as the late 1940s, was "ancient"—a term of endearment but also recognition that the park seemed at odds with the times. It was "ancient," the "ancient ball park in St. Louis," an "ancient arena," an "ancient landmark," and "ancient Busch Stadium."[89]

Something ancient, if not already dead, was clearly on its last legs. Many commentators anthropomorphized the park that teetered on the precipice of death. One referred to "the passing of ancient Busch Stadium" as though it were a person who had expired.[90] When personified, Sportsman's Park was often figured as an old woman.[91] Sportswriter Neal Russo of the *St. Louis Post-Dispatch* and the *Sporting News* wrote, "The belated face-lifting and later improvements gave Old Lady at Grand and Dodier a good luck that continued even though execution by the headache ball had been decreed."[92] Ed Wilks, also of the *Post-Dispatch*, penned an entire article extending the "Old Lady" metaphor after the last game there. He observed, "Oddly, the Old Lady wasn't dressed in her finery. Those 10 pennants were missing, folded away some place, on the Old Lady's final hour." He grimly observed the final rites, recounting, "The seats weren't filled on the Old Lady's last day. But those who were there groaned a bit when a bulldozer dug up her outfield grass. It was like watching 'em throw dirt on the coffin." He celebrated the park's presumably unfeminine resolve, writing, "The Old Lady just stood there, and took it like a man."[93]

The respect and affection commentators paid to this seemingly living ballpark were not extended to the city as a whole. A broader urban discourse conceived the city as a living thing, but one beset by blight, decay, disease, and rot; this was a city that was a living being on the brink of an unseemly death. Medical analogies were used often in postwar analyses of American cities and their problems; they were believed to have diseases, and it was the job of planners and developers, public and private, to save them by removing these infections, most commonly referred to as "blight." Agents of urban renewal imagined themselves as surgeons, battling heroically to save an urban patient.[94]

The new Busch Stadium and the monumental Arch were powerful symbols of urban renewal in St. Louis—surgical instruments to arrest urban disease. With these instruments, the city's progressive leaders would deliver the city from certain death, giving it a new life. This discourse of rebirth and rejuvenation animated much of the conversation about the stadium and downtown development. At the stadium groundbreaking, James Hickok proclaimed, "Look all around us," gesturing toward the Arch, the Third Street construction, Poplar Street bridge, and the Mansion House project. "You can see for yourselves the truth in the statement that our city is truly being reborn. We are replacing the old with the new."[95] The chairman of the Mercantile Trust Company, Kenneth R. Cravens, said of downtown, "A dying and decaying section has made a complete reversal."[96] As the stadium was being completed, the *St. Louis Post-Dispatch* announced in headlines, "A New Spirit of St. Louis Is Born . . . A Greater Tomorrow."[97] Writers celebrated "St. Louis' renaissance" and "the rebirth of downtown St. Louis."[98]

When the stadium opened in May 1966, the Cardinals' souvenir guidebook delivered a narrative of urban rebirth familiar to St. Louis residents—a story that had been told repeatedly through local newspapers over the previous half decade. The program recalled the visit of President Johnson on February 14, 1964, to officially celebrate St. Louis's two hundredth birthday. Johnson "saw in the so-called 'stadium area' . . . one big mass of blight and decay." It was an "eyesore" of vacant lots, empty and rundown buildings, industrial plants, warehouses, and parking lots. Those who knew the area best were the "police, fire marshals, and building and health inspectors." The only citizens who entered, the program stated, either worked there, had business there, or were simply "a few unfortunate human derelicts who had no place else to go. No visitors ever came . . . and nobody ever invited them." This sad condition would become transformed. "Today," readers were told, "more than any other single project this great stadium marks the determination of our community to grow and to prosper. It symbolizes the results of a unique partnership between private business, labor unions, various branches of the government, and long-range planning."[99]

The city's "rebirth" was also well noted by national media. The *Washington Post* described the "rejuvenation of the riverfront" and "downtown renaissance" that swept away "a warehouse-Skid Row area that spread blight along the waterfront for years."[100] The *New*

York Times noted hopes for "a new economic vitality" in an area that had been "an ugly picture of decay," while also recalling the city's image as a "dowager" for how rapidly it seemed to have aged in recent decades.[101] United Press International, too, called St. Louis the "Dowager City," known to be "once so set in its ways." But in the mid-1960s, it was "blasting out whole sections of blight and rot," replacing the "rotting levee" and "an area so decayed that St. Louis turned its back on it for a century." Urban renewal in St. Louis proved "a catalyst in the rejuvenation of the once-dowdy and depressed 'Dowager City.'"[102] Not all commentaries on downtown change were positive. Ada Louise Huxtable said of downtown, "All of the stages of decay, death, rebirth and rebuilding are currently visible—with the usual success and failures, ironies and anachronisms."[103] And yet, even in critiquing most of the renewal developments, Huxtable too employed this discourse of urban death and birth that associated the old with decay and the new with the vital.

These polarizing equivalences were reinforced by visual representations of the stadiums and the downtown area. The baseball Cardinals made an explicit comparison between the two stadiums in the 1965 souvenir yearbook. A two-page spread, titled "The Old . . . and the New," pitched the two structures against one another in visual terms. On one page was an aerial photo of Sportsman's Park—branded "The Old" with a decorative, anachronistic Old English typeface. The park seemed to be an open-end box, but with angles slightly askew. The light standards stuck out like rusty nails. The geographic contexts were almost wholly cropped out of the scene, as though the club was embarrassed to reveal what lurked outside the grounds—cars crammed in every nook and cranny of an old neighborhood, dirty brown roofs, and wholesale visual irregularity. Facing this was "The New" (in sleek, modern cursive)—an aerial illustration of the new Busch Stadium. The tight framing was gone here, as the vista opened up to a radically geometric and rational downtown—the curves of the stadium, the Arch, a new high-rise hotel, and the old courthouse (a final remnant of the old city) were set against the tidy boxes of office buildings and parking garages. The predominantly African American East St. Louis, across the Mississippi River, had been erased and painted over with idyllic farmland. The brown and jagged ballpark was replaced by a sculpted, modern womb that was blazingly white.[104]

This would be the visual vernacular of stadium renewal in St. Louis, a curved and glowing whiteness that distinguished the new from the old, the reborn from the decayed—a vital womb replacing the infertile dowager. The stadium's visual and sculptural purity was again celebrated on the cover of the 1966 club yearbook.[105] Hand-drawn illustrations of the stadium and downtown, used in news stories and advertisements, often featured a wide frame that captured the whole area post–urban renaissance. It was a rational landscape of orderly streets and new white structures—particularly the stadium.[106] Actual photographs of a downtown-under-construction usually employed much tighter framing, excluding the stadium's surrounding area, particularly to the industrial and unredeemed south. And yet

ST. LOUIS **CARDINALS**

OLD BUSCH STADIUM 1920-1966

1966
SOUVENIR
YEARBOOK

$1.00

FIGURE 66. The cover of the Cardinals' 1966 club yearbook featured a virginally white Busch Stadium—a stark contrast to the "old dowager" of Sportsman's Park. A. BARTLETT GIAMATTI RESEARCH CENTER, NATIONAL BASEBALL HALL OF FAME.

the stadium, even when photographed, seemed to glow against its brown, urban margins.[107] A full-page Anheuser-Busch advertisement, printed in a special *St. Louis Post-Dispatch* insert on the stadium and downtown redevelopment, combined photo and illustration. The ad asked readers, "What would the world be without the imagination of men combined with a will to win?" Filling the page was an aerial photograph of St. Louis shot from the southeast, pre-renewal. The blackened, boxy landscape was brightened by seemingly hand-drawn, white outlines of the urban renewal projects being constructed atop this visually lifeless city—freeways, the Arch, the stadium, new hotels, and apartment towers. It was a dreamy visualization of progress, a reauthored white city to replace a black one.[108]

Like its visual and rhetorical representation, the material stadium itself seemed a beacon of the clean, the modern, the breathing vital—a reproach to the black, heavy, and rotten city. Unveiling his plans in March 1963, architect Edward Durell Stone noted that the thin columns would "give an impression of light weight and wide open spaces," as a St. Louis reporter recounted it.[109] An editorial for the *St. Louis Post-Dispatch* agreed, claiming that the design "adds lightness and grace to mass and bulk."[110] Many observers noted these qualities once the stadium had been built. "The completed stadium bears out the promise of giving the impression of light weight and open spaces through the 2-by-3 foot supporting columns," one reporter noted, adding, "The brightness is accentuated by the concrete shell covering." The stadium was thus light and bright, contrasting with the dark, heavy, brick structures that had recently blighted the area.[111] In his syndicated column, sportswriter Red Smith ventured, "Perhaps the most striking feature of the stadium, seen from the outside, is its open work appearance. Instead of a solid wall of masonry, the facade has been left open between slender columns, leaving the inner ramps visible."[112] The "Sunday Pictures" insert of the *St. Louis Post-Dispatch* featured a cover photo shot from one of the interior ramps, framing the inclined pedestrian way flanked by thin columns, titled "Grandeur in Concrete." The setting was wholly un-stadium-like, resembling the glass-enclosed lobby of a new museum or a plaza beneath an office tower perched atop modern piers.[113] Like these analogical spaces, the openness and lightness of the Busch Stadium exterior expressed modernity, spaciousness, and order.

Many interpreted the stadium's modern characteristics as indicators of sophistication and beauty. Mrs. Claudia Hanebrink, a resident of suburban Affton, uttered, "This is the most beautiful thing I have even seen"—praise broadcast as a headline on the front page of the *St. Louis Post-Dispatch*.[114] A reporter called it "a decorative hub . . . more magnificent than envisioned in any dream because no lay dreamer could have imagined the final monumental design, the brilliant scalloped canopy and the delicacy of the slender piers. It took inspired architects to do that."[115] Busch was a "huge, luxurious circle of concrete" to New York sportswriter Leonard Koppett and "a steep, elegant gray concrete pile" for Roger Angell.[116] Player Nelson Briles likened it to the Taj Mahal—a common enough comparison for modern stadiums, though in this case, given the blinding whiteness of each, a justifiable one.[117] Busch was beautiful, luxurious, elegant, monumental; it was also, simply, "bright, clean and slightly antiseptic," in the words of a *Sports Illustrated* writer.[118]

The conspicuous openness of the exterior was balanced against a near-complete enclosure of the interior. While only the Astrodome fully sealed its inhabitants inside—a necessary condition for the climate control—Busch Stadium was the third outdoor stadium with a complete circle of stands (Washington's D.C. Stadium, opened in 1961, was the first; the Atlanta-Fulton County Stadium opened in 1965). The circular Busch effected a sense of enclosure for people inside, broken only for those sitting in the southeastern portion of the stadium who could see the top of the Gateway Arch peeking over the rim of the stadium. A thin band of roof around the stadium rim, leaning out over the top portions of the upper level, accentuated this sense of protection. The enveloped spectator enjoyed little of the visual relief allowed those at Dodger Stadium, where one drank in the rugged scenery of the hills beyond, or at Shea Stadium, where one could view the uneven spaces of Flushing outside. She certainly witnessed nothing like the various and chaotic scene outside Sportsman's Park. Inhabitants were sheltered from the unpredictable city outside, made to look at other consumers—often middle-class visitors in from the suburbs—rather than the urban landscape beyond.

Stadium discourse and materiality in St. Louis overlapped with broader conceptions of and conversations about the city—in fact, exemplifying them. The city was coded as diseased, decaying, dying, blighted—at a time when blight was, as historian Colin Gordon notes, "a near-synonym for black residency."[119] Illustrations and photographs marked it as dark, even black, when St. Louis was increasingly racially black. The remedy for these diseases of blight and blackness was a renewal program that extricated this tumorous decay and replaced it with new, rational, clean, and *white* projects like Busch Stadium. Urban change was understood through the lens of not only race but gender as well. The old ballpark and the depressed city were both figured as "dowagers"—presumably women that were beyond their "productive" years as mothers or wives.[120] The heroes of this story would be men of vision and action, corporate captains dragging their vassals into a progressive future by using sport—that prominent stage of traditional masculine prowess—as an anchor.

The Meaning of Progress

Interwoven with this discourse of death and life, blackness and whiteness, was another one regarding the past and the future: "progress" and its costs. The Astrodome expressed "progress" as technological advancement in the service of physical comfort and convenience. Busch Stadium, too, was celebrated as an icon of "progress," though in St. Louis the

FIGURE 67. A view from inside Busch Stadium in 1965, with the Gateway Arch just visible beyond the stadium walls. ARTHUR WITMAN, S0702, 702.776, STATE HISTORICAL SOCIETY OF MISSOURI/ RESEARCH CENTER–ST. LOUIS.

new modern stadium signified a city emerging from the nineteenth century into modernity—reflected both in the "rebirth" and "New Spirit" of downtown and in the move from Sportsman's Park to the new Busch Stadium.

At the stadium groundbreaking in May 1964, Preston Estep, executive committee chairman of the Civic Center Redevelopment Corporation, called the project the "spark that will kindle fires of progress"—words amplified in a *St. Louis Post-Dispatch* headline.[121] Companies eagerly linked themselves to the new stadium, treating it as a symbol of the new, the progressive, the modern imagination. One newspaper advertisement for two lo-

cal banks told readers that the new stadium "gives dramatic evidence of the new spirit which is transforming the destiny and changing the destination of this 200-year-old Gateway City. *It's concrete evidence of the distance we've come* [emphasis original]."[122]

"Civic progress" didn't come easy, of course. Men and their unwavering visions drove the project. When baseball's Cardinals moved to the new Busch Stadium, a *St. Louis Post-Dispatch* front-page headline announced, "Public Apathy, Other Barriers Surmounted by Dedicated Men." The reporter assured readers, "Men responsible for the stadium responded to every threatened delay with renewed energy that has overcome many obstacles." Busch Stadium "came into being because of the labors of dedicated men who overcame public apathy, the opposition of displaced businessmen, investors' doubts, rival proposals, architects' fears, high construction costs, strikes and a fire." These, it seemed, were the obstacles that dedicated men had to overcome—myopic citizens, doubt, fear, expense, worker unions, and fate—in converting what they saw as an old dowager into a bountiful and modern beauty.[123]

But progress in St. Louis was different from progress in Houston—a difference seemingly rooted in how many in those communities collectively understood and valued the past. In broad terms, Houstonian culture embraced a "purer" sort of modern ideology, readily casting aside the past as shabby and retrograde. Houston journalist and author George Fuermann claimed, "Houstonians have shown little compassion for their city's past." It was a city that always seemed new because few buildings existed long enough to become old. They were knocked down; the past was "scrubbed away as though it were an embarrassment."[124] St. Louisans seemed to labor under a more complicated relationship with their history. Though "progress" was celebrated in full throat, it was also experienced more ambivalently.

Just as the Gateway Arch was an ambivalent symbol—utterly modern and historically reflective—the transition from Sportsman's Park to new Busch Stadium mixed memory and anticipation. The move provoked a wave of nostalgia and imaginative recovery of all the oddities the old park had collected over the years. The baseball Cardinals, no doubt officially ecstatic over the earning potential of the new stadium, struck a reverential tone as they shifted grounds, memorializing the park in team publications. The club, like commentators, emphasized that it was the "oldest playing grounds of the game anywhere," baseball having been played there for a century.[125] Arthur Daley of the *New York Times* wrote two consecutive columns on Sportsman's Park, which was "one of baseball's most colorful outposts and contributed vastly to history and legend."[126] The passing from one stadium to the other prompted a series of articles, locally and nationally, accompanied by cartoon illustrations that recounted many events both verifiable and apocryphal. A reporter for *Sports Illustrated* wrote, "When they move into bright, clean and slightly antiseptic Busch Memorial Stadium next week, the St. Louis Cardinals will become the 10th big league team in the last 11 years to take up new digs. Happily, all the concrete west of the Mississippi can't bury baseball's storied past, which was never more vivid than in old Sportsman's Park (Busch Stadium to latecomers), where memorable things always seemed to be happening." This was a common trope—the stadium as a vesicle of quirky memories—at a time when quirkiness was seemingly being squeezed out of the game. Writers recalled the outrageous antics of the infamous "Gashouse Gang"; fights between players, coaches, and umpires; the legendary African American pitcher Satchel Paige, in his dugout rocking chair; Stan Musial's five home runs in a doubleheader; superfan Mary Ott and her "horse laugh"; "brew bombs," or bean bags filled with beer, thrown at straw hats in the stands; Chris Von der Ahe's refusal to roof the stands because he wanted fans hot and buying beer; the bullet from a holdup that passed over player Ken Boyer's head and landed in a thirteen-year-old fan's blouse; the former striptease joint, Club Boulevard, located under the stands on Grand Boulevard; and, of course, Eddie Gaedel's infamous base on balls (or as one writer put it, "Bill Veeck's midget").[127]

The city's baseball fans let the park go with a sense of restraint and perspective. The final game at the park was played on May 9, 1966. Ushers and police lined the field in the bottom of the ninth to discourage vandalism of the field and stands. After the closing ceremonies, they moved aside and many fans went on the field. Some took souvenirs—cups of dirt, a few numbered seat backs, some signs. But the scene was markedly different from the one at the Polo Grounds in 1957, after the Giants had played their final game there, when fans swarmed the field, chased the players, and looted the stadium of base pads, plaques, seats, telephones, and patches of grass. Cardinals fans largely treated the "Old Lady" with respect—more, one might say, than the Cardinals organization did. A bulldozer rammed through the outfield wall even before the last people had departed the grounds.[128]

Sportsman's Park was a memorial to baseball's origins by virtue of its age, but it was also a memorial to a passing age of baseball and sport more generally. By the mid-1960s, commentators were increasingly questioning the direction of sports business, as the impact of television and the construction of new, modern stadiums were altering the experience of sport—the product on the field, the experience in the stadium, and the amounts of money involved. Critics accused sport of becoming spectacle and mere "show business," losing its ethical compass that put the games and their traditions first, selling out to television and casual but more affluent audiences of largely suburban consumers. Sportsman's Park was a symbol of both a previous age and the loss of it.[129]

Cardinals player Nelson Briles recalled the shift from the park—"small, close to the fans, electric atmosphere"—to the stadium as "a compromise for everybody because you are removed from the field, and you lose that intimacy and the closeness to the action." This shift, he claimed, coincided with a new marketing of the game.

> It began the end of the age of innocence for baseball where it was just a game, where you opened the gates and the fans came and you played for the pride of the game and the win. And that was the real focus, balls and strikes, home runs, outs, base hits. Once marketing became a more integral part of the total operation, there was a focus on promotions. In the past, you didn't see too much of that because the older opinion seemed to be that it was too gimmicky. Promotions made too much a circus of the game. Back then we were there for the pure baseball people. Today you can't survive with just the purists. Today you must market to the masses.[130]

While we might question Briles's historical claims that baseball had been played merely for pride and victory in a bygone era, his characterization nonetheless marked the late

1960s as a moment of spiritual transition, regarding both the settings for the games and the production of those games as entertainment. Briles's complaint, a good example of a purist's lament, was dismissed by others who embraced the new money, new culture, and new comforts. The 1967 World Series was staged in stadiums that represented the old and the new: Boston's Fenway Park, opened in 1912, and the new Busch.

John Hall of the *Los Angeles Times* used the occasion to bat away the complaints of purists. "Some people," Hall claimed, "resent the new ballparks, insisting they are too antiseptic, too cold and too commercial. But there are some people who resent everything, including progress, peace and heaven." As the Series transitioned from one venue to the other, it moved "from the Stone Age to the Moon Age." He said of Boston's old ground, "Fabled Fenway Park . . . is quaint and colorful in its way, but it's a fading and obsolete relic and would be better off being put out of its misery. Or at least officially declared to be what it is, a museum displaying artifacts from another age." It was a "dishonest park," in Hall's opinion, because of its peculiar wall angles and field dimensions. Busch Stadium, conversely, "does it all. It's comfortable, convenient and true with balanced fences . . . and has all the modern touches." "If this is antiseptic," Hall concluded, "pass the iodine."[131]

Hall's gag line—"pass the iodine"—captured the hubristic spirit of the modern stadium and urban renewal, in St. Louis and elsewhere. His unapologetic celebration of cleanliness, comfort, and convenience—as well as his easy dismissal of tradition—articulated the approach of modern progressive thinkers in the 1960s. Busch Stadium was the bulkhead of downtown redevelopment in St. Louis, a massive material and ideological project designed to reinvent the downtown, to cleanse it of its age, of its industry, of its diseased blackness—to make parts of the city itself like a modern stadium. While other modern stadiums like Shea represented the geographical, material, and ideological suburbanization of the previously urban stadium form, Busch Stadium took that newly suburbanized form back to the city. St. Louis used the stadium to suburbanize the urban, sanitizing it, drawing affluent white suburbanites and their consumption dollars back into the decayed city, making the urban experience a safely consumable one again.

CHAPTER 6

MACHINES FOR SPORT

THE STADIUM SINCE THE 1970S

ROGER ANGELL TRAVELED TO PITTSBURGH IN 1970 to cover the Pirates' playoff series with the Cincinnati Reds. Pittsburgh's Three Rivers Stadium had opened earlier that year, and after a "study" of the new stadium, Angell wondered "how ballplayers nowadays can remember which town they are playing in as they look up at the same tiered, brightly painted circles of seats that, rising above fields of fake grass, identically and anonymously surround them in so many big-league cities." Three Rivers, home to both baseball's Pirates and football's Steelers, was yet another in a wave of new multipurpose stadiums built in the mold of Busch Stadium, D.C. Stadium, and Atlanta Stadium—each circular, enclosed on all sides by banks of seats. "More and more these stadia remind one of motels or airports in their perfect and dreary usefulness," Angell observed. "They are no longer parks but machines for sports."[1]

As Angell suggested, many big-league cities owned, or had plans to build, a "machine for sport" by 1970. New stadiums were modeled on structures like Shea Stadium, the Astrodome, and Busch Stadium, buildings that had been admired for their sense of novelty and ambition. And yet by 1970, stadiums that appeared futuristic and forward-looking just years before now increasingly seemed, ironically, behind the times. Many boosters and reporters continued to celebrate new stadiums as expressions of modern progress. But for a growing number of people, each new stadium represented another step in the dour march

FIGURE 68. The modernist Three Rivers Stadium—Pittsburgh's "machine for sport"—opened in 1970. Its circularity helped it convert between baseball and football formats, to host both the Pirates and Steelers. But this circularity also pushed fans for each sport farther from the field than had the Pirates' Forbes Field and the oval Pitt Stadium, the Steelers' home for the previous decade. ALLEGHENY CONFERENCE ON COMMUNITY DEVELOPMENT PHOTOGRAPHS, MSP 285, DETRE LIBRARY & ARCHIVES, HEINZ HISTORY CENTER, PITTSBURGH.

of modernist standardization, replicating the same spaces and sports experiences in city after city—derivative concrete cylinders dropped into lots swept clean by urban renewal, outfitted with artificial turf, squawking scoreboards, and private restaurants and luxury suites. Many of the tenets of postwar modernism—rationalism, symmetry, monumentalism, an abiding faith in new technologies, and a blind belief that all of these things signified "progress"—seemed increasingly out of step with the times, as more Americans were concerned with ecological integrity, historical roots, and authenticity.

A dreary placelessness born of modern standardization wasn't the only thing Angell noticed when he first visited Three Rivers Stadium in 1970. He was also struck by the

FIGURE 69. The Pirates' old ballpark, the irregularly shaped Forbes Field (opened in 1909), is in the foreground, adjacent to the University of Pittsburgh's Cathedral of Learning. The Steelers played at Forbes from 1933 until 1963, though in 1958 they began playing some games in the classic football bowl of Pitt Stadium (opened in 1925), seen here in the center of the image. They played all their games at Pitt Stadium between 1964 and the opening of Three Rivers in 1970. Downtown Pittsburgh is visible in the distance. The future location of Three Rivers Stadium was directly to the right of downtown, across the Ohio River.
AERIAL PHOTOGRAPHS OF PITTSBURGH COLLECTION, C. 1923–1937, AIS.1988.06, ARCHIVES SERVICE CENTER, UNIVERSITY OF PITTSBURGH.

"immense glassed-in dining room and bar called the Allegheny Club" that broke up the monotonous concrete cylinder of plastic seats. This private club lorded high over first base on the third and fourth tiers of the stadium, a fortress "permitting affluent locals (who may also lease private boxes, at a price of $38,000 for five years) to take their baseball a la carte."[2] There were forty-two pricey private boxes ringing the stadium. In Pittsburgh's new, publicly funded, $55 million stadium, the well-to-do and socially connected could assemble, screening themselves out of the stadium public, and take their sport in small doses—a sports-themed buffet item among other diversions.

Characteristically perceptive, Angell's portrait identifies the state of the stadium in 1970 and also anticipates the shape of things to come. The era of postwar modernist stadium building—envisioned by Geddes beginning in the late 1940s, enabled by the Braves' move to a new County Stadium in Milwaukee in 1953, and fully launched with the concrete style of Candlestick Park in 1959 and the multipurpose functionality of the District of Columbia Stadium in 1961—had run its course with the opening of Minneapolis's Metrodome in 1982. Stadium planning and design moves in cycles, and the next wave of stadium building exploded in the early 1990s. Those postmodern stadiums—initially and most famously Baltimore's Oriole Park at Camden Yards—demonstrably rejected the placeless, cookie-cutter modernism of the previous decades, celebrating above all else a *sense of place*. But snuggled into the new designs were even more private clubs and suites at a scale that would make Three Rivers look communistic, as well as an ethic of sports "à la carte" that has come to define the stadium "mallpark" experience.[3]

The Pirates called Three Rivers Stadium home for just three decades—half the time they had played at their previous ballpark, Forbes Field. Their new baseball-specific facility, PNC Park, was opened a few hundred feet east of Three Rivers in 2001. It was one in a wave of "retro" ballparks that had been built in or near downtowns over the previous decade, beginning with Baltimore's Camden Yards in 1992.[4] These were facilities designed as throwbacks to a previous era—that of the now-deemed "classic" ballparks like Forbes Field. The NFL's Steelers, former roommates of the Pirates at Three Rivers, got a new football stadium of their own, Heinz Field, directly west of its predecessor. Like the new baseball park, this open-ended horseshoe's signature quality was its enthusiastic expression of place. Both new stadiums looked directly across the Ohio River to the city's "Golden Triangle," a corporate spectacle of soaring glass skyscrapers. Fans and players weren't trapped in an anonymous web of plastic seats like their counterparts in Cincinnati, St. Louis, Atlanta, and Philadelphia—this was *Pittsburgh*.

The modern stadium had been split in two. No longer would fans have to endure the circular and plastic utility of the multipurpose stadium, which in accommodating both the rectangular gridiron of football and baseball's diamond complemented neither all that well. The anonymous cylinder was broken apart to reveal the world outside. Steel, brick,

FIGURE 70. The private, glassed-in Allegheny Club hovers over the scene as Steelers running back Franco Harris charges toward the end zone. AP PHOTO/NFL PHOTOS.

and limestone—the materials of prewar stadiums and ballparks like Ebbets Field, the Polo Grounds, and Pittsburgh's own Forbes Field—replaced smooth concrete walls and columns. On the face of it, this seemed the revival of an era of more democratic stadiums from a seemingly more authentic era of sport—a real revolution in stadium design.

But the rediscovery of the local, the intimate, and the seemingly authentic accompanied—and even masked—countervailing developments in stadium design. As architects, politicians, reporters, and fans celebrated the return of stadiums that seemed idiosyncratic expressions of local communities, they overlooked the ways new stadiums replicated and amplified many of the traits of their modernist predecessors. The private luxury suites and stadium clubs that Angell had pointed out in Three Rivers metastasized in the postmodern stadium. So too did an ethic of sport "à la carte," through which the game on the field became simply a thematic anchor to a broader consumption experience, marked by souvenir shops, restaurants, bars, art installations, and sports-themed museums and memorials. The stadium experience burst with sensory stimulation—every moment filled with distractions competing with the game on the field, from advertisements and cheerleaders to video-board action and wireless connectivity. These were stadiums built not for fans but consumers—designed not to meet existing needs but to create and satisfy new ones. In the postmodern stadium, the aesthetics and rhetoric of democratic inclusion and traditionalism ran aground the realities of increasing economic inequality and consumerist spectacle. New stadiums certainly didn't look like modernist machines for sport, but they had learned plenty from their predecessors. Technologies of exclusion, segmentation, and distraction define the contemporary stadium—all legacies of the modernist machines.

Cookie-Cutter Modernism

The modernization of stadium space since World War II converted the idiosyncratic urban ballpark into a placeless machine. Professional sports had been ripped from old neighborhoods and implanted in modernist cylinders—what sportswriter George Vass referred to in 1967 as "superficially attractive yet 'soulless' heaps of steel and concrete" that were being "stamped out" as if "with a cookie cutter" across the country.[5] This term—"cookie cutter"—would become a standard pejorative for a whole generation of stadiums, not all of which exactly fit the bill. At the time of Vass's writing, multipurpose and roughly circular modern stadiums had been built in the District of Columbia (opened in 1961), Queens (1964), Houston (1965), Atlanta (1965), St. Louis (1966), Oakland (1966), Anaheim (1966), and San Diego (1967). In truth, this was a more distinctive group of structures than it might have seemed—some with unique rooflines, some with openings in the seating bowl that allowed visitors' eyes to wander outside. And yet, with the opening of Three Rivers Stadium and Riverfront Stadium—Angell's "machines for sports"—there was a clear sense that each new stadium was less an adventure in modernism than a dutiful routine of concrete and plastic enclosure. Philadelphia's Veterans Stadium debuted the following year. San Francisco's open-ended Candlestick Park—the first major league stadium to adopt fully the engineered concrete idiom—was enclosed prior to the 1971 season to accommodate the NFL's 49ers.[6] This was followed by a string of urban domes in New Orleans (1975), Seattle (1976), Montreal (1976), Minneapolis (1982), and Toronto (1989). These were the apotheosis of the modern form—man the engineer, it seemed, had pacified unruly nature; the total obliteration of context was the price paid for this victory.

Stadium architect James Finch explained the trending routinization of the stadium form in 1971: "The current rash of stadiums is typical of the cycles architecture goes through. They are generated by developers; what goes well in one place is assumed to go well in another."[7] Expertise was spread from project to project and, unsurprisingly, stadiums increasingly resembled one another. Emil Praeger worked with Norman Bel Geddes on the stadium published in *Collier's* in 1952 and designed Dodger Stadium in Los Angeles. His firm, Praeger-Kavanagh-Waterbury, designed Shea Stadium and worked on the modernization of Yankee Stadium (completed in 1976). The firm teamed with two others on the Seattle Kingdome (1976), and consulted on the District of Columbia Stadium (1961) and the Astrodome (1965). The Osborn Engineering Company designed the District of Columbia Stadium and worked with two Pittsburgh firms on Three Rivers Stadium (1970). Osborn's project manager at D.C. Stadium, Noble Herzog, designed Anaheim Stadium

(1966). Atlanta Stadium (1966), Riverfront Stadium (1970), and Buffalo's Rich Stadium (1973) were designed by the Atlanta firm Finch and Heery. Skidmore, Owings & Merrill produced the Oakland-Alameda County Stadium (1966) and the Minneapolis Metrodome (1982). Kivett and Myers designed Kansas City's Arrowhead Stadium (1972) and Royals Stadium (1973), and also worked on New Jersey's Meadowlands complex (1976). The contractor for D.C. Stadium and Philadelphia's Veterans Stadium (1971) was McCloskey & Company. Huber, Hunt & Nichols, Inc., was the contractor for Riverfront Stadium, Three Rivers Stadium, and the Louisiana Superdome (1975). With such cross-pollination, it is no wonder that stadiums increasingly resembled one another.

The monotonous regularity of the stands was echoed in the overwhelming symmetry of baseball's outfield dimensions. In the older parks, of course, the layouts were all different, making game play different in each venue. However, in the modern stadiums built between 1962 and 1973, all baseball fields had even outfield dimensions, with center-field distances between 400 and 414 feet, and foul-pole distances between 329 and 338 feet.[8] Thus almost every ballpark played the same. Though the football gridiron had long been standard from stadium to stadium, its layout within old stadiums was not, as it was wedged into parks designed for baseball and flanked by temporary banks of stands. This made for a variety of vistas, depending on the seat of the fan. The modern stadium removed the idiosyncrasies of play in baseball and perspective in football, regularizing a view of fellow fans, far afield in cantilevered decks.

The idiosyncrasies of the playing surface—at least theoretically—had been removed as well. The idea of using artificial grass in a stadium was nothing new; Norman Bel Geddes had pitched it for his proposed indoor stadium for Brooklyn in the early 1950s.[9] The Astrodome was the first major stadium to put it to use, installing it during the 1966 baseball season.[10] The original playing surface there was a lab-designed grass hybrid that could grow under the dome's translucent Lucite panels. It was soon apparent that during day games the panels amplified daylight rather than diffused it, making it nearly impossible to see baseballs hit with a high trajectory. The Houston Sports Association responded to the problem short-term by painting over the panels. This, of course, killed the natural grass inside. The rest of that season was played on dead grass. A new artificial playing surface—designed by Chemstrand, a division of Monsanto Chemical Company—was installed in 1966.[11]

The artificiality of the grass marked a symbolic final severance with the natural world in the dome. For Roy Hofheinz, it was just another reason to celebrate: "Everything about the Astrodome is unparalleled and trail-blazing," he boasted. Artificial turf "not only enhances our own facilities here," he predicted, "but should also launch a new and wondrous era in recreational engineering. The Astrodome is honored to be the original site of this extraordinary experiment." Manager Grady Hatton claimed that the new surface was a

FIGURE 71. The Astrodome installed AstroTurf in 1966, after the Lucite panels in the roof were painted over. The zippered seams of each section are visible in this photo. MSS 0157-0062, HOUSTON PUBLIC LIBRARY, HOUSTON METROPOLITAN RESEARCH CENTER.

victory for fairness and predictability, ensuring the meritocratic nature of sport. He told stadium visitors, "This puts the icing on the cake. The Astrodome now becomes a real Utopia for baseball. No wind, no sun, no rain, no heat, no cold, and now no bad bounces."[12] Echoing the praise of modern stadiums more generally, advocates saw artificial turf as a symbol of progress. Richard Nixon, a visitor to the 1970 All-Star Game in Cincinnati's new Riverfront Stadium, predicted, "AstroTurf is the playing field of the future."[13]

Indeed it was, as every one of the stadiums constructed in the 1970s had artificial turf. It was installed in Pittsburgh, Cincinnati, Philadelphia, Irving, Kansas City, New Jersey, Seattle, Minneapolis, Foxborough, and Buffalo. St. Louis, San Francisco, and Miami's old

Orange Bowl replaced natural turf with synthetics in 1970. The financial bottom line, unsurprisingly, drove this trend. Surfaces like AstroTurf or Tartan Turf, its main competitor, were relatively expensive up front, requiring about two hundred thousand dollars for a football field. [14] However, after this initial investment, the field was much more durable and thus cheaper to maintain. Artificial fields could be used more frequently than delicate grass surfaces—an advantage for multipurpose stadiums hosting not only football and baseball but mass revivals, music concerts, and circuses. During the construction of Three Rivers Stadium, the Pittsburgh Pirates boasted of the many advantages of synthetic grass over the real thing. The new Tartan Turf field would provide "increased functionality" because it could be quickly adapted to other events; it would produce a "uniformity of the playing surface" that would allow for more consistent footing, more consistent ball bounces, and the "possibility of fewer ankle and knee injuries"; it would cut down on postponements "because water could be drained more quickly"; it would eliminate "muddy and otherwise undesirable field conditions that tend to detract from the superior performance of professional teams"; and, finally, it would "improve aesthetic appearance." [15] This litany of dubious justifications didn't include the true motivating factor: artificial surfaces cost less in the long run.

Synthetic grass seemed a logical step in the modernization of sports spaces—a process that eliminated oddities and idiosyncrasies in the name of multipurpose functionality and the economic bottom line. *Sports Illustrated*'s William Johnson mused in 1969, "Perhaps it was inevitable in this, the Synthetic Century . . . in an age when people quite readily embrace plastic wedding bouquets and electric campfires and spray-on suntans." Even yet, it was "still a shock" for Johnson to see football played on a "grassless gridiron, lush as a rug and flawless as a hotel lobby." [16]

It was inevitable, perhaps—but not always welcomed. "Grass, the old-fashioned, common, green growing stuff, is dying out," Peter Carry, also of *Sports Illustrated*, wrote in 1970. It was "a lamentable death wrought of ambiguity and polyester progress." [17] He noted that the cost savings might impress club owners and city councils, but most everyone else lost out. Though some baseball fielders claimed the turf produced more predicable bounces, Carry found that most players opposed this form of "progress." Unlike natural grass surface, which absorbed heat, the asphalt foundations reflected it, yielding extreme field temperatures. Cincinnati's Riverfront Stadium reported temperatures of up to 160 degrees on the surface; on a 90-degree day in Busch Stadium, it was 114 degrees six feet above the field. In some cases, such temperatures could cause blisters, melt shoe bottoms, and even lead to heatstroke. The asphalt base was also unforgiving to players' joints. Though early on many advocates claimed that the fields would cut down on injuries because of their uniformity—beliefs encouraged by research presented by its manufacturers—independent studies increasingly showed that the synthetic grass was responsible for all sorts of physical problems. Cleats got caught in the turf, resulting in ligament and knee injuries. The underlying asphalt surface resulted in more head injuries. Friction burns and blisters became common as well.[18]

But it was baseball fans, Carry claimed, who were the real losers in new stadiums defined by "even bounces and inorganic sterility." While the violence wrought by synthetic turf in some ways matched the violence of football, baseball's "lasting attraction must be its atmosphere of relaxation and naturalness." For evidence, he pointed to the young, friendly crowds at those traditional baseball-first, natural-grass ballparks, Boston's Fenway Park and Chicago's Wrigley Field. There, he wrote, "the atmosphere is warm, unhurried, occasionally exciting and generally very healthy."[19] But while artificial turf could influence the feel and pace of the stadium—rendering it cold, rushed, and unhealthy, as Carry suggested—new electronic technologies would more radically reshape the traditional stadium experience, dominating the eyes and ears of ballpark visitors.

Television and the Stadium

At the end of the 1950s, a scoreboard was largely what it sounded like—a vertical board where scores were posted, likely accented with an advertisement for a regional brewer. Scoreboards of the 1960s, like those at Shea Stadium and the Astrodome, increasingly played a more invasive role in the stadium experience. By the mid-1970s, scoreboards were hosting video screens that commanded the attention of visitors nearly as much as the game on the field. The development of the scoreboard—from a silent and functional tool to a multimedia competitor to the main event—was incremental and uneven from stadium to stadium. Enhanced scoreboards produced exploding spectacles of light shows and fireworks. They entreated fans to cheer. They trotted out rudimentary animations. Such features indeed drew fans' eyes and encouraged a more systematic and directed involvement in the game below. But with more sophisticated video-board technologies, evident in the opening of the Louisiana Superdome in 1975, the scoreboard increasingly became an outsized television—a screen that replicated the viewing experience from home. Accordingly, the ways the games were produced—on television and in the stadium—converged as well.

Ironically, the inspiration for the modern scoreboard was installed in one of baseball's oldest grounds, Chicago's Comiskey Park. Unsurprisingly, it was the brainchild of one of the game's most notorious promoters over the previous two decades: Bill Veeck. Veeck, who had worked his way back into the major leagues as a part owner of the White Sox in 1959, introduced his famous exploding scoreboard in 1960. The elaborate pinball machine in William Saroyan's play *The Time of Your Life* provided the model. When a player hit the jackpot, Veeck remembered, "the machine practically exploded. The American flag was unfurled; battleships fired guns; music blared. It was just so silly, you know, that it was unforgettably funny. I began to imagine something like that on a big scale, like a scoreboard."[20] Veeck's new scoreboard, nicknamed "the Monster" and "the Thing," cost three hundred thousand dollars. It soared above Comiskey's center-field bleachers, topping out 130 feet from the ground. Slender columns rose above the board, loaded with fireworks, set to go off upon a White Sox home run. When the scoreboard exploded, one reporter wrote, "Lights flash, sirens scream, whistles blow, fireworks light up the sky and aerial bombs shake the ball park as the slugging hero trots around the bases."[21] Veeck's invention was the first in a stadium scoreboard arms race that would quickly escalate.

Electronic messaging was one of the first features of the modern scoreboard; it debuted at Yankee Stadium in 1959 and was built into the District of Columbia Stadium in 1961.[22] Dodger Stadium, opened in 1962, employed two message boards above the outfield pavilions. One delivered lineups, scores by inning, and game statistics. The other gave results from other games, announced attendance figures, made special announcements, greeted visiting groups of fans, and delivered crowd instructions.[23] Such computer-controlled messaging might seem quaint today, but the impact then was considerable, commanding the attention of spectators and dictating their responses to the game. Roger Angell observed the influence of the "huge, hexagonal sign" on Los Angeles crowds in October 1962. "The fans respond to its instructions with alacrity," he noted, "whether they are invited to sing 'Baby Face' between innings or ordered to shout the Dodger battle cry of 'CHARGE!' during a rally."[24]

Each new stadium boasted a new scoreboard that attempted to outdo the last one; it was "the new status symbol," as a reporter visiting new Shea Stadium claimed in 1964.[25] Shea's freestanding Stadiarama Scoreboard, with its eighteen-by-twenty-four-foot rear projection screen Photorama video board, was taken down a peg by the Astrodome's two-million-dollar scoreboard, 474 feet long and four stories high. The Astrodome set a standard that was difficult for most to match, though this didn't stop the lips of local boosters who claimed to surpass it with each new stadium. John Hall, a columnist for the *Los Angeles Times*, told readers that while fans in Anaheim weren't going to get a dome when the new stadium opened in 1966, they wouldn't "have to take a rumble seat to Houston in the scoreboard department."[26] The nickname of Anaheim Stadium, "The Big A," actually derived from its scoreboard: a 230-foot A-frame scoreboard sited just beyond the left-field wall, topped with a revolving halo. Hall joked that future astronauts might mistake the halo for a ring of Saturn, adding vaguely, "Progress is wonderful," as if this towering board was evidence of the peak of human accomplishment.[27] A writer for the *Sporting News* branded it "the world's largest teleprompter" and "electronic cheerleader"; it seemingly relieved fans of the burden of deliberation, telling them precisely when to shout "Charge!"[28] Scoreboards in other new stadiums in Oakland, Pittsburgh, and Cincinnati struggled to keep up, though their promoters assured local fans that their new scoreboards were cutting-edge.[29]

The exploding scoreboard at Philadelphia's Veterans Stadium, opened in 1971, was particularly notorious. Baseball's Phillies claimed their new scoreboard to be "the most expensive, largest and most sophisticated scoreboard in the history of sports."[30] Costing three million dollars—a figure the club advertised with pride—it was a "magic lantern of incandescence, images, and information; flashing forth with statistics, scores, rulings, group names, ticket information, coming events, and enhancing every game with caricatures, cartoons, commentary, and even commercials to help pay for itself."[31] It had, according to local sports writers, "the color and excitement of Disneyland."[32] The main attraction of the Magic Scoreboard was the home run spectacular. The Phillies noted some of the more memorable home run celebrations around the league—particularly the "war dance" in Atlanta after a Braves home run and the "cattle stampedes when an Astro puts one in orbit" in Houston. "But nowhere in the history of baseball," promoters promised, "can one find a greater Homerun Spectacular than right here in Veterans Stadium." The Phillies' celebration featured two fifteen-foot-tall fiberglass animatrons, Philadelphia Phil and sibling Philadelphia Phillis, a fifteen-foot-tall replica of the Liberty Bell, a cannon, and water fountains. It was the stadium version of a Rube Goldberg machine; its elaborate mechanical display began with animatron Phil whacking a ball off the Liberty Bell, cracking it in the process. The caroming ball then hit Phillis "in the fanny," as Phillies executive Bill Giles described it; as she fell down, she accidentally pulled a lanyard to an exploding cannon. A revolutionary-era American flag subsequently unfurled, water spurted from an outfield fountain, and the sound system blasted "Stars and Stripes Forever."[33] This chaotic scene was enough to impress many visitors. Maury Allen of the *New York Post*, mesmerized by the display, claimed, "No more bad jokes about Philadelphia. Any town that can build a $45 million ball park, featuring a $3 million scoreboard with Philadelphia Phil, Philadelphia Phillis, the Liberty Bell, a Revolutionary War cannon and Betsy Ross' original flag . . . can't be all bad."[34] The routine failed to properly come off in the stadium's early days, prompting visiting sportswriter Roy Blount Jr. to remark, "Phillis struck a warranted blow for Women's Liberation by declining to fall down." When he asked Phillies manager Gene Mauch how he felt about "baseball's greater and greater reliance upon such gimmickry," a cowed Mauch replied, "It's here."[35]

Animatronic gimmickry did not become the norm, but it expressed widespread and profound changes in the production of the stadium experience. Filling the traditional pauses in game action with electronic content reworked the relationship between fans and the game, and thus the expectations and behavior of the crowd. Following his introduction to the Astrodome in 1966, Angell reflected on how "planned distractions" like cheerleading scoreboards and home run celebrations affected the experience of the game. "It will transform the sport into another mere entertainment," he suggested, "and thus guarantee its swift descent to the status of a boring and stylized curiosity." He saw it as an attempt to "build a following by the distraction and entire control of their audience's attention" and branded it a "vulgar venture"; baseball, he argued, "has always had a capacity to create its own lifelong friends."[36] The scoreboard took the lead in reprogramming the stadium experience—and this even before video boards had reached a basic level of sophistication.

Kansas City's Arrowhead Stadium—a football-specific stadium opened in 1972—pioneered the first legitimate instant replay scoreboard that could immediately show a previous play. The image was not particularly crisp—one reporter noted that when the board displayed the Chiefs' mascot horse, Warpaint, "it reminded one of an old sepia western . . . and out of focus at that."[37] And yet the impact on fans and players was significant. Michael Oriard, a player for the Chiefs in the early 1970s, compared the experience of playing at

FIGURE 72. Philadelphia Phil and Phillis (upper left and upper right, respectively) of the Veterans Stadium Homerun Spectacular. SPECIAL COLLECTIONS RESEARCH CENTER, TEMPLE UNIVERSITY LIBRARIES, PHILADELPHIA. ANTHONY BERNATO, PHILADELPHIA EVENING BULLETIN.

old Municipal Stadium—a traditional, baseball-first park located in the midst of the city's African American district—to that of the modern Arrowhead. The new stadium was more comfortable for both players and fans, he recalled, "but it also meant an altered relationship" between the two. "There were few distractions at the old ballpark to draw attention away from the contest on the field," he observed. "I felt that we players were the focal point of all our fans' attention. I sensed the fans' presence, felt bound to them by a common passion." At Arrowhead, this relationship between player and fan seemed to evaporate. Visitors to the new stadium "seemed less fans than spectators now, having paid ten dollars apiece to be entertained for three hours." Their attention was divided: "The huge electronic scoreboard behind one end zone, with all its showy displays, competed with the players for the spectators' attention."[38] This competition between players and scoreboard unraveled the connection between fan and game, converting visitors to passive spectators, no longer active participants in the contest and the moment.

No modern stadium scoreboard possessed the capacity for drawing attention and clipping the cord between fan and player like that of the Louisiana Superdome. The stadium itself, opened in 1975, was remarkable for a number of reasons—among them its monumental size (spanning 680 feet and topping out at 273 feet), its extravagant cost ($163 million), and the well-publicized political intrigue and corruption accompanying its development.[39] One of its most discussed characteristics was its space-age aesthetic: writers called it "a giant spaceship from a distant planetoid" and "Starship Superdome." The "most futuristic feather of the whole mind-boggling building," Jep Cadou of the *Saturday Evening Post* claimed, was its "giant-screen television."[40]

The "television" was in fact six televisions, one for each side of the massive six-sided gondola hung from the roof. The apparatus weighed seventy-five tons and cost $1.3 million—a veritable bargain when compared to Philadelphia's $3 million animatronic display. In addition to replays, the twenty-six-by-twenty-two-foot screens could also provide "isolated camera" and "slow-motion shots" that "television viewers have become used to." The screens possessed, a stadium consultant noted, a color image "superior to a home television set."[41] Thus visitors to the Superdome, Cadou claimed, "will have the best of both worlds. They will have the excitement of being present 'live' and participating in all the action, without sacrificing the luxury of instant replays, isolation and slow-motion shots."[42]

The Superdome was self-consciously modeled after the home. When still in its planning stages, a writer for *Sports Illustrated* reported that the stadium would have screens that "will show spectators instant replays and locker-room interviews just as if they were back in their living rooms."[43] Dave Dixon—a co-owner of the NFL's Saints and key player in the building of the Superdome—imagined the space as a fusion of living room and stadium, claiming, "The viewer will have the best of both worlds: all the physical and emotional excitement of being there *and* the best seat in the house."[44] The creative use of cameras and replay in recent years had made watching games at home better than being in a stadium, a reporter for the *Los Angeles Times* noted. But the Superdome turned this on its head: "Watching football in here is just like being at home, only more so," he wrote.[45]

Stadium managers planned to use the screens to simulcast the game on the field, for the benefit of those high in the stands and far from the field below. They also hoped to broadcast other games, attracting crowds to the Dome simply to watch huge televisions with others. They also sold advertising spots; ads for car dealers, banks, and resort communities were aired in between plays, prompting disgust from players and coaches.[46] These commercials, many noted, were as invasive as advertisements on the television in one's living room, and they were broadcast so loudly that those on the field were startled and distracted. A lineman for the Saints complained: "When we were calling plays or talking things over during time outs, it was pretty hard to hear." Another player called the scoreboard "a damn nuisance."[47] And players weren't the only ones criticizing the stadium invasion of the video screen. J. D. Reed of *Sports Illustrated* sarcastically suggested that the Superdome was a solution to the isolating capacity of television. "For years sociologists have been poor-mouthing television, noting that it separates people," he wrote. "Americans don't gather socially anymore because they are in apartments and in detached houses watching TV." But in New Orleans, "now tens of thousands can gather in one room on a Sunday afternoon. To watch television."[48]

Television bent the stadium and sport to its logic. Stadiums like the Astrodome and Superdome became living-room analogues—comfortable seats assembled around screens in air-conditioned rooms. Outdoor stadiums couldn't model the living room so exactly, though they could mimic the logic of television's incessant commercialized programming. But increasingly, the virtual identity of the stadium was surpassing its material significance. Lucrative television rights deals, particularly for professional football, redefined the economic significance of the stadium; the people physically present became relatively less important to those "attending" through televised broadcasts.

The debut of *Monday Night Football* on ABC in 1970 exemplified this shift. The program was under the steerage of Roone Arledge, who had honed his football production skills on college football broadcasts throughout the 1960s, developing a production style that, in his words, brought "the viewer to the game rather than the game to the viewer."[49] To do this, Arledge and ABC shot the game in innovative ways: from blimps, cranes, and helicopters, using handheld cameras to capture close-ups of cheerleaders and coaches; rifle microphones recorded the smashing of pads on the field and the buzz of the stands. His philosophy was to fill dead time, constantly engaging the television viewer with shots of the scene and commentary from broadcasters. *Monday Night Football* enhanced the televisual spectacle of ABC's football production with nine different cameras, cutting-

edge slow-motion technologies, and commentators who were stars in their own right—
the opinionated Howard Cosell, the irreverent good-old-boy Don Meredith, and the
winning Frank Gifford. *Monday Night Football* became the standard for televised professional football, and by the mid-1970s, NBC and CBS had embraced the Roone approach as
well.[50] Football was being produced less as sport than entertainment, celebrating the show
around the game as much as the contest on the field.[51]

These new priorities fueled an increasing sense that the stadium itself hardly mattered
except as a stage set for television drama. Some had anticipated, or at least speculated
about, such a development since the late 1950s. An American League official had told
sportswriter Roger Kahn in 1959 that baseball would survive competition from television
by making ballparks "TV studios," asking Kahn, "Do you know a better way to sell cigarettes and beer?" When a critic suggested that this plan seemed "unromantic," the official
responded, "It's too late to worry about that now. The mistakes have been made. We went
into the television business and now we have to make a living in the only way we can."[52]
Frank Lane, an executive for the Baltimore Orioles baseball club, had told *Newsweek* in
1965, "Within ten years, the baseball parks of America will be mere studios for pay television."[53] Mark Harris—author of the acclaimed *Bang the Drum Slowly*, considered among
the best sport-themed novels ever—argued this in a 1969 article in the *New York Times
Sunday Magazine*. He claimed football stadiums were nothing more than a stage set for
made-for-television drama, and the fans there were simply studio audiences designed "to
give the illusion of a crowd enthralled, as canned laughter gives the illusion of humor."
The real interest of team owners were "the unseen millions in parlors, dens, family rooms
and taverns, lulled by the illusion that they were spying upon an actual game, at no cost
to themselves."[54] Most knowledgeable observers, like television critic Ron Powers, thought
that stadiums had become "vast super-studios" by the 1970s, filled with fans who were no
more than "paying extras"; by then, most club revenue came from television rights fees,
not stadium gate receipts.[55] With the construction of each new "cookie-cutter" stadium,
there was a persistent and escalating sense that the average paying fan at the game was less
important than the television consumer far from it.

If you can't beat them, join them: architects and sports entertainers produced stadiums
in the image of television and suburban comfort. Elaborate scoreboards and new video
screens pumped advertising into the cracks of game play. Instant replays fixed people's
eyes upward. Visitors were told when to cheer and how to do it. Many of the stadiums'
residents—including sportswriters, fans, and players—outwardly objected to what they
saw as a disruption to the game experience, sports' subtle rhythms of play, and the relationship between players and their supporters. But team owners weren't particularly concerned about the traditionalists; they had their eyes on the casual consumer who, in their
eyes, might yawn during a game's natural pauses. Clubs certainly enjoyed the additional

revenue from video-board advertising—demonstrated by their eagerness to invest heavily in these expensive toys. Enough fans—a silent majority, it seemed—were willing to suffer through those ads in exchange for instant replay and other electronic amusements between plays.

Just as stadiums increasingly resembled one another materially, so too was the stadium experience routinized across the country. Scoreboard operators took their cues from other stadiums and spread this new logic of sports entertainment. Back in 1966, Houston's Roy Hofheinz had boasted that thanks to all the stadium add-ons—the scoreboard, the clubs and restaurants, the padded seats, the air-conditioning, and the attractive usherettes—one didn't have to "make a personal sacrifice to like baseball" in the Astrodome. In 1982, Dick Davis was hired to manage the Minneapolis Metrodome scoreboard, after spending the previous ten years operating the one at Cincinnati's Riverfront Stadium. Davis explained his scoreboard philosophy in terms that Hofheinz would have appreciated: "I want to use it as a reward for fans to be there in the first place."[56]

Suites and Second-Class Citizens

If the exuberant scoreboard was a reward, it was a relatively democratic one, bestowed on all visitors (whether they wanted it or not). But modern stadiums like the Metrodome were also noteworthy for heaping particular "rewards" on thin slices of their most affluent patrons. Luxury stadium space—private suites, clubs, restaurants, and other forms of premium seating—achieved its greatest notoriety in Houston's Astrodome, though it has existed in various forms throughout the history of stadium construction in the United States. Chicago's Lakefront Park, built in 1878 and refurbished in 1883, boasted an early form of the luxury suite. The home of the National League's White Stockings featured eighteen roofed boxes with armchairs and curtains, isolated from stadium riffraff atop the grandstand.[57] Larry MacPhail's exclusive Stadium Club at Yankee Stadium gained national attention in 1946. It was a "ritzy lounge beneath the stands where a select clientele of season boxholders can sup and sup in comfort far removed from the hoi polloi," in the words of a *Los Angeles Times* columnist, who noted that this was an adaptation of private clubs at horse-racing grounds.[58]

Nearly all of the stadiums built in the 1960s had private clubs; Candlestick Park, District of Columbia Stadium, Dodger Stadium, Shea Stadium, Anaheim Stadium, and Busch Stadium each had spaces removed from the public and reserved for dues-paying members. Of course, Houston's expansive outlay of fifty-three themed luxury suites, private clubs, and public restaurants inspired the envy of other cities' civic leaders and sports businessmen beginning in the mid-1960s. By the 1970s, such envy was being materialized in stadium after stadium. When Pittsburgh's Three Rivers Stadium opened in 1970, stadium promoters claimed its three-hundred-seat Allegheny Club and forty-two luxury boxes were "the epitome of spectator luxury."[59] Each eighteen-by-thirteen-foot box, accessible via elevator, accommodated nine visitors in its "completely private domain."[60] Philadelphia's Veterans Stadium, opened in 1971, also housed a private stadium club for three hundred, as well as twenty-eight "Superboxes" on the press level.

But it was another Texas stadium that really doubled down on Houston's model. Upon the opening of the Astrodome, Dallas Cowboys general manager Tex Schramm had told a Dallas reporter, "Everyone in sports is complaining that television is hurting their attendance . . . which it is, but that's shutting the barn door after all the animals are out. Promoters have got to restyle their product to the times, and that means ultra-luxury stadiums, weather-conditioning, theater-style seats, private clubs, maybe even a night club atmosphere where people watch the game while waiters in tuxedos serve champagne and lobster. It's not a civic responsibility for people to come out and watch us play. It's our responsibility to get them out."[61] Texas Stadium, the Cowboys' new home opened in 1971, materialized what for Schramm was the central lesson of the Astrodome—most provocatively in its soon-famous Circle Suites. Each of the 176 suites—"ranged on two levels . . .

FIGURE 73. Frederick Waggoner spent fifty-seven thousand dollars on his suite at Texas Stadium, which featured blue velvet chairs and drapes, commissioned art, and a crystal chandelier. AP PHOTO/FERD KAUFMAN.

like the promenade decks of some gleaming ocean liner," as described by a reporter—demanded a $50,000 bond, plus $1,680 for twelve season tickets and membership privileges in the Cowboy Club. What box holders got in return was "your own piece of real estate," a sixteen-by-sixteen-foot empty concrete box to outfit as desired. Suite holders enjoyed easy and exclusive access to their boxes, with reserved parking places near elevators that escorted them up to soft-lit and carpeted corridors leading to their private rooms. Half of the purchasers were corporations, the other half individuals.[62]

A commentator anticipated that the opening of the stadium "should be something like opening night at the Met." "The double row of millionaire suites should see a classic contest of one-upmanship as stoutly fought as any in the famed Diamond Horseshoe," the writer continued, facetiously adding as an afterthought, "There will also be football." Indeed, for many the football took a backseat to the Circle Suite luxury. The most "lavish" of the boxes was arguably that of Frederick Waggoner of Eldorado Oil & Gas. He spent fifty-seven thousand dollars on his suite, outfitting it with blue velvet drapes, empire-style chairs, wall-to-wall carpeting, velvet barstools, a glass-topped table with a massive gold vase of artificial roses, and commissioned wall paintings in oval gold frames. Combined, the decorations conspired to create an atmosphere "distinctly boudoir-like and 18th century [without] a hint of football in sight," as a *Los Angeles Times* reporter described it. Neighboring boxes played on other themes, "from the antique to the modern, the businesslike to the sporting." One holder outfitted his box like a Victorian saloon in old Ireland, with a solid brass bar rail, an old oak table carved with various names, a mirror advertising a whisky distillery, and a sign that warned, "Beware of pickpockets, drunks and loose women." A financier outfitted his suite like a boardroom, with wood-paneled walls, regency-style leather chairs, and thick green carpet.[63]

For many, the Texas Stadium Circle Suites were conspicuous symbols of a distinctly Texan extravagance. Articles chronicled the design high jinks of wealthy Texans with much of the same fascination that accompanied the opening of the Astrodome six years before. "In true Texas style," a writer for *Travel* magazine described the setting, "some of these suites, all with great views of the playing field, have elegant furnishings, original oil paintings, crystal chandeliers, walnut paneling and overstuffed chairs."[64] The home editor of the *Dallas Morning News*, after walking her readers through various Circle Suite design choices and details, concluded, "The glamour of the individual boxes carries on the tradition of the free-wheeling, Texas big rich!"[65]

For others, who noted the increasing frequency of the stadium luxury box across the national landscape, the "precious status symbol" of the Circle Suite spoke to a broader economic segregation within the modern stadium—and throughout American society more fully.[66] Stadium operators hoped, one commentator explained, "to increase stadium revenue by soaking the rich for the satisfaction of sitting in opulence, separated from the commoners."[67] The proliferation of exclusive spaces within the stadium didn't sit well with some. Charles Maher of the *Los Angeles Times* claimed, "The separation tends to dramatize class distinctions, and much more than the traditional separation between box seats and bleachers." Unlike the simple spatial segregation of sports space, which had scaled seating by cost since the earliest days of grounds enclosure and admittance fees, "now the wealthy are separated by real walls, sitting in splendid isolation, presiding like princes at the joust."[68]

Though the Circle Suites garnered much of the attention, becoming a symbol of socioeconomic stratification within the stadium, Texas Stadium was also notable for how it redefined access to the stadium more completely. The Cowboys' previous home was the Cotton Bowl, in Dallas's Fair Park, an area surrounded by neighborhoods that were almost entirely African American. Its crowds were eclectic and rough-and-tumble, shaped by the team's blue-collar faithful. The new stadium was built in the white suburb of Irving, surrounded by parking lots and expressways. The Cowboys' brash owner, Clint Murchison Jr., had hoped for a new stadium in downtown Dallas but had made enemies of the mayor and city council.[69] Instead the Cowboys decamped for Irving, where an innovative financing scheme funded much of the new stadium. To buy season tickets, fans were first required to purchase stadium revenue bonds. The suites required the purchase of $50,000 bonds and brought in about one-quarter of the stadium's total cost of $30 million.[70] But much of the stadium was paid for through bonds attached to regular seating in the stadium bowl. Over three-quarters of the stadium's 65,000 total seats required the additional purchase of low-yield bonds. To buy a ticket between the 30-yard lines ($63 dollars for the season), a Cowboys fan also had to buy a stadium bond worth $1,000.[71] Seats outside the 30-yard lines required a $250 bond. Just 15,000 seats, located at the tops of the end-zone sections, were sold on a game-by-game basis; these required no bond but were quickly purchased at a cost of $7 per game. It was relatively easy for a working-class Cowboys fan to pick up a ticket for a game in the Cotton Bowl; it was quite difficult to attend a game at the new stadium, where access to tickets required season-long investment.

Texas Stadium epitomized the increasingly tightened access to NFL tickets across the league. Although professional football's clubs continued to reap the rewards of escalating television contracts, the clubs also repeatedly raised ticket prices through the 1960s (and would continue to do so through the 1970s), claiming increased operational costs. League averages in 1970 were $6 per ticket, but most of these were scooped up by season-ticket holders—a system that priced out the young and working classes who couldn't afford to buy an entire season's worth of games.[72] In Dallas, the average reserved season ticket had risen from about $4.60 per game in 1960, to $5.50 per game in 1965, to $7.00 per game in 1970.[73] The additional burden of a ticket bond for the new stadium pushed this expense even higher. The Cotton Bowl's masculine and often raucous crowd, shaped by its working-class fans, didn't follow the Cowboys to the new stadium. Player Jethro Pugh remarked, "We gave up the shoeshine guy for the lawyer."[74]

The pricing-out of many of the game's hard-core fans was a troubling sign for many. "Watching the Cowboys play at home," a columnist wrote, "has become the equivalent of joining a country club—and a darned expensive country club at that." The title of an article in *Esquire* asked, "Wanta Buy Two Seats for the Dallas Cowboys? Struck Oil Lately?" Longtime Cowboys fans were priced out of seeing their beloved team—which many had followed through the club's lesser years in the early 1960s at the old Cotton Bowl. Some took to calling the club's new home "a rich man's stadium" and "Millionaires' Meadows."[75] A Cowboys supporter said of the stadium, "It kind of makes the whole thing a private club for the fortunate. You know the Cowboys have a lot of support among people who could never come up with $1,000, or even $250 for the privilege of buying season tickets. This is supposed to be a public stadium and yet its cost is well beyond most of the public's reach."[76] Cowboys owner Clint Murchison admitted that because of the financing scheme the club "lost a whole group in the $12,000-to-$20,000-a-year salary range who could afford tickets at the Cotton Bowl but couldn't afford to buy bonds." However, he philosophized, "all America discriminates against people who don't have enough money to buy everything they want."[77]

Murchison's justification certainly didn't calm the angst of those either locked out of the stadium or put under a considerable financial squeeze to be there. The luxury suites were a conspicuous symbol of this new modern order. One Cowboys fan complained: "We keep hearing about those fabulous private boxes with the instant television replay systems. But how many people do you think have $100,000 to spend to get that kind of service?"[78] The sense of a two-class stadium was only exacerbated when the City of Irving, located in a dry county, passed a special law that allowed liquor to be sold only in the Circle Suites and stadium club areas.[79] A fan said, "They don't serve alcohol to us poor slobs in the stands. Let's face it, at Texas Stadium, I'm a second-class citizen."[80]

When Miami Dolphins owner Joe Robbie began planning for a new 70,000-seat stadium north of the city in the late 1970s, he hoped to finance the project by selling $50,000 investment bonds to supporters—a plan devised from the financing of Texas Stadium earlier that decade. Broward County commissioner George Platt opposed such an approach, calling it "repugnant, because we wouldn't want to build a facility for the needs of the wealthy." Robbie defensively claimed that the bond approach didn't cater to the rich; of his potential buyers, he said: "They're not corporations or people who have inherited great wealth. They're mostly upper-middle class people who are making $50,000 to $100,000 a year."[81] The Dolphins owner's categorization of "upper-middle class" was predictably skewed; less than 4 percent of households made over $50,000 per year in 1979, when the national median income was $15,229.[82]

In spite of the complaints, team owners and architects increasingly committed stadium space to luxury suites and private clubs. The 83 suites in Kansas City's Arrowhead Stadium, opened in 1972, rivaled those in Texas Stadium for opulence. Michael Oriard remembered, as a player at Arrowhead in the early 1970s, looking up to the suites from the field below and thinking that "behind the glass the social elite of Kansas City were sipping cocktails, nibbling on hors d'oeuvre, and following the game on closed-circuit television sets when it was not convenient to look down on the field—if they followed the play at all."[83] Thirty-three suites were installed at Rich Stadium in suburban Buffalo. New Orleans's Superdome hosted 64 boxes—big party rooms for 30 people costing on average $25,000 per year.[84] Ron Labinski, a stadium designer who would later found the influential architectural firm HOK Sport, noted in 1980 that nearly all stadiums built after 1967 had incorporated suites, "and in many of the older stadiums, we're coming back and putting them in where we can." San Diego's Jack Murphy Stadium was adding 29 suites that year, and Anaheim Stadium was set for 112 as the stadium expanded to accommodate the relocating Rams of the NFL.[85] Even Minneapolis's Metrodome, endlessly celebrated by its promoters as a frugal antidote to some of its extravagant predecessors when it opened in 1982, housed 115 suites.[86]

In a decade of economic turmoil and stagnant working- and middle-class wages, the suite allowed the privileged a retreat from the stadium public into a private realm of food, drink, television sets, and personalized service. The inclusion of private luxury spaces in the stadium cultivated a new type of spectator: one who required certain standards of physical and social comfort to watch a game. These spaces also privileged a certain way of watching games: seated, dispassionately critical, expecting to be entertained by either the game on the field or the other entertainments at hand.[87] These were spaces where, as a *Los Angeles Times* reporter said of Arrowhead Stadium's suite holders, "If he or his friends don't like the way a game is going they can always retire behind the glass-doored suite and shut out the world."[88] The slow and mundane, it seemed, was being programmed out of sport with the cultivation of a new kind of fan: a fickle consumer of highlights with no appetite for the subtle bridges between them.[89]

Stadium Spectacles

Plastic, loud, unrelenting, undemocratic, and standardized: these were qualities that disgusted traditionalists who valued sports as something more than a mere diversion. As old ballparks were torn down and new modern ones built to replace them in the name of progress, many thought the stadium had been corrupted, removed from its traditional status as an urban landmark, as an anchor of community identity, and as a site where great athletes did great things. To the purists, television seemed to be killing sport. Imagining a time when money and marketing seemed to take a backseat to the games, they called for a return to roots. Such complaints were at home among broader social critiques of capitalist waste, environmental degradation, and dehumanizing modernist belief systems reflected in everything from the war in Vietnam to urban planning and design.[90]

Baseball traditionalists, of course, saw plenty to dislike in the artificial turf, noisy scoreboards, and symmetrical outfields. In 1969, Mark Harris lamented how baseball's "proprietors" had adopted the frenetic logic of television and the example of football. "Baseball is slow," Harris reasoned. "It always was. It was slow in 1869." He entreated baseball owners to look backward for inspiration, writing, "The man you need may be Henry David Thoreau, and what you need may be, not expansion but contraction, not speed but the nourishment of old roots, not closer fences or lowered scoreboards but a renewed connection between the game and its essential followers, not the eye of the camera but the vision of Time Past and Time to Come."[91]

Emergent critiques of sport and the stadium weren't limited to the boys of summer. Michael Oriard, just three years after concluding his playing career in the NFL, also lamented sport's modern disconnection with the natural. In a 1976 essay, he argued that the ballpark and stadium were traditionally sources of psychic compensation for the loss of the frontier, antidotes to the worst effects of industrialization and urbanization. Sports like baseball and football were "symbolic reenactments of our struggle to survive in wild nature and vestigial clingings to our intimate relationship to pastoral nature." This psychological need and relationship was undermined by the "artificiality of modern stadiums." The standardization and denaturalization of stadiums degraded the quality of experience there, for both players and fans. As a player, Oriard recalled the "non-experience" of playing in artificial spaces like Busch Stadium, the partially roofed Texas Stadium, and, most of all, the enclosed Astrodome, which provoked a sense of "constriction" and "unreality." In the monumental modern stadiums like Three Rivers Stadium and Riverfront Stadium, he felt alienated from the spectators. Conversely, "In the less pretentious stadiums," he remembered, "we players seemed the focal point. . . . We were bound to our fans in a common undertaking. We were not merely ornaments or objects of the spectators' amusement." The stadium was losing its capacity to be "a source of psychic regeneration"; instead, it had become "a theater in which the spectator demands to be entertained by showmanship and victories, and where the player simply earns a salary." Commercialized sport had maintained its "pastoral aspects" since the 1920s, but in recent years a new "dominance by technology signals a fundamental revision of American sport—a shift from mythic game to ostentatious spectacle."[92]

When Roger Angell visited Pittsburgh's Three Rivers Stadium in 1970, he found a building that was no longer a park but a machine—an anonymous non-place whose only distinguishing mark was an enormous stadium club hovering over the field, where the consumption of steak and cocktails rivaled the game. By the end of the decade, most major league cities had a new stadium like Pittsburgh's—an engineered concrete cylinder filled with plastic seats, plastic grass, private clubs, luxury suites, noisy scoreboards, and sometimes a roof to block out the weather. Television, above all, ruled the games and the stadium experience, its logic of continual stimulation redefining in-stadium production. Many mourned the seeming loss of traditional sport, in which fans were engaged with the game, each other, and not much else—fans like those from Ebbets Field or Sportsman's Park, where crowds were embodied participants in the game, talking to players on the field, jangling cowbells, and bellowing like farm animals.

The famed "Battle of the Sexes"—Billie Jean King's 1973 tennis triumph over Bobby Riggs in the Astrodome—perhaps expressed the state of sport, the stadium, and its culture at this time as well as any other event. Historian Bruce Schulman would later claim that the match "signaled the arrival of the women's movement as a broad cultural force."[93] And yet it could as easily be seen as a farce. For any other match, King would walk out from the locker room to the court; on this day, she rode in on a gold divan borne by four bare-footed, bare-chested men. Her rival—the fifty-five-year-old former Wimbledon champion—arrived in a rickshaw pulled by five buxom women he called the "bosom buddies." Divan and rickshaw ran an outrageous gauntlet of costumed characters from the nearby AstroWorld theme park; elegant women in evening dresses; men in the front-row seats wearing suits and holding signs with messages like "Whiskey, Women and Riggs" and "Who needs women?"; an eclectic mix of celebrities, including artist Salvador Dalí, singer Glenn Campbell, actress Janet Leigh, and football legend Jim Brown; and thirty thousand fans, many holding large banners that certainly distinguished the atmosphere of this match from most of the sport's country-club affairs.[94]

The match was undoubtedly among the great spectacles of American sports history, a made-for-television event splattered across front pages of newspapers and magazine covers across the country. Roone Arledge, who had played such a pivotal role in making football a darling of television, paid over seven hundred thousand dollars for broadcast rights and raked in over one million in advertising for ABC. The heavily sponsored match was broadcast to a television audience of more than forty-eight million, in thirty-six foreign countries. Three hundred reporters covered the event.[95]

Those reporters drew many different conclusions from the match. Most focused on its theatricality—comparing it to Barnum's circus.[96] Many dismissed the event as mere show business.[97] Gladys Heldman, the founder of the women's professional tour, asked reporters before the match, "What do we get if Billie Jean wins, 30 Senators?"[98] But others thought the match more significant. "Mrs. Billie Jean King struck a proud blow for herself and women around the world," Neil Amdur wrote on the front page of the *New York Times*. "Most important, perhaps for women everywhere," he claimed, "she convinced skeptics that a female athlete can survive pressure-filled situations and that men are as susceptible

FIGURE 74. Billie Jean King emerges for the "Battle of the Sexes" atop a gold divan.
RGD 0006-1973-0714, HOUSTON PUBLIC LIBRARY, HOUSTON METROPOLITAN RESEARCH CENTER.

to nerves as women."[99] After the match, King described the win as a turning point in women's sports and called it the apex of her career.[100] Senator Hugh Scott, a Republican from Pennsylvania, said that King had "ratified the 26th Amendment" through her victory, ensuring passage of the proposed (and ultimately defeated) Equal Rights Amendment, which would ban discrimination based on sex.[101]

The "Battle of the Sexes" would come to signify in shorthand a broader grassroots movement in women's sport. King would be the face of that movement, which overlapped with a feminist agenda asserting women's rights to control and enjoy their own bodies.[102] But this event also suggested the state of big-time sports in the 1970s. Sports became out-and-out show business, both in the stadium and on television. The game itself was often secondary to the circumstances about it—shiny objects that competed with sports performances, crowding them out, so that spectator sport often seemed just sports-themed entertainment. For those who looked to sport for something more than mere entertainment, they found it had lost much of its transcendental capacities. Though today the Battle of the Sexes is remembered by many as an iconic social moment, an expression of the women's movement and a repudiation of male chauvinism, its symbolic significance was muddled at the time by its carnivalesque production. It was an event both deeply meaningful and completely meaningless, a sporting event that, for many, had as much to do with sport as the kiss that King and Riggs shared—at the insistence of photographers—after the match.[103]

The Astrodome's televised spectacle occurred at a time when the world was in the midst of profound economic, political, and cultural upheavals, changes that dramatically impacted urban life and the design of cities. The standardization of the stadium and its culture in the late 1960s and through the 1970s coexisted with increasingly prevalent critiques of the modern city and its design. Modernist architects and planners had wrought new downtowns of austere office towers, open plazas, and automobile throughways. Like the "machines for sport," such spaces were criticized as placeless and anonymous, starkly functional and monumental, designed at a scale that dwarfed their users.[104] As disgust with modernist planning and design gained steam, American cities—particularly in the industrial Rust Belt of the Northeast and Midwest—were also forced to grapple with a series of profound and escalating economic and social challenges. The loss of manufacturing jobs—to the Sun Belt, suburban areas, and increasingly abroad—wreaked havoc on urban economies and city residents. As demands for social services grew, tax revenues declined alongside federal support. Suburbanization continued apace, further concentrating poorer Americans in old urban neighborhoods that encircled central business districts rewritten by urban renewal and modernist planning. With the loss of manufacturing jobs, urban governments increasingly turned to culture as an engine of economic development. Public-private alliances developed new mixed-use entertainment districts featuring shopping malls, cocktail bars, themed restaurants, conference centers, gentrified housing, and sports stadiums. Some modernist stadiums served as anchors to such redevelopment projects—like Busch Stadium in the mid-1960s and the ostentatious Superdome in New Orleans a decade later. But as cities pivoted from making things to producing experiences, planners and architects turned to new forms of urban design.

Architecture made a "romantic turn," rejecting the uniformity and cold rationalism of modernism. Unlike postwar modernists who scorned the styles of the past for a progressive and futuristic internationalism—a universal style that transcended all historical styles—postmodernists embraced local heritage and traditions. In a world that seemed ever more globally connected—marked by freer flows of people, goods, ideas, culture, and capital across regional and national boundaries—many Americans felt disconnected and looked to the past for stability and comfort. Designers tapped into these longings, insisting on the importance of place, as they attempted to materially construct a sense of community and security—while also distinguishing their cities from others in the competition for corporate investment. San Francisco's Ghirardelli Square, Boston's Faneuil Hall, New York's South Street Seaport, and San Antonio's Riverwalk were all prominent examples of a new postmodern urbanism that celebrated place at a human scale; such developments often repackaged old and abandoned spaces of industry and commerce into outdoor pedestrian malls and entertainment zones. They directly challenged the tenets of modernism, deploying ornamentation, stylistic eclecticism, and historical reference in their new designs. The spaces could work as stage sets for visitors craving expressions of community and a sense of the past, of simpler times. It was a nostalgic architecture of not just function but fiction.[105]

Stadiums fit perfectly into this new brand of urban redevelopment. Sports teams are anchored geographically to specific cities and work as rallying points for broad and diverse communities of people. Thus they work particularly well at producing and amplifying a sense of place-based identity that can serve the growth strategies of politicians and business leaders.[106] Just as cities compete for capital investment, their teams battle it out in city stadiums. City status is most easily marked in shorthand by the presence of "big-league" teams; this is as true today as it was in the 1950s when Milwaukee's civic leadership lured the Boston Braves westward. The postmodern redesign of the stadium followed closely after the reinvention of American cities, and its symbolism overlapped seamlessly with the symbolic reconstitution of those cities. The new stadium—the postmodern stadium—could express a sense of history, tradition, and authenticity that seemed increasingly absent in a postindustrial age of political, social, and economic change.

A Ballpark, Not a Stadium

When Baltimore unveiled plans for a new, downtown, baseball-specific stadium in 1989, *New York Times* architectural critic Paul Goldberger rejoiced, writing, "If it is half as good as the models and renderings suggest, it will represent a return to baseball as it should be; a game played on grass, not turf; under the sky, not a dome; in the middle of a city, not out on an interstate highway. This is a building capable of wiping out in a single gesture 50 years of wretched stadium design, and of restoring the joyous possibility that a ball park might actually enhance the experience of watching the game of baseball."[107] Goldberger's reading of the planned ballpark perfectly channeled the intention of stadium designers: to build the antimodern, anti-artificial stadium; architects HOK Sport called it a "reaction to the cookie-cutter stadia of the 1960s and 1970s."[108] Plans called for a structure dominated by arched brick and steel trusses; the architects would avoid what a reporter called the "mausoleum effect of unrelieved concrete," as expressed in the modern stadiums. Janet Marie Smith, Orioles vice president for planning and development, said that the designers wanted an intimate setting, with seats closer to the field than those at modern, multi-purpose structures. "We studied the old ballparks to see what made them special," Smith explained. They planned to blend the stadium into the cityscape rather than place it distinctly apart. The continual subtext, in describing the plans, was that the ballpark would *not* be another modern stadium but one that seemed to be from baseball's past—the era of

FIGURE 75. The view from behind home plate at Camden Yards in 1992. The old B&O Warehouse, integrated into the ballpark, flanks the right-field wall. The urbanoid scene of Eutaw Street, inside the stadium gates, runs between field and warehouse. The corporate spectacle of downtown Baltimore is framed by the stands. AP PHOTO/TED MATHIAS.

Ebbets Field, the Polo Grounds, and Sportsman's Park. Orioles president Larry Lucchino emphasized this point, claiming, "We refer to it as 'the ballpark,' not a stadium. We try not to use the S-word."[109]

Oriole Park at Camden Yards—a name that shoehorned two pastoral references and an industrial-era nod into five words—was the official title of the new stadium when it opened in 1992.[110] Roundly celebrated, Camden Yards, as it was commonly known, was located in Baltimore's Inner Harbor, near the city's Harborplace festival marketplace. Harborplace, designed by influential developer James Rouse, was one of the first histori- cally themed, consumption-oriented, gentrified urban spaces when it opened in the early 1980s. Such developments were what Goldberger, writing seven years after his enthusiastic reception of the Camden Yards plans, would term "urbanoid environments"—carefully planned and sheltered places that seemingly bristled with urban energy and unpredict-ability.[111] Pitched to middle-class, often suburban, consumers, these urbanoid spaces provided risk-averse, middle-class suburbanites with a sense of adventure.[112] People gleaned textures of the authentic from gentrified urban spaces—festival marketplaces like Harbor-place among them. Visitors were afforded a simulated city experience in a built environ-ment that signified authenticity and tradition through a historicist aesthetic.[113]

A new generation of stadium embraced an old urban idiom.[114] Camden Yards featured heavy brick arches and revealed steel trusses. Its irregular dimensions fit into the existing streetscape. It integrated the adjacent railroad warehouse into the design, which seemed to stitch the park into the urban fabric. It employed a whole range of accents to signify pastness—ironwork details, retro-styled advertising, sand-blasted signage painted on brick, costumed service workers. Camden Yards expressed, in the words of cultural his-torian Daniel Rosensweig, "the fundamental and magical simplicity of an earlier era."[115]

Camden Yards seemed to be everything the modern stadium wasn't. It was a return to roots, recalling the early twentieth-century baseball parks that the modern stadiums had replaced. Comparisons to these old parks seemed endless. One commentator claimed, "Left field . . . is a homage to Yankee Stadium's most memorable features. . . . Center field is an obvious nod to Wrigley. . . . Right field is pure Ebbets Field."[116] Another argued, "The asymmetrical playing field contains nooks and crannies in the outfield that will make playing defense there a thoughtful and artful vocation, in the mold of trying to learn all the angles at Boston's Fenway Park."[117] A third wrote, "To most, the huge brick B&O Ware-house provided the park's signature touch, looming large behind a sign-festooned right field fence reminiscent of Ebbets Field's."[118] Though brand-new, the park seemed well-worn, well used, and thus more real and authentic. Baltimore Orioles general manager Roland Hemond admitted, "I feel like there's already history here. It's like we transported the tradition and didn't lose it."[119] Baltimore star Cal Ripken said, "This may be the first game, but it feels like baseball has been played here before. It's kind of strange. And really beautiful."[120]

Many celebrated the connection of the park to the city around it. Physically and visu-ally, Camden Yards seemed a sibling of the old traditional ballparks locked in their urban landscapes—parks like Ebbets Field and Fenway Park. Orioles owner Eli Jacobs claimed, "This is the city. The park is an integral part of the whole experience. It's a natural part of the cityscape. It feels like it's been here a long time."[121] Architects HOK Sport claimed that parks like Camden Yards "provide authenticity and symbolism, forging a bond between community and resident by illustrating a city's best features."[122] Of the Baltimore park par-ticularly, Tim Kurkjian of *Sports Illustrated* wrote, "It's a real ballpark built into a real downtown of a real city."[123] Amid all this realness and authenticity, it was easy to forget that the stadium was brand-new.

The new park wasn't celebrated as just a physical fit with the city but a spiritual and ideological one as well. Kurkjian argued, "It's fitting that the new age of retropark is being celebrated already in Baltimore, a provincial, blue-collar, crab-cakes-and-beer town with thick roots and a thicker accent." Orioles pitcher Mike Flanagan also linked the city's blue-collar identity with a new stadium that seemed blue collar as well, claiming, "It's a working-class park in a working-class town."[124] *Washington Post* writer Eve Zibert called it "the most embracing, class-leveling, elbow-rubbing baseball stadium of our dreams" and an expression of "democracy."[125]

For all its seeming traditionalism and hardscrabble lineage, however, Camden Yards was luxurious—and in many ways quite modern—compared to its predecessor, Memorial Stadium. Though downtown, Camden Yards was adjacent to a freeway, convenient to suburban visitors; by the 1980s, Memorial Stadium was lodged into a majority-black residential neighborhood, notorious for its postgame traffic jams. The upper deck at Camden Yards was cantilevered; at Memorial Stadium, the second deck sat atop two-foot-wide support posts that obstructed plenty of sight lines. Camden Yards allowed its visitors more personal space; leg room for spectators in the new grounds varied between thirty-two and thirty-three inches, compared to the twenty-four to twenty-six inches at Memorial Stadium, and seats were nineteen to twenty-one inches wide, compared to sixteen to nineteen at the old place. Camden Yards featured sixty-one luxury suites, a private lounge, and a video screen. It was perhaps the best "stadium-as-studio" in the nation, boasting thirty-seven television camera locations staged throughout (compared to six at most parks), a television production studio, and an impressively framed view of downtown skyscrapers. Herb Belgrad, chairman of the Maryland Stadium Authority, asserted, "In the end we came up with state of art facilities and amenities as well as a traditional stadium"—though what made it "traditional" appeared to be as much about style as substance.[126]

Camden Yards became a national fixation and the envy of baseball executives and civic leaders across the country. Baseball commissioner Bud Selig would later call it "one of the two or three most powerful developments in the history of baseball," after a number of cities had adopted its style to profitable results.[127] HOK Sport designed retro baseball parks, and even some retro football stadiums, in city after city for the next two decades, including Cleveland, Denver, Detroit, San Francisco, Pittsburgh, Cincinnati, Philadelphia, San Diego, and the Bronx. The firm designed Enron Field (now Minute Maid Park) for Houston, a downtown retro ballpark opened in 2000 that featured a retractable roof. In 2006, a new Busch Stadium, also designed by HOK Sport, opened adjacent the old modern one in downtown St. Louis. Featuring massive brick towers—references to the landmark Eads Bridge crossing the Mississippi River nearby—this historicist park opened up to the city, providing most fans views of the iconic Gateway Arch. HOK Sport—renamed Populous in 2009, perhaps a gesture toward the populist accents of its ballparks—also devised

Citi Field for a lot adjacent Shea Stadium in Queens. Opened in 2009, it was "a blend of modern-day amenities and historic charm," masquerading as Brooklyn's old Ebbets Field with a replica of that park's main-entry rotunda.[128] This new retro ballpark boom was accompanied by the construction of new football-specific stadiums nationwide—with HOK Sport/Populous again leading the way. The firm designed stadiums in Jacksonville, Charlotte, Landover (Maryland), Tampa, Nashville, Cleveland, Foxborough (Massachusetts), Pittsburgh, St. Louis, Houston, and Baltimore (directly south of Camden Yards). Some of these stadiums adopted the historicist styles of the retro baseball parks, harkening back to early twentieth-century collegiate football stadiums; others took on a more contemporary corporate design mixing glass, brick, concrete, and steel.

Whether retro or contemporary in style, new ballparks and stadiums alike—most designed by HOK Sport/Populous and a few other major firms—foregrounded a sense of place.[129] In terms of structure, this meant breaking up the modern concrete cylinder so that the stadium opened out onto views of the landscape around it—often a framed ensemble of downtown skyscrapers. In terms of style, this often meant using materials like brick and steel seemingly borrowed from the old industrial city. Some stadium designs referenced the local through ornamental allusions. Coors Field in Denver, the Mile High City, possesses a line of purple seats at one mile of elevation. Gillette Stadium, home of the New England Patriots, features a futuristic lighthouse in deference to the region's coastal landmarks. Place was also constructed through stadium representation: designers, team representatives, journalists, and politicians rhetorically and visually highlighted these references to "place" in the public stadium conversation. Never again would people think these costly public investments were just anonymous "machines for sport," the same as in the next city over. Or so it seemed to those building them.

Designing Sport, the Stadium, and the Public

The fundamental project of the postwar modern stadium, from the 1950s through the 1970s, was to reshape the stadium public and experience. It removed sport from racially and ethnically diverse urban settings, relocating it to accommodate an emergent suburban population. It redefined the stadium public not only by changing sports space but also by catering to a new type of clientele—not just sports die-hards but casual or even sports-illiterate consumers who would need more than just the game to keep them entertained. And so, the game experience was reshaped around this targeted broader audience. New exploding scoreboards and massive video screens were installed to distract consumers during lulls in game play. New restaurants and souvenir stands encouraged visitors to splurge for more than just a hot dog and beer. Private clubs and luxury suites catered to a more upscale crowd, providing them premium service, status, and physical separation from the sporting masses. This project redesigned stadiums in the hubristic style of post-war modernism, rejecting the tired and traditional idiosyncrasies of the neighborhood, instead embracing the bold and forward-looking monumentalism of engineering and urban renewal. It was heroic architecture for an aspirational age. Nearly all this reengineering of the stadium, its experience, and the public within was paid for with public money. As the public funded the expansion of the suburbs and the infrastructure that served it—to the benefit of developers, construction companies, the auto industry, and the white middle class—so too would the public pay to reinvent the stadium for sports teams hoping to expand the number and spending power of their consumers.

Most references to modernist stadiums since the early 1990s have quickly dismissed them as drab and anonymous compromises to multipurpose economy—good for neither baseball nor football, players nor fans. By today's conventional wisdom, they were merely less expensive than their replacements, and thus ends the list of their advantages.[130] This position echoes Paul Goldberger's initial impressions of Camden Yards—that it might be "a building capable of wiping out in a single gesture 50 years of wretched stadium design." But when we don't wipe out those fifty years of design, instead considering Camden Yards and the navy of stadiums it launched as part of a broader historical evolution, a different picture emerges—one in which the social project of the postmodern stadium seems less a rejection of modernist values than an amplification of them.

Pittsburgh's machine for sport, Three Rivers Stadium, was replaced by two new stadiums in 2001: Heinz Field for football's Steelers and PNC Park for baseball's Pirates. They were both built in the spirit of Camden Yards, designed by the same architectural firm, HOK Sport. The design of Heinz Field—and the language used to describe it—framed the stadium as undoubtedly Pittsburgh. "We wanted people to be aware, when they were sitting in it, that they were in Pittsburgh," Steelers vice president Art Rooney II explained. The architects called it the "Steel City Stadium." Twelve thousand tons of structural steel "honored the region's history." At ground level, "we wanted to anchor the building to the site, and for that we used stone," a designer said, adding, "that came from looking at a lot of the buildings and bridges [in Pittsburgh], which have a heavy stone base." The horseshoe shape represented "the historic link to football as it originated on the college campus." Breaks between stands—unlike the continuous enclosure of Three Rivers Stadium—provided views in and out of the stadium, "establishing a dynamic link to the surrounding areas." The open south end—if one could see past the 2,800-square-foot video board—provided views across the Ohio River to the central business district, creating "a connection between the stadium and downtown." The FedEx Great Hall (formerly the Coca Cola Great Hall) on the stadium's east side—home to sports memorabilia, a team store, and various concessionaires—solidified "the uniqueness of the fan experience" while "establishing a physical tie between fan and facility, contributing to a grander experience of a unique atmosphere." According to the Steelers, the stadium wasn't just the team's home but "a monument to the outstanding Western Pennsylvania football tradition and its loyal fans." In theory, the stadium was supposed to represent "an understanding of what 'downtown is'—integrating places of working, living, gathering and celebrating into a comprehensive experience that ultimately symbolized the personality of Pittsburgh." In truth, it buzzed on game day—as just about any NFL stadium would—and lay fallow the rest of the week.[131]

Like that of Heinz Field, PNC Park's design was "rooted in Pittsburgh's architectural traditions," according to its architects. The masonry archways around the stadium's base, accented with terra cotta tiles, recalled old Forbes Field, the Pirates' home from 1909 to 1969. The Pirates called it "a classic-style ballpark, an intimate facility that embraces the progressiveness of Pittsburgh while saluting the spirit of early ballpark originals such as Forbes Field, Wrigley Field and Fenway Park." In deference to the old parks, it featured asymmetrical outfield dimensions. In the fashion of the new ones, it included a winking

FIGURE 76. Three Rivers Stadium hosts its final Pirates game in 2000. To the right is the new Heinz Field under construction; to the left, across the freeway, is the new PNC Park.
AP PHOTO/KEITH SRAKOCIC.

reference to local lore—the right-field wall was twenty-one feet tall, in honor of Pirates legend Roberto Clemente, who wore that number. Like Heinz Field, it featured views across the Ohio River to downtown Pittsburgh.[132]

There are clear differences between the new stadiums and the old ones in style and form. Each is designed in a way that self-consciously looks to a more distant past for inspiration. Three Rivers Stadium adopted the style and form of the previous two decades—engineered rationalism and monumental geometries. PNC Park and Heinz Field looked nearly a century back, adopting the angularity of the city block, the asymmetry of the old ballparks, the openness of the gridiron horseshoe, and older building traditions in materials and ornamentation. This could be a bit disorienting—an odd mash-up of 1909 pastiche and twenty-first-century technology. But most have celebrated this turn to the distant past—an understandable response. Place and localism have been central components to sports identity since leagues were organized in the nineteenth century—it is how we distinguish one team and its fans from another. Sporting traditions are learned and passed from person to person, generation to generation in the stadium; it makes sense that a design embracing the past would be a popular one for sports fans. These changes in style were matched with arguably more important changes in form. Multipurpose Three Rivers had to be circular to accommodate the gridiron and the diamond. Pittsburgh's willingness to finance and build separate sport-specific stadiums enabled HOK Sport to draw the seats of each closer to the game. This particularly impacted visitors to PNC Park, where grandstands could hug the diamond—a playing surface that was nearly 20 percent smaller than at the old, circular stadium—and thus replicate the sense of intimacy that marked old ballparks like Forbes Field.[133]

These new stadiums undeniably improved the stadium experience in significant ways. But these celebrated differences have also obscured the ways that the contemporary stadium has extended and even intensified the modern stadium project—from game experience to the people who experience it. While sight lines were improved and designs tickled the imagination, the in-stadium experience has replicated that of the modernist stadiums. Writers, players, and fans alike have long complained of an overproduced game atmosphere since the Astrodome's scoreboard debuted in the mid-1960s—conditions powered by increasingly sophisticated electronic audiovisual technologies. And though the new stadiums made design claims on the past to manufacture a sense of place-based authenticity, they rejected the traditional pacing and crowd-generated atmosphere that distinguished "classic" ballparks like Griffith Stadium and Cincinnati's Crosley Field. New stadiums instead doubled down on the Hofheinzian approach to sport: a belief that the games and the organic energies of the crowds would bore a general audience, whose main appetite was for constant stimulation. Shortly after the opening of PNC Park, a writer for the *Pittsburgh Post-Gazette* described such a scene there: music blasting over the sound system at any pause in game action; the "sensory overload" of cartoon pirates on the Jumbotron; and hot dogs and T-shirts being fired from cannons on the field into the stands, sending his neighbors into feeding frenzies. If they can have "Magnetic Schedule Night" and "Kids Replica Jersey Day," he wonders, why couldn't the Pirates host a "NOTHING-EXCEPT-THE-BALL-GAME Night?" He fantasizes experiencing "just the game with its quiet rhythms" and an atmosphere "where, say, a father might explain to his daughter the finer points of the game, and if something exciting happens, well, the crowd could—get this—make noise on its own."[134]

There was a time when crowds made their own noise, at places like Sportsman's Park and Ebbets Field. This was before stadiums were removed from old urban neighborhoods and rebuilt on suburban freeways and in "renewed" corporate downtowns—before diverse ballpark scenes were disciplined and narrowed, reshaped into whiter, more affluent stadium publics. The suburbanization of the stadium population was followed quickly by the installation of exclusive stadium spaces—symbols of upscaled stadium publics and the aspirations of sports entrepreneurs. When Roger Angell first surveyed Three Rivers in 1970, he noted the encroachment of new luxury spaces into the stadium—the private Allegheny Club and 42 suites. Today's stadiums have amplified and normalized such class distinction. Though PNC Park is about 25 percent smaller than Three Rivers in seating capacity (38,362 compared to 50,235), it significantly expanded its upscale luxury spaces, with 69 suites and an additional 2,900 club seats. Suite owners and club members enjoy a range of exclusive amenities, including private street-level entrances to the ballpark; a private concourse separated from the stadium's general public; and private dining, bar, and lounge areas.[135] Heinz Field boasts 129 suites and 7,300 premium club seats; these ticket holders buy access to the stadium's three exclusive clubs and private stadium entrances.[136] The wealthy and well connected in both new stadiums can rope themselves off from the general stadium public almost entirely.

PNC Park and Heinz Field are typical of American stadiums built in the last quarter century. Stadiums like Shea, the Astrodome, and Busch blazed trails that have been paved into freeways. Today's facilities are less accessible to the general public than ever before, as designers and teams increasingly pack them with more premium spaces like luxury suites, club seats, restaurants, and bars—a tendency initiated in the postwar era that has become much more pronounced over the last twenty-five years. While the stadiums built since Camden Yards have typically been much larger in size than those they replaced, they have also reduced standard seating by 15 percent, replacing regular seats with premium club seats and luxury suites. Architectural firms have tried to calm those anxious about the pricing out of the middle class by claiming that new premium seating subsidizes non-premium seating, making it more affordable to the "regular" fan. But the declining number of non-premium seats suggests otherwise. As the number of non-premium seats has dropped, the ticket price has risen consistently, greatly outstripping wage gains.[137] The cost of attending Pittsburgh Steelers games, for example, rose nearly 10 percent from 2013 to 2014 alone.[138] It is increasingly difficult for middle-class fans—to say nothing of the working class—to afford trips to major league stadiums.

The gentrification of the stadium might be less objectionable if the public wasn't funding it. The practice of publicly funded construction of stadiums for professional sports teams became normalized beginning in the 1950s; the public investment in stadiums is higher today than it ever has been. In the 1990s, cities invested nearly $8 billion in constructing fifty-five new stadiums and arenas; between 2000 and 2010, the public paid $12 billion on fifty-one new facilities. Thirteen new major league ballparks were opened in the 1990s, with average public costs—including capital and operating expenses—of $301 million per structure. The average public cost went up to $423 million the following decade, when eleven facilities opened. Public costs for twelve new professional football stadiums were, on average, $355 million in the 1990s; fifteen new stadiums were built between 2001 and 2010, costing the public, on average, $448 million each (all figures in 2010 dollars).[139]

Pittsburgh's new stadiums were largely paid for by the city, county, and state: $296 million for PNC Park (82 percent of the capital costs, $363 million in 2010 dollars) and $266 million for Heinz Field (76 percent of the capital costs, $349 million in 2010 dollars). Three Rivers Stadium, paid for entirely by the public, cost $55 million ($335 million in 2010 dollars). While modern multipurpose stadiums like Three Rivers might have made for less "intimacy" and compromised sight lines, at least they boasted an economy of cost compared to today's specialized facilities, doubling as two stadiums in one. Better sight lines and the pleasures of nostalgic designs cost Pennsylvanians $712 million, more than double the cost of the structurally sound stadium replaced.

More troubling than the public investment was the process that secured it. Pittsburghers voted by a nearly two-to-one margin in 1997 to reject "plan A"—the referendum that would increase regional sales taxes to finance the stadiums. Hours before the vote, Mayor Tom Murphy had warned, "There will be no plan B." But hours after the defeat of plan A, Murphy and his stadium allies—emboldened by the support of the city's powerful and unified growth coalition of corporate leaders—were assembling plan B. The stadiums were built in spite of voter rejection, channeling public tax dollars—euphemistically referred to as "revenue streams"—into the projects.[140] Murphy justified this end run on voters with logic and language that seemed straight out of the 1960s stadium games: "These teams are a symbol of Pittsburgh. They're a symbol of moving forward or moving backward. Something is at stake far bigger than what they're worth financially. The larger value is being a major league city."[141] An editorial in the *Pittsburgh Post-Gazette* celebrated the opening of PNC Park by calling it a "people's stadium—built largely with public funds and open for business to thrill the public."[142] It's a rhetoric that doesn't match the reality—a willful reinvention of a stadium built through the circumvention of the democratic process, a stadium built by the public for society's most privileged and powerful. The benefits of stadium subsidies like those in Pittsburgh disproportionately go to the wealthy who can afford to go the most, the developers whose investments in downtown real estate are augmented, the corporations that can trot out major league sports to recruit executives into the fold, and the team owners whose franchise values explode with the building of a new stadium.[143] This model of urban investment recalls Larry McMurtry's observation about Houston and the Astrodome in 1965: "Here, it is customary to build in order to steal."[144]

This gentrification of stadium space is disguised by formal and stylistic changes in design that manufacture a sense of place. Invoking the lessons of the old urban ballparks like Pittsburgh's Forbes Field, today's stadiums celebrate the local through architectural allusion and visual contextualization. The city again seems just beyond the stadium walls—though unlike in "classic" parks like the Polo Grounds and Fenway Park, this is usually a corporate spectacle—a judiciously framed view of business district skyscrapers. The city becomes spectacle and consumer item. Carefully controlled stadium "villages"— like those around Camden Yards and PNC Park—give visitors access to urban energy without the threat of urban unpredictability and any real experience of socioeconomic or racial diversity.[145] A simulation of urban space and an urban public is joined to a rhetoric of inclusion, intimacy, and community. This discourse matches the strategies of stadium advocates pushing for public funding, who have shifted their campaigns from economic development justifications to invocations of intangible community spirit.[146] In a society that has become increasingly stratified economically over the previous decades, the new generation of stadiums "provide[s] authenticity and symbolism, forging a bond between community and resident by illustrating a city's best features," according to HOK Sport/ Populous.[147] But with each new stadium seemingly more exclusive than the last, such claims about authenticity and community are increasingly more tired and transparent. These stadiums aren't anchors of community spirit but instruments of manipulation. Aesthetic appeals to local memory—at this point, often formulaic clichés—paper over the basic and obvious destabilizing effects of not only ruthless and monopolistic sports leagues that hold cities for stadium ransom but ever-restless capitalism and modern change. In spite of stylistic and rhetorical appeals to place, the retro postmodern stadium is arguably as formulaic as its modernist predecessors ever were—a series of urban "mallparks" clad in shabby chic, sandblasted brick. They aren't exactly "cookie cutters," but the postmodern adventure of Camden Yards has become postmodern routine in many cities.

Stadium gentrification has made it increasingly difficult for most Americans to see sport in person; as significant, it has robbed us of experiencing the thrilling energy of being among a genuine public of people from different neighborhoods, backgrounds, and experiences. This gradual reshaping of the stadium public has occurred unevenly across geography and time—it happened in Brooklyn in 1957, Philadelphia in 1970, and Baltimore in 1991. It appears to be happening even today, as the Atlanta Braves leave a ballpark opened in 1997, near downtown, for suburban Cobb County. Across this broad period, some stadium publics—particularly in older stadiums—have retained a more democratic, cross-class character.[148] But the genuinely diverse and organic stadium crowd and experience is largely a thing of the past—and a distant past in most cities.

Rod Sheard, a founder and senior principal for Populous—by far the most influential stadium builder—has said of today's stadiums, "These buildings aren't just stadiums . . . anymore. They're destinations. We want to design the most spectacular buildings or experiences, the ones that set a team or a city apart. We want to create places of magic."[149] But magic doesn't come from the stadium—it comes from what people do in it. A sense of place isn't hatched from a blueprint; it's developed over time as fans and players invest joy and suffering into a space and each other. We could demand that stadiums be affordable. We could start new leagues if they aren't. The stadium could again live up to its image as a democratic space where we experience our whole communities. We can have a society, inside and outside the stadium, in which citizenship isn't measured in income but in engagement—in stadium terms, a crowd that makes its own noise, not one pulverized by the Jumbotron. Professional stadiums once were great public spaces, and they can be again. When pitching for public funding in Pittsburgh, the mayor argued that sport "can cut across economic, ethnic, and racial boundaries. It's a reflection of how society ought to work."[150] Sport *can* do these things, and so too could our stadiums.

NOTES

INTRODUCTION

1   Edward D. Sargent, "University Expansion Changes LeDroit Park Neighborhood," *Washington Post*, February 28, 1983.

2   Blair A. Ruble, *Washington's U Street: A Biography* (Baltimore: Johns Hopkins University Press, 2010), 4, 9, 13–14; "Text of Wender Segregation Survey," *Washington Post*, May 8, 1949. It is worth noting that the owners of Griffith Stadium's two major tenants were both notorious racists, though of different stripes. Clark Griffith of baseball's Senators resented Jackie Robinson's desegregation of the major league game, arguing that it would destroy the Negro Leagues (and in doing so erode one of his great income sources: the leasing of his park to black clubs like the famous Homestead Grays). Shirley Povich, "Griffith Wishes He Had a Suitcase Simpson," *Washington Post*, May 22, 1953; Brad Snyder, *Beyond the Shadow of the Senators: The Untold Story of the Homestead Grays and the Integration of Baseball* (New York: Contemporary Books, 2003). Griffith was slow to desegregate baseball's Senators. But he also often made the park available to the black community, turning it into one of the neighborhood's predominant outdoor spaces, and allowed African American kids into the games for free on Sundays (Snyder, *Beyond the Shadow of the Senators*, 286). His son and successor, Calvin Griffith, moved the Senators to Minnesota in 1960 and would later famously say that he was attracted by the fact that there were "good, hard-working white people out here." Shirley Povich, "Griffith Shows Colors," *Washington Post*, October 6, 1978; Nick Thimmesch, "Baseball Plantation," *Washington Post*, October 7, 1978; Jon Kerr, *Calvin: Baseball's Last Dinosaur, An Authorized Biography* (Dubuque, Iowa: Wm. C. Brown Publishers, 1990). *Washington Post* sportswriter Shirley Povich noted of both Clark and Calvin Griffith, "They had a southern strain," speculating that the Griffiths weren't virulently racist but that their views were in concert with traditional southern attitudes that constructed and maintained overt racial hierarchies (Povich quoted in Kerr, *Calvin*, 137). George Preston Marshall, the owner of the city's National Football League team, was the more virulent kind. He didn't field a black player until 1962—under pressure from the Kennedy administration. See Thomas G. Smith, "Civil Rights on the Gridiron: The Kennedy Administration and the Desegregation of the Washington Redskins," in *Sport and the Color Line: Black Athletes and Race Relations in Twentieth-Century America*, ed. Patrick B. Miller and David K. Wiggins (New York: Routledge, 2003).

3   Loretta Parker Brown, "Growing Up in LeDroit Park in the 1950s," *Washington Post*, March 21, 1985.

4   Snyder, *Beyond the Shadow of the Senators*.

5   Kristin M. Anderson and Christopher W. Kimball, "Minnesota Twins," in *Major League Baseball Clubs*, ed. Steven A. Riess (Westport, Conn.: Greenwood, 2006).

6   Kerr, *Calvin*, 49.

7   District of Columbia Stadium was renamed after Robert F. Kennedy in January 1969, following his assassination the previous summer.

8   "New District Stadium Takes Shape and It's an Admirable Figure," *Washington Post*, June 18, 1961. Residents of Kingman Park and Lincoln Park were forced to deal with not only the overflow parking, as visitors parked on the streets outside their homes, but the accompanying noise and garbage as well. Brett L. Abrams, *Capital Sporting Grounds: A History of Stadium and Ballpark Construction in Washington, D.C.* (Jefferson, N.C.: McFarland, 2008), 202.

9   Dave Brady, "37,767 See Skins Lose in Stadium," *Washington Post*, October 2, 1961.

10   Bob Addie, "Cold Hot Dogs," *Washington Post*, October 26, 1961.

11   Thomas Hine, *Populuxe: The Look and Life of America in the '50s and '60s, from Tailfins and TV Dinners to Barbie Dolls and Fallout Shelters* (New York: Alfred A. Knopf, 1989).

12   I refer to stadiums as "public" space, though they share qualities of the public and the private. As Chris Gaffney explains, stadiums are really quasi-public, in that they allow access to a general public, though only under certain economic, behavioral, and temporal conditions. Undoubtedly, the exclusive qualities of stadium space—qualities that are amplified over time, as I show—qualify it as quasi-public space. But I refer to American stadiums of the postwar era as public because (1) they assemble large groups of people who see themselves as members of a larger community and (2) they are entirely or significantly funded by the public. Christopher Thomas Gaffney, *Temples of the Earthbound Gods* (Austin: University of Texas Press, 2008), 32–34. My project focuses particularly on urban stadiums used for professional sport. College football stadiums are, of course, monumental structures as well; however, their development, particularly until the late twentieth century, is quite different than that of the urban, professional stadiums in terms of geographical location, funding, ownership, and stadium culture.

13   Edward Relph, *The Modern Urban Landscape* (Baltimore: Johns Hopkins University Press, 1987), 8–10; John Bale, *Sport, Space, and the City* (London: Routledge, 1993); John Bale, *Landscapes of Modern Sport* (Leicester: Leicester University Press, 1994). Bale uses Relph's work in *Place and Placelessness* (London: Pion, 1976) and *Rational Landscapes and Humanistic Geography* (London: Barnes and Noble Books, 1981).

14   Michael Gershman, *Diamonds: The Evolution of the Ballpark* (Boston: Houghton Mifflin, 1993), 191.

15   There is an extensive body of literature on the economics and politics of the stadium, including Joanna Cagan and Neil deMause, *Field of Schemes: How the Great Stadium Swindle Turns Public Money into Private Profit* (Lincoln: University of Nebraska Press, 2008); Kevin Delaney and Rick Eckstein, *Public Dollars, Private Stadiums: The Battle over Building Sports Stadiums* (New Brunswick, N.J.: Rutgers University Press, 2003); Charles Euchner, *Playing the Field: Why Sports Teams Move and Cities Fight to Keep Them* (Baltimore: Johns Hopkins University Press, 1993); Judith Grant Long, *Public-Private Partnerships for Major League Sports Facilities* (New York: Routledge, 2012); Roger G. Noll and Andrew Zimbalist, eds., *Sports, Jobs, and Taxes: The Economic Impact of Sports Teams and Stadiums* (Washington, D.C.: Brookings Institution, 1997); Mark S. Rosentraub, *Major League Losers: The Real Costs of Sports and Who's Paying for It* (New York: Basic Books, 1997); Kenneth L. Shropshire, *The Sports Franchise Game: Cities in Pursuit of Sports Franchises, Events, Stadiums, and Arenas* (Philadelphia: University of Pennsylvania Press, 1995); Jay Weiner, *Stadium Games: Fifty Years of Big League Greed and Bush League Boondoggles* (Minneapolis: University of Minnesota Press, 2000).

16   David Harvey, *The Urban Experience* (Baltimore: Johns Hopkins University Press, 1989), 45.

17   Houston Sports Association, *Astrodome: Eighth Wonder of the World* (Houston: Houston Sports Association, 1966), 1.

18   Elliott J. Gorn and Warren Goldstein, *A Brief History of American Sports* (Urbana: University of Illinois Press, 2004), 184.

19   Robert Lipsyte, "Astrodome Opulent Even for Texas," *New York Times*, April 8, 1965.

20   Henri Lefebvre, *The Production of Space*, trans. Donald Nicholson-Smith (Malden, Mass.: Blackwell, 1991); Tim Cresswell, *Place: A Short Introduction* (Malden, Mass.: Blackwell, 2004), 31–32.

21   Stuart Hall calls popular culture "the arena of consent and resistance. It is partly where hegemony arises, and where it is secured." This ideological hegemony "stems from the ability of those in power to make their own interests appear to be synonymous with the interests of society at large," as George Lipsitz argues. The

stadium is then, both metaphorically and literally, an "arena" where hegemony is secured and where certain interests become universalized. Hall repeatedly invokes spatial metaphors to explain the significance of popular culture. He writes, "Popular culture, commodified and stereotyped as it often is, is not at all, as we sometimes think of it, the arena where we find who we really are, the truth of our experience. It is an arena that is *profoundly* mythic. It is a theater of popular desires, a theater of popular fantasies. It is where we discover and play with the identifications of ourselves, where we are imagined, where we are represented, not only to the audiences out there who do not get the message, but to ourselves for the first time." Stuart Hall, "Notes on Deconstructing 'the Popular,'" in *People's History and Socialist Theory* (London: Routledge, 1981), 239; George Lipsitz, "The Meaning of Memory: Family, Class, and Ethnicity in Early Network Television," in *Time Passages: Collective Memory and American Popular Culture* (Minneapolis: University of Minnesota Press, 1990), 67; Stuart Hall, "What Is This 'Black' in Black Popular Culture?" *Social Justice* 20, no. 1/2 (Spring–Summer 1993): 113.

22   See Stuart Hall, "Encoding/Decoding," in *Culture, Media, Language*, ed. Stuart Hall, Dorothy Hobson, Andrew Love, and Paul Willis (London: Hutchinson, 1980), 128–38.

23   Lefebvre, *The Production of Space*; Edward Soja, *Thirdspace: Journeys to Los Angeles and Other Real-and-Imagined Places* (Oxford: Blackwell, 1996).

24   Most scholarly work on stadiums approaches them from economic and political angles. The work of geographer John Bale is a notable exception, particularly his *Sport, Space, and the City*. Daniel Rosensweig's *Retro Ball Parks: Instant History, Baseball, and the New American City* (Knoxville: University of Tennessee Press, 2005) is a dynamic and multidisciplinary approach to late twentieth-century baseball parks. David John Kammer's "Take Me Out to the Ballgame: American Cultural Values as Reflected in the Architectural Evolution and Criticism of the Modern Baseball Stadium" (PhD diss., University of New Mexico, 1982) is a baseball-centered cultural history of the ballpark as told through Yankee Stadium, Dodger Stadium, and the Astrodome. My project elaborates on some of the same themes he engages, particularly increasing customer affluence and stadium standardization. I expand as well on some of the observations of Brian J. Neilson, who perceptively works through the taxonomy of baseball parks—including postwar stadiums—in "Baseball," *The Theater of Sport*, ed. Karl B. Raitz (Baltimore: Johns Hopkins University Press, 1995). Phil Gruen delivers a sharp interpretation of the modern stadium in its historical contexts—something few people have done in their rush to embrace the retro ballpark of the late twentieth century—in "Postwar Stadiums: Will We Miss Them When They're Gone," *Baseball Research Journal* 25 (1996): 16–20. Robert C. Trumpbour examines stadium construction as a product of urban growth ideology and media coverage in *The New Cathedrals: Politics and Media in the History of Stadium Construction* (Syracuse, N.Y.: Syracuse University Press, 2007). Finally, my understanding of the stadium and its role in the urban landscape shares much with that of Eric Avila's treatment of Dodger Stadium in *Popular Culture in the Age of White Flight: Fear and Fantasy in Suburban Los Angeles* (Berkeley: University of California Press, 2004). There are also, of course, many popular trade books on stadiums; my personal favorite is Gershman, *Diamonds*.

25   Clark Griffith's Senators never called the District of Columbia Stadium home, moving to suburban Minneapolis in 1960 before the new stadium opened. An expansion franchise—the second coming of the Senators—lasted hardly a decade, from 1961 to 1972, before relocating to "Turnpike Stadium" in Arlington, Texas. The professional football team moved seven miles east to FedEx Field, a nondescript stadium designed for football and parking lots in suburban Landover, Maryland.

26   Rich Campbell, "With New Park, Team Is Finally Safe at Home," *Fredericksburg Free Lance-Star*, March 30, 2008; Michael Zitz, "Pain at the Park? One Man's Take on the New Ballpark," *Fredericksburg Free Lance-Star*, March 27, 2008; David Nakamura and Thomas Heath, "For Some Fans, Stadium Designers Whiffed Big-Time," *Washington Post*, March 18, 2006.

27   HOK was the architectural firm, and Joe Spear was the lead designer. Spear had also worked on Camden Yards, as well as numerous other retro ballparks. David Nakamura, "Architects Promise Visionary D.C. Ballpark; HOK Sport Considers Such Encompassing Themes as 'Transparency of Democracy' for Design," *Washington Post*, April 1, 2005.

28   Jim McConnell, "It's Not Just Baseball That Brings Out Fans: Concessions at Nationals Park as Enjoyable as the Game," *Fredericksburg Free Lance-Star*, March 31, 2008.

29   Michael Todd Friedman, "The Transparency of Democracy: A Lefebvrean Analysis of Washington's Nationals Park" (PhD diss., University of Maryland, College Park, 2008), 191–92. The statues were originally installed at the center-field gate in 2009 but were relocated to the home plate side of the stadium before the 2015 season. Dan Steinberg, "Nationals Move Player Statues from Center Field Gate," *Washington Post*, March 30, 2105.

30   There are 78 luxury suites, 5,600 premium seats, and 3 private clubs.

31   The total cost of the stadium project was reported as $769.6 million in 2008. Major League Baseball and the Nationals paid $31 million. Federal contributions in road, bridge, and subway improvements amounted to $82.6 million. The D.C. Commission on the Arts and Humanities contributed $2 million in artwork. The city initially pledged $440 million for a new ballpark but would ultimately pay $654 million. "Paying for the Ballpark," *Washington Post*, http://www.washingtonpost.com/wp-dyn/content/graphic/2008/03/24/GR2008032400073.html/ (accessed February 26, 2016).

32   "The Business of Baseball: Washington Nationals," *Forbes*, http://www.forbes.com/teams/washington-nationals/ (accessed March 23, 2016); Friedman, "The Transparency of Democracy."

CHAPTER 1

1   Louis Effrat, "Chandler Bars Durocher for 1947 Baseball Season," *New York Times*, April 10, 1947; Roscoe McGowen, "Double by Reiser Beats Boston, 5–3," *New York Times*, April 16, 1947; Arthur Daley, "Opening Day at Ebbets Field," *New York Times*, April 16, 1947; Harold C. Burr, "Hatten Faces Sain in Dodger Opener," *Brooklyn Daily Eagle*, April 15, 1947. Many issues of the *Daily Eagle* have been scanned and posted here: http://fultonhistory.com/my%20photo%20albums/All%20Newspapers/Brooklyn%20NY%20Daily%20Eagle/index.html. Harold C. Burr, "'Old' Reiser, 'New' Hermanski Stars of Dodgers' Opening Day Triumph," *Brooklyn Daily Eagle*, April 16, 1947; David Quentin Voigt, *American Baseball*, vol. 3, *From Postwar Expansion to the Electronic Age* (University Park: Pennsylvania State University Press, 1983), 93.

2   Lester Rodney, "White Dodgers, Black Dodgers," in *Jackie Robinson: Race, Sports, and the American Dream*, ed. Joseph Dorinson and Joram Warmund (Armonk, N.Y.: M. E. Sharpe, 1998), 86.

3   Daley, "Opening Day." The NFL's Los Angeles Rams had signed two black players for the 1946 season; the league had also fielded black players in the 1920s and 1930s.

4   See Jules Tygiel, *Baseball's Great Experiment: Jackie Robinson and His Legacy* (New York: Oxford University Press, 1997), 182–89.

5   Rodney, "White Dodgers, Black Dodgers," 88.

6   Tygiel, *Baseball's Great Experiment*, 196–97.

7   Michael Benson, *Ballparks of North America: A Comprehensive Historical Reference to Baseball Grounds, Yards and Stadiums, 1845 to Present* (Jefferson, N.C.: McFarland, 1989), 63.

8   Steven Riess, *Touching Base: Professional Baseball and American Culture in the Progressive Era* (Westport, Conn.: Greenwood, 1980).

9   Doris Kearns Goodwin, *Wait Till Next Year* (New York: Simon and Schuster, 1997), 46–48.

10   Bob McGee, *The Greatest Ballpark Ever: Ebbets Field and the Story of the Brooklyn Dodgers* (New Brunswick, N.J.: Rivergate Books, 2005), 285.

11   The rotunda was, in a sense, an architectural failure; when the stadium opened, it was one of only two entrances and funneled both ticket holders and ticket buyers into the same space, creating intractable bottlenecks. The club would soon install additional entrances to relieve the pressure ("Ebbets Field Opening Victory for Superbas," *New York Times*, April 6, 1913). Years later, when New York Mets owner Fred Wilpon proposed constructing a replica Ebbets Field for his club, sportswriter and historian Robert Creamer disparaged the idea: "The rotunda that Fred Wilpon remembers so fondly was a small crowded area that looked more like the peanut concession at an amusement park than the entrance to a ball park." Creamer couldn't tolerate Ebbets Field or the Polo Grounds. Robert W. Creamer, "The Brooklyn Myth: Why Do You Think They Were Called the Bums?" *New York Times*, May 24, 1998.

12   Gershman, *Diamonds*, 111.

13   Philip J. Lowry, *Green Cathedrals: The Ultimate Celebration of All 271 Major League and Negro League Ballparks Past and Present* (Reading, Mass.: Addison-Wesley, 1992), 117–20.

14   Harvey Frommer, *New York City Baseball: The Last Golden Age, 1947–1957* (New York: Macmillan, 1980), 97–99.

15   Robert Gruber, "It Happened in Brooklyn: Reminiscences of a Fan," in *Jackie Robinson: Race, Sports, and the American Dream*, ed. Joseph Dorinson and Joram Warmund (Armonk, N.Y.: M. E. Sharpe, 1998), 44.

16   Myrna Katz Frommer and Harvey Frommer, *It Happened in Brooklyn: An Oral History of Growing Up in the Borough in the 1940s, 1950s, and 1960s* (New York: Harcourt Brace and Company, 1993), 36.

17   Peter Golenbock, *Bums: An Oral History of the Brooklyn Dodgers* (New York: G. P. Putnam's Sons, 1984), 577.

18   Ibid., 11; Frommer, *New York City Baseball*, 97–99.

19   This wasn't always a pleasant ride; it was sometimes charged with interethnic friction. See Peter Levine, "Father and Son at Ebbets Field," in *Jackie Robinson: Race, Sports, and the American Dream*, ed. Joseph Dorinson and Joram Warmund (Armonk, N.Y.: M. E. Sharpe, 1998).

20   Gruber, "It Happened in Brooklyn," 43.

21   Neil J. Sullivan, *The Dodgers Move West* (New York: Oxford University Press, 1987), 15.

22   Dick Young, "Hodges Erupts," in *A Brooklyn Dodgers Reader*, ed. Andrew Paul Mele (Jefferson, N.C.: McFarland, 2005), 133.

23   Arthur Daley, "Sports of the Times: Digging Up Dirt," *New York Times*, October 31, 1961.

24   Frommer, *New York City Baseball*, 99.

25   Gruber writes of Brooklynites, "They were ridiculed outsiders. They were underdogs who could sympathize with an underdog" ("It Happened in Brooklyn," 45).

26   Carl E. Prince, *Brooklyn's Dodgers: The Bums, the Borough, and the Best of Baseball, 1947–1957* (New York: Oxford University Press, 1996), 105.

27   Goodwin, *Wait Till Next Year*, 49.

28   McGee, *The Greatest Ballpark Ever*, 13.

29   "Gladys Goodding, Organist, Is Dead," *New York Times*, November 20, 1963.

30   Murray Robinson, "The Death of Ebbets Field," in *From Cobb to "Catfish": 128 Illustrated Stories from "Baseball Digest,"* ed. John Kunester (Chicago: Rand McNally, 1975), 207.

31   Frommer, *New York City Baseball*, 102.

32   Robinson, "The Death of Ebbets Field," 206.

33   Frommer, *New York City Baseball*, 100.

34   Golenbock, *Bums*, 20, quoted in Avila, *Popular Culture in the Age of White Flight*, 147.

35   Frommer, *New York City Baseball*, 98–100; Robinson, "The Death of Ebbets Field," 205.

36   Robin Roberts and C. Paul Rogers III, from *My Life in Baseball*, in *A Brooklyn Dodgers Reader*, ed. Andrew Paul Mele (Jefferson, N.C.: McFarland, 2005), 136–37.

37   Prince, *Brooklyn's Dodgers*, 103.

38   Sullivan, *The Dodgers Move West*, 38–39.

39   Ira Henry Freeman, "Out Where the Boo Begins—The Bleachers," *New York Times*, July 18, 1948.

40   Dorothy O'Keefe, "She Still Remembers Lincoln—And Roots for the Dodgers," *Brooklyn Eagle*, October 1, 1952.

41   Abraham & Straus advertisement, "For Ladies Only!" *Brooklyn Eagle*, June 25, 1952; Prince, *Brooklyn's Dodgers*, 82–83.

42   Prince, *Brooklyn's Dodgers*, 83–85.

43   Sociologist Michael Messner argues, "Sports as a mediated spectacle provides an important context in which traditional conceptions of masculine superiority . . . are shored up." Athletes can serve as "heroes who 'prove' that 'we men' are superior to women." Michael Messner, "Masculinities and Athletic Careers," *Gender and Society* 3, no. 1 (March 1989): 79. See also Michael A. Messner, "When Bodies Are Weapons: Masculinity and Violence in Sport," *International Review for the Sociology of Sport* 25, no. 3 (1990): 203–18.

44   Prince, *Brooklyn's Dodgers*, 120–21, 133–34.

45   Earlier acceptance of black players in organized professional baseball reached an apex in 1887, but by 1892 "the color line was firmly in place," according to Jules Tygiel. Tygiel, *Baseball's Great Experiment*, 14–15.

46   Tygiel, *Baseball's Great Experiment*, 130–32, 226, 266–67. Robinson aside, the presence of black players had an uneven effect on attendance. Other black stars, like Satchel Paige, brought out massive crowds. But other black players didn't always stimulate black attendance. See Tygiel, *Baseball's Great Experiment*, 222, 224, 230. Sociologists R. Saylor Breckenridge and Pat Rubio Goldsmith found that the racial integration of teams impacted attendance variously, depending on the city. They show that cities with relatively larger populations of African American, Latino, and Jewish players generally produced lower rates of white, non-Jewish attendance. They argue that white fans in these markets, where the "threat" of racial and ethnic otherness was more immediate, might have stayed away either because of the integrated crowds at the ballpark or because integration weakened "symbols of White supremacy." In short, the more people of color in the city, the less likely white fans were to attend the games of integrated clubs there—particularly if the team was performing poorly on the field. R. Saylor Breckenridge and Pat Rubio Goldsmith, "Spectacle, Distance, and Threat: Attendance and Integration of Major League Baseball, 1930–1961," *Sociology of Sport Journal* 26 (2009): 296–319.

47   Tygiel, *Baseball's Great Experiment*, 83–86.

48   Roger Kahn, *The Boys of Summer* (New York: Harper and Row, 1987), 164.

49   Ivan W. Hametz, "A Ten-Year-Old Dodger Fan Welcomes Jackie Robinson to Brooklyn," in *Jackie Robinson: Race, Sports, and the American Dream*, ed. Joseph Dorinson and Joram Warmund (Armonk, N.Y.: M. E. Sharpe, 1998), 66.

50   Bill Veeck, *Veeck—As in Wreck: The Autobiography of Bill Veeck* (Chicago: University of Chicago Press, 2001), 175.

51   Gruber, "It Happened in Brooklyn," 47.

52   Prince, *Brooklyn's Dodgers*, 21.

53   John Lardner, "Would It Still Be Brooklyn?" *New York Times*, February 26, 1956.

54   Karal Ann Marling, *As Seen on TV: The Visual Culture of Everyday Life in the 1950s* (Cambridge, Mass.: Harvard University Press, 1994), 134.

55   Christopher W. Wells, "Automotive Industry," in *The Oxford Companion to United States History*, ed. Paul S. Boyer (Oxford: Oxford University Press, 2001), *Oxford Reference Online*.

56   "No agency of the United States government," historian Kenneth T. Jackson writes, "has had a more pervasive and powerful impact on the American people . . . than the Federal Housing Administration." Formed in 1934, the FHA was intended to improve housing standards, enable affordable home financing, stabilize the mortgage market, and stimulate depression-era employment in the construction industry. The agency would become the basis for American home ownership by insuring long-term mortgage loans made by private institutions for home purchase and construction. The impact of the FHA—whose influence lowered down payments, extended repayment periods, established minimum construction standards, and effected a decline in interest rates—was to substantially increase the number of Americans who could purchase a home. Kenneth T. Jackson, *Crabgrass Frontier: The Suburbanization of the United States* (New York: Oxford University Press, 1985), 203.

57   Jon C. Teaford, *The Twentieth-Century American City* (Baltimore: Johns Hopkins University Press, 1993), 100.

58   Michael Johns, *Moment of Grace: The American City in the 1950s* (Berkeley: University of California Press, 2003), 92.

59   Jackson, *Crabgrass Frontier*, 206.

60   Ibid., 207–9. Though the Supreme Court deemed these covenants illegal in the 1948 *Shelley v. Kraemer* ruling, the FHA didn't stop insuring mortgages on properties subject to racial covenants until 1950.

61   Craig Steven Wilder, *A Covenant with Color: Race and Social Power in Brooklyn* (New York: Columbia University Press, 2000), 202.

62   Mapping racial characteristics on Brooklyn facilitated the practice of "redlining," whereby lending, leasing, and sales decisions were based on the racial makeup of an entire neighborhood rather than the specific merits of individual applicants and properties. Redlining, in turn, motivated unscrupulous real estate specula-

tors to engage in "blockbusting," in which they would place black residents in a previously all-white block. This was designed to create a panic among white homeowners, who might think the neighborhood was "turning" and thus quickly sell to the speculator at deeply discounted prices. Speculators could then systematically convert the block from white to black, selling properties at a premium to African Americans desperate for better housing or subdividing properties into multiple residences and charging above-market rental rates. William Thompson, who grew up in Brooklyn at this time, recounted how these discriminatory policies worked on the ground: "The speculating was a conscious and deliberate thing, no question about it. Starting in the 1950s, there was redlining and sophisticated blockbusting. The people who came in via blockbusting busted the houses up, rented out rooms, created illegal rooming houses. . . . The shutout was very subtle. Nobody said where you could and couldn't live, but where a bank might give a black person a mortgage on Hancock Street, it would never give him a mortgage in Bay Ridge. Blacks could only move out in concentric circles: to Crown Heights, then to East Flatbush, Flatbush." Frommer, *New York City Baseball*, 226.

63   Virginia Sánchez Korrol, "Puerto Ricans," in *The Encyclopedia of New York City*, 2nd ed., ed. Kenneth T. Jackson (New Haven, Conn.: Yale University Press, 2010), 1059.

64   Harold X. Connelly, *A Ghetto Grows in Brooklyn* (New York: New York University Press, 1977), 130.

65   Wilder, *A Covenant with Color*, 177; Ron Miller, Rita Seiden Miller, and Stephen J. Karp, "The Fourth Largest City in America: A Sociological History of Brooklyn," in *Brooklyn USA: The Fourth Largest City in America*, ed. Rita Seiden Miller (New York: Columbia University Press, 1979), 32.

66   Though Bedford-Stuyvesant was home to just 10 percent of the Brooklyn population in 1957, a quarter of the borough's relief cases were from that neighborhood. There were twice as many occurrences of tuberculosis than the borough-wide rate, four times as many cases of venereal disease, and seven times the rate of juvenile delinquency. Wilder, *A Covenant with Color*, 214.

67   Frommer and Frommer, *It Happened in Brooklyn*, 226.

68   "Suit Charges Plot in Mortgage Loans," *New York Times*, August 7, 1946; "Consent Judgment in Mortgage Suit," *New York Times*, June 17, 1948; Wilder, *A Covenant with Color*, 204.

69   Wendell Pritchett, *Brownsville, Brooklyn: Blacks, Jews, and the Changing Face of the Ghetto* (Chicago: University of Chicago Press, 2002), 99; "Brownsville," in *The Neighborhoods of Brooklyn*, ed. Kenneth T. Jackson and John B. Manbeck (New Haven, Conn.: Yale University Press, 1998), 40–43.

70   Wilder, *A Covenant with Color*, 193–94.

71   Three examples from the early 1940s illustrate this point. Midtown Real Estate Association president Thomas H. Doyle claimed, "Government handouts for the past decade have been all this new generation has ever seen. They know nothing of the strength and independence derived from working for a living." In response to a 1943 Kings County Grand Jury inquiry regarding Mayor LaGuardia's response to crime and poverty in Bedford-Stuyvesant, the mayor parried the conversation toward race, offering, "Let's be more frank about it—this is the negro question we are talking about. . . . When a neighborhood changes its complexion that way there is bound to be trouble." After the grand jury's report was released, Robert Moses wrote to LaGuardia, also pointing to race as the problem of central Brooklyn: "The urban negro problem exists all over the country. It has been aggravated by the war. It is not confined to New York City or to the Bedford-Stuyvesant neighborhood. The City can't do everything. Individual families, churches, and social organizations must do their part." All quotes from Wilder, *A Covenant with Color*, 195–97.

72   Jackson, *Crabgrass Frontier*, 214. See Charles Abrams, *Forbidden Neighbors: A Study of Prejudice in Housing* (New York: Harper, 1955), 229–35.

73   Henry Goldschmidt, *Race and Religion Among the Chosen Peoples of Crown Heights* (New Brunswick, N.J.: Rutgers University Press, 2008), 86–93; Ellen Marie Snyder-Grenier, "Crown Heights," in *The Encyclopedia of New York City*, 2nd ed., ed. Kenneth T. Jackson (New Haven, Conn.: Yale University Press, 2010), 301; "Crown Heights," in *The Neighborhoods of Brooklyn*, ed. Kenneth T. Jackson and John B. Manbeck (New Haven, Conn.: Yale University Press, 1998), 78–82; Michael Shapiro, *The Last Good Season: Brooklyn, the Dodgers, and Their Final Pennant Race Together* (New York: Doubleday, 2003), 99. Roger Green, who likely moved into the area in the early to mid-1950s, remembered:

We were first-generation New Yorkers, and we were mindful of that. I had a healthy childhood.

Still, it was inevitable there'd be times when I'd be confronted with racism. When we moved from Bed-Stuy to Carroll Street in Crown Heights [two blocks north of Ebbets Field], we were one of the first black families in that neighborhood. Everybody was very civil. The only incident I recall happened at P.S. 222, where a white student once called my friend and me "nigger," and nobody said anything. But when we were bused into Winthrop Junior High, which was near the Rugby section of Brooklyn [East Flatbush], we made sure not to wear our better clothes on Fridays, because we knew we would have to fight our way home. The white kids from Pigtown, as they used to call it—because people used to raise pigs in their backyards— would waylay us. (Frommer and Frommer, *It Happened in Brooklyn*, 167–68)

74   "Prospect-Lefferts Gardens," in *The Neighborhoods of Brooklyn*, ed. Kenneth T. Jackson and John B. Manbeck (New Haven, Conn.: Yale University Press, 1998), 180–83.

75   Charles G. Bennett, "Our Changing City: Flatbush-Coney Island," *New York Times*, July 25, 1955.

76   "East Flatbush," in *The Neighborhoods of Brooklyn*, ed. Kenneth T. Jackson and John B. Manbeck (New Haven, Conn.: Yale University Press, 1998), 103–9.

77   Golenbock, *Bums*, 430–32.

78   Goldschmidt, *Race and Religion Among the Chosen Peoples of Crown Heights*, 94.

79   Arnold Markoe, "Brooklyn Navy Yard," in *The Encyclopedia of New York City*, 2nd ed., ed. Kenneth T. Jackson (New Haven, Conn.: Yale University Press, 2010), 180.

80   Norman Bel Geddes, "Presentation to Brooklyn Dodgers," 1948, Flat file, folder 577.5, Norman Bel Geddes Papers, Harry Ransom Center, University of Texas at Austin.

81   Gruber, "It Happened in Brooklyn," 47.

82   Goodwin, *Wait Till Next Year*, 49.

83   Tommy Holmes, "A Couple of Fans Answer a Question," *Brooklyn Eagle*, June 22, 1951.

84   Golenbock, *Bums*, 577.

85   Levine, "Father and Son at Ebbets Field," 63.

86   Frommer and Frommer, *It Happened in Brooklyn*, 15.

87   Gruber, "It Happened in Brooklyn," 44.

88   Frommer and Frommer, *It Happened in Brooklyn*, 38.

89   Ibid., 39–40.

90   Golenbock, *Bums*, 556–57.

91   Golenbock, *Bums*, 561.

92   Kahn, *The Boys of Summer*, xix.

93   Prince, *Brooklyn's Dodgers*, 113.

94   This point is clearer when we consider the reaction to the increasing black presence on the field. Robinson, Campanella, and Newcombe were all stars in 1950, and with two promising black players in Dan Bankhead and Sam Jethroe deserving major league spots, sportswriters speculated about a "saturation point" beyond which a black presence might negatively impact economics or team morale. Branch Rickey would later admit that Dodgers ownership were unwilling to have a fifth black player on the big-league squad, for fear of its impact on the team. Tygiel, *Baseball's Great Experiment*, 306.

95   James Rubin, "The Brooklyn Dodgers and Ebbets Field—Their Departure," in *Brooklyn USA: The Fourth Largest City in America*, ed. Rita Seiden Miller (New York: Columbia University Press, 1979), 167.

96   Roger Kahn, *The Era, 1947-1957: When the Yankees, the Giants, and the Dodgers Ruled the World* (Lincoln: University of Nebraska Press, 2002), 327.

97   Ibid. Buzzie Bavasi was the Dodgers' general manager; Fresco Thompson was director of the Dodgers' minor league system. Kahn and others have noted that O'Malley was uncomfortable around Jackie Robinson because, in Kahn's words, "he was a challenging, defiant black. Walter liked blacks docile. He preferred Pullman porters to Jackie Robinson."

98   Rubin, "The Brooklyn Dodgers and Ebbets Field," 168.

99   Frommer, *New York City Baseball*, 2–3.

100   Emanuel Perlmutter, "Our Changing City: Northern Brooklyn," *New York Times*, July 22, 1955.

101   Jason Barnosky, "The Violent Years: Responses to Juvenile Crime in the 1950s," *Polity* 38, no. 3 (July 2006): 314–44.

102   Neil Sullivan argues that many have overemphasized the role of race in explaining the Dodgers' departure from Ebbets Field. He points to Yankee Stadium in the Bronx. It, too, was in an area that transitioned from ethnic white to African American, and yet it continued to draw customers thanks to the parking lots and access roads that connected the stadium to the city's freeways. Yankee Stadium was an urban stadium, Sullivan notes, but not a neighborhood stadium like Ebbets Field. This final point, I think, is vital. Suburbanites could avoid the full consequences of urban disinvestment more easily at Yankee Stadium than they could in Brooklyn, where they were forced to more fully engage the city streets intimately—even if they were arriving by car. Sullivan, *The Dodgers Move West*, 40–41.

103   Golenbock, *Bums*, 430.

104   Quoted in Frommer, *New York City Baseball*, 38.

105   Rubin, "The Brooklyn Dodgers and Ebbets Field," 168.

106   Fresco Thompson and Cy Rice, *Every Diamond Doesn't Sparkle* (New York: David McKay Company, 1964), 147.

107   Ibid., 144–45.

108   Shapiro, *The Last Good Season*, 10.

CHAPTER 2

1   Red Smith, *To Absent Friends from Red Smith* (New York: Atheneum, 1982), 377.

2   Sullivan, *The Dodgers Move West*, 29.

3   Murray Polner, *Branch Rickey: A Biography* (New York: Atheneum, 1982), 218.

4   Kahn, *The Boys of Summer*, 426.

5   Ibid., 423–24.

6   Ibid., 428.

7   Walter F. O'Malley, "O'Malley Stresses Need for Arena," *Brooklyn Eagle*, October 1, 1952.

8   Walter O'Malley, "Concord Village," January 26, 1948, box 45, folder 577.4, "Memos, correspondence, ms. notes, clipping, brochure 1948–1954," Norman Bel Geddes Papers, Harry Ransom Center, University of Texas at Austin.

9   Norman Bel Geddes, *Magic Motorways* (New York: Random House, 1940), 3.

10   Jeffrey L. Meikle, *Twentieth Century Limited: Industrial Design in America, 1925–1939* (Philadelphia: Temple University Press, 1979), 200–203; Joseph J. Corn and Brian Horrigan, *Yesterday's Tomorrows: Past Visions of the American Future*, ed. Katherine Chambers (Baltimore: Johns Hopkins University Press, 1984), 47–50.

11   Geddes, *Magic Motorways*, 4.

12   Norman Bel Geddes to Branch Rickey, December 17, 1947, box 45, folder 577.1, "Correspondence 1947–1954," Norman Bel Geddes Papers, Harry Ransom Center, University of Texas at Austin.

13   Norman Bel Geddes to Walter O'Malley, January 12, 1948, box 45, folder 577.1, "Correspondence 1947–1954," Norman Bel Geddes Papers, Harry Ransom Center, University of Texas at Austin.

14   Geddes seemed committed to rethinking the ballpark, at least aesthetically. He highlighted a quote from Dodgers' co-owner John L. Smith at the end of a newspaper profile: "Ballparks don't have to look like they did 30 years ago any more than an automobile or a chemical plant." See Michael Gaven, "Who Owns the Dodgers?" *New York Journal American*, February 25, 1948, box 45, folder 577.9, "Clippings 1948–1954," Norman Bel Geddes Papers, Harry Ransom Center, University of Texas at Austin.

15   Midget auto races feature smaller cars over shorter distances than conventional races.

16   Geddes, "Presentation to Brooklyn Dodgers."

17   Ibid.

18   Allen Guttmann writes of women as civilizing agents in nineteenth-century parks. Owner and league president A. G. Spalding tried to attract women to elevate the National League's status in the 1800s. Allen Gutt-

mann, *Sports Spectators* (New York: Columbia University Press, 1986), 114–15; Peter Levine, *A. G. Spalding and the Rise of Baseball: The Promise of American Sport* (New York: Oxford University Press, 1985). Geddes's interest in attracting women prefigured Roone Arledge's, stated in his famous 1960 manifesto to ABC's Ed Sherik. In that often-cited document ("We are going to add show business to sports!"), Arledge identified the need to appeal to the casual fan through broadcast elements peripheral to the game on the field; he cast the casual fan as woman. Ron Powers, *Supertube: The Rise of Television Sports* (New York: Coward-McCann, 1984), 145–46.

19   Geddes, "Presentation to Brooklyn Dodgers."

20   Gaven, "Who Owns the Dodgers?"

21   Walter O'Malley, "Memorandum," February 26, 1948, box 45, folder 577.4, "Memos, correspondence, ms. notes, clipping, brochure 1948–1954," Norman Bel Geddes Papers, Harry Ransom Center, University of Texas at Austin.

22   Leonard Lyons, "The Lyons Den," *New York Post*, March 15, 1948; "Dodgers Deny Field Plan," *New York Times*, March 16, 1948; "Dodgers Plan Park to Seat 80,400 Fans," *Brooklyn Eagle*, March 16, 1948. Though not reported, the Dodgers were also considering—at the suggestion of Emil Praeger—a site near Brooklyn's Fort Greene Park that would allow for a 58,000-seat stadium and cost $1.3 million. Michael D'Antonio, *Forever Blue: The True Story of Walter O'Malley, Baseball's Most Controversial Owner, and the Dodgers of Brooklyn and Los Angeles* (New York: Riverhead Books, 2009), 111.

23   "Dodgers Plan Park to Seat 80,400 Fans."

24   Doug Kennedy, "Geddes Still Intent on Selling Dodgers on 'New Look' for Park," *New York Herald Tribune*, March 17, 1948.

25   Lester Rodney, "On the ScoreBoard," *Daily Worker*, March 18, 1948.

26   Steve Snider, "Something New in Ballparks," *Portland Press Herald*, March 18, 1948. Snider was syndicated.

27   Ibid.

28   "Los Angeles Dodgers Year-by-Year Results," *The Official Site of the Los Angeles Dodgers*, http://los-angeles.dodgers.mlb.com/la/history/year_by_year_results.jsp (accessed February 1, 2015).

29   Roscoe McGowen, "Dressen Receives O'Malley Support: Dodgers' Chief Denies Report That Frisch Will Be Pilot—Stadium at Camp Planned," *New York Times*, February 25, 1952.

30   "Emil Praeger, 81, Engineer, Is Dead," *New York Times*, October 17, 1973.

31   "Geddes Ball Park Has Portable Roof," *New York Journal American*, March 6, 1952.

32   The Brooklyn Dodgers football team of the All-American Football Conference, owned by the Dodgers baseball club, lost $399,000 during the 1948 season. It was sold after one season. Craig R. Coenen, *From Sandlots to the Super Bowl: The National Football League, 1920–1967* (Knoxville: University of Tennessee Press, 2005), 132–33.

33   Box 45, folder 577.9, "Clippings 1948–1954," Norman Bel Geddes Papers, Harry Ransom Center, University of Texas at Austin.

34   "The New Stadium," *Providence Rhode Island Journal*, March 9, 1952.

35   "Brooklyn Selected for Experimental Ultra-Modern Baseball Park," *Akron Beacon Journal*, March 9, 1952.

36   "New Ebbets Field to Have Hot Dogs and Hot Seats," *New York Times*, March 6, 1952. "Dream Park Concocted for Flock," *Newark Star-Ledger*, March 7, 1952.

37   "The New Stadium."

38   "New Ebbets Field to Have Hot Dogs and Hot Seats," *New York Times*, March 6, 1952; "Geddes Ball Park Has Portable Roof."

39   Bill Dougherty, "Bel Geddes Has Big Plans for Brooks," *Newark News*, March 6, 1952.

40   M. Jeffrey Hardwick, *Mall Maker: Victor Gruen, Architect of an American Dream* (Philadelphia: University of Pennsylvania Press, 2004), 79–80.

41   Tom Meany, "Baseball's Answer to TV," *Collier's*, September 27, 1952, 60–62.

42   Television ownership had climbed from .02 percent to 9 percent of American households between 1946 and 1950. Most of those sets were in the Northeast, which had far more television stations than in other regions; this was due to restrictions in place by the Federal Communications Commission between 1948 and

1952. The number of stations exploded nationwide after the lifting of the freeze. By 1955, 65 percent of homes owned a television. Lynn Spigel, *Make Room for TV: Television and the Family Ideal in Postwar America* (Chicago: University of Chicago Press, 1992), 32.

43   Spigel, *Make Room for TV*, 100, 112. See also George Lipsitz, "The Meaning of Memory: Family, Class, and Ethnicity in Early Network Television," in *Time Passages: Collective Memory and American Popular Culture* (Minneapolis: University of Minnesota Press, 1990).

44   Sylvester L. Weaver, "Thoughts on the Revolution: Or, TV Is a Fad, Like Breathing," *Variety*, July 11, 1951, 42, quoted in Spigel, *Make Room for TV*, 134.

45   The term "vehicular ecosystem" is Dave Croke's, from "On the Road to the Future," in *Norman Bel Geddes Designs America*, ed. Donald Albrecht (New York: Abrams, 2013), 95.

46   O'Malley, "O'Malley Stresses Need for Arena."

47   Kahn, *The Era*, 311.

48   Ibid., 312.

49   Avila, *Popular Culture in the Age of White Flight*, 154.

50   Henry McKenna, "Braves Move to Milwaukee; Perini Confident of Approval," *Boston Herald*, March 15, 1953.

51   "Atlanta Braves Year-by-Year Results," *The Official Site of the Atlanta Braves*, http://mlb.mlb.com/atl/history/year_by_year_results.jsp (accessed February 16, 2010).

52   Lester Smith, "Braves Set Sail on Sea of Red Ink," *Sporting News*, March 25, 1953; Louis Effrat, "Braves Move to Milwaukee; Majors' First Shift Since '03," *New York Times*, March 19, 1953.

53   Smith, "Braves Set Sail on Sea of Red Ink."

54   Effrat, "Braves Move to Milwaukee."

55   "Boston Red Sox Year-by-Year Results," *The Official Site of the Boston Red Sox*, http://boston.redsox.mlb.com/bos/history/year_by_year_results.jsp (accessed February 16, 2010).

56   By 1960, Milwaukee's urban population was 741,324; Boston's was 697,197.

57   Gaffney was a member of Tammany Hall. After he purchased the club in 1911, people began calling them the "braves" in deference to Tammany's Indian logo. Gershman, *Diamonds*, 126–29, 224.

58   Smith, "Braves Set Sail on Sea of Red Ink."

59   Al Hirshberg, "Mistakes Helped Lose Braves for Hub, Says Scribe," *Sporting News*, March 23, 1953.

60   McKenna, "Braves Move to Milwaukee."

61   Smith, "Braves Set Sail on Sea of Red Ink."

62   Jack McCarthy, "Man in Street Sorry, But Most Don't Blame Owner of Braves," *Boston Herald*, March 19, 1953.

63   "Atlanta Braves Year-by-Year Results."

64   Bob Buege, *The Milwaukee Braves: A Baseball Eulogy* (Milwaukee: Douglas American Sports Publications, 1988), 12.

65   The power alleys are where hitters generally drive the ball most powerfully, about halfway between the foul poles and center field.

66   Effrat, "Braves Move to Milwaukee"; Sec Taylor, "Fine New Home of the Braves," *Baseball Digest*, June 1953, 63–64.

67   The Braves voluntarily tore up this contract on June 27, upping their contribution to the county to $25,000. The club had been overwhelmed by the positive reception and attendance. See "Braves Increase Their Stadium Rent," *New York Times*, June 28, 1953. Perini again upped his rent in 1954, voluntarily giving the Milwaukee County Park Commission a check for $225,000 before a meeting to discuss enlarging the stadium. See "Braves Raise Their Rent," *New York Times*, September 24, 1954.

68   "Happy Milwaukee Flocks for Seats," *New York Times*, March 19, 1953.

69   Taylor, "Fine New Home of the Braves."

70   "Sausages, Sauerbraten and Sympathy," *Life*, July 6, 1953, 39–42; Tim Cohane, "None But the Braves," *Look*, August 25, 1953, 86–89; Al Hirshberg, "Home-Run Mathews—the Idol of Milwaukee," *Saturday Evening Post*, August 1, 1953, 32–45.

71   Buege, *The Milwaukee Braves*, 5.

72   Cohane, "None But the Braves."

73   As football rose in popularity and prestige, it too would be a signifier of "big-league" status by the late 1960s.

74   Milwaukee had been a "major league" city four separate times, in four different leagues, but only for one year each time: the National League (1878), the Union Association (1884), the American Association (1891), and the American League (1901).

75   "A Prospectus of a Metropolitan Sports Area for the Twin Cities" (Minneapolis: Minneapolis Chamber of Commerce, Major League Baseball Committee, 1954).

76   "New Stadium Lured Team to Milwaukee," *Houston Chronicle*, August 6, 1959.

77   Ibid.

78   Veeck, *Veeck*, 50; Buege, *The Milwaukee Braves*, 10.

79   Melvin Durslag, "A Visit with Walter O'Malley," *Saturday Evening Post*, May 14, 1960, 31, 104–6.

80   Cohane, "None But the Braves," 87.

81   McKenna, "Braves Move to Milwaukee."

82   Cohane, "None But the Braves," 86.

83   "Site" and "situation" are foundational geographical terms useful in refining understanding of a place. Site references the physical characteristics of a place. Situation references that place's relationship with other places around it. See Karl B. Raitz, *The Theater of Sport* (Baltimore: Johns Hopkins University Press, 1995), 18.

84   Veeck, *Veeck*, 221–29; William A. Borst, "Baltimore Orioles," in *Encyclopedia of Major League Baseball Clubs*, vol. 2, *The American League*, ed. Steven A. Riess (Westport, Conn.: Greenwood, 2006), 479.

85   "Many-Purpose Giant Stadium Is Advocated," *Baltimore Sun*, May 2, 1945.

86   Herbert H. Stevens Jr. was the project designer; his roof would rely on tests run at New York University for the United States War Production Board in 1944, which found that air-supported roofs could work for "long-span building construction." Herbert H. Stevens Jr., "Roofs Supported by Air Pressure," *Nature* 161 (April 17, 1948): 613–14; "Super-Stadium May Be Built in Baltimore," *Washington Post*, September 2, 1945; "Poof! And the Roof Rises," *Milwaukee Journal*, May 2, 1945.

87   "Many-Purpose Giant Stadium Is Advocated"; Mike Klingaman, "Baltimore First Put Lid on Dome Debate in 1945: Martin's Idea Predated Astrodome by 20 Years," *Baltimore Sun*, February 27, 1996, http://articles. baltimoresun.com/1996-02-27/sports/1996058051_1_dome-covered-stadium-baltimore/ (accessed February 2, 2016).

88   "Baltimore Plans Inclosed [*sic*] Stadium for Grid, Baseball," *Washington Post*, May 2, 1945.

89   "Many-Purpose Giant Stadium Is Advocated"; "Council Gets Stadium Plan from War Memorial Group," *Baltimore Sun*, October 23, 1945; "War Memorial Stadium Dream Recalled by Repairs Plan," *Baltimore Sun*, August 16, 1946. The seven-million-dollar stadium would be paid for with state and federal funds and with private contributions from industry and individuals. In spite of early backing from the mayor and many of the city's most powerful businessmen, the project was abandoned. Klingaman, "Baltimore First Put Lid on Dome Debate in 1945"; "Lane Snags Baltimore Stadium Plan," *Washington Post*, June 8, 1947. The veteran is quoted in Klingaman, "Baltimore First Put Lid on Dome Debate in 1945."

90   John Steadman, "You Can Still Hear the Echo," in *The House of Magic, 1922–1931: 70 Years of Thrills and Excitement on 3rd Street*, ed. Bob Brown (Baltimore: The Orioles, Inc., 1991), 44–63; Michael Oriard, *Brand NFL: Making and Selling America's Favorite Sport* (Chapel Hill: University of North Carolina Press, 2007), 2, 40.

91   Joseph M. Sheehan, "Baltimore Goes 'All Out' Today to Celebrate Return to Majors," *New York Times*, April 15, 1954.

92   Joseph M. Sheehan, "Baltimore Hails Return to Majors; Orioles Respond by Beating White Sox," *New York Times*, April 16, 1954.

93   *Life*, April 26, 1954, quoted in James Edward Miller, *The Baseball Business: Pursuing Pennants and Profits in Baltimore* (Chapel Hill: University of North Carolina Press, 1990), 36.

94   "Orioles Win as 46,354 Whoop It Up," *Los Angeles Times*, April 16, 1954.

95   Shirley Povich, "This Morning," *Washington Post*, April 16, 1954.

96   Sheehan, "Baltimore Hails Return to Majors."

97   Thomas Boswell, "Just Around the Corner: Memorial as Memory," *Washington Post*, September 10, 1987.

98   Miller, *The Baseball Business*, 70.

99   Ibid., 39.

100   The club's first manager and general manager both came from the segregated Philadelphia Athletics. It released the only black player on the roster, the legendary Satchel Paige. When Maryland's governor asked Baltimore hotels to allow black major leaguers into their rooms, the Orioles didn't support him. Black patrons reported that when they bought tickets at the window, they would find that the seats sold to them were among other African Americans. The gleaming whiteness of the Orioles roster—and most of its fans—was made all the brighter by the growing number of black stars on the Colts, Memorial Stadium's other major tenant. Miller, *The Baseball Business*, 39–40, 66; James H. Bready, *Baseball in Baltimore: The First 100 Years* (Baltimore: Johns Hopkins University Press, 1998), 214.

101   U.S. Census Bureau, "Race, 1950, Tract 32, Jackson County, Missouri," Prepared by Social Explorer, http://www.socialexplorer.com/5fcbefd263/view (accessed January 27, 2015).

102   Gershman, *Diamonds*, 174.

103   Robert F. Lewis II, "Oakland Athletics," in *Encyclopedia of Major League Baseball Clubs*, vol. 2, *The American League*, ed. Steven A. Riess (Westport, Conn.: Greenwood, 2006), 777.

104   Walter F. O'Malley to Norman Bel Geddes, January 8, 1954, Norman Bel Geddes to Walter F. O'Malley, September 30, 1955, and Walter F. O'Malley to Norman Bel Geddes, October 13, 1955, all in box 45, folder 577.2, "Dodger Stadium—Data and Correspondence 1953–1957," Norman Bel Geddes Papers, Harry Ransom Center, University of Texas at Austin.

105   Aline B. Louchheim, "New Ways of Building," *New York Times*, August 31, 1952; Leigh White, "Buck Fuller and the Dymaxion World," *Saturday Evening Post*, October 14, 1944; "The Dodgers' Dome," *Sports Illustrated*, October 31, 1955.

106   "Art: Fuller Future," *Time*, October 20, 1958.

107   Louchheim thought that Fuller would need to pay more attention to appearances and "woo beauty" for his structures to pass from "building" to "architecture."

108   Elie Abel, "Atom Lights Mark Ford's 50th Year," *New York Times*, June 17, 1953.

109   "The Dodgers' Dome."

110   Mark Langill, *Dodger Stadium* (Charleston, S.C.: Arcadia Publishing, 2004), 9.

111   "Dodgers Study Possibility of Dome-Covered Stadium," *Washington Post*, October 1, 1955.

112   "A Geodesic Dome for Brooklyn Dodgers," *Progressive Architecture* 36, no. 11 (1955): 95; "Stadium with Dome Studied by Dodgers," *New York Times*, October 1, 1955; "Dodger Head Hails Studies Made for Domed Stadium," *New York Times*, November 23, 1955; "Dodgers Study Possibility of Dome-Covered Stadium."

113   "Dodgers' Dome (Cont.)," *Sports Illustrated*, November 28, 1955.

114   "Student Designs a Stadium for Dodgers; Princetonian's Idea May Affect Blueprint," *New York Times*, January 22, 1956.

115   "Indoor Park Plans Studied," *Washington Post*, January 22, 1956.

116   "Dodger Head Hails Studies Made for Domed Stadium." The image would be used elsewhere as well, including "Plastic Dome for Stadium," *Popular Mechanics*, July 1956, 104.

117   "A Geodesic Dome for Brooklyn Dodgers," 95.

118   Frank Tinsley, "A Dome Grows in Brooklyn," *Mechanix Illustrated*, July 1956.

119   Shapiro, *The Last Good Season*, 20.

120   Sullivan, *The Dodgers Move West*, 54.

121   Charles G. Bennett, "Big Dodger Stadium Outlined to Mayor," *New York Times*, July 25, 1956.

122   Sullivan, *The Dodgers Move West*, 48.

123   Ibid., 51.

124   Ibid., 80.

125   Neil J. Sullivan gives a comprehensive accounting of O'Malley's sparring with Moses in *The Dodgers*

Move West. Others cover it as well, including Shapiro, *The Last Good Season*; D'Antonio, *Forever Blue*; Kahn, *The Era*.

126 Arthur Daley, "Sports of the Times: Men in Motion," *New York Times*, August 18, 1955.

127 "Jack Envisions New Ball Park for the Giants," *New York Daily News*, March 5, 1956; "Proposes 'Stadium in Sky' for Giants over RR Tracks," *New York Mirror*, March 6, 1956.

128 "'Surprise' for Railroad," *New York Times*, April 6, 1956.

129 Al Buck, "Only Giants' OK Needed for West Side Stadium," *New York Post*, April 4, 1956; Harold Weissman and Wilfred Alexander, "Biggest Arena Planned Here," *New York Mirror*, April 5, 1956; Joseph C. Ingraham, "TV Center Added to Stadium Plans," *New York Times*, May 15, 1956; Marvin Sleeper, "New Field for Giants Stirs Feud," *New York Journal American*, May 18, 1956.

130 Arthur Daley, "Sports of the Times: Baseball's Passing Parade," *New York Times*, May 15, 1956.

131 Local papers reported that the original concept for a new stadium had been presented to Mayor Wagner at the Baseball Writers Dinner in February; however, Wagner had hoped to keep plans for a privately financed Manhattan stadium quiet, having already asked for state support to create a Brooklyn Sports Center Authority that would help the Dodgers build in downtown Brooklyn. But Jack, seemingly eager to stake his name to the grandiose project, scooped the mayor, angering him. Sleeper, "New Field for Giants Stirs Feud."

132 Daniel's Dope, "Tough on Giants: 120,000 Seat Park Stays in Dreamland," *New York World-Telegram-Sun*, June 4, 1956. Sportswriter Roger Kahn later claimed that Jack was an "eccentric" who "had no plan to raise construction money." Kahn, *The Era*, 334.

133 Avila, *Popular Culture in the Age of White Flight*, 29.

134 George Lipsitz, "Sports Stadia and Urban Development: A Tale of Three Cities," *Journal of Sport and Social Issues* 8, no. 2 (1984): 7–8; Teaford, *The Twentieth-Century American City*, 91–92.

135 "Historical Census Populations of Counties and Incorporated Cities in California, 1850–2010," California Department of Finance, http://www.dof.ca.gov/research/demographic/state_census_data_center/historical_census_1850-2010/ (accessed August 27, 2013).

136 Avila, *Popular Culture in the Age of White Flight*, 55–58. Poulson quoted in ibid., 58.

137 "Let's Build an Auditorium!" *Los Angeles Times*, February 9, 1950.

138 Avila, *Popular Culture in the Age of White Flight*, 60, 176.

139 Ibid., 158; Thomas S. Hines, "Housing, Baseball, and Creeping Socialism: The Battle of Chavez Ravine, 1949–1959," *Journal of Urban History* 8, no. 2 (February 1982): 123–38; "Three Fired as Housing Aides Silent," *Los Angeles Times*, September 27, 1952.

140 Cary S. Henderson, "Los Angeles and the Dodger War," *Southern California Quarterly* 62, no. 3 (Fall 1980): 264–67; Hines, "Housing, Baseball, and Creeping Socialism."

141 Joseph M. Sheehan, "Dodgers, Giants Win Right to Shift If They So Desire," *New York Times*, May 29, 1957.

142 "L.A. Ravine: Fertile Soil for O'Malley," *Los Angeles Times*, June 4, 1978.

143 For the most thorough account, see Henderson, "Los Angeles and the Dodger War." See also Avila, *Popular Culture in the Age of White Flight*, 164–66.

144 Dodgers attendance at Ebbets Field in the two years preceding their relocation was 1,213,562 (1956) and 1,028,258 (1957). In the first two years in Los Angeles, it was 1,845,556 (1958) and 2,071,045 (1959). "Los Angeles Dodgers Year-by-Year Results," *The Official Site of the Los Angeles Dodgers*, http://losangeles.dodgers.mlb.com/la/history/year_by_year_results.jsp (accessed August 29, 2013).

145 Gene Blake, "High Court Approves Dodgers Chavez Pact: Tribunal Upholds Contract with L.A. for New Ball Park," *Los Angeles Times*, January 14, 1959.

146 Quoted in Avila, *Popular Culture in the Age of White Flight*, 165–66.

147 Burton H. Wolfe, "The Candlestick Swindle," *Bay Guardian*, May 14, 1968; Maureen Smith, "From the 'Finest Ballpark in America' to 'The Jewel of the Waterfront': The Construction of San Francisco's Major League Baseball Stadiums," *International Journal of the History of Sport* 15, no. 11 (September 2008): 1530.

148 "Topics of the Times," *New York Times*, September 28, 1957.

149 "San Francisco Giants Year-by-Year Results," *The Official Site of the San Francisco Giants*, http://mlb.mlb.com/sf/history/year_by_year_results.jsp (accessed July 27, 2015).

150   Robert W. Snyder, "Washington Heights," in *The Encyclopedia of New York City*, 2nd ed., ed. Kenneth T. Jackson (New Haven, Conn.: Yale University Press, 2010), 1380; Antitrust Subcommittee (Subcommittee No. 5) of the Committee on the Judiciary, *Organized Professional Team Sports: Hearings Before the Antitrust Subcommittee (Subcommittee No. 5) of the Committee on the Judiciary House of Representatives Eighty-Fifth Congress First Session on H.R. 5307, H.R. 5319, H.R. 5383, H.R. 6876, H.R. 6877, H.R. 8023, and H.R. 8124 Bills to Amend the Antitrust Laws to Protect Trade and Commerce Against Unlawful Restraints and Monopolies*, 85th Cong., 1st sess. (1957), 1945–46; Noel Hynd, *The Giants of the Polo Grounds* (New York: Doubleday, 1988), 380; Kahn, *The Era*, 333–34.

151   Orr quoted in Stew Thornley, *Land of the Giants: New York's Polo Grounds* (Philadelphia: Temple University Press, 2000), 112.

152   Andrew Goldblatt, "San Francisco Giants," in *Encyclopedia of Major League Baseball Clubs*, vol. 1, *The National League*, ed. Steven A. Riess (Westport, Conn.: Greenwood, 2006), 377.

153   Joseph M. Sheehan, "Football Giants Quit Polo Grounds for Ten-Year Lease of Yankee Stadium," *New York Times*, January 28, 1956.

154   Smith, "From the 'Finest Ballpark in America,'" 1531; Wolfe, "The Candlestick Swindle."

155   Wolfe, "The Candlestick Swindle."

156   Smith, "From the 'Finest Ballpark in America,'" 1531; Gershman, *Diamonds*, 182; Wolfe, "The Candlestick Swindle."

157   John Drebinger, "Sports of the Times: San Francisco or Bust," *New York Times*, July 21, 1957. Though attendance perked up slightly in each of those pennant-winning seasons—just over one million in 1951 and just under 1.2 million in 1954—the team had drawn fewer than 700,000 in 1956 and 1957.

158   Goldblatt, "San Francisco Giants," 378.

159   Milton Bracker, "Souvenir-Hunting Followers of Baseball Club Rip up Polo Grounds After Team Is Defeated There in Its Final Game," *New York Times*, September 30, 1957.

160   Ibid.

161   Howard M. Tuckner, "Two Trumpets and a Trombone Sound Dirge in Empty Ballpark," *New York Times*, September 30, 1957.

162   Bracker, "Souvenir-Hunting Followers of Baseball Club."

163   Ibid.

164   Smith, "From the 'Finest Ballpark in America,'" 1533; "Cement Pouring Hailed: But Work on Baseball Giants' Park Also Draws Protest," *New York Times*, October 29, 1958; "Mayor Sued by Juror," *New York Times*, January 1, 1959.

165   Wolfe, "The Candlestick Swindle."

166   Gershman, *Diamonds*, 182; Bucky Walter, "Showplace . . . Candlestick Park—A Dream Come True," in *Sports in North America: A Documentary History: Sports, Prosperity, Conformity, Cultural Stirrings, 1950–1960*, ed. Joel S. Franks (Gulf Breeze, Fla.: Academic International Press, 2004), 24. Bolles specialized in commercial and industrial buildings, largely in Northern California; for example, he had designed the Bay Area's suburban Macy's stores.

167   The Pacific Coast League was essentially a minor-major league. Concentrated, as the name suggests, on the Pacific coast, the league enjoyed strong support from growing western cities. However, as major league games became nationally televised in the 1950s and jet travel allowed the Brooklyn Dodgers and New York Giants to relocate in California, the league became "minor" in status to the increasingly nationalized National and American leagues.

168   Brian J. Godfrey, "Ethnic Identities and Ethnic Enclaves: The Morphogenesis of San Francisco's Hispanic 'Barrio,'" *Yearbook: Conference of Latin American Geographers* 11 (1985): 45–53.

169   McCabe quoted in Robert H. Boyle, "Wind, Mai Tai, and Sam Jones," *Sports Illustrated*, April 25, 1960.

170   *Giants 1960 Yearbook: Mid-Season Edition* (San Francisco: San Francisco Giants, 1960), 8, A. Bartlett Giamatti Research Center, National Baseball Hall of Fame.

171   Ted Atlas connects Candlestick to Googie in *Candlestick Park* (Charleston, S.C.: Arcadia Publishing, 2010), 34.

172   Ibid., 37.

173   *Giants 1960 Yearbook: Mid-Season Edition*, 4.

174   There were some seats at the rear of the first level beneath the upper deck that were blocked by supporting posts. Red Smith, "Giants Simply Need Pennant for Stadium," *Washington Post*, August 28, 1959.

175   Harold Rosenthal, "Saluting Hardiest of All Fans—You," *Baseball Digest* 19, no. 4 (May 1960): 60.

176   Bob Stevens, "Wait Till Lefty Hitters Get Wind of This!" *Baseball Digest* 19, no. 1 (February 1960): 13–16.

177   "Hot Seat for Giant Fans," *Popular Science*, September 1959, 106. The heating system is noted in Tom Parkinson, "Heated Ball Park," *Billboard*, December 28, 1959, 35.

178   John Drebinger, "A 'Giant Miracle' Coming," *New York Times*, August 7, 1959. When Larry MacPhail, one of sport's most influential innovators, joined the Yankees in 1945, he quickly installed a private club at Yankee Stadium. These clubs were for box holders, individuals and businesses, who received brass nameplates for their boxes, first call on tickets for other stadium events like prizefights and football games, and "a magnificent feeling of aloofness," in the words of Arthur Daley. The club had no problem selling access to 2,500 seats. Arthur Daley, "More Stars, More Fans, More Everything," *New York Times*, April 14, 1946.

179   Atlas, *Candlestick Park*, 46.

180   It was typical for sportswriters to speak of female ushers as if they were inanimate objects, akin to other forms of luxury. Al Wolf, "Sportraits: S.F. Ball Park Quite a Place," *Los Angeles Times*, April 11, 1960.

181   "95 Fans Felled by Heat on Coast Before the Gale Brings Balm," *New York Times*, July 12, 1961. Female ushers might have caught the eye of out-of-towners, but San Franciscans were well accustomed to their presence in the stadium. The San Francisco Seals, a member of the Pacific Coast League, was among the first sports clubs to try to take advantage of the supposedly innate sense of refinement women supplied to commercial spaces, beginning in 1945. See Al Wolf, "Sportraits," *Los Angeles Times*, April 27, 1945; Al Wolf, "Sportraits," *Los Angeles Times*, April 9, 1948; Dick Dobbins and Jon Twichell, *Nuggets on the Diamond: Professional Baseball in the Bay Area from the Gold Rush to the Present* (San Francisco: Woodford Press, 1994), 170.

182   Robert Lipsyte, "An Image in Concrete," *New York Times*, July 7, 1963.

183   Atlas, *Candlestick Park*, 34.

184   Roger Angell, *The Summer Game* (New York: Viking, 1972), 76–77.

185   The 1962 thriller *Experiment in Terror* used Candlestick Park as the setting for its climatic ending. The film ends with police shooting a man dead on the pitcher's mound following a game between the Giants and rival Dodgers. On-screen, the stadium is a site of palpable anxiety and uncertainty, where an anonymous crowd harbors a nervous energy.

186   Bob Addie, "Windblown All-Star Classic," *Washington Post*, July 13, 1961; Frank Finch, "The Bull Pen: Gale Still Blowing at Candlestick," *Los Angeles Times*, April 15, 1961; Arthur Daley, "Sports of the Times: Life in a Wind Tunnel," *New York Times*, July 12, 1961; Al Wolf, "Sportraits: Giants Getting Rich at Home," *Los Angeles Times*, May 29, 1960; Art Rosenbaum, "Candlestick Wind Key Topic, But What's to Be Done About It?" *Los Angeles Times*, May 10, 1961; Frank Finch, "The Bull Pen: Giants Freeze in Candlestick Climate," *Los Angeles Times*, September 3, 1960; Arthur Daley, "Sports of the Times: Gone with the Wind," *New York Times*, July 13, 1961; Frank Finch, "The Bull Pen: It's an Ill Candlestick Wind Blowing No Good," *Los Angeles Times*, July 16, 1960.

187   Roy Terrell, "Old Pals in a Cold Wind," *Sports Illustrated*, September 26, 1960, 80–89.

188   Atlas, *Candlestick Park*, 22; Arthur Daley, "Sports of the Times: Thar She Blows!" *New York Times*, February 14, 1962; Smith, "From the 'Finest Ballpark in America,'" 1535.

189   Addie, "Windblown All-Star Classic"; Daley, "Sports of the Times: Gone with the Wind."

190   "Giants' Park Not 'Intimate,'" *Spokane Spokesman-Review*, April 3, 1960.

191   Atlas, *Candlestick Park*, 46; "Row Me Out to the Ball Game: Candlestick Park, San Francisco," *Life*, April 25, 1960, 40–41.

192   *Sports Illustrated*'s Terrell wasn't the only one to note San Franciscans' affection for a baseball cocktail. Roger Angell of the *New Yorker* observed that fans came to 1962 World Series games—noontime starts to avoid the afternoon winds as much as possible—"bearing picnic baskets and gin-and-tonic fixings." Angell, *The Summer Game*, 76–77.

193   "Giants' Park Not 'Intimate.'"

194   "'Candlestink' New Name for Giants' Park," *Washington Post*, January 10, 1960.

195   "Full of Drips: Leaking Pipes Chase Fans at Giants Park," *Los Angeles Times*, May 12, 1960.

196   "Giants Awaiting Final Approval of Plan for 45,400-Seat Stadium," *New York Times*, February 9, 1958; "Coroner Stricken at Candlestick Park," *Washington Post*, May 25, 1960; "Giants Plan New Ramp to Curb Heart Attacks," *Washington Post*, May 26, 1960.

197   "Candlestick Going Under," *Los Angeles Times*, May 18, 1960.

198   Gershman, *Diamonds*, 182.

199   Emil Praeger to Robert Moses, May 6, 1960, folder, Stadium-Land Construction, M–R, box 183, C3.615, New York World's Fair 1964–1965 Corporation Records, Manuscripts and Archives Division, The New York Public Library.

200   Golenbock, *Bums*, 442–43.

201   Walter Bingham, "Boom Goes Baseball," *Sports Illustrated*, April 23, 1962.

202   Frank Finch, "O'Malley Set to Make Bid for Coliseum," *Los Angeles Times*, December 10, 1957.

203   "A Vote in Favor of Everybody," *Los Angeles Times*, June 1, 1958.

204   Walter Ames, "Rundberg Changes Mind and Opposes Chavez Deal," *Los Angeles Times*, May 16, 1958.

205   Finch is quoted retrospectively in John Hall, "Around Town," *Los Angeles Times*, April 29, 1977.

206   Thompson and Rice, *Every Diamond Doesn't Sparkle*, 152–53, 193.

207   Henderson, "Los Angeles and the Dodger War," 281.

208   Avila, *Popular Culture in the Age of White Flight*, 167.

209   Quoted in ibid., 167.

210   Charlie Park, "Newest Stadium Baseball Marvel," *Los Angeles Times*, April 10, 1962.

211   Writers valued the stadium at $18 million, though this appears to have just accounted for O'Malley's spending on the stadium, not land value or preparation costs.

212   Al Wolf, "Tight Squeeze, But Dodger Stadium's Ready," *Los Angeles Times*, April 8, 1962; Jim Murray, "O'Malley's Mahalley," *Los Angeles Times*, January 29, 1962; Frank Finch, "Reds 'Crash' Dodger Stadium Party," *Los Angeles Times*, April 11, 1962.

213   Wolf, "Tight Squeeze, But Dodger Stadium's Ready"; Art Ryon, "Ham on Ryon: All This and Mr. O'Malley, Too!" *Los Angeles Times*, April 9, 1962.

214   Bingham, "Boom Goes Baseball," 23.

215   Paul Zimmerman, "City to Benefit by New Stadium," *Los Angeles Times*, April 15, 1962. The Dodgers had wanted an "all-girl staff" but had been rebuffed by the local service union. "25 Usherettes All Set for Chavez Ravine," *Los Angeles Times*, April 4, 1962.

216   Avila, *Popular Culture in the Age of White Flight*, 171.

217   Hine, *Populuxe*. Architectural critic Reyner Banham, a celebrant of the seeming freedom of Los Angeles automobility, argued, "The language of design, architecture, and urbanism in Los Angeles is the language of movement." Reyner Banham, *Los Angeles: The Architecture of Four Ecologies* (London: Penguin, 1971), 23. Thomas Pynchon seemed less enthusiastic about Southern California's spatiality and means of interconnectedness, comparing freeways to hypodermic needles that keep Los Angeles "happy, coherent, protected from pain, or whatever passes, with a city, for pain." Thomas Pynchon, *The Crying of Lot 49* (New York: Penguin, 2012), chapter 2.

218   *Los Angeles Dodgers 1962 Souvenir Yearbook*, A. Bartlett Giamatti Research Center, National Baseball Hall of Fame.

219   Teaford, *The Twentieth-Century American City*, 99.

220   "Holding Together Until Monday," *Los Angeles Times*, October 2, 1957.

221   "At Last: The New Ball Park," *Los Angeles Times*, April 9, 1962.

222   This point is well made by Avila, *Popular Culture in the Age of White Flight*, 174–75.

223   Charlie Park, "Stadium Hailed by Players," *Los Angeles Times*, April 10, 1962.

224   Bob Addie, "Shea Stadium Spectacular," *Washington Post*, April 2, 1964.

225   Avila, *Popular Culture in the Age of White Flight*, 175–76.

226   Angell, *The Summer Game*, 73.

227   Ibid.

228   Ibid., 73, 147.

229   Lipsyte, "An Image in Concrete"; Robert Lipsyte, "Wonderful! Old Folks Find a Home in the Ravine," *New York Times*, October 6, 1966.

CHAPTER 3

1   Frederick Exley, *A Fan's Notes* (New York: Vintage Contemporaries, 1988), 68, 132–33.

2   Stew Thornley, *Land of the Giants: New York's Polo Grounds* (Philadelphia: Temple University Press, 2000), 112; "City Eyes Housing at Polo Grounds," *New York Times*, September 5, 1957.

3   William J. Ryczek, *Crash of the Titans: The Early Years of the New York Jets and the AFL* (Kingston, N.Y.: Total Sports Illustrated, 2000), 119.

4   Leonard Lewin, "Plans for New Home Interest Giant Boss," *New York Mirror*, April 11, 1956.

5   "H. B. Herts Dead; Noted Architect," *New York Times*, March 28, 1933.

6   Thornley, *Land of the Giants*, 65–66.

7   Ryczek, *Crash of the Titans*, 120–21.

8   Ibid., 120.

9   Joe Gergen, "When Shea Stadium Meant Class," *Newsday*, December 7, 1983.

10   Charles G. Bennett, "Polo Grounds Doomed to Make Way for Low-Rent Housing Project," *New York Times*, March 10, 1961.

11   Louis Effrat, "National League Admits New York, Houston for 1962," *New York Times*, October 18, 1960.

12   John Drebinger, "Mets Sign Four Players and Start $300,000 Refurbishing of Polo Grounds," *New York Times*, January 12, 1962.

13   Leonard Shecter, *Once upon the Polo Grounds: The Mets That Were* (New York: Dial Press, 1970), 138.

14   George Vecsey, *Joy in Mudville: Being a Complete Account of the Unparalleled History of the New York Mets from Their Most Perturbed Beginnings to Their Amazing Rise to Glory and Renown* (New York: McCall Publishing, 1970), 9–14.

15   Shecter, *Once upon the Polo Grounds*, 61, 138–39.

16   Ibid., 59–62.

17   Vecsey, *Joy in Mudville*, 10.

18   Arthur Daley, "Sports of the Times: With Proper Finality," *New York Times*, September 18, 1963.

19   Robert Creamer, "The Quaint Cult of the Mets," *Sports Illustrated*, May 6, 1963, 61–63.

20   Ibid., 62.

21   Leonard Koppett, *The New York Mets: The Whole Story* (New York: Macmillan, 1970), 12; Frommer, *New York City Baseball*, 85; Goodwin, *Wait Till Next Year*, 61–63.

22   Vecsey, *Joy in Mudville*, 9; Koppett, *The New York Mets*, 12.

23   Frommer, *New York City Baseball*, 87.

24   Koppett, *The New York Mets*, 13–14.

25   Kahn, *The Era*, 45, 189.

26   Robert Lipsyte, "Sports of the Times: The Burdens of History," *New York Times*, June 19, 1969.

27   Howard M. Tuckner, "Mrs. Payson in Group Seeking 2d Team Here," *New York Times*, June 10, 1959; Joseph Durso, "Joan Whitney Payson, 72, Mets Owner, Dies," *New York Times*, October 5, 1975.

28   Vecsey, *Joy in Mudville*, 16.

29   Alfred Wright, "Happy Blend of Sport and Cash," *Sports Illustrated*, May 14, 1962, 82–94.

30   New York Mets, *New York Mets Revised Year Book 1964*, A. Bartlett Giamatti Research Center, National Baseball Hall of Fame.

31   Robert L. Teague, "Close-Up of the Met Fan: Loud, Happy Desperation," *New York Times*, June 3, 1962.

32   Shecter, *Once upon the Polo Grounds*, 71.

33   Koppett, *The New York Mets*, 64.

34   Vecsey, *Joy in Mudville*, 62.

35   Ibid., 56–57.

36   Koppett, *The New York Mets*, 58–59.

37   Vecsey, *Joy in Mudville*, 61–62.

38   Robert Lipsyte, "Yankee Fans vs. Met Fans: Tinker to Evers to Freud," *New York Times*, April 28, 1963.

39   Ibid.

40   Creamer, "The Quaint Cult of the Mets," 62.

41   Vecsey, *Joy in Mudville*, 61–62.

42   Ibid., 61.

43   George Weiss traded Throneberry to Buffalo in 1963. Leonard Shecter claimed that Weiss was never able to understand what Throneberry meant to Mets fans, "just as he didn't understand why huge crowds fought their way into a crumbling, obsolete ball park to cheer for a losing team." Shecter, *Once upon the Polo Grounds*, 114.

44   Shecter, *Once upon the Polo Grounds*, 110–11.

45   Roger Angell, "A Clean, Well-Lighted Cellar," in *The Summer Game* (New York: Viking, 1972), 67–68. This was originally published in the *New Yorker* in May 1964.

46   Teague, "Close-Up of the Met Fan"; Leonard Koppett, "Mets' Attendance Passes Million Here as Reds Win, 1–0, After 5–3 Defeat," *New York Times*, September 3, 1963; Shecter, *Once upon the Polo Grounds*, 124.

47   Koppett, *The New York Mets*, 51–52.

48   Vecsey, *Joy in Mudville*, 56–58.

49   New York Mets, *New York National League Baseball Club Official Year Book 1962*, A. Bartlett Giamatti Research Center, National Baseball Hall of Fame.

50   City of New York Department of Parks, *Dedication: William A. Shea Municipal Stadium*, 1964, folder P4.0—Opening Day—1964 Special Events, box 380, New York World's Fair 1964–1965 Corporation Records, 1959–1971, New York Public Library; Stan Isaacs, "No Bleachers in Mets' Split-Level Palace," *Newsday*, April 20, 1964; Leonard Shecter, "Yea Shea," *New York Post*, April 18, 1964; "Everything Is Ready for Opening Day," *Long Island Star Journal*, April 16, 1964; Leonard Koppett, "Soggy Shea Stadium Bails Out for Dedication Ceremony Today," *New York Times*, April 16, 1964; Jack Mann, "Shea Stadium Dedicated—Mets in Home Debut Today," *New York Herald Tribune*, April 17, 1964; Bob Addie, "New Breed Has Fun," *Washington Post*, July 9 1964; Milton Gross, "Casey Knows What's Missing," *New York Post*, April 20, 1964.

51   "Stadiums: City Status Symbol," *Newsweek*, September 30, 1963, 74–75.

52   Robert Caro, *The Power Broker: Robert Moses and the Fall of New York* (New York: Alfred A. Knopf, 1974), 6, 829.

53   Murray Schumach, "Mets' Euphoria Means All's Well in Flushing," *New York Times*, October 8, 1969.

54   "Flushing Meadows" is singularized by some speakers and writers to "Flushing Meadow."

55   Claudia Gryvatz Copquin, *The Neighborhoods of Queens* (New Haven, Conn.: Yale University Press, 2007), 55–57.

56   Schumach, "Mets' Euphoria." Many Japanese, Korean, and Chinese moved to Flushing in the 1960s. Vincent Seyfried and Jeffrey A. Kroessler, "Flushing," in *The Encyclopedia of New York City*, 2nd ed., ed. Kenneth T. Jackson (New Haven, Conn.: Yale University Press, 2010), 462.

57   Fred Powledge, "'Mason-Dixon Line' in Queens," *New York Times Sunday Magazine*, May 10, 1964, 12; Jason D. Antos, *Shea Stadium* (Charleston, S.C.: Arcadia Publishing, 2007), 55.

58   Caro, *The Power Broker*, 1113.

59   Antos, *Shea Stadium*, 7.

60   Caro, *The Power Broker*, 1113.

61   Robert Moses to Board of Estimate, September 28, 1959, Stadium-Land Construction folder, M-R, box 183, C3.615, New York World's Fair 1964–1965 Corporation Records, 1959–1971, New York Public Library.

62   Paul Crowell, "Approval Due Today for Study of Flushing Baseball Site," *New York Times*, October 22, 1959.

63   Edmond J. Bartnett, "Shea Wants Roof on Baseball Park," *New York Times*, November 18, 1959.

64   The National and American leagues each admitted two clubs from the proposed Continental League in 1960, cutting the league in half and effectively eviscerating it as a viable entity. Effrat, "National League Admits New York."

65   Many sportswriters commented on Moses's extravagant speech. For a particularly colorful description, see Lou O'Neill, "The Touting and the Tumult," *Long Island Star Journal*, October 31, 1961. Moses had his speech printed as a pamphlet and sent far and wide. He ordered his assistant to send copies to Port Authority members and staff (300 in all); World's Fair directors, members, staff, and consultants (1,000); State Park commissioners and executives (80); Triborough members and staff (25); Long Island State Park Commission staff; members of the New York City Planning Commission; New York politicians; "carefully selected sports reporters, editors, etc."; and "baseball and other athletic leaders." Robert Moses, "Remarks of Robert Moses at the Groundbreaking of the Flushing Meadow Municipal Stadium," October 28, 1961, box 450, Folder Moses, Robert—10/28/61, Speeches, New York World's Fair 1964–1965 Corporation Records, 1959–1971, New York Public Library.

66   City of New York Department of Parks, "Flushing Meadow Park Municipal Stadium: Groundbreaking Ceremony," October 28, 1961, box 380, Folio P4.0, New York World's Fair 1964–1965 Corporation Records, 1959–1971, New York Public Library.

67   A cartoon by Gallo of the *Daily News* celebrated the groundbreaking and Young's advocacy through the pages of that newspaper, putting Young's influence on par with Shea's. Gallo, "Thanks, Fellas," *New York Daily News*, October 28, 1961.

68   Joe Williams, "Maybe It's Guile, Bob, Not Bile," *New York World-Telegram-Sun*, October 30, 1961; Joe Williams, "Story of a Stadium . . . From 10 to 340 Million," *New York World Telegram*, October 28, 1961.

69   Roger Angell, "S Is for So Lovable," in *The Summer Game* (New York: Viking, 1972), 55–56. This was originally published in the *New Yorker* in May 1963.

70   Jane Jacobs, *The Death and Life of Great American Cities* (New York: Random House, 2002).

71   Charles Abrams, "Washington Sq. and the Revolt of the Urbs," *Village Voice*, July 2, 1958; Robert Fishman, "Revolt of the Urbs: Robert Moses and His Critics," in *Robert Moses and the Modern City: The Transformation of New York*, ed. Hilary Ballon and Kenneth T. Jackson (New York: W. W. Norton, 2007), 122–29.

72   Graham Hodges, "Lower East Side," in *The Encyclopedia of New York City*, 2nd ed., ed. Kenneth T. Jackson (New Haven, Conn.: Yale University Press, 2010), 769–70; Andrew S. Dolkart, "The Biography of a Lower East Side Tenement: 97 Orchard Street, Tenement Design, and Tenement Reform in New York City," 2001, http://www.tenement.org/documents/Dolkart.pdf (accessed January 11, 2017); Charlie Chin and Cecilia Magnusson, "Chinatown," in *The Encyclopedia of New York City*, 2nd ed., ed. Kenneth T. Jackson (New Haven, Conn.: Yale University Press, 2010), 241–42.

73   DeSalvio quoted in Fishman, "Revolt of the Urbs," 127. In spite of his claim, Moses was not the only advocate for the LME—Mayor Robert Wagner would support it, and then his replacement, John Lindsay, who initially opposed it, would propose alternative tunnel-and-ditch designs. The project wouldn't be officially defeated until 1969, in the face of considerable local resistance. Ray Bromley, "Lower Manhattan Expressway," in *Robert Moses and the Modern City: The Transformation of New York*, ed. Hilary Ballon and Kenneth T. Jackson (New York: W. W. Norton, 2007), 213–14.

74   Gerard Genette's concept of the "paratext" is useful in thinking about how sportswriters' rhetoric might have influenced the public's interpretations of stadium spaces. According to Genette, the "paratext" is what enables a book to be a book—elements surrounding a text that aren't the text itself but through which people experience the text. Paratexts can be attached to texts (like covers, typeface, prefaces, indexes) or separate from the text (reviews, interviews, advertisements). Paratexts set up meanings and interpretive strategies for readers, helping them make sense of the text itself. Gerard Genette, *Paratexts: Thresholds of Interpretation*, trans. Jane E. Lewin (Cambridge: Cambridge University Press, 1997). For an example of the use of paratexts in action, see Jonathan Gray's analysis of television advertising. Jonathan Gray, "Television Pre-views and the Meaning of Hype," *International Journal of Cultural Studies* 11, no. 1 (2008): 33–49.

75   Gross, "Casey Knows What's Missing."

76   Stan Isaacs, "No Bleachers in Mets' Split-Level Palace," *Newsday*, April 20, 1964.

77   Jimmy Breslin, "It's Metsomania," *Saturday Evening Post*, June 13, 1964, 22. Philadelphia-area developer Ralph Bodek and University of Pennsylvania marketing professor William T. Kelley found in a 1955 study that there were particular social-class associations with certain suburban home types. Split-level homes were considered solidly middle income and popular among young couples who considered themselves modern but more traditional than those willing to buy the single-level ranch house. See Lizabeth Cohen, *A Consumer's Republic: The Politics of Mass Consumption in Postwar America* (New York: Vintage, 2003), 208–9.

78   Lipsyte, "Yankee Fans vs. Met Fans."

79   Lipsyte, "An Image in Concrete."

80   Robert Lipsyte, "An Era Ends, Perhaps," *New York Times*, April 19, 1964.

81   Angell, "S Is for So Lovable," 55–56.

82   Roger Angell, "Farewell," in *The Summer Game* (New York: Viking, 1972), 57–58. This was originally published in the *New Yorker* in April 1964.

83   Phil Gruen makes this point in "Postwar Stadiums: Will We Miss Them When They're Gone?" *Baseball Research Journal* 25 (1996): 16–20.

84   City of New York Department of Parks, *Dedication: Shea Stadium*, folder P4.0—Opening Day—1964 Special Events, box 380, New York World's Fair 1964–1965 Corporation Records, 1959–1971, New York Public Library.

85   New York Mets, "Ticket Application," 1964, folder P4.0—Opening Day—1964 Special Events, box 380, New York World's Fair 1964–1965 Corporation Records, 1959–1971, New York Public Library.

86   City of New York Department of Parks, *New York City's Flushing Meadow Park Municipal Stadium*, 1962, Stadium Brochures Stadium Construction folder, box 183, C3.615, New York World's Fair 1964–1965 Corporation Records, 1959–1971, New York Public Library; City of New York Department of Parks, *Dedication: William A. Shea Municipal Stadium*; City of New York Department of Parks, *Dedication: Shea Stadium*; New York Mets, *New York Mets Revised Year Book 1964*.

87   Herbert Shuldiner, "A New Home for the Mets," *Popular Science*, April 4, 1964, 86–88; Vincent Butler, "All-Purpose Stadium Being Built in New York," *Chicago Tribune*, January 12, 1964; Bob Addie, "Views from Shea Stadium," *Washington Post*, July 8, 1964.

88   "Yes, Virginia, There Is a Shea Stadium," *New York Times*, April 18, 1964.

89   Koppett, *The New York Mets*, 77.

90   New York Mets, "Ticket Application."

91   "All Roads Lead to Shea Stadium," *New York Times*, April 12, 1964.

92   "Traffic Plan Set for Shea Stadium," *New York Times*, April 17, 1964; "Barnes Maps Road Lineup for Games at Shea Stadium," *Long Island Press*, April 14, 1964; "Barnes Shift to Zip Stadium Traffic," *Long Island Star Journal*, April 14, 1964; "Make Room for the Mets," *New York Post*, April 14, 1964.

93   Leonard Koppett, "Shea Stadium Opens with Big Traffic Jam," *New York Times*, April 18, 1964.

94   City of New York Department of Parks, *Dedication: Shea Stadium*.

95   City of New York Department of Parks, *Dedication: William A. Shea Municipal Stadium*.

96   Frank Litsky, "Team of 15 Architects Planning 'Airy' Arena," *New York Times*, April 28, 1960.

97   "Escalators at Mets Park to Take Toil Out of Grandstand Climbing," *New York Times*, April 13, 1963.

98   "Stadiums: City Status Symbol," 74–75; Butler, "All-Purpose Stadium Being Built in New York"; Mickey Herskowitz, "Domed Stadium Puts Shea in Shade," *Houston Post*, June 5, 1964.

99   New York Mets, *New York National League Baseball Club Final Revised Official 1963 Year Book*, A. Bartlett Giamatti Research Center, National Baseball Hall of Fame.

100   "Escalators at Mets Park to Take Toil Out of Grandstand Climbing."

101   Antos, *Shea Stadium*, 25.

102   Lipsyte, "An Image in Concrete."

103   City of New York Department of Parks, *Dedication: William A. Shea Municipal Stadium*.

104   New York Mets, "Ticket Application."

105   Litsky, "Team of 15 Architects Planning 'Airy' Arena."

106   Howard M. Tuckner, "Last-Place Mets Are Getting a First-Class Ball Park," *New York Times*, August 15, 1962.

107   Clifford Edward Clark Jr., *The American Family Home, 1800–1960* (Chapel Hill: University of North Carolina Press, 1986), 211–12, 223; Gwendolyn Wright, *Building the Dream: A Social History of Housing in America* (Cambridge, Mass.: MIT Press, 1983), 254; Christine Hunter, *Ranches, Rowhouses & Railroad Flats* (New York: W. W. Norton, 1999), 256.

108   Isaacs, "No Bleachers in Mets' Split-Level Palace."

109   Vecsey, *Joy in Mudville*, 93.

110   Angell, "A Clean, Well-Lighted Cellar," 61.

111   For some, Shea Stadium's internal transportational logic was no example of modern rationalism but existentialist absurdity. A writer for the *Village Voice* covering a 1970 music festival wrote:

> If anybody out there is looking for a convenient, already built set for a film of Kafka's "The Castle," I've got just the thing—Shea Stadium. Endless ramps that lead nowhere in particular, mysterious passageways, sudden twists and turns that lead from grubby kitchen areas in to stark daylight. It's even equipped with guards who have an innate feeling for Kafkaesque logic: "Press room? Well, now I heard something about a room like that once; why don't you try going up that ramp over there and then down the other side to level C and then take the elevator up to the fourth level. But then you better ask somebody when you get there." For Kafka?—terrific. For the Summer Festival for Peace? Ha.

But there were no other real alternatives in the city—a place "large enough or secure enough to hold 40,000–50,000 people. So, Shea Stadium it was." "Danger: Music for Peace," *Village Voice*, 1970, Flushing Shea Stadium 1964–1988 bound clippings, pp. 53–55, Long Island Division, Queens Library.

112   Vance Packard, *Status Seekers: An Exploration of Class Behavior in America* (Harmondsworth: Penguin, 1959), 12, 267.

113   Homeowners were thus very wary of who was moving in and out of the area. Home pricing became a primary sorting mechanism for neighborhood homogeneity. In the American suburb, a world determined by "the drive for . . . high-value property," according to political scientist Robert Wood, to overlook the income and race of one's neighbors was "to invite financial suicide." As such, not only were suburbs socioeconomically homogeneous; they were also racially homogeneous. While racial exclusion and segregation in public accommodations was receding more generally into the 1960s, it was being accentuated residentially through suburban development. Cohen, *A Consumer's Republic*, 202, 210, 218, 253.

114   Clark, *The American Family Home*, 233–35. Clark invokes Herbert J. Gans's study of Levittown, New Jersey, *The Levittowners: The Ways of Life and Politics in a New Suburban Community* (New York: Pantheon, 1967).

115   New York Mets, *New York National League Baseball Club Official Year Book 1962*; New York Mets, *New York National League Baseball Club Final Revised Official 1963 Year Book*.

116   Vecsey, *Joy in Mudville*, 93–94.

117   The 1965 program for the Houston Astrodome would baldly express this sentiment, collapsing the luxury and middle classes, telling readers that with the stadium's padded seats, "Sports fan is now a king!" At the dome, "You will be able to sit in a chair as comfortable as any found in the world's finest theatres and opera houses." *Inside the Astrodome* (Houston: Houston Sports Association, 1965), 41.

118   Isaacs, "No Bleachers in Mets' Split-Level Palace."

119   Angell, "A Clean, Well-Lighted Cellar," 61.

120   Benson, *Ballparks of North America*, 257.

121   Packard, *Status Seekers*, 168.

122   Daley, "More Stars, More Fans, More Everything."

123   New York Mets, "Ticket Application"; "The Mets Score in Restaurants," *New York Times*, August 23, 1964.

124   Gross, "Casey Knows What's Missing."

125   Vecsey, *Joy in Mudville*, 93–94.

126. Breslin, "It's Metsomania."

127   Mann, "Shea Stadium Dedicated." This is corroborated in a memo written by Bill Denny, of the Parks Department, who noted that the Diamond Club was "one of the most critical phases" of the stadium. See Bill Denny, "Memo to file," September 13, 1963, Stadium-Land Construction folder, A-L, box 183, C3.615, New York World's Fair 1964–1965 Corporation Records, 1959–1971, New York Public Library. As plans to roof Shea Stadium continued after its opening, stadium expansion also called for a "gigantic restaurant" at the top level. Sports Commissioner Ben Finney explained, "This restaurant would be for the average guy going to a ball game, at prices he could afford to pay. Unless he's a season ticket-holder or a member of the Diamond Club, he can't get into the restaurants now on the grounds." Finney's words suggested that there was some anxiety about the exclusive clubs in Shea, and it could also be read as a response to the Houston Astrodome's well-publicized and well-developed range of clubs and restaurants that each catered to a different socioeconomic slice of customer. Carl Lundquist, "Roof on Shea by '66, Sports Boss Forecasts," *Sporting News*, June 5, 1965, 7.

128   Richard L. Coe, "Gotham's Got 'Em at the Fair," *Washington Post*, June 7, 1964; Lester Bromberg, "Shea Stadium Fulfillment of a Promise," *New York World-Telegram*, April 16, 1964.

129   Addie, "New Breed Has Fun."

130   Richard Sandomir, "Stadium's Appeal Lay in Futuristic Functionality," *New York Times*, September 28, 2008.

131   City of New York Department of Parks, *Dedication: William A. Shea Municipal Stadium*.

132   Dick Young, "Young Ideas," *New York Daily News*, April 17, 1964.

133   Angell, "A Clean, Well-Lighted Cellar," 61.

134   Hine, *Populuxe*.

135   Herbert Shuldiner, "A New Home for the Mets," *District of Columbia Stadium Official Dedication Magazine*, 1961, George Washington University, Gelman Library, Special Collections Research Center, Washington, D.C.

136   City of New York Department of Parks, *Dedication: William A. Shea Municipal Stadium*.

137   New York Mets, *New York National League Baseball Club Final Revised Official 1963 Year Book*.

138   City of New York Department of Parks, *Dedication: Shea Stadium*.

139   New York Mets, *New York Mets Revised Year Book 1964*.

140   Jerry Levine, "Shea, Fair Run Dead-Heat," *New York Journal American*, April 4, 1964; "Mets to Use Giant Movie Screen to Introduce Stars," *New York Times*, March 29, 1964.

141   "A Spectacular," *New York World-Telegram-Sun*, March 28, 1964; "Mets to Use Giant Movie Screen to Introduce Stars."

142   Ed Rumill, "When Play Is On, Scoreboard Should Be Seen, Not Heard," *Baseball Digest*, August 1966, 65–66.

143   Angell, "A Clean, Well-Lighted Cellar," 61.

144   Angell wrote, "Still, I doubt whether Shea Stadium will ever see the likes of those steamy old midsummer doubleheaders at the Polo Grounds, when visiting outfielders used to stare up in wonder at the screaming sans-culottes, and had to brave summer thunderstorms of trash and firecrackers while catching a fly." Ibid., 66.

145   Addie, "Shea Stadium Spectacular."

146   Will Lissner, "City Improves Facilities for Shea Stadium Fans," *New York Times*, March 15, 1964.

147   Larry Van Gelder, "Mets Live It Up—Then Die," *New York World-Telegram*, April 17, 1964.

148   Robert Lipsyte, "'Fabulous' Stadium Delights Fans," *New York Times*, April 18, 1964; Robert Lipsyte, "Metchicks Have All the Answers," *New York Times*, April 21, 1964.

149   Kathleen M. Barry, *Femininity in Flight: A History of Flight Attendants* (Durham, N.C.: Duke University Press, 2007), 158.

150   Betty Friedan, *The Feminine Mystique* (New York: W. W. Norton, 2001); Joanne Meyerowitz, "Beyond the Feminine Mystique: A Reassessment of Postwar Mass Culture, 1946–1958," *Journal of American History* 79, no. 4 (March 1993): 1455–82.

151   The club was also organized to help the Mets sell tickets. A reporter wrote, "It is hoped that area clubs will be formed that will compete in selling tickets for games, with the best club winning a prize." Tania Long, "Mets Field Fast Questions from Women Fans," *New York Times*, July 4, 1965.

152   City of New York Department of Parks, *New York City's Flushing Meadow Park Municipal Stadium*; City of New York Department of Parks, "Flushing Meadow Park Municipal Stadium: Groundbreaking Ceremony"; City of New York Department of Parks, *Dedication: Shea Stadium*; New York Mets, *New York National League Baseball Club 1963 Official Program and Score Card*, A. Bartlett Giamatti Research Center, National Baseball Hall of Fame.

153   Litsky, "Team of 15 Architects Planning 'Airy' Arena."

154   Elaine Tyler May, *Homeward Bound: American Families in the Cold War Era* (New York: Basic Books, 1988), 12.

155   Breslin, "It's Metsomania," 20.

156   Ibid., 20, 22.

157   William N. Wallace, "Jets Turn Back Broncos, 30–6, Before 52,663 Here," *New York Times*, September 13, 1964; Robert Lipsyte, "Wahoo Hopes to Put Indian Sign on Big Town," *New York Times*, September 27, 1964; Edwin Shrake, "'Wahoo! Wahoo! Wahoo!'" *Sports Illustrated*, October 26, 1964.

158   Angell, "A Clean, Well-Lighted Cellar," 66, 67–68.

159   Koppett, *The New York Mets*, 87–88.

160   Vecsey, *Joy in Mudville*, 95.

161   Koppett, *The New York Mets*, 84–85.

162   Robert Lipsyte, "Fans Arise! It's Mets vs. Yanks Tonight," *New York Times*, May 3, 1965.

163   Shecter, *Once upon the Polo Grounds*, 129.

164   Vecsey, *Joy in Mudville*, 93–94.

165   Angell, "A Clean, Well-Lighted Cellar," 66, 67–68.

166   Koppett, *The New York Mets*, 138.

167   Ibid., 137–38.

168   Benjamin G. Rader, *In Its Own Image: How Television Has Transformed Sports* (New York: Free Press, 1984), 94.

169   Oriard, *Brand NFL*, 38–53; Dan Jenkins, "The Sweet Life of Swinging Joe," *Sports Illustrated*, October 17, 1966; John Skow, "Joe, Joe, You're the Most Beautiful Thing in the World," *Saturday Evening Post*, December 3, 1966, 99–103.

170   Robert H. Boyle, "Show-Biz Sonny and His Quest for Stars," *Sports Illustrated*, July 19, 1965.

171   John Lake, "Two for the Football Show: The Swinger and the Square," *New York Times*, November 5, 1967. Namath's contract reportedly was for three years at $100,000 per year plus bonuses and a $5,000 annual pension at the end of his career. "Jets Hand Namath $400,000 Package," *Washington Post*, January 3, 1965.

172   Oriard, *Brand NFL*, 43, 53.

173   Nancy Moran, "For Women, Home Is Where the Plate Is," *New York Times*, September 26, 1969.

174   Vecsey, *Joy in Mudville*, 242–43.

CHAPTER 4

1   Lasswell quoted in Jason Mellard, *Progressive Country: How the 1970s Transformed the Texan in Popular Culture* (Austin: University of Texas Press, 2013), 41.

2   "What Writers Are Saying About Dome," *Houston Post*, April 10, 1965.

3   Diliberto quoted in "What Nation's Writers Think of Our Dome," *Houston Chronicle*, April 11, 1965.

4   I use "enclosed" to mean that the stadium field was encircled by stands, precluding views of the outside world beyond what could be seen above the stands. Thus Shea Stadium would not be a fully enclosed stadium because it had an open end with views of Flushing. "Roofed" stadiums were both enclosed and topped, fully sealing stadium inhabitants inside.

5   Astrodome propaganda never listed the runner-up in this contest. The Belgrade Fair dome, opened

in 1957, was reinforced concrete and had a diameter of 340 feet. The Charlotte Coliseum was a steel-framed dome with a 332-foot expanse, opened in 1955. Harrison E. Salisbury, "Building Pattern Set by Belgrade," *New York Times*, August 22, 1957; "Uncovered Steel Is Gaining Favor," *New York Times*, August 18, 1957; "Several Area Florists Attend 9th Convention," *Gadsen (Alabama) Times*, November 4, 1958.

6   *Inside the Astrodome*, 130.

7   The stadium also introduced synthetic grass to the sports world, AstroTurf, in 1966, after the glare problems with the roof forced the county to paint over the translucent panels, thereby killing the grass below. For more on synthetic playing surfaces, see Benjamin D. Lisle, "Materiality and Meaning: Synthetic Grass, Sport, and the Limits of Modern Progress," in *Material Matters: Selections from the 2012 Material Culture Symposium for Emerging Scholars*, http://sites.udel.edu/mcses2012/papers/paper-i/ (accessed September 29, 2014).

8   Roger Angell, "The Sporting Scene: The Cool Bubble," *New Yorker* 42 (May 14, 1966): 141.

9   *Inside the Astrodome*, 8.

10   Joe R. Feagin, *Free Enterprise City: Houston in Political-Economic Perspective* (New Brunswick, N.J.: Rutgers University Press, 1988), 6–10, 71.

11   Teaford, *The Twentieth-Century American City*, 108–9.

12   David G. McComb, *Houston: A History* (Austin: University of Texas Press, 1981), 138–39.

13   Quoted in George Fuermann, *Houston: The Feast Years* (Houston: Premier Printing Company, 1962), 6.

14   Ibid., 24.

15   Jetero Airport would later be renamed Houston Intercontinental Airport; Houston International would become William P. Hobby Airport.

16   McComb, *Houston: A History*, 132–33.

17   Houston City Planning Department, *Houston: CBD Today* (Houston, 1964), 14–15.

18   Ibid., 14–15, 18, 24.

19   Fuermann, *Houston: The Feast Years*, 34.

20   Houston City Planning Department, *Houston: CBD Today*, 36–38, 40–43.

21   McComb, *Houston: A History*, 124.

22   Kirkpatrick Sale, *Power Shift: The Rise of the Southern Rim and Its Challenge to the Eastern Establishment* (New York: Vintage, 1976), 53.

23   Ibid., 13, 35.

24   Feagin, *Free Enterprise City*, 6, 109; Lipsitz, "Sports Stadia and Urban Development."

25   Jesse H. Jones was at the center of the "Suite 8F crowd." Jones had been Houston's largest prewar developer, responsible for most of the city's major prewar construction, and had interests in real estate, banking, Humble Oil, the Ship Channel, and the *Houston Chronicle*. As chairman of the Reconstruction Finance Committee from 1933 to 1939, he was among the most influential men in the country—a position that empowered him to dictate federal investment and assist the development of the steel and chemical industries in Texas. Jones was joined in the Suite 8F crowd by figures like Herman and George Brown—whose Brown and Root construction firm built military bases, roads, dams, bridges, petrochemical plants, offshore drilling platforms, and the Manned Spacecraft Center—and Judge James A. Elkins Sr. of the influential Houston law firm of Vinson and Elkins, who had also founded one of Houston's major banking firms and served as a director for a wide range of companies. The name "Suite 8F crowd" referred to George Brown's suite in the Lamar Hotel. Feagin, *Free Enterprise City*, 107–10. Also, see the Texas State Historical Association's *Handbook of Texas Online*, http://www.tshaonline.org/handbook/online/search.html (accessed October 8, 2016).

26   Roy Terrell, "Fast Man with a .45," *Sports Illustrated*, March 26, 1962, 32–42.

27   "Debut of the Dome," *Texas Sunday Magazine*, April 4, 1965.

28   Sale, *Power Shift*, 34.

29   One of Hofheinz's first acts as mayor was to remove the "White" and "Colored" signs over city water fountains. City employees threatened to strike, so Hofheinz ordered the return of the "White" signs (but not the "Colored"). Some white employees, in support of desegregation, began using the non-marked fountains. After six to eight months, they removed the "White" signs, and it was no longer an issue. William Sherrill, former

mayoral aide to Hofheinz, remembered, "That was one of the very early and very small steps toward social justice in Houston." Edgar W. Ray, *The Grand Huckster: Houston's Judge Roy Hofheinz, Genius of the Astrodome* (Memphis: Memphis State University Press, 1980), appendix.

30   *Inside the Astrodome*, 99.

31   Dan Cook, "Domed Stadium Among World's Wonders," *San Antonio Express*, April 30, 1964.

32   Dick Blue, the former director of marketing for the Astros, claimed, "I heard that in one county judge race Roy was called a 'fuehrer.' I never heard it said in my presence, but I can't help comparing him with Hitler in many ways, not from a derogatory standpoint, but from an oratory standpoint. There were three men that I have heard in my lifetime that I thought were the greatest orators—Franklin D. Roosevelt, Hitler, and—by far the best—Hofheinz. I listened to Hitler on the radio, and, although I didn't speak German, I could feel the tension as he built his speeches. Hofheinz followed the same pattern of speech. It was incredible." Ray, *The Grand Huckster*, appendix.

33   "The Business of Baseball," *Newsweek*, April 26, 1965, 66–70; Frank X. Tolbert, "The Incredible Houston Dome," *Look*, April 20, 1965, 96–98; Wells Twombly, "Money Flows Like Oil into Astrodome," *Sporting News*, April 10, 1965.

34   Terrell, "Fast Man with a .45," 32.

35   Angell, "The Cool Bubble"; Robert Lipsyte, "Hofheinz Says Yanks Will Be Awed in Game Tomorrow," *New York Times*, April 8, 1965; Harold Scarlett, "Goldphone," *Houston Post Sunday Magazine*, June 13, 1965, 12–13; "Debut of the Dome"; Liz Smith, "Giltfinger's Gold Dome," *Sports Illustrated*, April 12, 1965, 45–63. Smith referred to Hofheinz as an owl, a metaphor echoed in Robert Altman's 1970 film *Brewster McCloud*, which featured a fictionalized version of Hofheinz, whose car bore the license plate OWL 180.

36   Smith, "Giltfinger's Gold Dome," 45.

37   Lipsyte, "Hofheinz Says Yanks Will Be Awed in Game Tomorrow." Estes was an extravagant, wealthy, and corrupt Texan under federal indictment for fraud in the early 1960s.

38   Terrell, "Fast Man with a .45," 34.

39   Bob Gray, "Bonds for Sports Center Win Heavy Endorsement," *Houston Post*, July 27, 1958, 16A. Plans for the sports center anticipated it being located on 230 acres off South Main—where the stadium ended up being constructed. The Parks Commission had wanted to build it at Memorial Park, but Ima Hogg, who had sold the land to the city at a discount, was opposed. The city feared that the title to the park might be revoked if they pushed forward to try to use it as something besides a public park, so they backed off. Ray, *The Grand Huckster*, 259.

40   Hofheinz and Smith became increasingly involved with the bid, particularly after the HSA won the new franchise. New teams were required to make a $5 million deposit to cover start-up costs; they also needed an additional $1.75 million to spend on players in an expansion draft set to follow the 1961 season. Cullinan offered ownership roles to Smith and Hofheinz after twelve of the original twenty-seven HSA stockholders backed out of their initial pledges. Smith and Hofheinz each then owned 33 percent of the enterprise (with Smith financing Hofheinz's share—an arrangement that would become a point of contention and factor in Smith's departure from the club in the coming years). Cullinan owned 15 percent and Kirksey 2 percent. Benjamin D. Lisle, "Houston Astros," in *Encyclopedia of Major League Baseball Clubs*, vol. 1, *The National League*, ed. Steven A. Riess (Westport, Conn.: Greenwood Press, 2006), 163–65; Effrat, "National League Admits New York."

41   "New Stadium Lured Team to Milwaukee," *Houston Chronicle*, August 6, 1959.

42   Clark Nealon, "All-Weather Sports Stadium Planned for Site Off South Main," *Houston Post*, August 21, 1960; "Photo of Domed Stadium," *Houston Post*, December 6, 1960; Box 94-274/18, folder "magazine clippings, 1951–1965," Robert J. Minchew Houston Astrodome Architectural and Engineering Collection, 1958–1967, Center for American History, University of Texas at Austin; Dick Peebles, "$15 Million Domed Stadium Planned," *Houston Chronicle*, no date; Box 94-274/19, Robert J. Minchew Houston Astrodome Architectural and Engineering Collection, 1958–1967, Center for American History, University of Texas at Austin.

43   Harold Scarlett, "Bonds for Stadium Win in Record Vote," *Houston Post*, February 1, 1961.

44   *The Strange Demise of Jim Crow: How Houston Desegregated Its Public Accommodations, 1959–1963, A Documentary*, VHS, 60 min., Institute for Medical Humanities, University of Texas Medical Branch, Galves-

ton, 1997; Lisle, "Houston Astros," 165. Many in Houston struggled with the realities of Jim Crow throughout the 1950s, producing a gradual and uneven desegregation of public spaces. Five African Americans sued the municipal golf course in 1950. The public library was desegregated in 1953, without much publicity. Buses were desegregated in 1954. The desegregation of schools began in September 1960. The City Hall cafeteria began serving blacks in 1961. In 1963, city pools were opened. Some of these changes were carried out under cover of organized nonpublicity campaigns. Racial change in Houston was hardly quiet, however. For example, four hundred students of the historically black Texas Southern University rioted after a pep rally in November 1965, throwing rocks, beer cans, and vegetables at police. McComb, *Houston: A History*, 166–70.

45   George T. Morse Jr., "Roadblocks to Houston's Progress," *at work: monthly newsletter of the Houston Chamber of Commerce* 17, no. 6 (June 1962).

46   "Let's Build the Stadium," *Houston Chronicle*, May 20, 1962.

47   Ray, *The Grand Huckster*, 285.

48   Marshall Verniand, "Voters Approve Bond Issue for Domed Stadium," *Houston Post*, December 23, 1962; Lisle, "Houston Astros," 166. Robert C. Trumpbour and Kenneth Womack, *The Eighth Wonder of the World: The Life of Houston's Iconic Astrodome* (Lincoln: University of Nebraska Press, 2016), 95.

49   Ray puts the figure at $35.5 million for the entire project: $31.6 million from the county bond issues ($22 million for the stadium itself) and $3.75 million from the City of Houston and the Texas Highway Department for off-site improvements like paved streets, bridges, drainage, and storm sewers. He doesn't include the HSA improvements. Ray, *The Grand Huckster*, 285–86.

50   The original debt obligation wouldn't be fully paid off until 2001. Kiah Collier, "Money Still Owed on Dome Less than Previously Stated," *Houston Chronicle*, June 18, 2013, http://www.houstonchronicle.com/news/houston-texas/houston/article/Money-still-owed-on-Dome-less-than-previously-4608496.php (accessed October 8, 2016). For a comprehensive history of Astrodome planning and construction, see Trumpbour and Womack, *The Eighth Wonder of the World*.

51   McComb, *Houston: A History*, 188.

52   Baytown resident Ray Heinrich's complaint was cited in Bob Fenley, "Dome on the Range," *Dallas Times Herald Sunday Magazine*, April 4, 1965.

53   Gene Goltz, "Visitors Queue Up to Goggle at Dome," *Houston Post*, April 18, 1965.

54   Larry McMurtry, "Love, Death, and the Astrodome," *Texas Observer*, October 1, 1965, 2.

55   Buff Stadium was located on the southwestern edge of census tract 00350000. U.S. Census Bureau, "Census 1960 Tracts Only Set-Total Population: Black," http://www.socialexplorer.com/86535a9a44/view (accessed October 31, 2014); U.S. Census Bureau, "Census 1960 Tracts Only Set-Total Population: Puerto Rican or Spanish Surname," http://www.socialexplorer.com/ab99ff1322/view (accessed October 31, 2014); U.S. Census Bureau, "Census 1960 Tracts Only Set-Total Population: White," http://www.socialexplorer.com/f711230484/view (accessed October 31, 2014).

56   Harry Grayson, "The Judge: Veeck Looks Like Peanut Man," *Houston Post*, April 8, 1965.

57   Ray, *The Grand Huckster*, 283.

58   Frank Finch, "Gaily Decorated Colt Stadium Puts Most Ballparks to Shame," *Los Angeles Times*, May 8, 1962.

59   *Colt .45s Souvenir Program* (Houston: Houston Sports Association, 1963).

60   Joseph M. Sheehan, "Colts Open First Major League Season in Houston," *New York Times*, April 10, 1962; Finch, "Gaily Decorated Colt Stadium Puts Most Ballparks to Shame."

61   Walter Bingham, "Boom Goes Baseball: Ticker Tape, Dyed Grass, Blue Cowboy Hats," *Sports Illustrated*, April 23, 1962, 18–25.

62   Sheehan, "Colts Open First Major League Season in Houston"; Robert Reed, *Colt .45s: A Six-Gun Salute* (Houston: Lone Star Books, 1999), 74–75. Reed compares the Fast Draw Club to *Gunsmoke*'s Long Branch Saloon. See also Ray Sons, "Houston's Dome a Real Chicago Challenge," *Chicago Daily News*, February 6, 1964; Ray, *The Grand Huckster*, 280–81.

63   *Colt .45s Souvenir Program.*

64   Finch, "Gaily Decorated Colt Stadium Puts Most Ballparks to Shame."

65   Reed, *Colt .45s*, 106.

66   *Colt .45s Souvenir Program.*

67   Sons, "Houston's Dome a Real Chicago Challenge."

68   ".45s Fans Pop Off," *New York World-Telegram*, May 22, 1962.

69   Lipsyte, "An Image in Concrete," S3.

70   Reed, *Colt .45s*, 82–83.

71   Ibid., 77.

72   Ibid., 78.

73   Frank Finch, "Dodgers Happy to Leave Town After Summer Roasts Houston," *Los Angeles Times*, June 11, 1962; "Houston Heat Boosts Domed Stadium Hope," *Washington Post*, June 12, 1962.

74   "What Writers Are Saying About Dome"; Fenley, "Dome on the Range."

75   McMurtry, "Love, Death, and the Astrodome," 3.

76   *Inside the Astrodome*, 3. Use of letterhead was a common cliché for opening stadium programs. It seemed to lend the document (and stadium) a sense of occasion and gravity, as well as letting the reader in on some inside dope from one powerful man to another.

77   Ibid., 6. Stadium officials would have to paint the translucent panels of the roof because of a glare problem shortly after its opening, rendering Welch's metaphor an ironic commentary on the limitations of progress.

78   Ibid., 7. Kirkpatrick Sale claimed that the presidency of the chamber of commerce in Houston was a step up from being mayor in terms of political power. Sale, *Power Shift*, 53.

79   *Inside the Astrodome*, 33.

80   Ibid., 11.

81   "That Man McCarthy Plans 180,000-Seat Covered Stadium," *Washington Post*, January 20, 1950; Mc-Comb, *Houston: A History*, 187.

82   *Inside the Astrodome*, 11.

83   Ibid., 10–13.

84   For other examples, among many, see "Electricity Has Big Role in Operation of Our Dome," *Houston Post*, April 8, 1965; "Stadiums: City Status Symbol," 74–75; and just about any photo of Hofheinz appearing in the print media.

85   Marling, *As Seen on TV*, 50–84.

86   *Inside the Astrodome*, 19–27.

87   Ibid., 52.

88   Ibid., 49–51.

89   Ibid., 52–53.

90   Ibid., 28–31.

91   "Plastics Score in Stadiums," *Chemical Week*, April 17, 1965, 87–90.

92   *Inside the Astrodome*, 26.

93   Ibid., 76–77.

94   Lisle, "Materiality and Meaning."

95   *Inside the Astrodome*, 9, 40, 250.

96   Wells Twombly, "History in the Making," *Houston Chronicle*, April 10, 1965.

97   Red Smith, "Weather's Bad? Watch the Astros," *Washington Post*, February 16, 1965.

98   "Houston's Dream of a Domed Stadium Rapidly Nearing Conversion to Reality," *Chattanooga Times*, January 12, 1964.

99   Mickey Herskowitz, "Doctor, Lawyer, Indian, Chief, You Can Find a Home in the Dome," *Houston Post*, April 8, 1965.

100   Michael L. Smith, "Making Time: Representations of Technology at the 1964 World's Fair," in *The Power of Culture: Critical Essays in American History*, ed. Richard Wightman Fox and T. J. Jackson Lears (Chicago: University of Chicago Press, 1993), 239–40.

101   Fenley, "Dome on the Range."

102   *Inside the Astrodome*, 9, 93.

103   Michael L. Smith, "Selling the Moon: The U.S. Manned Space Program and the Triumph of Commodity Scientism," in *The Culture of Consumption: Critical Essays in American History, 1880–1980*, ed. Richard Wightman Fox and T. J. Jackson Lears (New York: Pantheon Books, 1983), 184–85.

104   Ibid., 192.

105   *Inside the Astrodome*, 6.

106   Lipsyte, "Astrodome Opulent Even for Texas." A subtitle of the article read, "Houston Club Chief Uses Gold Phones in Various Sizes."

107   *Inside the Astrodome*, 41.

108   Ibid., 33, 45.

109   This sort of attitude is of a piece with the post–World War II changes described by historian Lizabeth Cohen, whereby the categories of consumer and citizen were fused together. It also recalls the parable of a "democracy of goods" that historian Roland Marchand identified in prewar advertising. Of these marketing clichés, Marchand wrote, "By implicitly defining 'democracy' in terms of equal access to consumer products, and then by depicting the everyday functioning of that 'democracy' with regard to one product at a time, these tableaux offered Americans an inviting vision of their society as one of uncontestable equality." See Cohen, *A Consumer's Republic*, and Roland Marchand, *Advertising the American Dream: Making Way for Modernity, 1920–1940* (Berkeley: University of California Press, 1985), 218.

110   *Inside the Astrodome*, 58–59.

111   McMurtry, "Love, Death, and the Astrodome," 3.

112   Smith, "Weather's Bad? Watch the Astros."

113   *Inside the Astrodome*, 49.

114   Fuermann, *Houston: The Feast Years*, 3.

115   "The Place for Pleasure," *Houston Magazine* 29, no. 1 (1958).

116   Marsha E. Ackermann, *Cool Comfort: America's Romance with Air-Conditioning* (Washington, D.C.: Smithsonian Institution Press, 2002), 5–6, 47–53, 127; Jackson, *Crabgrass Frontier*, 281; Packard, *Status Seekers*, 68.

117   Smith, "Giltfinger's Gold Dome," 51.

118   *Inside the Astrodome*, 86.

119   Ibid., 80–82.

120   "Bigger and Better in Texas," *Economist*, June 10, 1967, 1125.

121   Jerome Holtzman, "New Houston Stadium Greatest of All," *Chicago Sun-Times*, September 13, 1964.

122   *Inside the Astrodome*, 80–82.

123   McMurtry, "Love, Death, and the Astrodome," 4.

124   Angell, "The Cool Bubble," 128, 130.

125   Ibid., 135.

126   Ibid.

127   Mike Vance, *Houston's Sporting Life: 1900–1950* (Charleston, S.C.: Arcadia Publishing, 2011), 14. Roger Angell concludes his assessment of the Houston Astrodome with a woman's memories of old Buff Stadium, where she had been a fan for over thirty years. She recalled the smells of a nearby bakery: "I'll never forget sitting in the stands in the afternoon and watching the games, and the sweet smell of fresh bread in the air all around." Angell, "The Cool Bubble," 142.

128   Fuermann, *Houston: The Feast Years*, 34.

129   Benjamin D. Lisle, "'We Make a Big Effort to Bring Out the Ladies': Visual Representations of Women in the Postwar American Stadium," in *The Visual in Sport*, ed. Mike Huggins and Mike O'Mahony (London: Routledge, 2011). Many of the ideas in this section were originally published in this article.

130   "Debut of the Dome," 23.

131   Dave Bruce, "Houston's Big Bubble: Rain or Shine Stadium," *Texas Parade*. This article was not dated but is located in the "Stadiums: Anaheim, CA" clippings folder at the A. Bartlett Giamatti Research Center, National Baseball Hall of Fame.

132 Dick Young, "Roy's Shack the Greatest," *Houston Post*, April 30, 1965, sec. 4, 3.

133 *Inside the Astrodome*, 37.

134 Angell, "The Cool Bubble," 125.

135 "What Writers Are Saying About Dome."

136 Mickey Herskowitz, "In a Mighty Splash, It's Open," *Houston Post*, April 10, 1965.

137 Smith, "Giltfinger's Gold Dome," 54, 56.

138 "Debut of the Dome."

139 Virginia Drane McCallon, "Fashions Under the Dome," *Houston Post*, February 28, 1965.

140 *Inside the Astrodome*, 39.

141 Ray, *The Grand Huckster*, 282; "Andy Frain, 'Usher King' Dies; Supervisor of Crowds Was 59," *New York Times*, March 26, 1964.

142 Twombly, "Money Flows Like Oil."

143 Teddye Clayton, "Spacettes Will Sparkle Under Dome," *Houston Post*, April 4, 1965.

144 Barry, *Femininity in Flight*, 47.

145 Ibid., 46.

146 Stewardesses, of course, underwent much more rigorous training beyond grooming and sociability; they were not merely airborne Spacettes but practiced professionals in ways that the stadium ushers were not.

147 Though the Spacettes were supposed to signify class, and did to many, not everyone was convinced. A writer for the *New York Times* argued, "The décor is on the garish side—the costumes of the usherettes, waiters and other servants of the public look like all the Gilbert and Sullivan operettas mixed together, and the physical furnishings might be termed Early Cinemascope—but the totality is festive and exciting." "Baseball Under Dome," *New York Times*, May 2, 1965.

148 We might find a parallel in automobile design and advertising. Historian David Gartman argues that both men and women wanted color and comfort out of their automobiles, but it was only acceptable for a woman to admit it. The standards of midcentury manhood wouldn't allow men to luxuriate in such frivolity, as much as they desired these luxuries. The automobile industry appeared to advertise to women, knowing that men were the actual decision makers when it came to purchasing cars. Men could then use their wives' tastes as cover for their own, blaming the non-utilitarian elements of their cars on the needs of their wives without compromising their masculinity by admitting to enjoying these elements themselves. David Gartman, *Auto Opium: A Social History of American Automobile Design* (London: Routledge, 1994), 167.

149 Ray, *The Grand Huckster*, 337.

150 Hofheinz refers to the New Breed of the Polo Grounds. See the previous chapter. Angell, "The Cool Bubble," 135.

151 Marling, *As Seen on TV*, 86–126.

152 The lines between promotion and independent interpretation were often crossed and mingled, as promotional materials for the stadium often cited newspaper and magazine writers, appropriating them as advocates. An inversion of that also occurred regularly, as writers quoted or repackaged the claims of promoters made through interviews, press conferences, and press releases.

153 *Inside the Astrodome*, 18.

154 Ibid., 144.

155 Press release, July 9 1965, box 94-274/19, folder "Press releases concerning Astrodome correspondence, 1966," Robert J. Minchew Houston Astrodome Architectural and Engineering Collection, 1958–1967, Center for American History, University of Texas at Austin.

156 Andy O'Brien, "The Stadium That Could Revolutionize Sport," *Montreal Star Weekend Magazine*, May 15, 1965, 30–32; "Houston's Dream of a Domed Stadium Rapidly Nearing Conversion to Reality."

157 John Cronley, "Some Dome!" *Daily Oklahoman*, December 22, 1964.

158 "Debut of the Dome."

159 "What Nation's Writers Think of Our Dome."

160 "What Writers Are Saying About Dome."

161 *Inside the Astrodome*, 16–17, 45.

162   Mickey Herskowitz, "A New Order Cometh to Baseball," *Houston Post*, April 9, 1965.

163   Finger Contract advertisement, *Houston Post*, April 8, 1965.

164   Smith, "Giltfinger's Gold Dome," 58.

165   *Inside the Astrodome*, 58–59.

166   Smith, "Giltfinger's Gold Dome," 52–53.

167   Architect Herman Lloyd recalled that the space on the ninth level "was an afterthought as far as we were concerned. Space at the top we had planned for transverse-travel for our duct work. When Roy saw that space he felt he could sell private boxes for what was then fabulous amounts. We didn't see how he could do it, but we put in the boxes. Ever since, there hasn't been a big stadium built without boxes." Ray, *The Grand Huckster*, 305.

168   Ann Valentine, *Houston Post*, box 94-274/18, folder "Magazine clippings, 1951–1965," Robert J. Minchew Houston Astrodome Architectural and Engineering Collection, 1958–1967, Center for American History, University of Texas at Austin.

169   *Inside the Astrodome*, 33.

170   Valentine, *Houston Post*. *Sports Illustrated*'s Liz Smith was less impressed with the boxes than Valentine, writing, "The rooms are decorated in a riot of astounding styles from western to southern to Oriental to heaven-knows-what, with much fake ivy and other plastic plant life and scenic wallpaper panels (there are no windows). Despite the conflicts and contrasts, they create an overall impression of motel modern." Smith, "Giltfinger's Gold Dome," 56.

171   Valentine, *Houston Post*.

172   *Inside the Astrodome*, 33–34. "Orientalism" as a discourse, as Edward Said described it, was a mechanism for post-Enlightenment European and American cultures to discipline, manage, and produce the Orient. Through it, Western cultures distinguished themselves from Eastern ones by ascribing certain characteristics—irrationality, mysticism, uncivilization—onto the Orient as a way of confirming their oppositional characteristics for rational Westerners. Orientalist discourse, thus, is a misrepresentation of the East in the service of Western identity. Edward Said, *Orientalism* (New York: Pantheon Books, 1978).

173   Angell, "The Cool Bubble," 135.

174   Scarlett, "Goldphone," 12; Ray, *The Grand Huckster*, 312.

175   Smith, "Giltfinger's Gold Dome," 46.

176   Ray, *The Grand Huckster*, 328.

177   Bill Roberts, "The Town Crier," *Houston Post*, December 23, 1964.

178   Finger Contract advertisement.

179   F. Talbott Wilson, "The City: Our Shame and Hope," address to the Houston Philosophical Society, March 18, 1965, box 94-274/18, Robert J. Minchew Houston Astrodome Architectural and Engineering Collection, 1958–1967, Center for American History, University of Texas at Austin.

180   Sociologist Joe R. Feagin makes the distinction between these two types of cities. Free-enterprise cities were disproportionately shaped not by market forces (as a free-market city would be) but by state intervention, often motivated by business leaders. He wrote, "The close relationship between the state and the business elite is one of the more revealing aspects of Houston's political-economic evolution." Feagin, *Free Enterprise City*, 5–6, 39, 44.

CHAPTER 5

1   "Goodby to Old Stadium, Hello to New Today," *St. Louis Post-Dispatch*, May 8, 1966.

2   Joseph Heathcott and Maire Agnes Murphy, "Corridors of Flight, Zones of Renewal: Industry, Planning, and Policy in the Making of Metropolitan St. Louis, 1940–1980," *Journal of Urban History* 31, no. 2 (January 2005): 161.

3   Katharine G. Bristol, "The Pruitt-Igoe Myth," *Journal of Architectural Education* 44, no. 3 (May 1991): 163–71.

4   George Lipsitz makes this point: "Racialized space enables the advocates of expressly racist policies

to disavow any racial intent." George Lipsitz, *How Racism Takes Place* (Philadelphia: Temple University Press, 2011), 35. For more on how racial ideology is spatialized, in St. Louis and elsewhere, see Joseph Heathcott, "Black Archipelago: Politics and Civic Life in the Jim Crow City," *Journal of Social History* 38, no. 3 (Spring 2005): 705–36; Joseph Heathcott, "The City Quietly Remade: National Programs and Local Agendas in the Movement to Clear the Slums, 1942–1952," *Journal of Urban History* 34, no. 2 (January 2005): 221–42; Heathcott and Murphy, "Corridors of Flight"; Colin Gordon, *Mapping Decline: St. Louis and the Fate of the American City* (Philadelphia: University of Pennsylvania Press, 2008); Thomas J. Sugrue, *The Origins of the Urban Crisis: Race and Inequality in Postwar Detroit* (Princeton, N.J.: Princeton University Press, 1996); Arnold R. Hirsch, *Making the Second Ghetto: Race and Housing in Chicago, 1940–1960* (New York: Cambridge University Press, 1983); Jackson, *Crabgrass Frontier*; Douglas S. Massey and Nancy A. Denton, *American Apartheid: Segregation and the Making of the Underclass* (Cambridge, Mass.: Harvard University Press, 1993); Kevin Fox Gotham, *Race, Real Estate, and Uneven Development* (Albany: State University of New York Press, 2002).

5   Gordon, *Mapping Decline*, 225.

6   "Pictorial St. Louis, the great metropolis of the Mississippi valley; a topographical survey drawn in perspective A.D. 1875," map, American Memory, Map Collections, http://hdl.loc.gov/loc.gmd/g4164sm.gpm00001 (accessed February 5, 2010).

7   William A. Borst, "Baltimore Orioles," in *Encyclopedia of Major League Baseball Clubs*, vol. 2, *The American League*, ed. Steven A. Riess (Westport, Conn.: Greenwood, 2006), 475; Jon David Cash, "St. Louis Cardinals," in *Encyclopedia of Major League Baseball Clubs*, vol. 1, *The National League*, ed. Steven A. Riess (Westport, Conn.: Greenwood, 2006), 421; "Baltimore Orioles Year-by-Year Results," *The Official Site of the Baltimore Orioles*, http://baltimore.orioles.mlb.com/bal/history/year_by_year_results.jsp (accessed February 2, 2015).

8   Claire Smith, "Color Issue Reaches People in Seats," *New York Times*, April 10, 1997; Benson, *Ballparks of North America*, 349.

9   For evidence of Dodgers support in St. Louis, see Roscoe McGowen, "Brooks Take 8th in Row, 7 to 2; Triple Play for St. Louis in 1st," *New York Times*, June 15, 1949; Roscoe McGowen, "Brooks' Roe Takes Night Contest, 2–0," *New York Times*, May 20, 1949; Roscoe McGowen, "Dodgers Break Even with Cardinals, Stay Game and Half Out of First Place," *New York Times*, September 22, 1949.

10   Though none of these players would last the entire season with the Browns—struggling at bat and, no doubt, with the trying racist environment—the thirty-six-year-old Brown would ultimately be voted into the Baseball Hall of Fame. Thompson joined the New York Giants in 1949 and won the 1954 World Series there.

11   Borst, "Baltimore Orioles," 475.

12   Rader, *In Its Own Image*, 27.

13   Gaedel was given number 1/8. Detroit pitcher Bob Cain was laughing so hard by the third pitch that he could barely throw it. Arthur Daley, "Sports of the Times: The Poor Relation," *New York Times*, May 31, 1966. The strike zone in 1951 would have been "that space over home plate which is between the batter's armpits and the top of his knees when he assumes his natural stance." See "The Strike Zone: A Historical Timeline," http://mlb.mlb.com/mlb/official_info/umpires/strike_zone.jsp (accessed February 2, 2010).

14   Cash, "St. Louis Cardinals," 421–22.

15   Neal Russo, "The Grand Years: Personalities and Pennants," *St. Louis Post-Dispatch*, May 8, 1966.

16   Cash, "St. Louis Cardinals," 423.

17   St. Augustine Catholic Church, organized in 1874, was constructed in the late 1800s to serve the area's population of German Catholics. Central High School, originally James E. Yeatman High School, opened in September 1904. Bethlehem Lutheran Church, organized in 1849, opened in 1895. Mount Moriah Masonic Hall opened in 1903. Many of the neighborhood details come from "History of St. Louis Neighborhoods," written by Norbury Wayman, a city planner, architect, and historian, for the St. Louis Community Development Agency in the 1970s, http://stlouis.missouri.org/neighborhoods/history/index.htm. (accessed February 5, 2010).

18   Roger Angell, "Two Strikes on the Image," in *The Summer Game* (New York: Viking, 1972), 105, originally published in the *New Yorker*, October 1964.

19   Louis Effrat, "Whatever Hilda Wants Hilda Gets in Brooklyn," *New York Times*, September 3, 1955; "Woman Rooter Takes Her Baseball Seriously," *Los Angeles Times*, August 21, 1938.

20   "Cardinals' Park Oldest in Majors," *Los Angeles Times*, March 5, 1958; Jerry Rombach, "Sport Scope," *Southeast Missourian*, May 22, 1962.

21   "Comprehensive City Plan 1947," Official Web Site of the City of St. Louis, http://stlouis.missouri.org/government/docs/1947plan/images/plate13.GIF (accessed May 25, 2010); Gordon, *Mapping Decline*, 186.

22   Barry Checkoway, "Revitalizing an Urban Neighborhood: A St. Louis Case Study," in *The Metropolitan Midwest: Policy Problems and Prospects for Change*, ed. Barry Checkoway and Carl V. Patton (Urbana: University of Illinois Press, 1985), 245.

23   Census reporting is uneven over the three decades from 1950 to 1970. However, the reports do reveal consistent differences between what was known as census tract 0010D (in 1950 and 1960) and 1104 (in 1970) and points directly southwest, south, and southeast in terms of housing values.

24   Gordon, *Mapping Decline*, 195.

25   United States Census Bureau, "State and County QuickFacts," http://quickfacts.census.gov/qfd/index.html (accessed February 5, 2010).

26   United States Census Bureau, "Missouri—Race and Hispanic Origin for Selected Cities and Other Places: Earliest Census to 1990," by Campbell Gibson and Kay Jung, Population Division, Working Paper No. 76, http://www.census.gov/population/www/documentation/twps0076/motab.pdf (accessed October 9, 2016).

27   James Neal Primm, *Lion of the Valley: St. Louis, Missouri, 1764-1980* (St. Louis: Missouri Historical Society Press, 1998), 476, 479.

28   Bristol, "The Pruitt-Igoe Myth," 164.

29   Heathcott and Murphy, "Corridors of Flight," 152–53; Gordon, *Mapping Decline*, 167–68.

30   Heathcott and Murphy, "Corridors of Flight," 157–59; Lipsitz, "Sports Stadia and Urban Development," 3. For a more general discussion of postwar capitalist urbanization and the emergence of the postindustrial city, see Harvey, *The Urban Experience*, 37–45.

31   Primm, *Lion of the Valley*, 465.

32   Lipsitz, "Sports Stadia and Urban Development," 4.

33   Nicholas Dagen Bloom, *Merchant of Illusion: James Rouse, America's Salesman of the Businessman's Utopia* (Columbus: Ohio State University Press, 2004), 28–37, 55.

34   Gordon, *Mapping Decline*, 156.

35   Ibid., 157.

36   Ibid., 162.

37   Ibid., 162–63.

38   Practically speaking, a private development proposal identified a parcel of land for redevelopment. Investors worked with the city to have the area designated as blighted and to authorize an urban redevelopment corporation (URC) that would redevelop the land. The Board of Aldermen would declare the area "blighted," using Chapter 353, Chapter 99, or both. Chapter 353 was generally used for single projects or buildings; a URC formed under Chapter 353 used the city's power of eminent domain to have properties blighted. Chapter 353 URCs could also buy, sell, hold, and lease property provided that the investors limited profits to 8 percent of overall project costs. Chapter 99 was used for larger projects; a Chapter 99 Land Clearance for Redevelopment Authority (LCRA) used federal funds to acquire and clear the plot.

    Land acquisition and development defined as a "public purpose" carried the added benefit of tax abatement. Chapter 99 land became city property, and was thus removed from the tax rolls. The LCRA could both clear the land for redevelopment and significantly improve it before selling the title to a private developer or URC. Chapter 353 gave URCs a sliding twenty-five-year property tax abatement on land redeveloped within an urban renewal area. For the first ten years, the property was assessed and taxed at its value before being designated as "blighted." For the following fifteen years, it was assessed and taxed at just half of its improved value. Gordon, *Mapping Decline*, 163–64.

39   Primm, *Lion of the Valley*, 467.

40   Historian James Neal Primm claimed that the city's primarily black wards voted 15,243 to 878 in favor of slum clearance, even knowing that they would be displaced by that clearance. Primm, *Lion of the Valley*, 467. However, for a city that was home to 153,766 black residents in 1950 and 214,377 by 1960, this seems only a partial portrait.

41   Bristol, "The Pruitt-Igoe Myth," 166.

42   Gordon, *Mapping Decline*, 167–68. Gordon puts the figure at twenty thousand, Lipsitz at thirty thousand. Lipsitz, "Sports Stadia and Urban Development," 4.

43   Gordon, *Mapping Decline*, 167. Plans to get affluent suburbanites to relocate downtown failed. Mansion House Apartments would be burdened by low occupancy. It was the last attempt to cultivate upscale downtown living for many years. By most accounts, however, nonresidential downtown developments flourished.

44   Technically the Arch was a catenary, not a parabola. Many, however, mistook the shape for a parabola—a form with a broader cultural resonance.

45   Though the Gateway Arch wouldn't be completed until the mid-1960s, the competition for the memorial was conducted in 1947–48. Suggestions for the memorial, like Dickmann's stadium, preceded that.

46   Carl R. Baldwin, "Public Apathy, Other Barriers Surmounted by Dedicated Men," *St. Louis Post-Dispatch*, May 8, 1966.

47   "Proposed County Stadium," *St. Louis Post-Dispatch*, no date; Box 94-274/19, Robert J. Minchew Houston Astrodome Architectural and Engineering Collection, 1958–1967, Center for American History, University of Texas at Austin.

48   Carl R. Baldwin, "Chance to Build a Dream," *St. Louis Post-Dispatch*, December 12, 1958. For an image of the structure, see "Studying Sketch of Proposed Stadium," *St. Louis Post-Dispatch*, December 10, 1958.

49   "Stadium a Part of $80,935,000 Downtown Plan Ok'd by C. of C.," *St. Louis Post-Dispatch*, September 10, 1959.

50   Baldwin, "Public Apathy, Other Barriers Surmounted by Dedicated Men."

51   "Bid to Declare Stadium Site Blighted Meets Hot Opposition," *St. Louis Post-Dispatch*, January 27, 1960.

52   Gordon, *Mapping Decline*, 168.

53   Lipsitz, "Sports Stadia and Urban Development," 5.

54   "Stadium Design Unveiled; Wins Backers' Praise," *St. Louis Post-Dispatch*, March 12, 1963; Baldwin, "Public Apathy, Other Barriers Surmounted by Dedicated Men."

55   Brian Burnes, Dan Viets, and Robert W. Butler, *Walt Disney's Missouri: The Roots of a Creative Genius* (Kansas City, Mo.: Kansas City Star Books, 2002), 142.

56   Burnes, Viets, and Butler, *Walt Disney's Missouri*, 150.

57   Ibid., 151; John Hannigan, *Fantasy City: Pleasure and Profit in the Postmodern Metropolis* (London: Routledge, 1998), 47–48; Peter Bart, "Walt Disney Eyes a 2D Disneyland," *New York Times*, July 3, 1964; "2nd Disneyland Proposal Refused," *Los Angeles Times*, July 7, 1965.

58   The proposed Disneyland site was filled by the Spanish Pavilion. While celebrated at the fair, the pavilion would largely be seen as an economic failure in St. Louis.

59   The newness of the stadium accentuated the aged condition of the area around it, putting pressure on city officials to broaden downtown redevelopment. The area was designated blighted, block by block, into the late 1960s. This enabled the development of a series of office towers north of the stadium. All of downtown (from the river west to Twelfth Street, Chouteau to Cole) was declared blighted under Chapter 353 in 1971, as officials grew weary of the tedious block-by-block blight approach. Gordon, *Mapping Decline*, 168.

60   Lipsitz, "Sports Stadia and Urban Development," 4.

61   Edward Durell Stone, *Recent & Future Architecture* (New York: Horizon Press, 1967), 30.

62   "Brilliant and Harmonious," *St. Louis Post-Dispatch*, March 13, 1963, 2c.

63   Frank Leeming Jr., "46,048 Attend First Game in New Stadium," *St. Louis Post-Dispatch*, May 13, 1966.

64   Neal Russo, "Something New in St. Louis—Spacious Stadium," *Sporting News*, May 28, 1966, 15.

65   Advertisement for KSD5-TV, *St. Louis Post-Dispatch*, May 15, 1966, 6d.

66   Leeming, "46,048 Attend First Game in New Stadium."

67   Russo, "Something New in St. Louis."

68   Ibid.

69   Ibid.

70   Neal Russo, "Site Near Arch, Stores, Hotels Hailed as Ideal for Ball Fans," *St. Louis Post-Dispatch*, May 8, 1966.

71   Angell, "Two Strikes on the Image," 177.

72   Russo, "Something New in St. Louis."

73   Leeming, "46,048 Attend First Game in New Stadium"; Russo, "Something New in St. Louis."

74   Stone, *Recent & Future Architecture*, 30.

75   Henry Evans, "Too Much Downtown," *St. Louis Post-Dispatch*, May 11, 1966.

76   Leeming, "46,048 Attend First Game in New Stadium"; Russo, "Something New in St. Louis."

77   Leeming, "46,048 Attend First Game in New Stadium"; Red Smith, "Stadium Isn't Pipe Dream," *St. Louis Post-Dispatch*, May 13, 1966.

78   Bob Broeg, "Stadium a Hot Item Without Gas," *St. Louis Post-Dispatch*, May 13, 1966. Like Shea, Busch had a private club but no luxury suites. Skyboxes weren't common in modern stadiums until the 1970s.

79   Russo, "Something New in St. Louis"; "Together We Built the New STADIUM," *St. Louis Post-Dispatch*, May 8, 1966.

80   Dave Lipman, "For Those Who Know the Score, Busch Board Adds Living Color," *St. Louis Post-Dispatch*, May 13, 1966.

81   Leeming, "46,048 Attend First Game in New Stadium."

82   Broeg, "Stadium a Hot Item Without Gas."

83   Ibid.

84   Angell, "Two Strikes on the Image," 103.

85   Lipsitz, "Sports Stadia and Urban Development," 5.

86   Ada Louise Huxtable, "St. Louis Success," *New York Times*, February 4, 1968.

87   "Dodgers Study Possibility of Dome-Covered Stadium," *Washington Post*, October 1, 1955; "Friend Triumphs on Six-Hitter, 9–1," *New York Times*, September 30, 1957; Creamer, "The Quaint Cult of the Mets"; Daley, "Sports of the Times: With Proper Finality"; John Hall, "Tale of Two Cities Tells Baseball Trend," *Los Angeles Times*, October 7, 1967; Arthur Daley, "Sports of the Times: Waiting for the Stars," *New York Times*, July 14, 1970.

88   Creamer, "The Quaint Cult of the Mets"; Hall, "Tale of Two Cities."

89   "Cardinals Seek Sportsman's Park, Offering to Pay $700,000 'or More,'" *New York Times*, December 2, 1947; Russo, "The Grand Years"; Daley, "Sports of the Times: The Poor Relation"; Jack Hand, "Baseball Begins with New Look," *Washington Post*, April 10, 1966; Arthur Daley, "Sports of the Times: Passing of a Landmark," *New York Times*, May 30, 1966; Neal Russo, "Million Memories—They're All That's Left in Cards' Old Park," *Sporting News*, May 21, 1966, 25; "Defeat Sours Nostalgia, But Cards Had Moments," *St. Louis Post-Dispatch*, May 9, 1966; Russo, "Site Near Arch."

90   Russo, "Site Near Arch."

91   As noted previously, Angell warmly referred to Sportsman's Park as "an old down-on-her-luck dowager" from a settlement house ("Two Strikes on the Image," 105). It is also worth noting that the "dowager" metaphor was not limited to Sportsman's Park; this was a trope applied to other old ballparks as well.

92   Russo, "The Grand Years."

93   Ed Wilks, "100 Years of Baseball End at Old Park," *St. Louis Post-Dispatch*, May 9, 1966.

94   Relph, *The Modern Urban Landscape*, 147. The affiliation of cities and disease has a much longer back-history in the United States. Thomas Jefferson wrote, in his *Notes on the State of Virginia*, "The mobs of great cities add just so much to the support of pure government, as sores do to the strength of the human body. It is the manners and spirit of a people which preserve a republic in vigour. A degeneracy in these is a canker which soon eats to the heart of its laws and constitution." Thomas Jefferson, *Notes on the State of Virginia*, ed. Merrill D. Peterson (New York: Library of America, 1781–82), 291, http://etext.virginia.edu/toc/modeng/public/JefVirg.html (accessed March 22, 2010).

95   "Ground Broken for Downtown Sports Stadium," *St. Louis Post-Dispatch*, May 25, 1964.

96   Donald Janson, "Arch Symbolizes St. Louis Revival," *New York Times*, August 4, 1963.

97   "Stadium Symbolizes City's Rebirth," *St. Louis Post-Dispatch*, May 8, 1966.

98   Busch Memorial Stadium Special Supplement advertisement, *St. Louis Post-Dispatch*, May 1, 1966; Baldwin, "Public Apathy, Other Barriers Surmounted by Dedicated Men"; "Sunday Pictures," *St. Louis Post-Dispatch*, May 8, 1966.

99   *St. Louis Cardinals 1966 Souvenir Yearbook*, 1966, A. Bartlett Giamatti Research Center, National Baseball Hall of Fame.

100   Jean M. White, "St. Louis Is Gracefully Dwarfing All High-Rises," *Washington Post*, March 28, 1965.

101   Janson, "Arch Symbolizes St. Louis Revival."

102   Maggie Bellows, "Two Cities Kick Up Heels in Missouri," *St. Petersburg Times*, April 20, 1967.

103   Ada Louise Huxtable, "St. Louis and the Crisis of American Cities," *New York Times*, June 28, 1964.

104   *The World Champions: St. Louis Cardinals Yearbook 1965*, A. Bartlett Giamatti Research Center, National Baseball Hall of Fame.

105   *St. Louis Cardinals 1966 Souvenir Yearbook.*

106   For an example, see Mississippi River Transmission Corporation advertisement, *St. Louis Post-Dispatch*, May 8, 1966.

107   For an example, see Busch Memorial Stadium Special Supplement advertisement, *St. Louis Post-Dispatch*, May 1, 1966.

108   Advertisement for Anheuser-Busch, Inc., *St. Louis Post-Dispatch*, May 8, 1966.

109   "Stadium Design Unveiled."

110   "Brilliant and Harmonious."

111   Baldwin, "Public Apathy, Other Barriers Surmounted by Dedicated Men."

112   Smith figured this was done to ventilate the stadium during hot St. Louis summers—a precaution not taken in Washington's D.C. Stadium, making Busch superior. Smith, "Stadium Isn't Pipe Dream." If that was the case, the feature wasn't particularly effective. When asked what he thought of the stadium by a young St. Louis writer, proud of the new stadium, Casey Stengel responded, "It holds the heat very well." Daley, "Sports of the Times: Waiting for the Stars."

113   "Sunday Pictures."

114   Leeming, "46,048 Attend First Game in New Stadium."

115   Baldwin, "Public Apathy, Other Barriers Surmounted by Dedicated Men."

116   Koppett, *The New York Mets*, 96; Angell, "Two Strikes on the Image," 177.

117   Peter Golenbock, *The Spirit of St. Louis: A History of the St. Louis Cardinals and Browns* (New York: Avon Books, 2000), 77.

118   "Gashouse Full of Memories," *Sports Illustrated*, May 9, 1966, 28–29.

119   Gordon, *Mapping Decline*, 225.

120   Thank you to Margaret McFadden for pointing this out.

121   "Ground Broken for Downtown Sports Stadium."

122   Advertisement for First National Bank in St. Louis and St. Louis Union Trust Company, *St. Louis Post-Dispatch*, May 8, 1966.

123   Baldwin, "Public Apathy, Other Barriers Surmounted by Dedicated Men."

124   Fuermann, *Houston: The Feast Years*, 24.

125   *The World Champions: St. Louis Cardinals Yearbook 1965.*

126   Daley, "Sports of the Times: Passing of a Landmark."

127   "Gashouse Full of Memories"; Russo, "The Grand Years"; Wilks, "100 Years of Baseball End at Old Park."

128   Bracker, "Souvenir-Hunting Followers of Baseball Club"; Eugene Bryerton, "Traffic Snarl Fails to Develop at New Stadium," *St. Louis Post-Dispatch*, May 9, 1966; Wilks, "100 Years of Baseball End at Old Park"; Benson, *Ballparks of North America*, 349.

129   For a handful of examples of this line of critique, see Angell, "Two Strikes on the Image"; Will Grims-

ley, "Being Big Business a Fact Baseball Today Must Face," *Eugene Register-Guard*, September 13, 1964; Lipsyte, "An Image in Concrete"; George Vass, "New Parks Have Symmetry; Old Ones Had Color," *Baseball Digest*, May 1967, 77–84.

130   Golenbock, *The Spirit of St. Louis*, 476–77.

131   Hall, "Tale of Two Cities."

CHAPTER 6

1   Roger Angell, "The Baltimore Vermeers," in *The Summer Game* (New York: Viking, 1972), 243, originally published in the *New Yorker* in October 1970. It was fitting that Angell would invoke the words of Le Corbusier, the Swiss modernist who claimed a proper house should be a "machine for living in" back in 1923. Designers shouldn't be burdened by old styles or historical prejudices, according to Le Corbusier; they should make buildings like machines—standardized and functional. It would take decades for American cities to fully adopt the austere, engineered modernism imported from Europe—and ironically, it was more often applied to corporate skyscrapers and office parks than worker housing, as Le Corbusier had planned. But the Corbusian "concrete cage" would eventually become an American standard, evident in stadium design as well. Le Corbusier, *Towards a New Architecture* (Mineola, N.Y.: Dover, 1986), 4. See also Reyner Banham, *Age of the Masters: A Personal View of Modern Architecture* (New York: Harper and Row, 1975), 19; Relph, *The Modern Urban Landscape*, 199.

2   Angell, "The Baltimore Vermeers," 243.

3   "Mallpark" is a common pejorative term used to describe the hypercommercialized ballpark today. The earliest record I can find of its use comes from a description of Toronto's SkyDome, an outlying exemplar of the modern stadium opened in 1989. Scott Ostler, "Take Me Out to the McBallpark," *San Francisco Chronicle*, October 7, 1992.

4   Buffalo's minor league Pilot Field is the first downtown "retro" ballpark of this era; Camden Yards was the first major league retro park and became the model for other cities building throwback baseball parks through the early 2000s. The hugely influential architectural firm HOK Sport (later renamed Populous) designed both.

5   Vass, "New Parks Have Symmetry."

6   Similarly, Anaheim Stadium, debuted in 1966 as an open-ended ballpark, was enclosed for the 1980 season and the arrival of football's Rams.

7   Clinton Page, "The Stadium: All-American Monument," *Progressive Architecture* 52 (November 1971): 78, quoted in Kammer, "Take Me Out to the Ballgame," 316. It should be noted that a single firm—Cleveland's Osborn Engineering Company—was responsible for many of the famously idiosyncratic ballparks built before World War I, including Pittsburgh's Forbes Field (opened in 1909), Cleveland's League Park (1910), Chicago's Comiskey Park (1910), Washington's Griffith Stadium (1911), Harlem's Polo Grounds (1911), Boston's Fenway Park (1912), Detroit's Navin Field (1912), Boston's Braves Field (1915), and Yankee Stadium (1923). Though baseball magnates of that era were politically connected, they didn't have the weapons that modernists worked with, particularly the ability to clear vast lots under the auspices of urban renewal.

8   Gershman, *Diamonds*, 202.

9   Norman Bel Geddes, "New Dodger Stadium to Replace Ebbets Field," May 9, 1952, box 45, folder 577.2, "Dodger Stadium—Data and Correspondence 1953–1957," Norman Bel Geddes Papers, Harry Ransom Center, University of Texas at Austin.

10   The first reported athletic use was at the Moses Brown School in Providence, Rhode Island, in 1964. Mark Bechtel and Stephen Cannella, "For the Record," *Sports Illustrated*, July 26, 2004, 20; "How We Got Here: Home in the Dome," *Sports Illustrated*, August 16, 1994.

11   "What a Wonder! What a Blunder!" *Life*, April 23, 1965, 76A; "Daymares in the Dome," *Time*, April 16, 1965, 97; Angell, "The Cool Bubble," 125.

12   Houston Sports Association, *Astrodome: Eighth Wonder of the World*, 24–25.

13   Shirley Povich, "This Morning," *Washington Post*, July 16, 1970.

14   AstroTurf was essentially a removable blanket of bristled, green, nylon tufts, laid atop foamed plastic. Tartan Turf was bonded to the surface below, a permanent, pile surface atop a padded mat. Poly-Turf, used in the Orange Bowl and Schaefer Stadium, was a third (but less popular) synthetic grass.

15   *Pittsburgh Pirate 1969 Yearbook*, 4, A. Bartlett Giamatti Research Center, National Baseball Hall of Fame.

16   William Johnson, "Goodby [*sic*] to Three Yards and a Cloud of Dust," *Sports Illustrated*, January 27, 1969, 37.

17   Peter Carry, "A Surface Case of Bugs in the Rugs," *Sports Illustrated*, September 14, 1970, 40.

18   Ibid. For a fuller study of artificial grass, see Benjamin D. Lisle, "Materiality and Meaning: Synthetic Grass, Sport, and the Limits of Modern Progress," *Material Matters: Selections from the Winterthur Material Culture Symposium for Emerging Scholars*, 2013, http://sites.udel.edu/mcses2012/papers/paper-i/ (accessed January 24, 2015).

19   Carry, "A Surface Case of Bugs in the Rugs," 45.

20   Gershman, *Diamonds*, 97.

21   "Scoreboard 'Adds Insult to Injury,'" *Washington Post*, May 22, 1960.

22   "Yankees to Get Biggest Scoreboard for $300,000," *New York Times*, February 12, 1959; Til Ferdenzi, "A Real Push-Button Manager!" *Baseball Digest*, December–January 1960, 97–98; *District of Columbia Stadium Official Dedication Magazine*, 16–17.

23   Charlie Park, "Newest Stadium Baseball Marvel," *Los Angeles Times*, April 10, 1962.

24   Roger Angell, "A Tale of Three Cities," in *The Summer Game* (New York: Viking, 1972), 73, originally published in the *New Yorker* in October 1962.

25   Addie, "Shea Stadium Spectacular."

26   John Hall, "Halo in the Sky," *Los Angeles Times*, May 29, 1965.

27   Ibid.

28   "Angel Scoreboard: A 23-Story Giant," *Sporting News*, September 11, 1965.

29   *1968 Oakland A's Premier Yearbook*, 49; *Three Rivers Stadium Souvenir Book*, 1970, 17; *Reds Review/1970 Yearbook*, 4, all at the A. Bartlett Giamatti Research Center, National Baseball Hall of Fame.

30   *Phillies Official 1970 Yearbook*, 52, A. Bartlett Giamatti Research Center, National Baseball Hall of Fame.

31   *Phillies 1972 Yearbook*, 5, A. Bartlett Giamatti Research Center, National Baseball Hall of Fame.

32   Ibid.

33   Roy Blount Jr., "Curtain Up on a Mod New Act," *Sports Illustrated*, April 19, 1971; *Phillies 1972 Yearbook*, 6.

34   *Phillies 1972 Yearbook*, 6.

35   Blount, "Curtain Up."

36   Angell, "The Cool Bubble," 141–42.

37   Chuck Woodling, "KC's Disneyland Arrives, But Don't Look at Lights," *Lawrence Daily Journal*, August 14, 1972. Instant replay in the stadium was a feature that worried NFL commissioner Pete Rozelle, who said, "There could be some serious consequences . . . football is a highly volatile sport. If a replay shown on a scoreboard should indicate a play had been called incorrectly, and if you have 60,000 or 70,000 persons in the stands, there could be bad effects. Unlike soccer stadiums in South America, we do not have moats around our playing fields." "Sudden Death Endings Supported by Rozelle," *Milwaukee Journal*, September 16, 1972.

38   Michael Oriard, *The End of Autumn: Reflections on My Life in Football* (Garden City, N.Y.: Doubleday, 1982), 197–98.

39   The Astrodome spanned 642 feet and rose 218 feet. Superdome promoters were fond of comparing their structure to Houston's.

40   Jep Cadou, "New Orleans' Dome Sweet Dome," *Saturday Evening Post*, April 1975, 62; J. D. Reed, "The Louisiana Purchase," *Sports Illustrated*, July 22, 1974, 68.

41   Real Estate Research Corporation, *Analysis of Stadium Alternatives: Twin Cities Metropolitan Area* (St. Paul: Real Estate Research Corporation, 1974), 67–71.

42   Cadou, "New Orleans' Dome Sweet Dome," 79.

43   Jerry Kirshenbaum, "Let Me Make One Thing Clear," *Sports Illustrated*, June 7, 1971, 39.

44   Reed, "The Louisiana Purchase," 72.

45   "Superdome Commercials Draw Player Complaints," *Los Angeles Times*, August 30, 1975.

46   Ibid.

47   Red Smith, "Sports 'Fringe Benefits' Are Not Unprecedented," *Sarasota Herald-Tribune*, August 16, 1975. The massive screens also interfered with play; because of their poor design, people at the back of the lower level couldn't see the gondola screens. The gondola was then lowered ten feet. After it was lowered, punter Ray Guy hit the screen with a ball, forcing the creation of a ground rule: re-kicks if one hit the screen. The NFL would bar simulcasts of the game on the field, believing it distracted players and officials. This was a bit unfair to those sitting at the top, who were so far away from the action. The NFL also censored replays involving questionable calls by officials, worried about their safety should their errors be displayed in slow motion to rowdy fans. J. D. Reed, "Really Running in the Red," *Sports Illustrated*, March 15, 1976, 26–30.

48   Reed, "The Louisiana Purchase," 72.

49   Rader, *In Its Own Image*, 116.

50   Powers, *Supertube*, 145.

51   Oriard, *Brand NFL*, 25.

52   Roger Kahn, "Something's Changing About Baseball," *New York Times*, April 5, 1959.

53   "The Business of Baseball," 68.

54   Mark Harris, "Maybe What Baseball Needs Is a Henry David Thoreau," *New York Times Sunday Magazine*, May 4, 1969, 66–73.

55   Powers, *Supertube*, 154. See also George Vecsey, "New Jersey, New Jersey," *New York Times*, September 29, 1983; Guttmann, *Sports Spectators*, 141.

56   *Metrodome: A Souvenir Section* (Minneapolis: Minneapolis Tribune, 1982), 28.

57   Gershman, *Diamonds*, 30–31; Rosensweig, *Retro Ball Parks*, 77–78.

58   Wolf, "Sportraits"; "Another MacPhail First—Baseball's Biggest Bar Room," *Chicago Daily Tribune*, April 22, 1946.

59   *Three Rivers Stadium Souvenir Book*, 7.

60   *Pittsburgh Pirate 1969 Yearbook*, 4.

61   Gary Cartwright, "The Dome Is Upon Us," *Dallas Morning News*, April 13, 1965.

62   John Crittenden, "Cowboy Ticket Plan: Struck Oil Lately?" *Miami News*, August 14, 1972; Charles Maher, "Stadium Suite: A Room with a View and a Bar (Only the Rich Need Apply)," *Los Angeles Times*, October 23, 1973; "Millionaires' Row: Rich Texans to Live It Up in $50,000 Stadium Suites," *Los Angeles Times*, November 25, 1971.

63   "Millionaires' Row."

64   James H. Winchester, "Superdomes!" *Travel*, November 1972, 65.

65   Jeanne Barnes, "Spectators Sport Luxury," *Dallas Morning News*, October 23, 1971.

66   "Millionaires' Row."

67   Maher, "Stadium Suite."

68   Ibid.

69   David G. McComb, *Spare Time in Texas: Recreation and History in the Lone Star State* (Austin: University of Texas Press, 2008), 86–87.

70   Crittenden, "Cowboy Ticket Plan"; Maher, "Stadium Suite"; "Millionaires' Row."

71   Mark S. Rosentraub and Samuel R. Nunn, "Suburban City Investment in Professional Sports: Estimating the Fiscal Returns of the Dallas Cowboys and Texas Rangers to Investor Communities," *American Behavioral Scientist* 21, no. 3 (January 1, 1978): 397.

72   William N. Wallace, "Pangs of Prosperity," *New York Times*, February 8, 1970.

73   "Season-Ticket Sales Start Tomorrow for Cowboys," *Dallas Morning News*, April 24, 1960; "Cowboy Season-Ticket Option Deadline April 1," *Dallas Morning News*, February 5, 1965; "Cowboy Season Ticket Sales Open Saturday," *Dallas Morning News*, April 23, 1970.

74   McComb, *Spare Time in Texas*, 86–87.

75   Crittenden, "Cowboy Ticket Plan."

76   Marlyn Schwartz, "Cowboy Fans Voice Complaints," *Dallas Morning News*, November 21, 1971.

77   Crittenden, "Cowboy Ticket Plan." The median family income in 1970 was $18,440 per year. U.S. Department of Commerce, Bureau of the Census, "Money Income of Families and Persons in the United States: 1979," Report P-60 No. 129, 2, http://www.census.gov/prod/www/abs/p60.html (accessed March 27, 2010).

78   Schwartz, "Cowboy Fans Voice Complaints."

79   Ibid.

80   Crittenden, "Cowboy Ticket Plan."

81   "Arvida in Talks for Stadium," *Boca Raton News*, November 14, 1979.

82   Bureau of the Census, "Money Income of Families and Persons in the United States: 1979," 2.

83   Oriard, *The End of Autumn*, 197–98.

84   Real Estate Research Corporation, *Analysis of Stadium Alternatives*, 48–52; Reed, "The Louisiana Purchase," 78.

85   Ruth Ryon, "Luxury Vantage Points: 'California Suite' Has a New Meaning at Anaheim Stadium," *Los Angeles Times*, July 29, 1980.

86   See Benjamin D. Lisle, "'You've Got to Have Tangibles to Sell Intangibles': Ideologies of the Modern American Stadium, 1948–1982" (PhD diss., University of Texas at Austin, 2010), 394–98.

87   Bale, *Sport, Space, and the City*.

88   Mal Florence, "Building Better Fantraps," *Los Angeles Times*, September 19, 1972.

89   This development prefigures the emergence of ESPN's *SportsCenter*, launched with the network in 1979. The use of highlights to tell stories about sport was nothing new—look no further than old newsreels for an example—however, the highlight-as-entertainment took on a new prominence in the *SportsCenter* era. See Raymond Gamache, *A History of Sports Highlights: Replayed Plays from Edison to ESPN* (Jefferson, N.C.: McFarland, 2010), 13. Another sports-themed development that seems to follow that of the "à la carte" stadium experience of the 1970s is the growing popularity of fantasy baseball, beginning in the early 1980s.

90   For example, see Buckminster Fuller, *Operating Manual for Spaceship Earth* (Carbondale: Southern Illinois University Press, 1968); Charles Reich, *The Greening of America* (New York: Random House, 1970); Frances Moore Lappé, *Diet for a Small Planet* (New York: Ballantine Books, 1971); and E. F. Schumacher, *Small Is Beautiful* (New York: Harper & Row, 1973).

91   Harris, "Maybe What Baseball Needs Is a Henry David Thoreau."

92   Michael Oriard, "Sports & Space," *Landscape* 21 (Autumn 1976): 32–40. For another incisive and contemporary critique of sport, television, and the stadium, see Michael Oriard, "Professional Football as Cultural Myth," *Journal of American Culture* 4, no. 3 (Fall 1981): 27–41.

93   Bruce J. Schulman, *The Seventies: The Great Shift in American Culture, Society, and Politics* (New York: The Free Press, 2001), 161.

94   Mark Goodman, "How King Rained on Riggs' Parade," *Time*, October 1, 1973, 110; Neil Amdur, "Mrs. King Defeats Riggs, 6–4, 6–3, 6–3, amid a Circus Atmosphere," *New York Times*, September 21, 1973; Charles Maher, "Barnum Would Have Loved It," *Los Angeles Times*, September 21, 1973.

95   King and Riggs were both guaranteed one hundred thousand dollars to play, with that figure doubled for the winner. The winning share of two hundred thousand dollars would nearly double King's yearly earnings, which were tops in women's tennis. Las Vegas odds-maker Jimmy the Greek Snyder put the odds at five-to-two for Riggs. One press pool had twenty-two of thirty-two reporters picking Riggs. Heavyweight boxer George Foreman, who was to deliver the ceremonial winner's check at the match conclusion, thought King would do the job. Maher, "Barnum Would Have Loved It"; Grace Lichtenstein, "Mrs. King Calls Victory 'Culmination' of Career," *New York Times*, September 21, 1973.

96   Goodman, "How King Rained on Riggs' Parade," 110; Curry Kirkpatrick, "There She Is, Ms. America," *Sports Illustrated*, October 1, 1973, 31; Amdur, "Mrs. King Defeats Riggs"; Maher, "Barnum Would Have Loved It."

97   Maher, "Barnum Would Have Loved It."

98   Kirkpatrick, "There She Is, Ms. America," 32.

99   Amdur, "Mrs. King Defeats Riggs."

100   Maher, "Barnum Would Have Loved It"; Lichtenstein, "Mrs. King Calls Victory 'Culmination' of Career."

101   "Leaders in Senate Acclaim Mrs. King," *New York Times*, September 22, 1973.

102   Susan K. Cahn, *Coming on Strong: Gender and Sexuality in Twentieth-Century Women's Sport* (New York: The Free Press, 1994), 252.

103   Goodman, "How King Rained on Riggs' Parade," 111.

104   Nan Ellin, *Postmodern Urbanism* (New York: Princeton Architectural Press, 1999), 16.

105   Ibid., 1, 13, 18. The phrase "romantic turn" is Ellin's. Harvey, *Condition of Postmodernity* (Cambridge, Mass.: Blackwell, 1990), 92–93, 97; Michael L. Silk, "Cities and the Cultural Politics of Sterile Sporting Space," in *A Companion to Sport*, ed. David L. Andrews and Ben Carrington (Malden, Mass.: Blackwell, 2013), 271–72; Heinrich Klotz, *The History of Postmodern Architecture*, trans. Radka Donnell (Cambridge, Mass.: MIT Press, 1988).

106   John R. Logan and Harvey L. Molotch, *Urban Fortunes: The Political Economy of Place* (Berkeley: University of California Press, 1987), 61–62.

107   Paul Goldberger, "Architecture View: A Radical Idea: Baseball as It Used to Be," *New York Times*, November 19, 1989.

108   Rod Sheard, *The Stadium: Architecture for a New Global Culture* (Singapore: Periplus, 2005), 88.

109   Robert Fachet, "Orioles' Ballpark Takes Shape," *Washington Post*, December 29, 1989.

110   The "yards" technically referred to the shipyards, as the park was located adjacent the city's harbor.

111   Paul Goldberger, "The Rise of the Private City," in *Breaking Away: The Future of Cities: Essays in Memory of Robert F. Wagner, Jr.*, ed. J. Vitullo Martin (New York: Twentieth Century Fund, 1996), 135–50. Rosensweig applies Goldberger's concept of the "urbanoid" to Cleveland's historicist ballpark in *Retro Ball Parks*, 45.

112   Hannigan, *Fantasy City*, 7.

113   Michael Sorkin, "Introduction: Variations on a Theme Park" and "See You in Disneyland," in *Variations on a Theme Park* (New York: Hill and Wang, 1992), xiv, 226.

114   Buffalo's Pilot Field is sometimes noted as the original "retro" park, though most accounts of the stadium upon its opening in 1988 didn't celebrate it as such. The new Comiskey Park (replacing the older version) opened in Chicago in 1991. It suggested the direction of future ballparks, fusing historical allusions to the old park with a modern look. HOK Sport designed both.

115   Rosensweig, *Retro Ball Parks*, 5.

116   Thomas Boswell, "Now That's the Way to Build a Ballpark," *Washington Post*, April 4, 1992.

117   Mark Maske, "For Players, Park Will Need Figuring," *Washington Post*, March 31, 1992.

118   William Gildea, "It's a Grand Opening for Camden Yards," *Washington Post*, April 7, 1992.

119   Boswell, "Now That's the Way to Build a Ballpark."

120   Ibid.

121   William Gildea, "Friendly and Familiar Confines," *Washington Post*, April 12, 1992.

122   Patrick Bingham-Hall, *HOK Sport + Venue + Event: 20 Years of Great Architecture, Colleagues, Clients and Community* (Sydney, Australia: Pesaro Publishing, 2003), 61.

123   Tim Kurkjian, "A Splendid Nest," *Sports Illustrated*, April 13, 1992, 34.

124   Ibid., 36, 41. In his study of Cleveland's retro ballpark, Rosensweig argued that older stadiums became increasingly "democratic" as they aged. They offered fewer amenities than the retro parks and exercised less spatial control between sections, opening space for more organic fan behavior. While there certainly would seem to be some truth in this, I think Rosensweig's argument is over-reliant on certain stadiums (that had a more horizontal scale of consumer options, like Cleveland Stadium) at the exclusion of others (like Three Rivers) and a presentist perspective that compared the consumption options of the 1970s to those that would follow

rather than those that preceded them. That said, his important broader point—that the retro parks offered a more socioeconomically stratified entertainment experience outfitted in a guise of working-class authenticity—remains convincing.

125 Not everyone bought into this discourse of democracy that, on the face of it, seemed absurd given the rough-and-tumble conditions of old Memorial Stadium. A seventy-one-year-old Orioles fan complained, "There's not a thing wrong with that ballpark [Memorial Stadium]. It's one of the best. The parking won't be better down in the Inner Harbor, maybe worse. And the seats for us fans won't be better, either. They're building it so that lawyer owner and his politician friends can sit in them lounge chairs in their sky boxes with their feet up, get served champagne and watch the game on TV." Eve Zibert, "In & Around the Ballpark," *Washington Post*, April 3, 1992; Thomas Boswell, "Just Around the Corner: Memorial as Memory," *Washington Post*, September 10, 1987.

126 Fachet, "Orioles' Ballpark Takes Shape." George Ritzer and Todd Stillman deliver a version of this argument—that Camden Yards is more rationalized than modern stadiums and uses style to distract from this—in "The Postmodern Ballpark as Leisure Setting: Enchantment and Simulated De-McDonaldization," *Leisure Sciences* 23 (2001): 99–113.

127 Bingham-Hall, *HOK Sport + Venue + Event*, 11.

128 "Projects: Citi Field," *Populous*, http://portfolio.populous.com/projects/citifield.html (accessed March 29, 2010).

129 Other significant stadium-building firms include HNTB, NBBJ, HKS, and Ellerbe Beckett.

130 For an example of this sort of treatment—though it has now become so common as to be cliché—see Jack Moore, "Throwback Thursday: Cincinnati's Riverfront Stadium and the Era of Multipurpose Mistakes," *Vice Sports*, July 2, 2015, https://sports.vice.com/en_us/article/throwback-thursday-cincinnatis-riverfront-stadium-and-the-era-of-multipurpose-mistakes (accessed October 9, 2016).

131 Patricia Lowry, "Heinz Field an Imposing Presence Poised on the Riverfront," *Pittsburgh Post-Gazette*, July 29, 2001; "Steel City Stadium," *Populous*, http://populous.com/project/heinz-field/ (accessed February 16, 2015); Heinz Field Tours, http://heinzfield.com/stadium/heinz-field-tours/ (accessed February 16, 2015).

132 "Major League Baseball Ballparks," *Populous*, http://populous.com/projects/type/major-league-baseball/ (accessed February 16, 2015); "PNC Park Information," *The Official Site of the Pittsburgh Pirates*, http://pittsburgh.pirates.mlb.com/pit/ballpark/information/index.jsp?content=overview (accessed February 16, 2015).

133 Fair territory at Three Rivers Stadium was 120,000 square feet; the entire area of the field was 140,000 square feet. At PNC Park, the playing surface is just under 97,000 square feet. Benson, *Ballparks of North America*, 318; "PNC Park: Facts," *The Official Site of the Pittsburgh Pirates*, http://pittsburgh.pirates.mlb.com/pit/ballpark/information/index.jsp?content=facts (accessed July 14, 2015).

134 Peter Leo, "PNC Park: Food, Fun, Rock 'n' Roll, Even Baseball," *Pittsburgh Post-Gazette*, April 30, 2001.

135 "Premium Seating," *The Official Site of the Pittsburgh Pirates*, http://mlb.mlb.com/pit/ticketing/premium_seating.jsp (accessed July 14, 2015); Benson, *Ballparks of North America*, 318.

136 "Heinz Field Facts," *Heinz Field*, http://heinzfield.com/stadium/heinz-field-facts/ (accessed July 14, 2015).

137 Historian Sean Dinces's revealing work on the expansion of premium spaces in sports facilities aggregates and quantifies the trends that many critics have qualitatively identified in recent decades. He includes NBA arenas in his data set. Sean Dinces, "The Reinvention of the Revanchist Stadium: Spectatorship and Stratification in Late Twentieth-Century American Sport" (paper presented at the annual meeting for the North American Society for Sport History, Glenwood Springs, Colo., May 30–June 2, 2014); Sean Dinces, "Fanfare Without the Fans," *Jacobin*, issue 15–16 (October 2014), https://www.jacobinmag.com/2014/10/fanfare-without-the-fans/ (accessed October 9, 2016).

138 Team Marketing Report, "2014 NFL Fan Cost Index," September 2014, https://www.teammarketing.com/public/uploadedPDFs/FOOTBALL_FCI_TWENTYFOURTEEN.pdf (accessed July 15, 2015).

139   Judith Grant Long, *Public/Private Partnerships for Major League Sports Facilities* (New York: Routledge, 2013), 37, 93–94.

140   Delaney and Eckstein, *Public Dollars, Private Stadiums*, 1, 155–67; Trumpbour, *The New Cathedrals*, 112–55.

141   Delaney and Eckstein, *Public Dollars, Private Stadiums*, 164.

142   "Birth of a Ballpark: PNC Park Debuts," *Pittsburgh Post-Gazette*, April 9, 2001.

143   Delaney and Eckstein, *Public Dollars, Private Stadiums*, 26, 39–40, 186–88.

144   McMurtry, "Love, Death, and the Astrodome," 2.

145   Rosensweig, *Retro Ball Parks*.

146   Delaney and Eckstein, *Public Dollars, Private Stadiums*, 38.

147   Bingham-Hall, *HOK Sport + Venue + Event*, 61.

148   Rosensweig writes about such a stadium crowd at Cleveland's Municipal Stadium, before it was replaced by the retro Jacobs Field in 1994. Rosensweig, *Retro Ball Parks*, 86–88, 140.

149   Bingham-Hall, *HOK Sport + Venue + Event*, 16.

150   Delaney and Eckstein, *Public Dollars, Private Stadiums*, 164.

INDEX

ACKNOWLEDGMENTS

THIS IS BASICALLY A BOOK ABOUT PEOPLE, places, and the relationship between the two. Stadiums and their people have always fascinated me. Many of my earliest memories are set in and around Owen Field at the University of Oklahoma. I can recall the rich smell of soup wafting from the thermos of the couple that sat next to us year after year. I can see the sheen of the wet artificial turf at night games, illuminated by the temporary light towers brought in for a nationally televised Big Eight matchup (usually with Nebraska, of course). I can mimic the gait and pace of the brisk walk from where my father parked by the railroad tracks down Jenkins Avenue to the stadium. How odd, then, that this book would start to take shape in Austin, less than a hundred yards from Darrell K. Royal Memorial Stadium at the University of Texas (though Royal himself was, after all, from Oklahoma). It was at the Center for American History that I found *Inside the Astrodome*, the remarkable souvenir magazine that accompanied the opening of Houston's iconic stadium. It would be the seed from which this book grew.

I was lucky to spend many years among great scholars and people at the University of Texas at Austin. Jeff Meikle, Steve Hoelscher, and Janet Davis modeled scholarship and teaching, showing me how to think about architecture, design, space, culture, and the past. Jan Todd introduced me to a community of sports historians; I thank her and Michael Kackman for their feedback on this project in its earlier stages. Those early versions of this book were forged in the cafés of Austin, often alongside Tracy Wuster, who was always willing to read and comment. Jason Mellard and Amy Ware also helped me work through the project's younger iterations. My thanks go to Ella Schwartz and Cynthia Frese for guiding me through the bureaucratic waters of the university. And thanks to Matt Hedstrom, Andrew Busch, and many others for counsel and companionship.

I say this book was born in Texas, but it also has roots in my years living in Boston. For someone accustomed to the western grid, the unruly paths of that old city were a revelation. And so too was Fenway Park, where baseball wasn't pastoral and leisurely but urban, electric, and quite serious business. The football fan within me felt at home. It was in Boston, and at Fenway, that I began thinking about how the stadium might be worth studying. I owe a debt to Alan Howard, at the University of Virginia, for selling me on the prospects of American studies as a way to explore the stadium, the city, and their cultures. And after a decade at Virginia and Texas, I have found myself back in the orbit of Fenway, in the land of the Red Sox. I arrived at Maine's Colby College with a manuscript; it has now been reshaped into a proper book, thanks in large part to my wonderful colleagues and comrades here. Laura Saltz, Lisa Arellano, and Cyrus Shahan have been great mentors and confidants. Lisa is no expert on stadiums but is much smarter than I am and helped me sharpen multiple chapters. I am especially indebted to Margaret McFadden, whose intellect, example, generosity, and friendship have not only improved this book but also made me a better person. Sherry Berard makes my life at the college easier in countless ways. I also owe thanks to research assistants Michael Perrault and Julia Butler, as well as Gordon Lessersohn (and family).

Many others have read versions of this text closely and provided crucial feedback: they include Bob Trumpbour, David Nye, Miles Orvell, and Klaus Benesch. Profound thanks to Bob Lockhart at the University of Pennsylvania Press, whose advice has always been excellent; I cringe to think what this would have been without his guidance and patience. The book has benefited greatly from the expertise of many others at the press, including Erica Ginsburg, Amanda Ruffner, Jennifer Backer, Elizabeth Glover, Will Boehm, John Hubbard, Susan Staggs, Tracy Kellmer, Gigi Lamm, Peter Valelly, Gavi Fried, and Laura Waldron.

I am grateful to the many others who have supported this project in different ways. Librarians and archivists have steered me through collections and dug up old photos at the Center for American History and the Harry Ransom Center at the University of Texas at Austin, the A. Bartlett Giamatti Research Center at the National Baseball Hall of Fame, George Washington University special collections, the New York Public Library Manuscripts and Archives Division, the Minnesota History Center, the Brooklyn Public Library, the Houston Public Library, the DC Public Library, the John F. Kennedy Presidential Library, the Jordan Schnitzer Museum of Art at the University of Oregon, the Boston Public Library, the Wisconsin Historical Society, the New York City Municipal Archives, the San Francisco History Center at the San Francisco Public Library, New York City Parks, the Missouri History Museum, the State Historical Society of Missouri Research Center at St. Louis, the St. Louis Mercantile Library at the University of Missouri–St. Louis, the Detre Library & Archives at the Heinz History Center, the Archives Service Center at the

University of Pittsburgh, and the Special Collections Research Center at Temple University. Bill Hancock generously provided me with a treasure trove of old Houston programs and scorecards. Many others have sent me newspaper articles on stadiums and ballparks. Thanks to Meredith Kelley Lesher, Mike Foley, Jenn Jefferson, and Tracy Wuster for their hospitality, housing me during research trips and conferences. Linda and Grif Lesher generously allowed me the run of their Rockport writer's retreat atop Barnswallow Books, where I grappled with the final chapter in the midst of a February blizzard. And thanks to the stadium anthropologists whose work I have relied on—incredibly insightful thinkers and writers like Roger Angell, Robert Lipsyte, Michael Oriard, and Larry McMurtry. Without voices like theirs, this would be a much thinner account of the stadium and what it has meant in American life.

Since I was a young boy, sport has shaped my relationships with those closest to me. I have shared stadiums countless times with family and friends: Okies, Texans, Minnesotans, Virginians, Mainers, Carolinians, and Coloradans. You know who you are. I thank you for those experiences, memorable and mundane, which have certainly worked their way into this text. My family has always supported me, whatever I have done, and for that I am immensely and continually grateful. I am not the easiest being to live with, and neither is my cat. Erin Murphy knows this. She has not only endured my dark moods and fits of anxiety but also dragged me through them. Whenever I have needed perspective and advice, she has listened and read; she tells me what doesn't work and what does. How lucky I am. In the end, this book is for her.